ADDITIONAL PRAISE
FOR *Virtual Banking*

"For too long financial services has lagged behind other industries in understanding and adapting to new consumer expectations of service. This book shows how they can stop falling behind by becoming part of the emerging new 'innovation eco-system' and adopting new ways of working, especially partnering with smaller innovative firms."

—David Milligan, CEO, Matchi.biz

"*Virtual Banking* is full of practical advice, built on careful analysis and thoughtful predictions, such as the future of mobile banking. A call-to-action for an industry that desperately needs deeper innovation-minded partnerships."

—Michael Strange, CTO, Mitek Systems

"Financial technology has advanced dramatically in the past two decades, but in recent years we've seen major banks and institutions embrace data processing technologies to be more efficient. In the 1990s, the limitations of mainframe technologies hampered the banking industry's ability to make automated decisions based on billions of data points. Today, parallel processing and scalable technologies have enabled an entire generation of alternative lenders, virtual banking products, emerging payment systems, and mobile tools for consumers, business owners, and the enterprise. Dan's book is a fantastic analysis of these evolutions and specifically how SMB's have become more inclined to use technology to grow fast."

—Darian Shirazi, CEO and Co-founder, Radius

Virtual Banking

Founded in 1807, John Wiley & Sons is the oldest independent publishing company in the United States. With offices in North America, Europe, Australia and Asia, Wiley is globally committed to developing and marketing print and electronic products and services for our customers' professional and personal knowledge and understanding.

The Wiley Finance series contains books written specifically for finance and investment professionals as well as sophisticated individual investors and their financial advisors. Book topics range from portfolio management to e-commerce, risk management, financial engineering, valuation, and financial instrument analysis, as well as much more.

For a list of available titles, visit our web site at www.WileyFinance.com.

Virtual Banking

A Guide to Innovation and Partnering

DAN SCHATT

WILEY

Cover image: ©Alex Belomlinsky/Getty Images
Cover design: Wiley

Published by John Wiley & Sons, Inc., Hoboken, New Jersey.
Published simultaneously in Canada.

For general information on our other products and services or for technical support, please contact our Customer Care Department within the United States at (800) 762-2974, outside the United States at (317) 572-3993 or fax (317) 572-4002.

Wiley publishes in a variety of print and electronic formats and by print-on-demand. Some material included with standard print versions of this book may not be included in e-books or in print-on-demand. If this book refers to media such as a CD or DVD that is not included in the version you purchased, you may download this material at http://booksupport.wiley.com. For more information about Wiley products, visit www.wiley.com.

Library of Congress Cataloging-in-Publication Data:

ISBN 9781118742471 (Hardcover)
ISBN 9781118742549 (ePDF)
ISBN 9781118742365 (ePub)

Printed in the United States of America
10 9 8 7 6 5 4 3 2 1

To my wife Suzan—for agreeing to give me a tour of Bucharest 22 years ago and who remains just as charming, talented, and beautiful 4 continents, 10 countries, and 2 kids later.

To Brianna and Demian—who regularly inspire me with their own innovations and awesomeness

Contents

Foreword

By Renaud Laplanche
Co-Founder and CEO of Lending Club

When I founded Lending Club in 2006, I saw the potential for a new model to deliver credit, in a way that would transform the U.S. banking system into an online marketplace where investors directly fund borrowers, earning a return in the process and creating savings for borrowers. This transformation would allow the system to operate at a lower cost, be more transparent and more consumer friendly. As I started building Lending Club I came to learn from people like Dan that my vision was part of an unprecedented wave of technological innovations in financial services. The task Dan took on–to provide a guide to such innovations–is enormously challenging, but as a former investment banker, industry analyst, and PayPal innovation executive, he was uniquely qualified to do so, and the result is a resounding success.

Today's financial services industry includes a plethora of technology companies, from new and innovative brokerage platforms like Stockpile, personal financial management platforms like Personal Capital and Wealthfront, new models for banking such as Simple, payments processors like Braintree, and business services such as Swipely. The common thread tying all of these innovations together is the customer-centric vision that brought them into being. Focusing on the consumer, rather than the product, as a starting point is one of the central themes of this book. Through its six chapters, Dan deftly outlines the landscape of the financial technology industry, acting as an accessible yet deeply thought-provoking tour guide to the rapidly changing financial technologies from mobile to social to Bitcoin.

Now more than ever customers demand immediacy, relevance, and personalization in their day-to-day behaviors. These trends are evident in the data and examples that Dan presents in the book. Consumers want to split checks with friends digitally at the restaurant (Venmo), request car service before getting onto the street (Uber), and access their Starbucks loyalty and payment card while waiting in line (Square). These trends will not only continue, but accelerate, as younger generations use their mobile phones for more transactions in their lives and are increasingly willing to share information and data with friends and financial institutions alike in order to get more customized service offerings.

Dan doesn't just describe the landscape at it exists today, he makes us consider the endless possibilities that tomorrow holds. What if your digital wallet not only pays for your purchase, but also automatically opts into your preferred method of getting rewarded, be it cash back or travel points, when you pay and redeem rewards? What if you received automatic budget alerts for spending on electronics when you either physically or virtually entered an Apple retail store? What if you never had to present your ID ever again to enter a bar or pay with your credit card? Dan invites us to imagine a world without friction, where banking is not an act or a destination but an enabler of everything that we do.

To achieve that vision, new and incumbent players in the financial services industry will need to collaborate, integrate, and innovate together. No one understands these types of partnerships better than Dan. One of the most clear themes of Dan's career—and, I would argue, one of the most important lessons for financial institutions looking to stay relevant to their customers—is the enlightened idea that banks should seek to actively partner with technology companies with complementary business models.

Dan weaves this point throughout the book with powerful examples, including the Mastercard-branded Google Wallet card and the Yodlee platform for a host of personal financial management tools. At Lending Club, we made the decision to partner and work with banks rather than viewing them as competition. We recognized that banks have competitive advantages in their low cost of capital and pre-existing customer relationships, while we can deliver a better customer experience at a lower cost. This creates the opportunity to partner, with traditional banks working with innovators for the good of the customer. History has shown that major innovations tend to come from outside the banking industry. It will be up to banks to decide whether they will open themselves up to innovation that will better serve their customers, and it will be up to technology companies to work constructively with incumbents.

With *Virtual Banking: A Guide To Innovation and Partnering*, Dan takes us on a journey through the technological advances occurring in the space today that every banker, investor, entrepreneur, and industry professional could benefit from. His rich anecdotes and interviews make it a colorful, entertaining read. Disruption in finance through technology is a complex subject, but Dan simplifies it and more importantly he encourages us–no, challenges us–to think differently about it.

Preface

"**Y**ou guys are the enemy!" As head of financial innovations for PayPal, I heard that pretty often in my first few years at PayPal. Even prior to my time at PayPal, when I headed the retail payments practice for financial research and consulting company Celent, I heard it regularly from my bank clients: "How should we think about PayPal, Google, Facebook, Apple, or any other institution innovating in the financial services space? Will they eat our lunch? What about the emerging start-ups that are getting into banking services without becoming banks?" More than once, I told myself that somebody should write a book on what's really happening in the world of tech and financial services—the fact that if you really peeled back the onion a few layers, what you would find is that co-opetition does exist, everyone is working out deals behind the scenes, and massive opportunities exist for banks to partner with nontraditional players. Many of the new partnerships forming are blueprints that give a glimpse into future financial services innovation and some really compelling customer experiences to come. You just wouldn't know it from the media hype that loves drama! In fact, it's companies like PayPal and the many innovative financial technology start-ups that are opening new opportunities for the banking industry, expanding the opportunity pie and keeping the financial services community more relevant to changing customer preferences, new technology trends, and significantly increased customer expectations.

As a professional running virtually any service for your retail bank, how can you position your institution to become a customer magnet instead of a repellent? Part of the answer lies in creative deal making, Silicon Valley style. New technologies and platforms are now available on a wide scale and those financial institutions who can strike deals with nonbanks can meet their regulatory requirements while offering valuable new experiences that consumers will happily pay for. Even more important, the right partnerships will not only help banks meet their requirements, it will make banks more competitive in "the new normal." I define the New Normal as an environment in which many nonfinancial entities are now entering the financial space and finding ways to attract customers with no branches, no checkbooks, or other brick-and-mortar services, historically seen as "must-haves" to attract customers. Banks must learn what they can outsource and what must remain a key part of their offering in order to compete and thrive in this environment.

This book is intended for those who would like to understand how to innovate and drive significant positive change in their organization though creative partnering. These opportunities to collaborate haven't always existed—it's a result of a unique collision of trends—today's ubiquity of the Internet and smartphones, the rise of open platforms and application programming interfaces (APIs), the growth of new commerce brought by social, local, and digital capabilities, network effects, and a fundamental change occurring in consumer expectations. This is meant to serve as a guide on how to exploit these trends to further innovation, whether you are part of a large bank, small bank, financial technology provider, or someone who would like to understand better how innovations in banking and payments can be shaped through the use of creative partnering.

As a member of the first large-scale payments company to make the shift to platform services, and to witness the tremendous amount of creative partnering that was happening, it became increasingly clear to me that what was holding financial services industry back from unleashing more innovation were really two things—a lack of focus on creative partnering, and a good understanding of the major technology and consumer shifts that have precipitated the needs for these major business model changes to occur. At PayPal, within a few short years, we went from no financial institution partnerships to several hundred, generating over $1 billion in payment volume. The opportunity for our bank partners to take advantage of PayPal platform capabilities for their own customers to generate new value was significant, and I realized that there was a macro trend taking shape—one that would allow the financial community to take advantage of open platforms and partnerships like never before to spur a new wave of innovation and value for their customers.

In light of many of the significant industry shifts happening—consumer expectations around commerce, the growth of mobile, the network effects of social commerce, it has never been more important to understand and anticipate what consumer expect from financial services firms in order to meet their needs. What often ends up happening is an inside-out approach to thinking about what's best for the customer—something I call "the military industrial complex of payments"—large technology departments at banks who advocate for continual proprietary development work that could be done in a more user friendly fashion, done cheaper and more efficiently by outside parties who listen more closely to the market. These insular projects often end up costing banks far more than money or time—they end up confusing large technology projects with true customer-focused "innovation" and doesn't end up solving a consumer pain point and usually disappoints. Too often, the first thought is to build a product, leverage a standard banking vendor, or engage in a coalition with other banks to build a common framework or utility. While that approach has worked well to create utility services—standard credit card and automated teller machine (ATM) networks—it works less well when it comes to differentiating product or service offerings, which is a must in order to stay relevant with customers. Instead, why not think "partner" before "build" or "buy," particularly in today's environment when there are so many companies with such a strong history of design and product innovation.

Financial services innovation often implies heavy investments in technology or operational process, which may or may not lead to positive, transformative change. Real innovation can be very low cost and leverage existing technology assets and processes, but it can often come in the form of creative partnerships that aren't always obvious on the surface. An untapped opportunity exists between the tech world and the financial world, which can work together to achieve more than they could separately.

I hope this book will provide you with a very hands-on approach to how banks can innovate and thrive by partnering and imitating the approach of some of the cutting-edge incumbent banks, technology providers, and other thought leaders.

Dan Schatt
April 2014

Acknowledgments

The original inspiration for this book really came as a result of my experience with the founding financial innovations team at PayPal—the most innovative, passionate, unstoppable folks out there who exemplify talent and teamwork: Arkady Fridman, Mamta Narain, Peter Amalraj, Katherine Wilson, Kareem Al-Bassam, Jeroen Van Son, Jonathan Knoll, Fred Alexander, and Maksim Rohkline. Thank you all for proving that a small group of people can make a huge impact in shaping the financial services landscape and demonstrating to banks that technology companies make worthy partners.

The latest and continued inspiration for this book has come from my partners at Stockpile, Inc., an exceptional group of people who are building the first ever "PayPal" for stock. A sincere thanks to Avi Lele and Sanjeev Kulkarni for their pioneering work in this area. It will most definitely have a significant impact on global financial inclusion.

I've been very fortunate to have numerous mentors along the way that without whom this book would not have been possible. A very big thank you to Scott Thompson, former president of PayPal. Scott is one of the best leaders I've had the pleasure to work with, a friend, a mentor, and a real innovator responsible for PayPal's largest innovations to date. Thank you to Alenka Grealish, who is responsible for my becoming an industry analyst with Celent, for helping me develop those analyst skills necessary to go below the surface and dig out those valuable insights! Thank you to Noel Kullavanijaya, for whom I had the pleasure of working at Citigroup and who has been extremely generous with his time, guidance, and friendship over the years. Thank you to Osama Bedier, a true inspiration to work with and a great big-picture thinker. Thank you to Matthew Mengerink for your guidance at PayPal, your insights for this book, and your never-ending energy.

Thank you to the highly talented contributors in the book—George Peabody of Glenbrook for authoring the chapter on math-based currencies, which is filled with interesting observations. Matt Harris—thank you for your very well-written piece on prepaid and your valuable perspective on trends in financial technology. Paul Steencamp, a real innovator formerly with First National Bank of South Africa, and Warren Bond, CEO and founder of Luminous, were also extremely helpful in outlining the many practical examples of how banks and start-ups can work together. Another big thanks to Neil Hiltz at Facebook, who put together a very thoughtful piece on how banks can take advantage of social trends, and Julie Ruggiero for helping with all the necessary approvals. I'd also like to express my appreciation to Peter Aceto and Charaka Kithulegoda, CEO and CIO of ING Direct Canada for their terrific contribution that discusses how they have successfully driven innovation at their bank, and to Aline Badr for putting it all together. JP Nicols, thank you for your encouragement, introductions, and contribution to how banks can think about partnering. A very big thanks to Anil Arora, Melanie Flanagan, Joe Poverari, and Eric Conners at Yodlee, who continue to push the envelope on bank innovation and always offer valuable thoughts for the financial services industry.

Thank you to the many thought leaders who agreed to be interviewed for this book: Hans Morris for the always insightful, relevant, and thoughtful feedback on financial services and payments; Russell Goldsmith, CEO, and Nate Wehunt, head of Digital at City National Bank; Bill Ready, of Braintree; Sergi Herrero of BNPP; Zilvinas Bareisis of Celent; and Dana Stalder at Matrix. Renaud Laplanche, CEO of Lending Club—thank you for sharing your insights on peer-to-peer lending and how banks might participate. Meyer Malka of Ribbit Capital—thank you for giving me a brand new perspective on Bitcoin and for your very unique and valuable perspectives on financial technology. I am also appreciative of Mike Strange, CTO of Mitek, for his contribution and insight for banks in how they might invest in their ecosystem. Brett King, author of Bank 3.0—thank you for your innumerable insights on book writing and your support. Chris Popple of RBS Bank—thank you for contributing your thoughts and time. Thanks to John Staley, COO of Equity Bank, who has opened my eyes to the many financial innovations taking place across Africa.

I want to thank the many industry colleagues and partners who have helped shape this book directly and indirectly through their insights, anecdotes, and content. Jim Bruene, founder and CEO of Online Banking Report and the Finovate conference—thank you for offering so much rich content, introductions, and encouragement during this process. John Schulte, CIO of Mercantile Bank of Michigan—a true thought leader and visionary—thank you for having your bank become the first bank to partner with PayPal for person-to-person payments and all of your excellent perspective. Carl Scheible, EVP at MoneyGram—a very big thank you for your collaboration and providing such rich material on behalf of MoneyGram. Thank you to John Valentine at LevelUp for pointing me to some great industry and media sources. Thank you to Chris Larson, Patrick Griffin, and Danny Aranda at Ripple for your contribution and support in researching math-based currencies. Danny

Shader and Billy Robins at PayNearMe—thank you for the strong content you've contributed and the insights into how banks can work with nontraditional partners. Thank you to John Hurley and Darian Shirazi, founder of Radius, for the unique data and insight you have made available for the book. Scott Dunlap, founder of 10th Dimension—thank you for your insightful contributions and quotes. Thank you to Shamir Karkal and Krista Berlincourt of Simple (now BBVA) for taking the time to discuss your company with me. I also want to thank Sarah Friar at Square for taking the time to discuss Square and sending me $1. May Meere and Ericson Chan of Standard Chartered—thank you for offering new perspectives on some of the challenges and opportunities in Asia. Thank you to David Greene at Technology Credit Union, one of the first movers to partner with PayPal and offer a unique perspective on partnering. Mike Boush, thank you for your support and for demonstrating that sometimes big card issuers can act like nimble start-ups. Thank you to Andy Spindler of FSVC for lending your perspective and the always unique vantage point on financial services in the emerging markets. I also want to thank Jenny Ceran, a trusted friend and former PayPal colleague, for all the support, encouragement, and terrific ideas along the way.

Several friends and colleagues from the research and consulting community were also instrumental to this book. To Daniel Wolfe, editor-in-chief at PaymentSource—I always learn something from every conversation we have. Thank you to Zachary Aron and the Deloitte financial services team for lending your time to offer your thoughts for the book. Thanks to Steve Mott at BetterBuyDesign, always an original thinker and a highly respected industry colleague. Also thanks to Jane Hennessy and Chuck Adams for the many suggestions and articles you've shared. I also appreciate the time and insights from my former analyst colleagues—thanks to Zil at Celent and Gwenn Bezard at Aite for your terrific insights.

I am very thankful to the editors at Wiley Finance—thank you to Susan McDermott and Bill Falloon, who sought me out and enlisted me on this adventure. Thank you very much to Judy Howarth, who painstakingly went through this manuscript and offered innumerable contributions to make the book better. Thank you to Vincent Nordhaus for running a tight ship with the production schedule, and to Katie McGowan for all of your creative distribution ideas. Thanks to Tiffany Charbonier for your support with the various marketing and administrative work for this book.

Last, but never least, to my wife and best friend over the past 22 years, Suzan Negip Schatt, who has been a true partner, comfortable with my leaving PayPal to write a book without the future mapped out, and just as comfortable with exploring the unknown on our fourth continent together as when we met. She is the uncommon master of common sense whose good judgment, humor, and patience deserves an entire book of praise.

Introduction:
Innovating Through Scarcity

"More money is rarely the answer to innovation. The best innovations actually come from a world of scarce resources."
—John Donahoe, CEO, eBay[1]

A few years ago, I had the privilege to be one of the early members of PayPal X, a division of PayPal owned by eBay Inc. PayPal X was a radical idea at the time—a complete shift in business and operating models, which put developers and partners at the center of everything PayPal did. It was an acknowledgment that despite the significant number of talented people working at PayPal, far more talent, business insight, and innovation existed outside PayPal's walls than from within. That's a tough realization for any company to grasp—the fact that the best ideas, business, product, marketing, and engineering talent will always live outside the walls of any particular company, regardless of how successful it is with its core business. It requires a lot of courage to invite outside talent to compete with your company's ideas and products, and that was certainly true for PayPal. It meant that other companies might have a better idea of how to serve their customers with your company's assets. It requires a very strong, forward-looking CEO to allow that creative destruction to take place—a company might disintermediate itself to some degree, but the trade-off is that it stays relevant and has its fingers on the pulse of where an industry may be headed.

Most financial services companies are not wrestling with this challenge. Hiring a "chief innovation officer" or forming an innovations group isn't sufficient because significant industry innovation and disruption happens outside the walls of a company. Just consider the average mortality of large, multinational firms—roughly 40 years, versus the 75+ years that humans live.[2] We live in a world of scarcity—there never seems to be enough talent, time, or resources for innovation beyond a core business. Ask any senior executive at a bank how many of their information technology (IT) and operations professionals are dedicated to risk and compliance initiatives, and chances are high that you'll hear that anywhere from 70 to 90 percent of their resources are tied up to ensure they are meeting regulatory and risk requirements, despite the fact that U.S. banks will spend close to $42 billion on technology.[3] They'll spend another 25 percent of their compliance budgets on new overseas regulation.[4]

Even at places like PayPal, which has a reputation for industry innovation and disruption, it's never easy to free up product and engineering resources to focus on new initiatives. In today's world, the only way to harness a critical mass of talent and stay relevant to consumer preferences and expectations is to open up and partner.

In the case of PayPal, that meant encouraging developers of all sizes to build new products with a "PayPal Inside" approach. They could create frictionless experiences by integrating them within their own mobile applications. And through the new JavaScript PayPal buttons, developers could add PayPal by copying and pasting five lines of code into their web site, shopping cart, or a QR (quick response) code[5]—leading to massive improvements and cost reductions in development and integration. Developers could have access to new application programming interfaces (APIs)[6] so that companies could accept credit cards while PayPal maintained the liability of handling the compliance aspects of the payment instrument. This was to include applications like peer-to-peer payments that could happen on multiple platforms besides PayPal.com. It allowed for split payments, enabling many recipients to receive funds at once, or payment preapprovals that allowed for automatic transfer of funds based on preset specifications, and even payment aggregation—allowing businesses to reduce the cost of transactions by aggregating payments to one lump sum.

Opening up a platform, however, is not trivial and not for the faint of heart. Key vetting processes, compliance, and risk capabilities need to be in place. It requires ceding some control of an institution's customers and brand. It also requires an understanding of what micro trends will become mega trends, and how to evaluate and build trust with the right partners.

The exercise we went through with PayPal was transformative for us. Too often, the bigger a financial services company gets, the easier it is to resort to an insular "build it and they will come" mentality, leading to mediocre thinking and products. At PayPal, the platform approach led us to develop a strong business development culture—scouting for companies that could leverage PayPal assets. We partnered with many types of companies—other platform providers, technology companies, kiosk providers, and various commerce enablers. One of the biggest shifts was our approach in partnering closely with the banking world. We realized early on that these partnerships generated win-win outcomes due to the complementary nature of business models and core competencies involved.

Fast-forward to today, and the financial services industry at large now has an opportunity to take advantage of a plethora of new services built by innovative companies that are recognizing trends faster than any larger company could. It requires a large company mind shift—an understanding that consumers or small businesses may not want to access their bank for a lending product; they may prefer Kabbage, Lending Club, Braintree, or Square to their banks. The only way to stay relevant is to embrace the fact that if you are one of the 14,000+ financial institutions not in the "top 10," faced with a scarcity of assets, you can embrace technology to create incredibly relevant and compelling experiences for your customers. This means making it incredibly easy for others to integrate to your channels through a common platform services approach (think Apple App store for banks), or make it incredibly easy to embed a bank's capabilities within a nonbank application. If you are involved in a strategy, innovations, or business development role with your institution, that will be important if you want to stay ahead of the curve. Stessa Cohen, a banking analyst with research firm Gartner Group recently tweeted her prediction that a full 25 percent of banks will have consumer app stores by 2016.[7]

So how are some financial institutions not just surviving but thriving in this environment, even with little to no IT staff? They are taking advantage of a few key shifts in the marketplace—changing consumer behavior (social, mobile, and local trends discussed later in this book), the rise of platform services, and open APIs. These shifts, if combined with good, creative partnering, can go a long way to ensure that any institution can stay relevant and thrive. There are a few other trends and influencers discussed briefly in this introduction that we'll weave throughout this book.

THE INFLUENCE OF CLOUD ON INNOVATION

Platform services, as we've just discussed, have been a tremendous enabler for anyone looking to innovate in the financial services arena. This has all come about as a result of "cloud services": the ability for software to be remotely hosted on servers and delivered through the Internet. This allows for traditional financial institutions to more easily take advantage of others' software and pair up offerings to create an almost unlimited number of software possibilities delivered through bank and nonbank channels. It has effectively lowered barriers and costs for anyone with a good idea to deliver their software. The cloud cuts across many areas of business but is tremendously valuable in the realm of financial services, where most people now bank online and money increasingly is managed in the form of digital information.

THE INFLUENCE OF SMARTPHONES

Much has been written on the smartphone revolution, and we'll explore some of ways the financial services industry can take advantage of new technologies, partnerships, and business models. To this day, 2.5 billion adults do not have access to the formal banking system, yet through smartphones, that is about to change very quickly.[8] Around the world, companies such as PayPal, Square, and iZettle are enabling small businesses that would have otherwise transacted in cash to accept electronic payments. Simple credit card readers that can plug into a consumer's existing smartphone make all this possible.

BIG DATA = BIG DRIVER OF INNOVATION

Big data is a big buzzword, but it's a powerful trend and concept that we'll discuss in more detail throughout the book. It refers to powerful analytics that can analyze massive amounts of information to detect patterns and correlations that most would not spot. It becomes particularly interesting these days given the information that can be unearthed in unconventional ways. Data are increasingly read from mobile phones (location, time, identity, mobile applications) combined with social data (e.g., LinkedIn, Facebook) and wearables (e.g., Nike's Fuelband, Jawbone "Up") that can give businesses and consumers the opportunity to better pair their financial and commercial needs with specific, tailored offerings.

Two notable areas worth watching relate to home automation and autos. Imagine getting an instant claim completed if there were a fire or flood in the house or a car accident. Leveraged in the right way, better data can also allow consumers to connect more directly with their banker, as they did 50 years ago. It used to be that your banker could sit down with you, view your history, and help you make your money work harder. That can create a digital dialogue that would have once happened in person. Sean Gilchrist, who led Barclays Digital Group, stated, "Interestingly, when you ask consumers if a bank can track your mobile data, and it's put in the right context, 90 percent of the customers will say yes. We did a test with geolocation through your phone and asked, 'Would you allow our bank to know where, so that if we spot a suspicious transaction, we can text you instead of call you?' It is very contextual, and we can build their trust in terms of how we're transparently using this information and it's relevant to their needs."[9]

Today's banking systems largely still run on technology and credit assessments built decades ago. Increasingly, we'll see more companies like Affirm on the landscape. Founded by Max Levchin, who was the founder and CTO of PayPal, Affirm is a service that uses nontraditional data sources such as social data—for example, Twitter, LinkedIn, and Facebook—to create a detailed portrait of someone as they live their life online, and by looking at these data with their permission, it's possible to assess the ability for someone to be responsible financially in an economy better than traditional credit reports can. As we'll discuss more in this book, the opportunity to partner with firms that are making credit more efficient can enable the financial services industry as a whole to create new markets and bring more financial inclusiveness into the economy.

TAKING A CUE FROM RETAILING

Remember Blockbuster? Circuit City? Borders? We can learn a lot about how the banking industry needs to adapt from the retailing industry. We'll discuss the changing landscape of commerce and how financial institutions fit in later, but it's worth mentioning here that one of the most important trends in retail is the rise of the omnichannel experience—retailers understand that increasingly consumers are buying through their mobile phone, and their expectations have increased dramatically. Why can't a retailer instantly check their inventory? Why can't the correct size and color be delivered from another store? Why can't I return this item just as easily as I bought it? If retailers can't satisfy their customers in the age of instant information access and transparency, then Amazon will. It remembers what you bought last time, what you looked at, and what you may need next. Retailers need to be just as sophisticated, and so do financial institutions if they want to stay relevant to their customers. Retailers also realize that if they don't find new channels to offer their goods or services, they face irrelevance.

There's a lot we can learn on how bank services will need to be delivered if financial institutions are to stay relevant. How inconvenient it is to go to a bank to deposit a check when many banks now offer the ability for me to use my mobile phone to take a picture of my check. How about requiring me to go into a branch when I'd love to just do everything on my phone or tablet? The good news is that there has never been a better or easier time to work with the many tech providers to build compelling experiences for customers. We'll hear from tech providers and offer up tips on how banks and financial technology firms can work together in new and unique ways.

THE ENEMY OF MY ENEMY IS MY FRIEND

The new age of partnering and innovation in the financial services arena is filled with brilliant shades of gray. The media would have you believe that any new up-and-comer in the financial services space is a disrupter to banks. I look at the media reports, and then at the 500+ partnerships we struck at PayPal in my tenure, and I just shake my head. There are really very few pure competitors in the financial services arena. The challenge is to recognize and seize new opportunities of every kind. Any institution a financial services company might view as a disintermediator for banks might just be what's keeping your financial institution relevant. The biggest risk for financial institutions is to remain static. There is a nonbank alternative product to most everything these days, including peer-to-peer payments, financing, investments, and payment services. What will keep consumers using their financial institutions is the level of service, convenience, and trust.

RECONCILING INNOVATION AND REGULATION

In the financial services industry, it's hard to discuss innovation without at least mentioning regulation. The two are not mutually exclusive concepts. What's important to note is that history has showed us that often what's good for the consumer wins the day and results in changes in the regulatory landscape. When PayPal started, some thought what it was doing was "illegal" as a nonbank. PayPal was considered by some state regulators as an illegal banking service and was shut off in some states early on until it received appropriate licenses.[10] Tesla, the electric car company, was viewed as illegally distributing its cars and bypassing dealer networks, until courts ruled in Tesla's favor.[11] Uber, a mobile taxi service that has taken the market by storm, has faced significant legal challenges, given that taxi companies did not want to let a newcomer in. Travis Kalanick, Uber's CEO, summed up the challenge of innovation and regulation well: "If you put yourself in the position to ask for something that is already legal, you'll find you'll never be able to roll out."[12]

This isn't true just in the developed world—consider the mobile payments company M-Pesa, offered in Kenya by Safaricom, owned largely by Vodafone. M-Pesa allowed every Kenyan who had a mobile phone to participate in the formal banking system and use the service to pay individuals or businesses. As Chris Bishko and Pearl Chan of the Omidyar Network discuss, the Central Bank of Kenya took a lean approach to regulation in the interest of consumers, and as a result, M-Pesa thrived. In five years, it now has 23 million customers, representing 74 percent of adults in Kenya.

Thirty-one percent of Kenyan gross domestic product (GDP) is now transacted through these mobile money services.[13]

While I would argue that it's important for banks to be regulated because they play such a central role in the economy, the details of how governments ultimately decide to impose capital requirements and encourage more efficient business models to surface is up for significant debate. New entrants can provide quicker and more valuable ways of connecting with the customer and provide enormous benefits, particularly if they can still leverage a bank's expertise and partnership to navigate the complex maze of compliance and regulatory requirements.

Banks and tech companies can leverage each other to ensure that innovation and regulation can be balanced, and while it's true that compliance does suction off significant product, IT, and operational resources, it's also true that through creative partnering and some ingenuity, banks and financial tech companies can rise to meet these challenges. One of the more challenging pieces of legislation that banks have had to contend with is the Durbin Amendment, which took effect in 2011. Card-issuing banks have made much of their revenue in recent years from interchange, paid by merchants in exchange for the ability to take credit card and debit card payments. The average interchange fee for debit cards has dropped from 50 cents to 24 cents since the law went into effect, translating into $8 billion a year of losses.[14] Aside from charging higher fees on other products, this has challenged the financial services industry to think about making up for this shortfall through new revenue streams or increased volume. The thinking this stimulates can lead to some creative opportunities, often introduced by nonbanks. One such example to be discussed later in this book involves Simple, a virtual bank, which has introduced its card through Braintree, a payment processor recently purchased by PayPal. Through Braintree, Simple cards will automatically be on file for consumers as they sign up for various services hosted by Braintree.[15]

There are over 9,000 pages of complex rules in the Dodd-Frank Wall Street Reform and Consumer Protection Act. Section 1073 of this act gives just one glimpse into the challenges financial institutions face as they reconcile compliance with business innovation. The rule is intended to give greater transparency to consumers related to the cost of international payments. The Consumer Financial Protection Bureau requires fair and transparent disclosures and when the funds become available. While well intentioned, the law poses serious IT challenges for most financial institutions. Since these transactions generally go through correspondent banks, it is challenging to get this information since no central database exists. In later sections we'll talk about some of the creative partnering that has come about to address regulations and even thrive as a result. Banks have partnered with

PayPal and MoneyGram and have seen tremendously positive results. Even start-ups can work with money transmitters who offer their state licensing portfolio, allowing them to get to market quicker.[16]

For those financial tech start-ups that are interested in becoming a part of the latest generation of virtual currencies, such as Bitcoin, the guidance issued by the Financial Crimes Enforcement Network (FINCEN) requires these companies to become licensed money transmitters.[17] It is otherwise costly and expensive to obtain close to 50 separate licenses, and as such, partnering can present a significant set of opportunities. Otherwise, not only can it be difficult to obtain licenses, but capital constraints can also challenge early-stage companies seeking money transmitter licenses. While companies have to split revenue and pay compliance fees, it is far more palatable than the alternative.

IN SEARCH OF NEW PAYMENT REVENUE STREAMS

As we've just discussed, in the United States, the Durbin Amendment has knocked down a major source of retail banking revenue—debit card interchange. Other countries have had these regulations in place for several years. Australia has a 12-cent debit card fee[18] while the European Union[19] and Canada[20] are offering debit transactions directly out of a bank account at cost. Considering that 25 to 40 percent of checking accounts at big banks are unprofitable[21] and banks aren't making interchange fees, where can they find new revenue? The answer increasingly is to issue prepaid cards, which aren't regulated, or work harder to provide more value to consumers on how to save or spend, and identify new partners that can bring consumers a new level of convenience and insight. Later in this book, we'll discuss how banks like Standard Chartered are bringing the concept of artificial intelligence to their consumers to give them more insight and information into their finances.[22]

American Express's decision to partner with Wal-Mart to offer a light-touch banking product based on a prepaid card, which can introduce new segments into more banking products and services, will be an increasingly common model. Banking products are increasingly becoming things you can pick up at any retailer—a prepaid card hanging up near the cashier can get you a bank account with direct deposit, a credit line, and an automated teller machine (ATM) card. Large retailers are seeing the benefits of this model around the world. Wirecard in Germany offers mobile network operators the ability to offer a banking service, just as M-Pesa in Kenya, a mobile service that is ultimately running on the back of an underlying bank. Bank services increasingly are powering channels that connect with customers in new ways. How can these partner tie-ups help financial institutions make up for revenue shortfalls? We'll discuss later in the book how opportunities to build digital wallets really give financial institutions an opportunity to rethink how they can leverage their payment infrastructure. What becomes far more valuable today is how all the nonpayment data—offers, coupons, promotions—can potentially be leveraged around the payment and flow through data rails. With the cost of debit processing going lower, partnering with unconventional partners will be critical.

NEW SKILL SETS FOR A NEW ERA

Those financial institutions that help consumers get what they want, when and where they want it, realize that this may mean consumers simply don't want to frequent their bank's branches, online banking, or mobile banking application to get what they need. They may very well want to access their bank through Facebook, or through one of a myriad of applications tied into the context of something tangentially related to banking. When looking for a house, wouldn't it be terrific if you could also find financing on the same app you're using for real estate? How about financing your car with the same app that allowed you to find the car you wanted in the first place? The latest virtual banks, such as Moven, employ consumer behavior specialists with degrees in psychology to better understand consumer needs and wants. Banks that have a keen sense of how they can help retailers drive more sales and demand for their goods or services will also be needed. What will also be needed are the competitive intelligence and market assessment skills to identify partners that are institutions that are creating highly compelling consumer experiences (e.g., think Uber, Square, and Apple). Other companies include those that manage activities around the payment versus the payment itself (think Amazon and Facebook). Finally, those companies that can create the most compelling, vertically integrated experiences through the mobile phone (think Samsung, Apple, and Google) can be very powerful partners as well, which we'll discuss at length. Honing in on skill sets that can identify categories of partners and creative partnering options will be key for the financial services industry to stay relevant with changing consumer expectations.

A ROAD MAP FOR THIS BOOK

We'll outline the most important trends we see impacting the growth of financial technology and consumer banking services, along with changing consumer expectations of what they expect from their financial services providers. As Peter Aceto, CEO of ING DIRECT* puts it, "It's clear everyone

---

*At the time of this writing, ING DIRECT changed its name to Tangerine.

is talking about mobile, social, cloud, and big data. But who knows what the next trend will be? And what do these buzzwords actually mean in the context of a business solution?" I will look to focus on the business solutions and context of partnership opportunities I've observed that could benefit the financial services world. We'll touch on technology enablers and consumer empowerment knocking over existing industries in a *huge* way and how fast these pivots occur. We'll also get into some of the divergent thinking that leads to innovation—how consumers rule the day and governments capitulate when an innovation catches hold.

We'll also examine mobile commerce and the rise of the digital wallet. Why is this trend so important? We're moving to an era where convenience and personalization will finally make a digital wallet more valuable than a physical wallet. Customers will gradually question whether it makes sense to keep their bank account and credit card if these same services are accessible by third parties. We will examine how some of the smaller, nimble providers of financial services are solidifying their position to dictate how future retail financial services are delivered. There are many young companies that are fundamentally rethinking how people pay, buy, sell, and access the foreign exchange markets.

As we'll discover, frictionless on-boarding, the use of social media, and partnering with nontraditional technology players will be a critical part of innovation in order to stay relevant in the new normal. The rise of nontraditional financial services companies over the past few years has been significant, given the financial crisis and low interest rates, and given birth to several non–financial services companies, that are serving a growing need for savers seeking higher returns. Lending Club, as an example, has already surpassed the $2 billion asset mark by fulfilling this need.[23] We'll then move on to some specifics in Chapter 5 of how to partner with these nontraditional players and discuss opportunities to leverage big data in these partnerships.

Do you have some IT resources you can put to work? In later chapters we'll examine some of the more innovative case studies with banks of all sizes, and how to leverage the power of mashups and platform services. We'll then move on to the new financial technology players and why they seem to be some of the scariest innovators of all: start-ups that don't need to monetize payments! We'll examine some of the implications their platforms will have for the banking industry and opportunities for collaboration.

We'll then move on to some of the specific opportunities in store for financial services companies that can seize the moment—opportunities to take advantage of a rapidly changing platform paradigm, in which mobile is the be-all and end-all platform for many future developments. Further, we'll discuss what is happening with tablet devices, and how tablet-centric providers can open the door for banks seeking new monetizable opportunities.

We'll also take a glimpse of math-based currencies and the Bitcoin phenomenon. take a look at where some of the financial technology shifts are heading and offer suggestions on how to take advantage of these trends. We'll also hear from several thought leaders in the financial technology and banking world to get a variety of perspectives and insight on how best to prepare for these trends.

Let's dive right in!

NOTES

1. Brad Stone, "eBay's John Donahoe on E-Commerce and Mobile Payments' Future," *Business Week,* www.businessweek.com/articles/ 2013-08-08/ebays-john-donahoe-on-e-commerce-and-mobile-payments-future. Accessed August 8, 2013.
2. "The Lifespan of a Company," *Business Week*. www.businessweek.com/ chapter/degeus.htm. Accessed February 7, 2014.
3. Ovum, 2013.
4. Protiviti, May 2012.
5. A QR code is a machine-readable code consisting of an array of black and white squares, typically used for storing URLs or other information for reading by the camera on a smartphone.
6. An application programming interface (API) specifies how some software components should interact with each other.
7. Tweet by Stessa Cohen, Industry Analyst at Gartner Group, https:// twitter.com/stessacohen/status/386882091054813185.
8. Asli Demirguc-Kunt and Leora Klapper, "Measuring Financial Inclusion," World Bank, www-wds.worldbank.org/external/default/WDSContentServer/ IW3P/IB/2012/04/19/000158349_20120419083611/Rendered/PDF/ WPS6025.pdf. Accessed February 7, 2014.
9. Interview with Sean Gilchrist.
10. Troy Wolverton, "Feds: PayPal Not a Bank," CNET, http://news.cnet .com/2100-1017-858264.html. Accessed February 7, 2014.
11. "Tesla Wins Another Round against Car Dealers," *Wall Street Journal,* http://blogs.wsj.com/corporate-intelligence/2013/04/11/tesla-wins-another-round-against-car-dealers/. Accessed February 7, 2014.
12. Brian X. Chen, "A Feisty Start-Up Is Met with Regulatory Snarl," *New York Times,* www.nytimes.com/2012/12/03/technology/app-maker-uber-hits-regulatory-snarl.html?pagewanted=all&_r=0. Accessed February 7, 2014.
13. Chris Bishko and Pearl Chan, "M-Pesa and GCash: Can 'Lean Regulation' Be a Gamechanger for Financial Innovation?" *Forbes,*

www.forbes.com/sites/kerryadolan/2013/10/03/m-pesa-and-gcash-can-lean-regulation-be-a-gamechanger-for-financial-innovation/.   Accessed October 3, 2013.

14. Martha C. White, "Why Banks Love Debit Cards Again," *Time,* http://business.time.com/2013/03/28/why-banks-love-debit-cards-again/. Accessed February 7, 2014.

15. Sarah Perez, "Braintree Expands Venmo Touch, Partners with Online Banking Startup Simple for One-Touch Mobile Payments," *TechCrunch,* http://techcrunch.com/2013/07/10/braintree-expands-venmo-touch-partners-with-online-banking-startup-simple-for-one-touch-mobile-payments/. Accessed July 10, 2013.

16. Bailey Reutzel, "In Money Transmitter Licensing, Is It Better to Own—or to Rent?" *PaymentsSource,*www.paymentssource.com/news/in-money-transmitter-licensing-is-it-better-to-own-or-to-rent-3015198-1.html. Accessed August 22, 2013.

17. Bailey Reutzel, "FinCEN's Virtual-Money Guidelines Add Roadblocks for New Companies," *PaymentsSource,* www.paymentssource.com/news/fincens-virtual-money-guidelines-add-roadblocks-for-new-companies-3013574-1.html. Accessed February 7, 2014.

18. "Proposed Changes to the EFTPOS Interchange Fee Standard," letter addressed to Ms. Michele Bullock, head of payment policy at the Reserve Bank of Australia, October 23, 2009, www.rba.gov.au/payments-system/reforms/debit-card-systems/submissions-pro-interchg-stds/epal-23102009-1.pdf

19. "What Is SEPA?" Factsheet published by MasterCard Worldwide, www.mastercard.com/us/company/en/docs/SEPA%20backgrounder_four%20party%20model_fact%20sheets.pdf

20. Interac, "Interac Fees," www.interac.ca/index.php/en/interac-about/interac-fees. Accessed February 7, 2014.

21. Halah Touryalai, "How Banks Are Getting Richer Off the Poor," *Forbes,* www.forbes.com/sites/halahtouryalai/2012/04/26/how-banks-are-getting-richer-off-the-poor/. Accessed February 7, 2014.

22. Matthew Sainsbury, "Artificial Intelligence Leading the Way for Financial Services Technology Innovation," *FST Media,* http://fst.asia/NewsArticle_details.aspx?Articlenewsid=56. Accessed February 7, 2014.

23. "Revenge of the Nerds," *The Economist,* April 1, 2013, www.economist.com/news/finance-and-economics/21582512-explosion-start-ups-changing-finance-better-revenge-nerds. Accessed February 7, 2014.

CHAPTER 1

Consumer Empowerment Knocking at the Door

How Mobile Is Reshaping Consumer Expectations in Financial and Retail

"The smartphone revolution is underhyped—more people have access to phones than access to running water. We've never had anything like this before since the beginning of the planet."

—Marc Andreessen, Andreessen Horowitz

"Our job is to make mobile the answer to everything."

—Eric Schmidt, Google

What happens when you equip billions of people with a computer in their pocket? Financial services and commerce will forever be reshaped. There are certain catalytic events that have such a major impact on consumer behavior that the downstream opportunities that come about create change at a much faster rate. Mobile is just such an event. Consumers are rapidly shifting to mobile as their primary computing device, with a staggering 51 percent of their Internet time happening through a smartphone or tablet![1] Yet we are still in the early stages of more dramatic changes that will come about as a result of the innate software and hardware combinations associated with mobile and tablet devices. The microphone, the camera, low-frequency Bluetooth, and biometrics will all have a significant and dramatic impact for financial institutions.

Aman Narian, global head of digital with Standard Chartered Bank, sums up this vast uncharted territory well:

> *We are at the beginning of the beginning when it comes to mobile . . . we have still not used the hardware and software integration of a mobile phone—voice message tags, talk to your mobile banking app . . . biometrics with touch ID coming to iPhone . . . there is much to do. . . ."*[2]

Aman sums up how much of the banking industry thinks about mobile— as a vast uncharted territory. Consider ING DIRECT Canada (recently re- named Tangerine). Eighteen percent of today's banking transactions are happening on mobile phones; that number was zero two years ago. More than 12 percent of all money transfers, 18 percent of all bill payments, and 17 percent of e-mail money transfers are now conducted using mobile phones.[3]

Mobile devices are becoming consumers' primary computing device, and with that, a new set of possibilities open up for financial institutions interested in capturing new markets. These new markets come about as a result of the unique software and hardware attributes associated with a mobile device.

Customer expectations have skyrocketed now that mobile can bring rich, personalized experiences to any smartphone. And as a result, it's more important than ever for financial institutions and commerce companies to operate with a "mobile first" mind-set. We are already seeing examples of how users are leveraging their mobile devices to disrupt the traditional re- tail commerce paradigm in the form of "showrooming." Consumers will look in physical stores, and then simply look up the item on the mobile phone and order it. The Comscore survey shown in Figure 1.1 helps explain why people are showrooming—72 percent simply find a better price online.

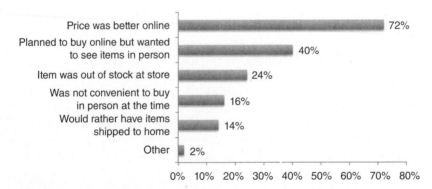

FIGURE 1.1 "Showrooming" Is Driving More Spending Online
Source: Business Insider, Comscore.

Increasingly, retailers that don't have a mobile presence will lose out to the Amazons of the world, who provide consumers with the ability to scan any item they see, and can facilitate the payment and shipping of the item with one click. Moreover, prior to even stepping foot in a store, most surveys suggest that close to 50 percent of consumers are researching products and services before they buy. As a result of consumers' using mobile devices to shop in these new ways, they have completely disrupted the traditional retail shopping paradigm. Aside from simply researching products, comparing competitors' prices, and buying goods from online sellers, consumers expect to review ratings and know their budget and bank balance—all while standing in the aisles of brick-and-mortar locations. Real-time access to products is the one significant competitive advantage physical stores have over digital ones, enabling consumers to head to a local store rather than order online and wait for the item to be delivered in days. Who needs to wait!

This disruption certainly isn't confined just to physical retailers. Most people can't remember the last time they were in a bank branch now that you can deposit checks, pay bills, send individuals money, and manage your personal budgets all from the comfort of your mobile phone. As a result, bank branches are going through similar radical changes, as is the overall mobile financial services experience. It's not just the bank branch that is affected; why go into a bank when you can instantly get approved for credit through your mobile phone?

Next, we'll discuss some of the models that are being developed to take advantage of the inherent capabilities associated with mobile and how they can ultimately benefit forward-looking financial services providers.

HOW MOBILE IS CHANGING CONSUMER BEHAVIOR

Globally, we now have more mobile connected devices on earth than people![4] As smartphones, data plans, and bandwidth continue to improve, those pocket computers, otherwise known as smartphones, have become a significant way for consumers to interact with the Internet. A few notable statistics from the Pew Research Center on U.S. consumers[5]:

- Sixty-three percent of adult cell owners use their phone to go online, doubling since 2009.
- Forty-four percent of cell owners have slept with their phone next to their bed because they wanted to make sure they didn't miss any calls, text messages, or other updates during the night.
- Thirty-four percent of cell Internet users go online mostly using their phones, and not using some other device such as a desktop or laptop computer.

- Twenty-nine percent of cell owners describe their cell phone as something they "can't imagine living without."
- Twenty-one percent of all adult cell owners now do most of their online browsing using their mobile phone—and not some other device such as a desktop or laptop computer.

Smartphones are expected to account for close to 70 percent of all smart connected device shipments by 2015. Mobile phones are not the only devices changing behavior-tablets are also impacting how consumers and businesses use technology. In fact, as of this writing, it appears that we will see more tablets shipped worldwide than personal computers.[6] A growing number of consumers are looking at two screens when they're home, such as watching TV while they use their tablet, and we are seeing a growing number of consumers who watch television and movies on their tablet or mobile phone.[7]

So what do all these statistics tell us? Given the ubiquity of these devices, consumers are entering a world in which transparency, information, and access are a given. Goods and services become commoditized unless the consumer experiences something more, whether it is convenience, loyalty, insight, or service. Banks can't possibly offer their customers a premium experience with their lending, payments, and deposit products unless they are offered in a way that adds context to the experience. For example, securing a traditional line of credit or bank account requires a fair amount of paperwork and certainly is not a real time. In a world where security and price are table stakes, consumers expect to be able to secure an instant auto loan if they are at a car dealership, pay someone in another country without walking into a branch, and deposit their checks by simply taking a picture of them. Young customers that grew up with a mobile phone in their hand will check the phone as part of their morning routine. Consumers will increasingly look to their mobile devices for insight, and to save time and money. Jack Dorsey, founder of Square, has often referred to design and simplicity as the cornerstones of any good customer experience:

> . . . And that's something we've always believed strongly in building our technology, building our product: is that we can fade the technology away, we can fade the mechanics away so that the people can focus on a very human, natural, personal interaction and a very simple exchange.[8]

Those companies that can help with this insight will be the companies worth partnering with!

MOBILE IS BLURRING THE LINES BETWEEN DIGITAL AND PHYSICAL

A few years ago, in the developed world, the distinction between e-commerce and commerce was fairly clear. E-commerce related to all those things consumers purchased using their desktop or laptop computer, or whatever device they used to shop online. "Physical" commerce was the art of buying something at a physical location—a retailer with real "brick and mortar," a cash register, large point-of-sale machinery, PIN pads, card swipers, and receipt printers. This clear distinction has made it easy for the U.S. Department of Commerce to report out the percentage of e-commerce sales that contributes to "total" retail sales. Judging by this measurement, the total impact online commerce has had on the economy seems quite paltry—less than 10 percent of total retail sales.[9]

Over the next few years, it will become very difficult to make this same distinction. Why? People are changing their shopping patterns in physical stores based on their mobile behavior. Purchasing something "online" and "offline" is very hard to judge now that retailers have been moving quickly to a multichannel environment. A customer may initiate a purchase online or pickup in a physical store. Or, increasingly, they may purchase something while they are in a store, and "check out" through their mobile phone. This is giving rise to what the retail and banking industry is calling multichannel commerce. Customers will use a channel most convenient to them to complete part of their experience, whether it is to research, purchase, or take ownership of an item. Kareem Al-Bassam, a friend and former PayPal colleague who headed PayPal's Point of Sale Business Development uses a nice analogy:

> *The current paradigm of large-format retail is focused on the retailer's wants and needs. Like large-scale cattle operations, consumers roam the aisles and eventually to the chute for their final moment—checkout and payment. The checkout process has been optimized for the retailer's needs: through-put, lower cost (i.e., staff), and high-margin add-on sales. It's not a very nice process for the cow. The new paradigm will force retailers to treat their consumers more like free-range chickens. If you've ever tried, it is hard to force a chicken to do much—they scratch and eat as they want. Today, empowered with technology, consumers roam the fields of retail, physical and online, creating complex and nonlinear shopping patterns. They are also in control of when, how, and where they actually finalize the purchase.*

While at PayPal, I delivered a number of presentations in which I often showed the chart in Figure 1.2. This chart shows that revenue derived by

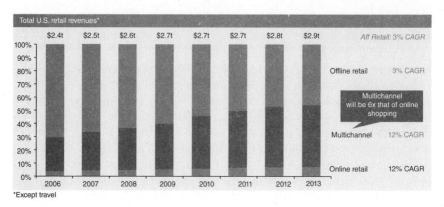

FIGURE 1.2 Total U.S. Retail Revenues
Sources: PayPal, Milo.com, Forrester Report ("U.S. Online Sales Forecast: 2008–2013," February 2, 2009).

pure online retail continues to be very small, and pure offline retail is actually shrinking, although it is over 10 times larger than online shopping today—approximately $3 trillion in the United States. Online shopping, in contrast, will account for just 10 percent of retail sales by 2017 according to Forrester Research.

However, what continues to grow significantly is multichannel shopping, which is six times greater than online shopping. That requires payment providers, retailers, and the financial services and commerce ecosystems to think deeply about how they can unite their channels. Mobile will most often be the connection point, the bridge between the world of physical and digital because, as we've seen, mobile is something that is always with most people, even when they sleep! All of these innovations point to the fact that with the invention of new ways to interact in a commerce context come with fundamental changes in the way we shop and pay for things. The mobile phone can allow the consumer to engage with the merchant when they walk in the store and know significantly more— your potential wish lists, how often you shop, what you shop for, and what promotions might be most relevant to you at the moment. It can make the process of shopping and connecting to the store much more personal. In the process, your card might already be on file, and at some point, as new ways of tagging inventory become available, payment could take place automatically upon leaving.

We also see blurring between offline and online with mobile applications that allow us to complete transactions for things in the physical world. For example, OpenTable, an application for online reservations and ordering, has recently started its own one-click capability.[10] Consumers order and pay using their mobile phone, while dining or picking up their food in a restaurant. Samsung and PayPal recently released the ability for a consumer to use their fingerprint on their mobile phone to check in and purchase goods at physical locations where PayPal check-in capabilities are present.

What are the implications to the banking world? Today, "card not present" rates that merchants must pay to accept online credit or debit cards is much higher than "card present" rates. The economics of a card transaction will no longer be based on whether the transaction is Internet-based or done at a physical terminal. The justification for higher rates used to be valid—identity thieves could steal credit card numbers and use them online, with merchants and banks none the wiser. With the advent of biometrics on the phone and new ways of making identity verification possible, these distinctions go away. Thanks to mobile, we are in an age when we may coin a new classification of transactions, "human present" and "human not present" transactions that could ultimately better dictate the level of risk a merchant is taking on a transaction. This could then better determine the transaction fees that merchants would ultimately pay for payment acceptance. As technology enables the transactions to become less risky, and authentication can begin to be federated to multiple devices, it will become easier for this to occur. Organizations such as Fast Identity Online (FIDO) are enabling standards for this to occur, which should move mobile commerce forward in the new world of "multichannel" commerce.

Mobile Learnings from PayPal and Square

While the banking industry and press love to view PayPal and Square as competitors capable of disintermediating a bank's customers, in reality, nothing could be further from the truth. Both have unlocked a significant portion of economic growth and profit for financial institutions as they have made it much easier for merchants to collect electronic payments that ultimately come from the banking industry. As a result, billions of dollars in credit and debit card volume have been generated over the years by these institutions that have contributed to interchange revenue for the banks. Both of these institutions understand that if you eliminate payment friction in a commerce-like setting and combine these things with offers and incentives, it can contribute to significant growth of commerce on the mobile phone. Both institutions recognize how consumers are changing the way they *buy* and *interact* with merchants and how that can significantly deepen the relationships and lead to better engagement. I would argue that both of these companies have been good at seeing what could exist around the corner, recognizing that mobile is the convergence point among commerce, the Internet, and traditional shopping at physical locations.

Square and PayPal both started out in a very similar manner, addressing a significant small business pain point—how to accept payments in a frictionless manner. Both saw an opportunity to help small businesses that often did not pass the underwriting criteria to obtain a merchant account to accept payments, usually because they were too new or too small. In the case of PayPal, its initial focus 15 years ago started with enabling online businesses to quickly accept payments in a secure manner. Square's initial focus started with serving underserved microbusinesses in the physical world that also needed an ability to accept credit card and debit card payments (see Figure 1.3). Serving these customers required completely altering the underwriting criteria used to assess merchant credit risk, and a deep understanding of design—a mobile or online experience that could be significantly better than anything on the market today. Economically reasonable,

FIGURE 1.3 Square Wallet's Virtual Punch Card
Source: Jim Bruene, Online Banking Report.

transparent, and user-friendly payment card acceptance and processing has historically been hard to find for many small businesses. However, what is really dramatic relates to the differences these businesses pay in card fees to the acquiring banks. As the cofounder of Square, Jim McKelvey recently remarked at a conference that if you were to calculate the ratio of fees small businesses pay for card processing, for every dollar Wal-Mart spends to process a credit card, a small business pays $45.[11] Paul Downs, a *New York Times* reporter, underscored the pain most small businesses face when he wrote a series of articles on his search for "reasonable and understandable credit card processing."[12]

Square focused on a "mobile first" payment system available to the masses, much like how PayPal has ultimately created an Internet layer over many existing and disparate payment and clearing systems. Square's ability to give small businesses a transparent fee structure, one that is the same for everyone, and allow businesses to quit anytime with no penalty addressed pain points felt by a critical mass of small businesses. Although the software it produced was not revolutionary, its brilliance related to its prescient timing, in seeing overarching trends in mobile and Internet, and a sea-wave of consumer behavior change. In a world with ubiquitous, real-time access to information, businesses and consumers expect complete transparency. Systems that misinform or obfuscate consumer pricing are going away, and the only way to truly compete is to embrace and partner with companies that are paving the way in solving significant consumer and business pain points.

Square hasn't stopped innovating; it has introduced a number of consumer-oriented innovations with mobile through its Square Wallet mobile application. It has introduced a number of capabilities that make using the mobile phone a better overall experience than using a card. Why? It goes back to somewhat of a recurring theme I'll mention throughout the book—payments really aren't such a big problem in the developed world, the big problem is how to include a powerful commerce context that can ultimately help the consumer gain valuable insight and save time or money. As illustrated in the mobile screenshot (Figure 1.3), courtesy of Jim Bruene, founder of Online Banking Report and the highly successful Finovate conference, digitizing the mobile punch card can add a level of convenience and insight that a physical wallet just can't do. In this case, Square is better than plastic because it can store your loyalty cards and receipts, and unlike a human being, it will not forget to bring your punch card with you and to give you that digital punch every time you frequent a store. According to Bruene:

> *This is where Square shines. . . . When its wallet is used, a virtual punch card is automatically started for you. And when enabled,*

the next time you are near the merchant, Square will automatically remind you (via popup message) to come back and buy from that merchant. And even if it's six months later, you get a second punch on that virtual card. And if all goes well for the merchant, the incremental sales mount up, and you are well on your way to a complimentary mocha. And all your previous transactions, with fully itemized receipts, are available within the Square app. It's truly the future of payments. . . .

How might a bank consider partnering with Square? Consider the recent announcement by U.S. Bank to add Square to its digital wallet options available to customers via their iOS and Android smartphones (see Figure 1.4). As mentioned in a recent article:

Customers can link their U.S. Bank credit, debit, or prepaid account to the Square application to make purchases from their smartphone.

FIGURE 1.4   Receiving Money in Your Bank Account through Square
Source: Dan Schatt (screen shot of author's Citibank account credited from Square).

Square's technology automatically manages the transaction from the customer's U.S. Bank payment account to the merchant. Transactions are then completed without the cashier ever having the customer's account number and other sensitive data, the bank said. U.S. Bank added that its customers can choose to register with one or more wallets and shop at any store that displays the wallet's logo.[13]

We will discuss the digital wallet in later chapters, but the opportunity that U.S. Bank surely sees is to align with a company that has brought to market some experiences consumers and merchants love. That alignment can ultimately translate into experiences in which a U.S. Bank credit card becomes the first payment instrument a consumer thinks about whenever they use their Square account. Partnering with innovative commerce providers to have "top of wallet" and "top of mind" standing can go a long way to ensure that a bank's bread-and-butter payment and lending products aren't treated as another commodity. U.S. Bank's decision to move ahead of the crowd to announce a friendly stance with Square is commendable; they've recognized that their core competency is not necessarily in design, rewards, couponing, promotions, and other areas surrounding commerce experience. Their competency lies with their banking products, their relationship with their customers, and how they continue to enable access of their products through channels and mediums that can resonate most with their customers. Dominic Venturo, chief innovation officer for U.S. Bank, has noted that the Square Wallet is complementary to U.S. Bank's payments business and is interested in enabling its banking customers to "pay where, when, and how they would like to with our products." That's great forward thinking as Square comes out with new products linked to its wallet, such as its most recent Square Cash capability, allowing consumers to pay through e-mail by simply cc'ing the e-mail address, for example, copy pay@square.com. Put the dollar amount in the subject line and add text in the body if you want and hit send. Sarah Friar, CFO of Square, was nice enough to send me a dollar, and it worked as advertised; I simply added my debit card number and expiration date, and the money was transferred (see Figure 1.5).

PayPal has also been busy looking at ways to remove consumer and small business pain points when it comes to "friction" as well.

The question becomes which friction points are mere annoyances, and which really have a significant impact. Swiping a card versus tapping or pressing a few buttons may not make much of a difference, but PayPal has been focusing on taking mobile commerce up a notch when it comes to

FIGURE 1.5   PayPal's In-Store Mobile Experience

convenience. One such feature expands "order ahead" functionality, allowing users to place orders via mobile and then pick up in-store. Some of these combine integrated offers and deals and the ability to check in to certain restaurants to pay and tip at the table via mobile device (see Figure 1.6).

One of PayPal's biggest innovations over the past couple of years has been its co-innovation with the banking industry. One such example allows bank customers to use their mobile phone to instantly send money around the world for a fraction of what it cost years ago, which offers significant value. Most research in the area of person-to-person payments indicates that a significant percentage of consumers who use such services rate speed highly, and a large percentage of users of person-to-person payment services want recipients to be able to access funds immediately. Potential adopters of outbound foreign money transfer and person-to-person real-time payments most often want to use real-time applications to send money as gifts, as payments, for emergencies, and more, to family members and friends.[14] Payment solutions that are geared toward this context can provide some significant value for financial institutions, which can take advantage of innovative partnering. At first glance, it might seem strange that PayPal would offer its payment network to banks for their use, yet peeling back the onion a few layers, what becomes apparent is PayPal's desire to be a provider of platform services, which is the thought behind their recent $800 million acquisition of Braintree, discussed later. Becoming a platform provider means that there might be some that use your assets for their own customers, and that you might not always control the user experience or the brand that is leveraging the service. However, what comes with being a platform is

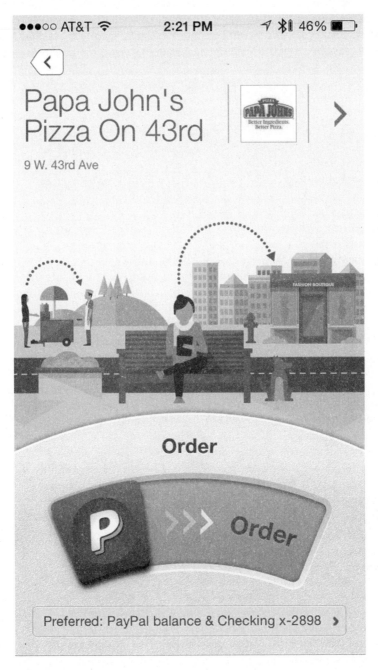

FIGURE 1.6   PayPal Mobile App

relevance to many use cases that may never have been contemplated. There are many examples of innovative use cases and channels that could benefit from the assets PayPal has built over many years, including risk, compliance, and payment infrastructure. Included in this infrastructure is PayPal's flagship e-mail payment service, which today can seamlessly whisk money across many borders within milliseconds. PayPal's payment architecture has always been geared toward Internet and mobile, and as such, it has enjoyed a technology and operations advantage in many of the ways it manages risk, fraud, and the myriad of anti–money laundering and compliance requirements that banks must adhere to.

Several hundred banks have partnered with PayPal over the past several years to make its person-to-person capabilities an asset for their own customers. The "Intel Inside" philosophy PayPal has developed has proven to be a strategic benefit to those innovative financial institutions that have recognized early that companies like PayPal can be accelerators to growth. Mercantile Bank of Michigan, one of the earliest banks to partner with PayPal as a result of its platform approach, continues to enjoy satisfied customers and a strong, innovative brand. According to John Schulte, chief information officer at Mercantile Bank of Michigan:

> *Our partnership with PayPal for mobile P2P was groundbreaking at the time we launched, as most financial institutions still saw PayPal as a competitor and not a potential collaboration partner. We saw an opportunity to work with an innovative leader in the payment space, and bring a unique value proposition in mobile payments to our customers that did not exist in the marketplace. By tapping the PayPal brand and its expansive base of users already set to receive mobile payments, we were able to offer a solution that took away a lot of the barriers to mobile payment adoption. Luckily, we were not saddled with the same biased perception against partnering with innovative nontraditional players. Given our status as a community bank, there was no real overlap in our business models and more ways to complement our combined services for the benefit of the customer.*

What are some of the concrete partnering examples PayPal has done with the banking industry? Take a look at some of the mobile screenshots shown in Figure 1.7. Union Bank, a $100 billion financial institution, has cobranded their person-to-person payment offering with PayPal. USAA, recognized as one of the most innovative institutions in the industry, has also partnered with PayPal to offer money movement capabilities. Credit unions such as Wescom and community banks like Mercantile Bank are all incorporating PayPal's capabilities in their mobile channels for their customers.

FIGURE 1.7 Mobile Screenshots
Source: Dan Schatt (iPhone screenshots of banks utilizing PayPal).

Money originates with a bank customer and arrives in a recipient's PayPal account, which can be opened immediately if the recipient does not have a PayPal account.[15] What's more, PayPal's highly innovative partnerships with companies such as MoneyGram allow the recipient to deposit or withdraw cash at many locations simply using their mobile phone. In the case of MoneyGram, a customer can simply indicate to the MoneyGram agent where they would like to pick up the cash, and can immediately withdraw money. What makes these innovations particularly interesting is that the banks can now charge their customers for real-time international money movement at a fraction of the rate of a normal wire transfer. What's more, the banks can, to a large degree, control the user experience on their mobile channel and can partner with a trusted provider, who can help them navigate the myriad of complex money transmitter laws. Often, technology companies such as PayPal can more easily architect their systems to help banks meet and exceed various regulatory requirements required of them.

Mobile Commerce through Tokenization

We've just discussed how banks can align with tech companies such as PayPal and Square to keep mindshare with their customers and develop possible revenue streams. While PayPal and Square both continue their push to unite e-commerce, m-commerce, and physical commerce, other democratizing elements of mobile commerce are beginning to light up that will allow financial institutions to play a bigger role in commerce than they have done historically. This will become increasingly important as mobile commerce spend continues to accelerate. Addressable spend for mobile commerce alone was valued at $100 billion in total volume in 2013, growing to over $200 billion in 2016.[16] Some research firms have predicted that we will see a full 25 percent of all online commerce happening through the mobile phone by 2017. These numbers could be considerably higher as businesses begin to think "mobile first" and design their experiences in ways that will allow a more seamless customer experience.

There is a lot of talk in the industry about where mobile payments are headed. What continues to be important is the value associated with payments results from the many services around the payment, which makes commerce more valuable. Since payments are largely a commodity business for banks, the opportunity to partner with those who can bring new, valuable experiences to their customers is what matters. Many of the drivers that will ignite mobile commerce will be discussed more in future chapters, but the single most important driver is the emergence of the digital or cloud-based wallet. That is, sensitive information no longer needs to be stored on a mobile phone. A bank ultimately stores that information somewhere far away on a network server behind a firewall at multiple undisclosed locations. A thief could steal the phone, but never actually steal your credit card—for that, they would have to know your online user ID and password. The emergence of "cloud" is so important because it can create a "token" in place of your payment instrument. Tokenization relates to the process of replacing your sensitive information with symbols that retain the information without compromising security. This is very important when it comes to commerce and security, since most small businesses want to minimize the amount of information they need to keep, to increase security and minimize the work they need to do to comply with government regulations.

Most payment experts are very familiar with the term PCI (payment card industry) standards, which specify that no credit card numbers can be stored within retailer point-of-sale terminals or in their databases. To be compliant, businesses either have to invest in expensive systems and encryption standards that allow them to be compliant or outsource payments to a provider that offers a tokenization option. The provider is responsible for issuing the token value, and ultimately is accountable for ensuring that sensitive card data stay safe. In this case, the provider will convert the numbers into randomly generated values (tokens) that can be used only within the context of a unique transaction.

This technology has become an enabler for the banking industry. It means that banks and retailers alike can now leverage very innovative service providers that can safely digitize payment instruments into various forms, allowing consumers and retailers to leverage the mobile phone for commerce. The mobile device has introduced unique qualities such as the portability of the technology and additional factors inherent to the mobile device, including multimedia services, global positioning system (GPS), Internet access, mobile telephony, camera, and social media, which could all impact the payments environment.[17]

The Mobile Camera—It's Not Just for Pictures Anymore!

These days, it might not seem so revolutionary to use your smartphone to take a picture, but it certainly is proving to be an incredibly powerful tool for banks and payment companies in a variety of ways. Aside from alleviating one of the main reasons consumers frequent the bank branch, depositing checks, the camera is playing an even larger role in how the commerce and payments experience will be forever altered. Imagine a future in which you can take a picture of a fabric with an intricate pattern in a store window and immediately access information about the item and purchase it instantly from the location of your choice. eBay's Red Laser is working on just such an experience. In the United Kingdom and Asia, you don't even have to imagine some of the opportunities that have now come about thanks to the mobile phone camera—truly virtual shopping. South Koreans, noted for their tech savviness, have been some of the first to sample what Tesco has in store for the future. Banks take note—Tesco found a way to become relevant in a new market in which it had not much of a brick-and-mortar presence. In this example, Tesco printed 500 of its most popular products on high-resolution paper with barcodes, and posted them at train stations. The intent was to allow busy consumers with no time to head to the supermarket to simply buy their groceries by taking a picture of the barcodes next to the pictures. In effect, it created virtual aisles featuring food on what was designed to look like grocery store shelves. Consumers would use the Tesco application to take pictures of the items and pay, and the goods would then be delivered to the customer's doorstep. As long as orders were placed before 1 P.M., their items could be delivered the same evening, making the virtual experience even less cumbersome than a real shopping trip! The shopping application is the number one application in Korea, with over 900,000 downloads since 2012. Tesco is now expanding to bus stops and other public areas that can enable customers to do their shopping from wherever they are. These initiatives point to the fact that it is increasingly important for banks to partner with companies that are actively making these new experiences possible and linking payment instruments to their applications.

Banks are continuing to leverage the camera to allow their mobile applications to take full advantage of new possibilities. Mitek, a leading provider of mobile services to financial institutions and a pioneer in enabling remote deposit capture of checks through the mobile phone, continues to come up with new opportunities for banks. U.S. Bank recently signed up for its latest service, allowing customers to conduct a balance transfer to a U.S. Bank credit card by taking a picture of a credit card payment coupon in the bank's mobile application.[18] Another popular application, mobile photo bill pay, allows bank customers to take a photo of a bill and pay. Mitek has indicated that bank customers in the 25-to-34 age range are three times more likely to use this service. With statistics like these, it's easy to see where social trends may be heading and how many customers will be gravitating to their mobile phone to fulfill most of their financial service needs.

The Mobile Microphone—Offers and Payments through Soundwaves!

One of the more exciting areas of financial innovation is the ability to conduct basic transactions with voice commands. Several banks offer voice control technology, and some, such as Standard Chartered, have been experimenting with artificial intelligence when it comes to customer service. Others, such as USAA have had Apple Siri-like customer service in place for a few years now, to great effect.[19]

However, as we are starting to see, there is much more that can be done with the mobile microphone than providing virtual customer service—it could very well be the way customers pay and are introduced to offers in the future. Traditionally, communicating between mobile devices has been challenging and complex, but companies like Chirp that offer an iPhone application today allow users to send links to each other using sound waves. Way2ride is another application produced by Verifone, a payment services company that already processes a significant amount of volume for New York City taxicabs. Clinkle is another company that has indicated it plans to offer payments through sound waves. It raised $25 million in funding on this promise from notable venture capital firms such as Accel Partners, Andreessen Horowtiz, Peter Theil, and Intuit. It appears it will use high-frequency sounds that smartphones and tablets can pick up to transmit data over short distances.[20] The Clinkle accounts will be tied to existing bank accounts or credit cards, and merchants would need the same application installed on their mobile devices. Why is there so much time and attention on sound waves with mobile devices? Most all devices have a microphone and speaker, the two prerequisites needed for widespread adoption. The technology is so widespread that this could work even beyond smartphone users to those who have lower-end devices.

Alipay, the payments company partly owned by China's e-commerce giant Alibaba, has also launched a sound wave mobile payments capability in the Beijing subway. It uses white noise generated by a smartphone-to-smartphone transaction to carry digital information to another device. As reported in *Techcrunch,* "to use the sound wave payment system, customers open the Alipay Wallet app on their handset while holding it close to a sensor on the vending machine, and wait for it to make a 'shoo-shoo-shoo' noise." Wang Yu-ming, Alipay's business development director, told Xinhua that each sound transmission is unique to the transaction and is valid for only five minutes because of security reasons (each transaction takes less than a minute). If the sound payment's Beijing subway launch proves successful, the system could potentially be implemented in convenience stores, supermarkets, and department stores.

While it is still too early to determine if there is a future for banking and payments through soundwaves, it is clear that we will see some disruption leveraging the mobile phone and speaker. If you are with a financial services institution, seeking out companies in this space who are gaining a following with customers, it is certainly worth developing potential partnership opportunities.

NFC's Rebound and the Promise of Host Card Emulation

One of the most hotly debated topics about mobile technologies over the past few years has been the development of near field communications (NFC) a wireless technology standard that is a close cousin to radio frequency identification (RFID). Both technologies use radio signals for tracking, but it is NFC that has been of most interest as a payment technology. Until now, NFC has required a costly set of terminal changes for retailers and mobile companies to agree on standards; the problem has historically been that both the telco world and the banking world would like to own the customer and control the secure element (SE), typically a microchip capable of securely hosting application and confidential data by a set of trusted parties. Both banks and telcos have wanted their own designs on the SE, to have control over the customer experience. This multi-industry battle has led analysts to reduce their forecasts by over 40 percent NFC's transaction value has been reduced by more 40 percent, and to account for just 5 percent of total transaction value in 2017.[21]

Google's recent innovations may have helped solve some of these underlying problems. In one of its recent Android releases, it focused on a term called *host card emulation* that effectively allows communication to happen from an NFC controller to an application running on the Android handset. Aside from potentially alleviating the need for specific phone architecture, it could also alleviate the need to have a significant number of ecosystem participants that would have to be involved to securely load credentials on a secure element. Cherian Abraham, an expert in the space and longtime commentator, recently wrote the following in his blog:

> *... It had become absurd that one must enquire upon Carrier, Platform, Issuer and Device support before installing an NFC payment app, much less use it. Talk about fragmentation. This was a problem only Google could begin to fix—by removing the absurd limitations put in place in the name of security—but in truth existed because of profit, control and convenience.[22]*

FIGURE 1.8 Discover Card

Google's challenge until recently has been the confinement of its own Google Wallet to Sprint handsets, since Verizon and others effectively blocked them from offering NFC capabilities, but their breakthrough could potentially mean much more merchant and consumer adoption of their Google Wallet. Banks would do well to consider Google as another potential mobile wallet partner to work with if consumer adoption picks up. How? Consider what Discover (see Figure 1.8) has done recently. The card company has marketed to its user base the ability to load up a Discover card to a Google Wallet account. As people gravitate to using mobile wallets to manage their everyday spending and their various offers and coupons, the card will naturally become one of the payment instruments top of mind when spending. This becomes increasingly important as the payment itself becomes increasingly invisible to the user—just another point of friction that is removed in the future through a simple tap, or even by simply having your phone with you. While Google's breakthrough is a terrific boost for the industry, it surely was also motivated to make its wallet work seamlessly to protect against its biggest potential competitor in the commerce world, Apple. If Google doesn't make it simple for banks, merchants, and consumers to utilize a digital wallet, then Apple might take its place with a larger digital wallet—the iTunes account and Passbook.

Apple's Passbook

If you haven't used Apple's Passbook yet and you travel a lot, you're in for a treat. This "container" of sorts on your iPhone allows you to add anything that has a QR code attached to it such as gift cards, tickets, coupons, boarding passes, and even your Starbucks card (see Figure 1.9). Passbook is stimulating an ecosystem of commerce providers; United Airlines, Starbucks, and Fandango all get more of their applications downloaded as a result of the Passbook application. What makes Passbook so interesting is that it already has about 600 million iTunes accounts, each with a credit card or debit card attached, and is adding another 500,000 per day.[23] Given the fact that so many consumers and businesses are using its products, most wonder when the moment will come when Apple will firmly become the mobile wallet of choice that is used to shop, pay, and receive offers and promotions. Consider that today Apple receives 30 percent of the price of a downloaded application. However, the reality is that the vast majority of payments are happening after applications are downloaded, also referred to as "in-app" payments. Consider Amazon's free iPhone app. Wouldn't Apple surely love to utilize its iTunes wallet to enable payments within that app and every other iPhone app that offers commerce? Surely it would, and it is certainly in a good position to dictate the future

FIGURE 1.9 Apple's Passbook

rules of payments within its ecosystem. In the physical world of commerce, of the many things Apple's future points to, many hope that the initial release of Apple's fingerprint sensor signals the demise of future user IDs and passwords. Could we be looking at a future environment where payments are only a fingerprint away? Quite possibly, but Apple hasn't made any definitive moves yet. While banks may be concerned about the subjugation of the brand inside Apple's Passbook application, the reality is that the digitization of payments offers just as many potential opportunities. We'll discuss some of the other notable developments with Apple in later chapters, but there are quite a few opportunities in store for the banking industry to leverage Passbook for offers and promotions similar to retailers. Consider Texas Roadhouse, a Texas restaurant chain that recently promoted its offers through texting, and got people to install their offer on Passbook. They claim to have generated a 37 percent installation rate, with 32 percent of users who clicked through actually redeeming the offers. These offers are particularly powerful when combining them with the location-aware feature of passes that alerts users when they're within a certain distance of the restaurant to redeem the offer. The loyalty club achieved a 45 percent net growth rate during its first six months and a 17 percent average offer redemption rate.[24] Now imagine if a bank's card is promoted in the same way. As my friend Jim Bruene has said, "The main reason Passbook is such a big deal, besides the Apple halo effect, is that it automatically opens your 'virtual card' when you walk in to the store. Yes, you read it correctly. Automatically. Opening. Mobile. Payment. Really, just having your receipt stored safely away in the Passbook app could make the difference between using the store card versus MC/Visa. . . ." We will see how far Apple goes to enable the next generation of commerce and payments, but it certainly can and will continue to be a very powerful platform that banks can leverage with enough thought and creativity.

The Apps Phenomenon

The battle for mobile platform supremacy is now down to three platforms: iOS, Android, and Windows. With that, it has become much easier to build mobile applications for the masses, particularly in the United States. As a result, providers of mobile banking applications, who a few short years ago had to wrestle with the many competing mobile platforms and operating systems, have found themselves in a very strong business position. They are in a position to take perfect advantage of the explosive growth of tablets and the heavy interaction consumers have with them. As a result, armed with the insights as to the tablet and mobile experience, it makes perfect sense that they would naturally usurp the role of online banking provider as well. In the commerce world, we're seeing many examples of smartphone users now entrusting many more companies with their payment information, so long as the company is providing significant convenience. With the advent of tokenization, and the increasing sentiment that payment on mobile may in many ways be safer, we're seeing several mobile services crop up that handle specific tasks. Small items like chargers are useful, but imagine larger-ticket items purchased in a similar manner. At PayPal, I witnessed tens of thousands of cars purchased every year through the eBay mobile application with the click of a button. As you can see in the chart in Figure 1.10, in 2013, 23 percent of consumers feel comfortable spending $200 or more on their mobile phone. Recent studies also suggest a high percentage of smartphone users have searched for a place to eat using their phone through companies like Yelp or OpenTable, and are often heavily influenced as to which restaurants they choose as a result. Mobile applications have revolutionized quite a number of industries, not the least of which are travel agencies, map publishers, camera makers, and taxi services. What role can a bank play in the fast-moving world of mobile apps? We'll next look at some interesting partnering opportunities that are arising as a result of these trends and where financial institutions might insert themselves.

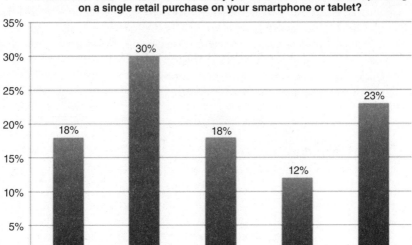

FIGURE 1.10   Consumers Are Purchasing Higher-Ticket Items with Their
Smartphones
Source: Data from maxymiser.com.

THE UBER-IZATION OF MOBILE

Uber is a very fast-growing transport services company, accessed through an
application on a smartphone (see Figure 1.11). It is also the poster child in
describing how the mobile phone is revolutionizing industries and the customer experience. Need to get somewhere? Want a car within the next few
minutes? Push a button on your Uber mobile application, and within 5 to
15 minutes a driver will show up at your door and take you anywhere you
need to go. Once you've arrived, simply get out of the car and leave. There's
no need to pay since your credit card is on file with your Uber account and
you'll be automatically charged. This "one-click" experience has inspired a
host of other one-click services that take friction out of many daily things
consumers do. Watching your Uber driver approaching your location on
GPS changes the experience of taxis and limos, while at the same time providing total transparency throughout the value chain, from dispatcher to
driver to fleet manager.

As apps with frictionless experiences continue to increase in popularity, we see that consumers are not afraid to spend significant amounts of

FIGURE 1.11   Uber App

money using their mobile phone. eBay's new eBay Now application (see Figure 1.12) allows consumers to receive their merchandise in an hour or less in a very personalized way. Thanks to location-based services, the courier who is immediately assigned for delivery can deliver the item to wherever the consumer happens to be. Not only do you know who your courier is, you can track them every step of the way, just as they can track exactly where the delivery should come. Not everything requires a real-time experience, but we'll see a growing number of use cases where real-time services can be incredibly valuable. More than once, I've landed in New York and forgot my iPhone charger. I don't want to have to find a store to buy it. I want it delivered to me so I can get my phone charged. In this case, not only is this a terrific experience, but mobile has fundamentally reshaped how distribution is done—a mobile-to-mobile delivery marketplace can provide significant efficiencies, and the delivery happens directly to the mobile device, so a courier can't miss where the recipient is. If the recipient walks across the street, the delivery person knows exactly where they are.

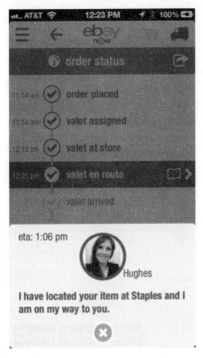

FIGURE 1.12 eBay Now

"TOP OF WALLET" TO "TOP OF MOBILE"

What is the relationship between Uber, eBay, and the impact of a growing mobile commerce trend on the financial services landscape? Today, companies like Braintree, which help enable the one-click payment services, may be some of the biggest potential partners for banks that need to find ways of encouraging use of debit or credit card accounts with their customers and the growing use of mobile apps their customers use. As it becomes increasingly easy to make purchases for any good or service, consumers will no longer have a need to reach inside their physical wallet and actively think about which payment instrument they intend to use. Over time, consumers will become immune to the marketing messages of various payment cards because they will no longer be consciously choosing which payment instrument to pay with; in many cases, the card will have already been uploaded to a cloud-based service. While companies like Uber make the payments experience nearly invisible to the consumer, the impact to issuers of credit and debit cards can be startling. How can a financial institution that issues debit and credit cards continue to grab more shares of a consumer's wallet and the accompanying interchange revenue that goes along with it?

The Case of Braintree and Simple

Let's give a concrete example of a very innovative deal recently struck between two companies, Simple (now BBVA) and Braintree (now PayPal). If you are not in the payments business, prior to the acquisition of both companies, it's unlikely you have heard of either, but the sort of partnership these two companies formed could very well help the banking industry think about a new blueprint to capture the significant amount of spend that is increasingly happening through tablets and mobile devices.

Who is Braintree? Braintree is a company recently purchased by eBay that was one of the first to offer one-touch purchasing across mobile apps with a large and growing two-sided network of merchants and consumers. They manage the payment infrastructure for thousands of merchants that need credit card processing. Other companies in this space include Stripe, Merchant e-Solutions and large bank entities such as Wells Fargo and Chase Paymentech. Braintree processes about $10 billion in payments annually, $2 billion of which are done through mobile. They also happen to power many of the most promising start-ups, such as Uber, Air BNB, Fab, Living-Social, Angry Birds, and OpenTable. Merchants in more than 40 countries throughout North America, Europe, and Australia accept payments in more than 130 currencies using Braintree and the power single-click purchasing for more than 40 million consumers. Since Braintree stores the payment cards on file for these companies, it started the Credit Card Data Portability initiative[25] to promote the ability to share customer payment credentials (card number, expiration date, etc.) between merchants. This is the foundation of a new product called Venmo Touch that will gradually lead to a consumer who has a card on file with one merchant, automatically having the their card on file with other merchants they sign up with. In Venmo's case, this includes companies like Hotel Tonight, TaskRabbit, and Wrapp. The firm argues that integrating their technology into their own apps offers a route to the coveted "top of wallet." It is now pitching the technology to card issuers and mobile banking providers. Who wants to type in their credit or debit card on a four-inch screen? If Braintree already has your card on file, why not just use that and get on with the service! In the case of Venmo Touch, sending money to friends and opening two new iPhone applications might require a user only to put in their payment information once.

What is Simple and its relationship with Braintree? Simple offers mobile-centric "virtual" banking with no physical branches. The company offers real-time budgeting and saving features that can forecast and automatically show a user what he can safely spend without overdrawing not only their present account balance but also their current and future financial goals. And their data suggest that these tools appeal to the consumer as more than a quarter of a million people have requested an invite to Simple. Its focus on user experience and digital money management tools offer some very elegant user experiences to manage a consumer's digital financial life. It contracts with federally insured banks to hold its customers' money. Simple customers are accessing their accounts an average of 2.5 times per day[26] as they are able bring their bank with them wherever they go. Simple's challenge has been to figure out how to leverage the Internet to get a disproportional amount of spend on its debit cards from customers, who might just look to use any particular payment card. Now, in its partnership with Braintree, as part of the customer enrollment process, Simple can keep its customers' Visa cards on file with the payments processor.

How do Simple and Braintree work together? They are creating a consumer experience that simply prompts their customers if they'd like to make the Simple debit card the default card for purchasing on a particular device. And with that, Simple and Braintree see three to four times the conversion of consumers' on-boarding to new services. Since the payment card is already on file, why not use it?

As a bank, wouldn't it be terrific if you could offer the same level of convenience to your customers? As people demand greater convenience when purchasing from mobile devices, the stakes are rising for banks and card issuers to compete in this growing mobile economy. As the battlefield for top of wallet quickly moves from consumers' pockets to their mobile phones, partnering with a company like Braintree and its Venmo Touch service can offer a way for banks large and small (especially small!) to stay competitive in the mobile economy. Once a card is entered and stored in the cloud, a consumer can use that card in all the apps on the network in one touch. Consumers are likely to make the first card they add their default for all future mobile purchases, thus banks and card issuers can make their card top of wallet and capture the mobile purchasing opportunity.

THE QR CODE

Until now, we've been talking about how banks can try to secure a digital top-of-wallet position with respect to mobile commerce—a market specifically relating to the payment of goods and services through the Internet, using one's mobile phone. As we discussed previously, one of the best ways a bank might position itself for future relevance and growth is to ensure that consumers find it as easy as possible to utilize a bank's payment instrument

FIGURE 1.13   PayPal's Mobile Experience at McDonald's France
Source: PayPal.

when paying on their mobile phone. Certainly, key partnerships with companies like eBay, Google, and Facebook (to be discussed later) can be important in this respect, to ensure that a bank's customers can permit their card to be used automatically in as many places as possible.

We haven't yet discussed what is happening in the case of face-to-face transactions, what I refer to as *proximity payments*. Those transactions require a common way of interacting with many legacy point-of-sale systems. And as we have seen from Apple's Passbook, perhaps the easiest technology to make universally available is the QR code. Although the bar code has been around for over 30 years, it is making a comeback in a big way, now that smartphones can tokenize the information and make it available on a high-resolution screen. As you can see from Figure 1.13, PayPal has been active with QR codes, having signed an agreement with McDonald's France that ultimately allows customers to pay at the point of sale by having the cashier simply scan the QR code in the application.

WHAT BANKS CAN LEARN FROM STARBUCKS

Starbucks is arguably the most advanced retailer in the United States when it comes to the number of their consumers that are using their mobile application to make payments at Starbucks locations (Figure 1.14). CEO Howard

FIGURE 1.14   Starbucks App

Schultz has gone so far as to declare that a combination of mobile payments and social networking are central to the company's blueprint for growth.

Starbucks is a unique retailer that is able to take advantage of its recurring, caffeine-addicted user base and its tremendous retailing competency. There is a lot banks can learn from its mobile payments success. Today, mobile payments account for a full 10 percent of all in-store purchases.[27] These purchases are done by holding the phone up to a scanner at the register, similar to how groceries are scanned. Given the high resolution associated with smartphones, and the general availability of scanners, QR codes have come back in force.

How can banks take advantage of this trend? Some companies such as Paydiant allow banks to build QR codes into their mobile banking experience, enabling them to present cards in this digital format. Paydiant does not have a consumer brand; its entire business model is associated with the building of a platform and a white-labeled solution for banks and retailers. Its message to banks is that it can help them launch their own mobile payment applications instead of letting wireless carriers, payment processors, and Internet companies get between banks and their banking customers.

While this can allow consumers to leave their wallet at home, it doesn't necessarily lead to more convenience—swiping a card is still faster than taking your phone, entering your password, and having the barcode appear.

The real interesting opportunities can take place when offers, coupons, loyalty points, and promotions are combined on this medium to ultimately give the consumer more insight into their physical wallet. The QR code is a business model enabler for a bank. Why? It allows the bank to be with its customers every step of the way, as they walk into a store and check out. If banks incorporate retail-oriented "wish lists" in conjunction with location-based services, a financial institution could begin to create deals with neighboring stores to help make consumers aware of items they normally buy, and offer coupons or other points to take advantage of the offer. It also can help banks build mindshare with customers to use their payment instrument, which is increasingly invisible in any checkout experience. You, as a financial institution, can digitize your customers' payment instruments and enable them to become QR code, but the value has to be more than the payment. Are you saving your customers money? Will they get valuable points they can use? Does it save them time? If you can't check the box on any of these items, implementing a QR code won't help financial institutions to engage their customers. In fact, in might just have the opposite effect.

This holds true for mobile payments in general—unless there is some value accruing other than the payment itself, having the transaction come from a mobile phone versus a card isn't valuable. In fact, the real opportunity with payments is commerce, whether it's building rich personalization capabilities that make consumers feel that they're getting offers that suit them personally to more valuable recommendations of goods or better offers. Financial services firms need to be thinking more about the value created around the payment, rather than the payment itself, and that requires thinking differently about design, products, and partnering.

LEVELING THE PLAYING FIELD WITH LEVELUP

For banks today, it's more important than ever to continuously scan the mobile landscape in search of any company that is showing early signs of attracting businesses and customers. Often, those companies may appear to be competitors on the surface, but in reality have completely different business models that can be highly relevant to financial services. LevelUp is one such example (see Figure 1.15). To some, it may seem like it is a payments company, enabling consumers to use its application to make purchases through their mobile phone using a QR code at the point of sale. However, in the case of LevelUp, it really is in the advertising business, making money by helping businesses generate targeted offers to consumers. LevelUp is a company that allows consumers to pay with their mobile phone at the point of sale with one tap on an application, at over 5,000 merchants that use its

FIGURE 1.15 LevelUp App

service. Although small, its recent partnership with Heartland Payment Systems should give it a larger reach into restaurants and convenience stores. It offers a combined loyalty, rewards, and payment experience that can potentially deepen bank relationships with its customers through more personalized offers. Its signature product offers deals and discounts at participating merchants. Users locate offers they'd like, and they generate QR codes on their phones that are scanned at the point of sale.

Consider how a $600 million asset bank, First Trade Union Bank, recently leveraged LevelUp's platform to drive consumer engagement on their mobile application. The bank released a mobile payment and loyalty app called FT Pay. The bank matches the savings from merchant discounts and deposits up to $25 as a new account bonus deposited directly into its customers' checking accounts. Existing bank clients can increase their savings by sweeping merchant credits into their savings accounts.[28]

Why is this interesting for banks? We continue to see new, innovative technologies that can generate more valuable commerce—more sales for the merchant and more money- and time-saving offers for consumers. While banks should really look to become a part of others' offerings, they shouldn't neglect the fact that they can take advantage of some compelling white labeling of their own. To stay relevant to consumers in this mobile-centric environment, you need to make sure you are everywhere they want you to be. Some might be interested in using their bank applications to take advantage of their commerce needs, and many more still will be interested in having their bank's payment capabilities integrated into other valuable time- and money-saving applications. How valuable could a mobile banking application that leverages partners like LevelUp be for banks? Today, LevelUp claims that its solution accounts for 4.5 percent of the volume a merchant sees when they use a LevelUp solution and 25 percent of volume with a white-labeled solution.[29] If merchants and consumers are seeing value in these transactions, then it is something banks should be a part of as well.

LevelUp is one of many great examples of how banks can leverage others' core competencies in mobile to produce compelling consumer mobile experiences.

FROM MOBILE BANKING TO TABLET BANKING

We've discussed many innovative applications that banks should consider becoming a part of, but is there really anything that banks should be building that others may want to be a part of? The answer generally is that the most innovative banks we see will make it easy for consumers to use them in whatever context they are in. If they want to pay using Uber or receive a loan through a mobile application, consumers will do so. It's therefore incredibly important for you to be where your customers are, rather than believing if you build, they will come. Banking via mobile is the fastest-growing segment in retail banking and payments, and by 2016 the average customer will have 300 digital transactions for every one face-to-face interaction with a bank.[30] The mobile banking application today is extremely important because at many institutions, the number of online banking sessions conducted from a mobile device exceeds the number through all nonmobile channels, including branch, call centers, and ATMs. Mobile also has become much more important with the Durbin Amendment and Dodd-Frank Act, which have regulated interchange fees and reduced profits on credit cards. As a result, most banks are charging greater fees to make up for the lost interchange fees, when what they really should be doing is closing down the traditional physical infrastructure once needed to open accounts and service customers, and create more compelling mobile experiences as Simple and Moven have done in the market. We'll talk in later chapters about some of the new business models that are out there, but taking a "mobile first" approach will go a long way to ensure that financial institutions can stay relevant.

To underscore that point, consider the changing consumer behaviors we have been discussing. According to a recent survey by AlixPartners, consumers say that branch location is the number one factor they consider when changing banks. Younger customers say a desire for mobile banking capabilities is their main motive for switching. A study commissioned by Cisco found that nearly half of banking customers would even be willing to close complex transactions such as mortgages through digital interactions.[31] USAA recently mentioned that its mobile banking growth is now two to five times faster than Internet banking, and that a significant number of their deposits now come through mobile remote deposit capture—simply taking a picture of a check. Mobile banking is already accessed by nearly half the banking population and will become the epicenter of banking and payments. It is especially important to recognize that as a dominant interaction point, the user interface becomes absolutely critical. Intuit recently found that over the past 12 months, they are seeing eight logins per week, a fundamental shift from the two logins per week they've seen over the previous 12 years! And given that one in four consumers who do mobile banking also own a tablet, in combination, consumers will log in as many as 50 times per month on multiple devices. In addition, they recently found that when it comes to mobile, the three reasons customers switch banks are (1) mobile remote deposit capture, (2) mobile payments, and (3) actionable offers.[32] What are people using the mobile phone for? Most banks and research firms point to the following:

- Checking balances
- Depositing checks
- Locating ATMs and branches
- Alerts and notifications
- Paying a bill on the go
- Managing rewards and reminders of what rewards you could be using

Mobile bill payment alone is expected to grow 44 percent in 2013[33] as friendlier user experiences make their way to the phone and facilitate a more frictionless experience. The context of what you might be interested in doing with your bank may not be right to leverage your mobile phone for everything, but this is where the tablet comes in. As consumers increasingly look to leverage multiple-size devices based on the type of their interaction, tablet banking can become increasingly important to a financial institution. What areas are ripe for tablet banking? Consider these areas that can help financial institutions build a deeper relationship with their customers:

- Registration for additional products and services
- New account opening
- Financial management

Tablets provide financial institutions an opportunity to build deeper relationships with their customers; the larger form factor allows users to see more data at one time. In addition, it provides ample real estate for cross-sell opportunities and a larger keyboard and camera to make data entry easier. The convenient size and weight contribute to a "layback factor" that might contribute to more time spent than usual, if the application is laid out in a very agreeable, user-friendly way. Intuit has found that bill payers that use a tablet pay more bills than those using their mobile phone or a computer. One thing is also clear: tablets are largely considered entertainment devices, and it therefore must be fun to garner engagement, more like a game. As a result, very engaging financial management tools often fit well with tablet banking experiences. Tablet banking needs to be full featured to create delight and drive returns for the financial institution. Here are suggestions about what is important for tablet consumers and how to appeal to them:

- A simplified login is key. It could make the difference between a consumer's logging into your application versus a third-party application to access their financial information.
- A single consolidated view of accounts is important to users who use tablets. They expect to be able to view charts, categorize information, and get more insightful information about their finances.
- Over half of tablet owners use it to compare prices, far more often than mobile phones. If you are considering a commerce-like service on your financial application, this will be important, particularly since tablets now account for 25 percent of online retail commerce.[34]
- Tablets can allow small businesses the ability to manage their business on the go and in the field. Consider taking a tablet-centric approach to small business and corporate banking.
- Tablets can reduce teller lines in a branch by creating self-service stations. Consider offering in-branch tablet experiences.

MOBILE MODELS FOR THE EMERGING MARKETS

Globally, there are approximately 7.2 billion people, 5 billion handsets, yet less than 1.8 billion formal bank accounts. The amount of cash still moving through our world accounts for a staggering 85 percent of global payment transactions, hard to believe in countries like the United States, where everything seems to revolve around a Visa, Mastercard, or American Express transaction. While we are still in the early phases of massive mobile payments and a banking revolution taking place, there are some very powerful examples we'll discuss that illustrate how profound an effect the mobile phone is making on emerging economies and its contribution to financial inclusion. Part of the reason individuals in emerging markets are quickly gravitating to mobile is for safety. Traveling with cash or storing it at home is simply a risk and often dangerous. Using the mobile phone eliminates a lot of risk; if your phone is stolen, thieves will have to know the code to unlock your phone and the one on your M-Pesa account. Business models that charge for low, frequent usage instead of generating revenue through penalty fees, float, and loans can be quite powerful in the emerging markets when they revolve around the mobile phone. As mentioned in the book *Money, Real Quick: The Story of M-Pesa,* Tonny K. Omwansa, Nicholas P. Sullivan, and *The Guardian* authors sum it up well:

> *The classic banking model doesn't map to the needs of the poor. Banks make money from a small number of relatively large transactions; mobile operators make money from a large number of relatively small transactions. The bank model is based on float, accepting deposits and lending them; the mobile operator model is based on usage, the more the better. Prepaid airtime, bought in very small increments, was the precursor and conceptual foundation for mobile money. Once you have minutes (airtime) in your phone, you are storing value, which you can use or send to others.*

As a result, many analyst firms are forecasting an explosion of mobile transfers, transferring money directly to individuals or businesses with a mobile phone. Individuals are transacting with their mobile phone much more frequently around the world (although at lower values) given the wider availability of mobile payment services, which are much lower cost than those of traditional bank services. In fact, Gartner, a research firm, forecasts mobile transfers will account for almost 69 percent of the total value of mobile payments, which is expected to surpass $721 billion in 2017, and account for more than 450 million users.[35] As financial institutions and mobile carriers alike focus more on the buying experience using the mobile phone, there should be continued growth, particularly in the emerging markets.

A few years ago, I served as a technology consultant for CGAP, an organization affiliated with the World Bank that was looking at how technology and new branchless banking models can help drive new banking models and financial inclusion. One country in particular, Kenya, has seen a dramatic impact in this area with the introduction of M-Pesa, a mobile payments service run by Safaricom, a telecommunications company backed by Vodafone, a large minority stakeholder. In Kenya, we are now seeing mobile virtual banking happening at scale. In fact, virtually every adult in Kenya has an account with M-Pesa and manages their money and their payments on their mobile phone. The fascinating thing about M-Pesa, aside from the

FIGURE 1.16 Dan Schatt (author) in Kenya with friend John Staley, COO of Equity Bank add "standing in front of an m-Pesa booth in Nairobi."
Source: Dan Schatt

fact that it is run by a mobile carrier, not a bank, is that it has literally "banked" an entire population of "unbanked" individuals. The number of bank accounts in Kenya increased from 2.5 million in 2007 to more than 15 million in 2011.[36] One study has demonstrated that the income of rural recipients of M-Pesa increased up to 30 percent as a result of money being sent more frequently. The study mentioned: "By breaking up their transfers, urban migrants end up remitting more money back home. Also, rural recipients save money when retrieving cash. They no longer need to pay for transport costs to urban centers, where most of the money transfer services are located. Instead, they make the withdrawal directly. Such an increase is vitally important for the rural recipients, who depend heavily on remittances for their livelihoods. The financial diaries reveal that such remittances constitute as much as 70 percent of rural household income."[37]

The number of branches or locations to collect and deposit cash is also staggering. M-Pesa went from 7,000 agents in 2007 to 87,000 agents in 2013 and now accounts for 60% of Kenyan GDP! Part of the secret sauce has been M-Pesa's unleashing of entrepreneurship; the creation of opportunities for enterprising individuals to run an M-Pesa agency. Those very familiar with the service have mentioned that some agents make more than doctors, lawyers, and other professionals, especially "aggregators" that operate multiple agencies and subagents (aka cash merchants).[38] These agents operate as human ATMs and have been so successful that now banks are building their own agent-based networks beyond branches to try to increase their own customer base. According to Tonny K. Omwansa and Nicholas P. Sullivan:

> *Every day, M-Pesa transactions in Kenya outnumber Western Union transactions globally. Every day, 60 percent of all electronics financial transactions in Kenya go through M- . . . . Those big numbers actually represent a very small slice of the Kenyan money supply, less than 1 percent. But the massive flow of a small stock of money is statistical proof of the pen-up demand for a more accessible system of payments. M-Pesa is a transactional rail that in five years has created a whole new financial ecosystem, much like the iPhone in Western markets.*[39]

While there is a bank that sits behind the account, everything is controlled by Safaricom. Perhaps most impressive with this model is that M-Pesa has demonstrated that its ability to do business with the poor in a responsible way can be profitable and sustainable. In Kenya, the banks are behind and in catch-up mode, and given the pace of change, it's even hard to see how others, including PayPal could get a large share of payments or banking volume, particularly given how quickly mobile operators have captured so much of the asset.

Are there opportunities for banks to partner with the likes of M-Pesa? Equity Bank, the largest private bank in Kenya, has partnered with Safaricom to offer M-Kesho accounts. This partnership could be the next evolution in financial services in Kenya with products beyond payments, including savings, insurance, and credit, to be offered over mobile, with agents, at scale. In addition, M-Pesa's agents face greater demands for cash as the service continues to grow. Banks like Equity have an opportunity to acquire M-Pesa agents as small business clients and provide low-cost loan products to grow the agent business and ensure reliable availability of cash at agents.

First National Bank of South Africa (FNB) has been able to thrive in the new world of "mobile first" banking in Africa. The bank recently launched a payment service aimed at Zimbabwean expats that allows them to send money back to Zimbabwe in ways that cost a fraction of what Western Union or a bank could charge. Using this new solution to send $1,000, a consumer would pay of the payment, a fraction of what it cost a year ago. Until recently, consumers paid about 10 percent of the face value to send money (e.g., sending $1,000 would cost $100); using this new solution, they pay about 43 basis points (sending $1,000 would cost just $4.30) and can send money anytime to a recipient, who doesn't need a bank account.

Recognizing that mobile would be the primary way it would be interacting with its customers, FNB did something not many banks would have considered. It began selling Apple products with its application preloaded. As a result, it became the largest reseller of Apple products in South Africa. Paul Steencamp, former head of FNB's Innovators program, summed up his bank's strategy:

> *If we could provide the means for our customer to migrate to electronic channels, we could then effectively rationalize and pass savings through these channels, offer smart devices customer to customer, get them to use our banking products and earn our rewards currency as well. . . . We are the biggest distributor of Apple products in South Africa. We have a distribution license for Apple and Samsung. Why? Our strategy is to help customers' self-service where possible. As such, we believe it is not enough to provide affordable, intuitive, easy-to-use electronic channels, but the means to afford the aspirational devices required to engage these channels. As such, we offer qualifying customers a selection of Samsung and Apple devices at heavily discounted prices, and zero to low interest rates over a variety of payback periods. This affords them the means to acquire these devices with our banking app (mobile/tablet) preloaded. Managing stock is now a core competency. The decision was a no-brainer given the strong alignment to strategy.*

WHAT'S NEXT? MORE OF THE SAME

Mobile is accelerating innovative business models faster than anything the financial services industry has ever seen. The best way to prepare for the changes coming is to develop a "mobile first" philosophy. Think about how a mobile device can be leveraged for any financial services interaction to deepen customer relationships and create a more frictionless, convenient experience. With the continued march toward greater bandwidth and resolution, better microphones and cameras, we can expect payments and other financial transactions to be most popular with customers when they don't require thought. Need to check your balance? Why input a user ID and password when you can just use your fingerprint. Need a loan? Why doesn't my virtual assistant already know that, since I'm at a car dealership? We can expect context banking to become more prevalent; bankers will need to anticipate the needs of their customers by where they are and what they're doing. Otherwise, customers will be able to leverage the many burgeoning services that better understand a customer's needs and may be that much closer to offering a one-click or no-click alternative to existing financial services products.

NOTES

1. "Jumptap and comScore Report 14% of Women 25–49 Access Internet Only through Mobile," Jumptap, Inc., www.businesswire .com/news/home/20130905005184/en/Jumptap-com Score-Report-14-Percent-Women-25-49#.UvFMW3ku6TA. Accessed February 4, 2014.
2. Interview with Aman Narian, head of Digital, Standard Chartered Bank, October 30, 2014.
3. Interview with Peter Aceto (CEO), and Charaka Kithulegoda (CIO), ING DIRECT Canada.
4. Cisco, "Cisco Networking Visual Index: Global Mobile Data Traffic Forecast Update, 2013–2018," www.cisco.com/en/US/solutions/collateral/ ns341/ns525/ns537/ns705/ns827/white_paper_c11-520862.html. Accessed February 4, 2014.
5. Joanna Brenner, "Pew Internet: Mobile," http://pewinternet.org/ Commentary/2012/February/Pew-Internet-Mobile.aspx. Accessed September 18, 2013.
6. IDC, "Tablet Shipments Forecast to Top Total PC Shipments in the Fourth Quarter of 2013 and Annually by 2015, According to IDC," www.idc.com/getdoc.jsp?containerId=prUS24314413. Accessed September 11, 2013.
7. "Survey Finds 14% of Mobile Device Owners Use Them for TV," Park Associates, www.bloomberg.com/news/2013-07-18/survey-finds-14-of- mobile-device-owners-use-them-for-tv.html. Accessed July 18, 2013.
8. Sarah Kessler, "Why Did Starbucks Choose Square?" www.fastcompany .com/3000291/why-did-starbucks-choose-square. Accessed February 4, 2014.
9. U.S. Department of Commerce, "Quarterly Retail E-Commerce Sales, 3rd Quarter 2013," www.census.gov/retail/mrts/www/data/pdf/ec_ current.pdf. Accessed November 22, 2013.
10. Shane Cole, "OpenTable Will Enable Diners to Pay for Meals through Its iPhone App," *Apple Insider,* http://appleinsider.com/articles/13/08/02/ opentable-will-enable-diners-to-pay-for-meals-through-its-iphone- app. Accessed August 2, 2013. Relax News, "PayPal Goes Biometric,"

http://www.ctvnews.ca/sci-tech/paypal-goes-biometric-1.1771848. Accessed April 12, 2014.

11. Cards and Payments Conference, 2013, produced by Terrapinn, www .terrapinn.com/exhibition/cards-and-payments-middle-east/.

12. Paul Downs, "My Search for Reasonable and Understandable Credit Card Processing," *New York Times*, http://boss.blogs.nytimes.com/2013/03/26/ my-search-for-reasonable-and-understandable-credit-card- processing/?_r=0. Accessed April 2, 2013.

13. Bryan Yurcan, "U.S. Bank Adds Square to Its Digital Wallet Options," *Bank Systems and Technology*, www.banktech.com/payments-cards/ us-bank-adds-square-to-its-digital-walle/240158523. Accessed July 18, 2013.

14. Emarketer, "Smartphones, Tablets Drive Faster Growth in Ecommerce Sales, www.emarketer.com/Article/Smartphones-Tablets-Drive-Faster- Growth-Ecommerce-Sales/1009835. Accessed April 24, 2013.

15. FIS, "Real-Time Payments Resonate with Consumers," www.fisglobal .com/ucmprdpub/groups/public/documents/document/c022390.pdf. Accessed May 1, 2013.

16. Tom McCrohan, Janney/Financial Tech, "Ten Frictionless Take-Aways from Our 2013 Digital Payments Bus Tour."

17. Marianne Crow, Susan Pandy, and Elissa Tavilla, "U.S. Mobile Landscape— Two Years Later," Federal Reserve Bank of Boston, Cynthia Jenkins, NACHA, May 2, 2013.

18. Jonathan Camhi, U.S. Bank Rolls Out Mobile Photo Balance Transfer," *Bank Systems and Technology*, www.banktech.com/channels/us-bank- rolls-out-mobile-photo-balance-t/240163226. Accessed October 28, 2013.

19. Nuance, "USAA Honors Nuance Award with Supplier Innovation Award for Nina Virtual Assistant," Nuance PR Release, www.nuance .com/company/news-room/press-releases/2013_08_12_USAA_ Supplier_Award_Web.docx. Accessed August 12, 2013.

20. Philip Ryan, "Clinkle Will Reportedly Process Payments Using High-Frequency Sounds," *Bank Innovation*, http://bankinnovation .net/2013/06/clinkle-will-reportedly-process-payments-using-high- frequency-sounds/. Accessed June 28, 2013.

21. "Gartner Says Worldwide Mobile Payment Transaction Value to Sur- pass $235 Billion in 2013, Gartner press release, June 4, 2013, www .gartner.com/newsroom/id/2504915. Accessed June 4, 2013.

22. Drop Labs, "Host Card Emulation: NFC's Tale of Redemption," www .droplabs.co/?p=938. Accessed November 3, 2013.

23. Daniel Eran Dilger, "Apple Now Adding 500,000 New iTunes Accounts per Day," *Apple Insider*, http://appleinsider.com/articles/13/06/14/apple-now adding-500000-new-itunes-accounts-per-day. Accessed June 13, 2013.

24. "Texas Roadhouse Generates 37pc Installation Rate for Passbook Pass Effort," *Mobile Commerce Daily,* www.mobilecommercedaily.com/texas-roadhouse-generates-37pc-installation-rate-for-passbook-pass effort. Accessed June 4, 2013.

25. www.portabilitystandard.org/.

26. Interview with Shamir Karkal, October 31, 2013.

27. Darrell Etherington, "Mobile Payment at U.S. Starbucks Locations Crosses 10% as More Stores Get Wireless Charging," *TechCrunch,* http://techcrunch.com/2013/07/26/mobile-payment-at-u-s-starbucks-locations-crosses-10-as-more-stores-get-wireless-charging/. Accessed July 26, 2013.

28. Philip Ryan, "First Trade Union Bank Releases Payment and Loyalty App Built on the LevelUp Platform," *Bank Innovation,* http://bankinnovation.net/2013/06/first-trade-union-bank-releases-payment-and-loyalty-app-built-on-the-levelup-platform/. Accessed July 26, 2013.

29. pymts.com, "LevelUp Builds First Bank Partnership Via Mobile App," www.pymnts.com/briefing-room/mobile/mobile-payments/2013/levelup-builds-first-bank-partnership-via-mobile-app/. Accessed June 27, 2013.

30. Interview with Brett King, author of *Bank 2.0.*

31. "The Financial Brand," http://thefinancialbrand.com/30129/cisco-banking-customer-experience/. Accessed May 23, 2013.

32. Kimberly Prieto, Intuit, "Tablets, A New Playing Field of Opportunities and Expectations," Presentation, NACHA, 2013.

33. Gartner, "Gartner Says Worldwide Mobile Payment Transaction Value to Surpass $235 Billion in 2013," www.gartner.com/newsroom/id/2504915. Accessed June 4, 2013.

34. University of San Francisco, "Mobile Payments a Growing Piece of the Retail Payments Industry," www.usanfranonline.com/mobile-payments-a-growing-piece-of-the-retail-industry/. Accessed November 3, 2013.

35. www.gartner.com/newsroom/id/2504915.

36. www.itu.int/dms_pub/itu-t/oth/23/01/T23010000200002PDFE.pdf.

37. Olga Morawczynski and Mark Pickens, CGAP Brief, "Poor People Using Mobile Financial Services: Observations on Customer Usage and Impact from M-PESA," www.cgap.org/publications/poor-people-using-mobile-financial-services. Accessed June, 2013

38. Tonny K. Omwansa and Nicholas P. Sullivan, *Money, Real Quick: The Story of M-PESA* (Bradford, Ontario: Guardian Books, 2012).

39. Ibid.

CHAPTER 2

Social and Financial Services

Maintaining Relationships and Relevance through Social Strategies

"Banking is necessary, but banks are not."

—Bill Gates, Microsoft

Some of you may remember what it was like to live in a small town 50 to 60 years ago. Your corner store knew you by name and probably had your preferences and shopping habits memorized. In fact, in the 1950s, it was common to have that relationship with half a dozen stores, including your local grocery store and pharmacy. Your local banker also knew you well and could often anticipate your needs and give you the level of attention and service that comes with years of interactions. You could tell the store manager to put the bill on your tab, to be settled at the end of the month. He knew you were good for it; after all, he knew your reputation in the community and even knew who your banker was. Interactions were extremely personal and relationship oriented.

How things have changed over the past few decades. A recent Harris Poll indicates the banking industry has a reputation that isn't much better than the tobacco industry.[1] That survey found that 51 percent of respondents indicated the financial services industry has a "very bad" reputation. Contrast this with technology companies, in which just 6 percent of respondents indicated this, and it is clear that banks need to do more than have Facebook pages. People trust their friends and family, but not their banks. How can the banking industry rebuild trust and relationships with its customers? Aside from some of the basic business model reformation that will happen, for example, finding ways of making money through value creation versus penalty fees, overdraft fees, automated teller machine (ATM) fees, and so on, understanding and fitting into a customer's lifestyle becomes very important. This is where social fits in.

Today, we're at an inflection point in which technology can be leveraged to bring back the highly personal and relationship-oriented interactions of the past. That same technology can also be used to dehumanize commerce and banking experiences, raise privacy concerns, and drive unwanted interactions. As a retailer, banker, or technology provider, your customers are looking to you to provide the right set of interactions to create the set of experiences that consumers have come to expect. Today, one in five couples meet online, and one in four divorces are blamed on Facebook. Things have changed; many relationships, social or otherwise, are often through online channels. Future banking has the potential to become much more integrated into everyday life, understanding and serving customers with the intimacy and attention of a medical doctor.[2] Susan Ochs, former Treasury Department adviser and a senior fellow at the Aspen Institute Banking, articulated this well, saying that "banking will feel more intimate like a medical relationship and this full frontal banking will be better for everyone."

And just what are those experiences and expectations that consumers are looking for? Later, we'll discuss how social banking, social commerce, and social in general are reshaping consumer expectations of how financial technology and services will be delivered. For financial institutions that have been delivering basic payment, lending, and account management services, the world we live in today will require dramatic changes to stay relevant to the consumer. The good news is that often these changes can happen through good partnering rather than heavy product development, but it will require thinking differently about brand, customer ownership, and what expectations consumers have today.

Nobody expects to come to their banks to do basic financial services transactions. It won't be long before nobody will expect to come to their banks even to do complex financial transactions. Today, people expect to do things with their money wherever they are, in the context of whatever they are actually doing—in a shop, in a stadium, at a restaurant, or car dealership—banks need to be there and embed their historical transaction capabilities differently to fit with a customer's life.

If you were born between 1945 and 1985, you may have the most disconnected relationships from your financial institution. Banks became much larger, globalization took place, and the constant march toward efficiency may have actually made you feel like a commodity to your bank. Before World War II, you knew your banker by name and he knew your birthday, In fact, he may have come to your wedding. He'd give you a free apple as you came through the door. All these relationships were very strong back then, and the past several decades have largely disconnected us. We are now at a point where industries are recreating those relationships and recreating communities online. Who would have thought that Zappos, an online shoe retailer (purchased by Amazon), could have such a large and rich relationship with its customers? Redeveloping that trust and social experience really comes down to a few simple concepts that technology and innovative partnerships can help the financial community reclaim. What are those concepts? They include the following:

- Greet the customer by name.
- Listen and learn. Understand (like Amazon does) that when they interact with you, you learn from them.
- Always offer suggestions—establish yourself as a personal subject matter expert for them.
- Be appreciative—thank the customer. Banks are used to doing this in private banking, but don't do this in a personal way for the masses.

Social technologies can help the financial community reclaim some of their lost relationships if, of course, it is done in a genuine way. What's important to understand is that you can own your experience with your customers, but it does not mean you own the many technologies and components necessary to create the strong relationship. Many people feel a strong affinity with Toyota, although they really are just assemblers of the overall automobile, their product. Apple doesn't manufacture a single component of its product; it owns the design and user experience.

If consumers can use financial products in their own environment, this will do more to build trust and the relationships that have been missing over the past decades.

One of the interesting observations that is true with most banks is that the further up the organization hierarchy, the more often bank executives lose touch with technologies that are relevant and meaningful to their customers. And often, it is the executives who are the ones making decisions on the technologies and partnerships for their partners to engage with. Those employees on the front lines, greeting customers and speaking with them regularly, may be relying on executives whose last time on the front line greeting customers was more than 10 years ago.

These days, decisions need to be made very quickly, particularly in a social networking environment, where a small number of tweets by those with large social and professional networks can hurt an institution's reputation. Part of becoming a responsive financial business is to use social technologies, not necessarily own them to be successful.

DIGITAL, DATA, AND THE FUTURE OF BANKING

A discussion about how social technology is impacting the financial services space wouldn't be complete without hearing from Facebook. Facebook now has over one billion monthly users and is still growing. Neil Hiltz, head of global vertical marketing for Financial Services, discusses some of the larger trends he is seeing and how banks might think about social in a different context:

> There's no doubt digital technology has changed our world in a very short period of time. Distinctions like "online" vs. "offline" are fading more every day; consumers have more choices than ever, and businesses have access to more data every day. This has fundamentally changed the way people bank and the ways banks do business.
>
> But a few things never change. In fact, all of these shifts in technology have created even more opportunity for financial institutions to achieve some of their longest-held objectives. In particular, the digital revolution has enabled entirely new levels of efficiency, scalability, and long-term profitability. Here's how the rise of social and digital technologies transform these opportunities:
>
> 1. Efficiency. Efficiency of business is an absolute must in Financial Services—it's the core driver of profitability. Digital technology and the abundance of data open up massive opportunities. Foremost for marketers is targeting. The type of marketing done through direct mail is massively wasteful because we often reach the wrong person at the wrong time—and with the wrong message. Better targeting gives us a much straighter path past each of those obstacles, at a much lower cost. Customer acquisition is also transformed because it is also dependent on this magic formula of reach + time + place. Add in now-rich profiles of authentic identity, and you can see how customer retention can also be a profoundly more efficient exercise.
> 2. Scalability. This seems obvious at first. If a business can't scale its impact with a global communications network to which almost half of the world is currently connected (the Internet), it's probably the business not the network. On Facebook in particular, more than one billion people are connected. They span every demographic you can imagine—a billion people is too large to generalize. So what does this mean for banks seeking scalability? First, brand preference. The same scale in communication that brought a billion people to one website has also commoditized much of the Financial Services industry. Yet, when an organization can tell its brand story and value

prop in an individually meaningful way at low cost—that's just scalable brand marketing. And it works. Second, consolidation is a factor. As retail locations for banks consolidate and consumer behavior shifts online, Financial Services marketers can invest in digital channels with much broader reach and impact than traditional channels like physical locations or television.

3. *Long-term profitability. This is where it gets really interesting, because the bottom line for Financial Services marketers is literally the bottom line. The first opportunity is full customer lifecycle marketing. Real identity-based networking (like Facebook) allows long-term relationships with customers that increase the ROI of each customer over time, allowing for upsell and co-marketing. Second is trust. Among other long-lasting setbacks of the 2008 financial crisis, trust between financial institutions and their clients plummeted. While 63 percent of people trust their financial institution, only 36 percent of people trust the Financial Services industry (Facebook Insights, Nov. 2012). This has been shown by several firms to affect profitability. And while financial institutions have scalable ways of determining trustworthiness of consumers (e.g., credit scores, FICO scores, etc.), the time has come to develop scalable ways to show and grow trustworthiness of financial institutions. Banks that leverage people-based networks as that scalable trust mechanism will see a corresponding effect on profit.*

The digital landscape does not reflect the industry zeitgeist—it defines it. In 2013, time spent on digital surpassed TV (eMarketer, August 2013). This should serve as a wake-up call for those in Financial Services still focusing largely on the retail footprint, traditional media, and direct mail. More specifically, the most significant change to this industry is and will continue to be mobile. As the number of people who connect and operate on some form of mobile device rise worldwide, businesses' approach to reaching [desired and potential] customers should reflect this. (As an example, by October 2013, 874 million people used Facebook on mobile—nearly $1/7$ of the world's population.)

People share their lives and are their authentic selves on Facebook, so implementing a people-centric rather than product-centric approach is the answer. The question is how to use the changing digital and mobile realities to take giant steps forward in efficiency and scalability—both of which drive profitability. This will not only yield greater results as more of the world connects online, but utilizing a platform the size of Facebook will help banks stay relevant because it is where their customers are spending their time.

SOCIAL MEDIA EXPERIENCES IN BANKING

As we've just heard from Facebook, integrating highly social, personalized marketing can be an effective way to build relationships with customers. Facebook claims that reaching a unique user on its channel is 40 to 60 percent cheaper than on other major advertisement networks or publishers, and it achieves significantly more accuracy, 90 percent versus an online average of 35 percent.

Facebook Connect, which allows consumers to log in to a site using their Facebook credentials, has created an interesting service to help it become an even stronger advertising platform—one that could ultimately allow it to offer a "pay per purchase" capability that could see how its advertisement could more precisely be turned into a sale. How? If consumers keep their credit card details linked to their Facebook account, Facebook can facilitate a payment through a one-button click at participating merchants, much like PayPal. The company clearly isn't interested in offering payment processing services and will use multiple processors, but it is interested in the data that can be translated back into insights potentially give Facebook keen insight into the shopping habits and preferences of the company's users. It could also provide its advertisers with valuable insight into what type of products its users are buying off of Facebook.[3] The consumer value proposition, much as we've discussed with Braintree, allows for more frictionless commerce to occur, particularly on the mobile phone, where entering a credit card number often is the biggest impediment to a potential sale.

While marketing through social media is interesting, it won't help if the material is not relevant to its customers or the financial products are outdated. There are several social-oriented financial products that nonbanks have been able to offer, which can lead to some fruitful bank partnerships. This is important, because as we will see, customers' expectations are changing; they want a social media experience in banking, as the blurring between online and offline continues to happen. Consumers are expecting relationships with the companies they patronize, as they move effortlessly between mobile phones, tablets, computers, and physical locations. Aside from expecting to have real-time access to their bank accounts, the ability to personalize services in a way that recognizes consumers for their loyalty and have offers and communication tailored to their needs is highly valuable.

Most banks are just waking up to the power of social media companies as a new standard for communication, delivering banking services within Facebook and other social media platforms. Today, a few thousand customers using Twitter could ruin the reputation of a bank within 20 hours. These social networks also represent a tremendous opportunity to connect and better understand customers and what they're interested in at a very individual level. This means far more than setting up a Facebook page, offering

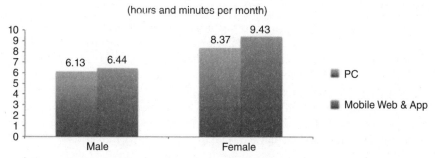

FIGURE 2.1   People Spend Lots of Time on Social Networks
Source: Nielsen Social Media Report 2012.

marketing information, or getting "Likes"—this is about becoming relevant to customers who may never plan to use a bank branch or would prefer to interact with their financial information through a nonbank. It's a necessity to connect with the younger generation since close to 90 percent of Gen Y has a social media profile.[4] Consumers today who have an active Facebook account spend over 6 hours per month on Facebook versus a little over 4 hours on Google. Even more important, they spend over 11 hours on Facebook mobile (see Figure 2.1)![5]

The idea is that banks don't have to wait for their customers to come to them; they can meet them where they are in the Web/mobile/social world. We have only seen the very beginning of social banking, but there are already some terrific examples from around the world. Germany's Fidor Bank used Facebook to tempt users into helping with its online promotion. The more Facebook likes it receives, the more interest users have on their savings. Danish Danske has used social media to ask how they could improve their mobile banking app. Their "Idebank" received hundreds of ideas and comments. They ask how to generate better consumer experiences and regularly engage with their customers to help define their product road map. American Express just rolled out a new feature that pushes alerts to its cardholders' Facebook pages.[6] Signing up will allow customers to receive notifications on Facebook when their statement is ready, when they need to make a payment, and when the payment has been received. American Express has also leveraged Twitter in some innovative ways, allowing customers to connect their American Express account to Twitter, allowing consumers to receive offers and purchase items using special hashtags. DenizBank from Turkey (now owned by Sberbank) launched a Facebook application that actually allows customers who have a Facebook account to transfer money 24/7 and monitor their credit card, deposits, and credit accounts.[7]

GAMIFICATION

Increasingly, we have seen more companies using "gaming" techniques to keep their customers engaged on their channels, and learning more about their business. Grow Financial, a credit union in the United States, installed a giant video screen outside a branch that allows passers-by to play a game and win money using interactive graphics on their mobile phones and a mirror that captures motion.[8] In Bulgaria, DSK Bank created an application that allows its customers to earn points redeemable for concerts and sporting events. Customers earn the points by setting up savings goals and learning about the bank's products.[9] mBank of Poland has made its entire user experience a type of game that can earn the consumer points as they learn financial management skills, as shown in Figure 2.2. Increasingly, if financial institutions are to attract the next generation to their online and mobile channels, gamification partnerships will become an important component of innovation, no different than any other retailer looking for creative ways to stimulate customer interest and engagement.

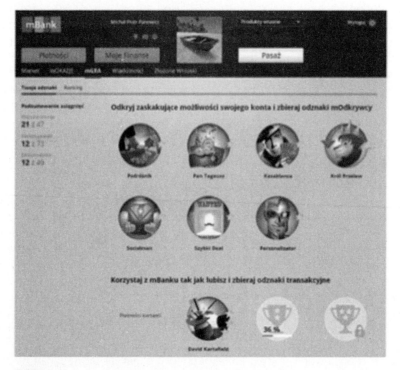

FIGURE 2.2   mBank of Poland
Source: thefinancier.uk.

PERSONAL FINANCIAL RELATIONSHIP MAPPING

Some of the most fundamental needs we have with our money relate to how we engage other people to pay, manage, and track our finances. When you start thinking about payments, tracking who pays you and who you pay, and having that information visually graphed, your payment network can quickly become a very social exercise. Detailed money management tools have always been available for the wealthy but for the mass-market banks have traditionally been very product-centric. The ability for consumers to see their entire financial snapshot in one place is now something they expect. They also expect to be able to categorize their own transactions to make them more personal. For example, I may not remember the $200 I spent at a restaurant, but I sure would remember exactly what it was if I could categorize that transaction as a lunch with coworkers. . . . Now that I've personally categorized this transaction the way I'd like it represented in my bank statement, I'd like to share this individual transaction with my accountant, or perhaps my employer.

Yodlee is one such company that is providing the next generation of financial services technology to its customers, tapping into a consumer's natural interest in their social financial relationships. Yodlee has its own personal financial management (PFM) offering called MoneyCenter, but Yodlee is most notably the plumbing behind many other popular brand-name PFM offerings, including Personal Capital, LearnVest, and seven of the top U.S. financial institutions, which gives them unique insight into how to make a PFM offering work (see Figure 2.3).

For financial providers, the role of trusted adviser has been seriously damaged in the last decade. People have used outside services for analysis, tools, and advice that used to be a financial institution's domain. PFM helps financial institutions move beyond checking an account balance or recent transaction into a deeper engagement model where customers can proactively manage their entire financial life, from setting goals to managing future cash flow, to protecting against fraud, to managing shared finances with others, all aimed to help customers become more informed about their finances.

Yodlee recently launched Tandem, a mobile app for managing financial relationships (see Figure 2.4). Tandem was designed to go beyond personal finances in order to help create order and peace of mind around how people manage finances within the context of other relationships (children, spouses, aging parents, teams, friends, roommates, etc.). What's unique about Tandem is the level of account sharing and access for different relationships. Through creating Financial Circles, people can engage in real dialogue around finances, share transactions, and send money, in a secure and controlled way.

FIGURE 2.3   Yodlee's MoneyCenter Application
Source: Yodlee.

The Financial Circles dictate the levels of account sharing access. So, for example, a child may have no access but a trusted financial adviser full access to a particular account. Tandem is especially compelling for people who are remote, such as kids in college, siblings and parents in different states, or friends and relations across the country and world. They can collaborate on shared expenses, ask for reimbursements, contribute to group goals, monitor others' accounts, and send cross-border remittances.

FIGURE 2.4   Tandem

Eric Conners, Yodlee's head of product, sees several banking uses for Yodlee's product:

> *A college student may tag several credit card transactions for reimbursement from mom and dad. Small business partners can upload and share loan documents with a bank officer. A suspicious set of transactions on mom's account can trigger action by siblings monitoring mom's affairs. There are hundreds of scenarios we all deal with every day. It's a very proactive and actionable app.*

CAPITALIZING ON SOCIAL BANKING

On first glance, Instabank may look like another virtual banking company, but it is leveraging social partnerships and trends in ways that may be a global blueprint of how financial institutions will leverage customer context, social, and the smartphone to offer a much more compelling set of experiences to customers (see Figure 2.5). Instabank is accessed entirely through a mobile application and uses Facebook and Foursquare data to make money transfers and bill tracking easier. Given that mobile is also becoming the primary way many access social networks, the combination of a mobile-only, social bank resonates. Customers' perceptions of the safety of online banking are also improving. Surveys show that 18- to 29-year-olds in America choose their banks mainly on the basis of their online offerings. Proximity to branches, the main criterion for people in their 70s, barely features, says Sherief Meleis of Novantas, a consulting firm.[10]

FIGURE 2.5 Instabank

Instabank's focus on mobile and social functions, relating in particular to Facebook, Instagram, and Foursquare, is a distinct advantage in Russia's social banking market, which, according to Instabank, is "very ample and almost untapped."[11]

The next set of banking experiences we will see will integrate itself deeply within a consumer's social web. Partnering with social companies will not only focus on marketing, it will also focus on allowing customers to utilize banking services more naturally within the context of what they are already doing such as chatting with friends on Facebook and remembering they forgot to pay them back for the concert, sending an immediate gift for a friend's birthday, or getting information about your bank account without having to remember another set of login credentials.

As social banking develops, we will surely see more integration with social commerce. Did your friend just find a great deal on a TV and share it on Facebook? Wouldn't it be great for your bank to know you're looking for a TV and offer instant financing to get the same TV? Offering these sorts of experiences will require deeper partnering and integration with social companies, and it will be very important. Offering the power of money management, both savings and spending management, is a powerful combination, particularly when connected with social. Most research available today concludes that a vast majority of consumers receive advice from friends and family relating to a product purchase through a social networking site, and most consumers rely on social networks to guide their purchases.[12] We already see the emergence of social peer-to-peer payments, whereby people chronicle their social timeline by what sorts of payments they're making (See Figure 2.6). Venmo, owned by Braintree and now PayPal, has made peer-to-peer payments a very social phenomenon.

As friends send payments with notes attached, payments themselves become a living commentary about how friends and acquaintances are spending time. While human nature hasn't changed much over the years, the medium by which this information is exposed certainly has, and financial institutions would do well to partner with those social commerce and social media companies that can make banking work in those environments.

MOVEN: DELIVERING BANKING THROUGH SOCIAL CONTEXT

One of the most well-known virtual banking institutions in the United States, Moven has incorporated a number of social elements to become contextually relevant for its customers. For example, it has integrated with a customer's Facebook social timeline so a customer can understand the impact of his or her social life on spending and updates these spending profiles in real time, alerting customers to spending trends. I sat down with

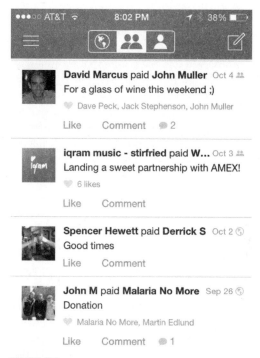

FIGURE 2.6 Venmo person to person payments app owned by PayPal

Brett King, CEO of Moven and best-selling author of *Bank 2.0,* to discuss what he thinks about the changing landscape and some of the social capabilities he has incorporated into his virtual bank:

Question: Can you share your perspective on some of the larger trends impacting financial services?

King: If you think about where banking sits right now and where it's going, everyone is focused on omnichannel or multichannel—serving the customer with less friction. We're entering a different phase of delivery of banking services. In the past, the branch was dominant, but now there is a major shift in consumer behavior. In the 1990s, I'd visit a branch twice a month; today, it's twice a year! We've seen a 90 percent contraction in activity! Today, to deposit a check or to send money to someone, you don't need to go to a bank. You can use Moven for a Facebook person-to-person payment!

Banking is becoming more of a platform—the thing that mobile does that is different is that it enables context. The problem of banking is that it is really dependent on location, event, or a trigger. I don't buy a credit card—I'm shopping or traveling, buying a home or car, and bank products are facilitating it. Ultimately, mobile and wearables like Google Glass give a financial institution the ability to understand where, when, and why their customers need banking services. The problem today is if you are looking for a car to buy, banks say: "Stop buying that car, that home; we don't know if we're going to lend the money. Come into the branch, fill out the paperwork. . . ." The banks won't be able to sustain their traditional model. If you are with your real estate agent and want to make an offer on a home, the bank should know me and if they can underwrite me at that moment.

Banking becomes widely distributed from a solution perspective. Here's the problem: as banking becomes distributed, it becomes integrated into your life, through data, data partnerships, mobile, geo tags, NFC, wearables, facial recognition, etc. Banking no longer becomes a physical place you go to, it is more of a utility that is provided, and it may be banks are not the best organizations to provide that utility—it might be a realtor or a search engine. As a bank, you may never be the first place the customer comes to and you might not be relevant unless the product is integrating into their life.

Where does that journey start for a customer? It could be at a shopping center, enabling me to get a flat-screen TV with an offer that helps me finance the TV, streamlining all the Know Your Customer (KYC), and making the experience very simple.

Question: How does Moven integrate social capabilities into its services, and why is that important?

King: Eighty percent of our customers already have integration with social networks. I would hazard a guess, as a bank, or as a banklike organization, we have the highest social integration of any organization. Eighty percent on their profile, linked their Facebook, Twitter, Google+ accounts. . . . About 40 percent of our customers use Facebook Connect for sign-in because they can use Facebook peer-to-peer payments right away. When they join Moven, they can send money to their friends by simply choosing a Facebook friend. The friend receives a message in their Facebook inbox that asks if they would like to accept it. Once the receiver clicks on it, they are pulled into the Moven environment. The receiver is then prompted if they would you like to keep the money in their Moven account or send to an existing bank through ACH. If the money is sent from one Moven account to another, it can be sent through FB instantly.

To enable this process with Facebook, we're simply enabling this process with their API and leveraging our relationship with our processor and partner bank to make most of this happen.

Question: What sort of benefits accrue to Moven when using Facebook?

King: The advantage for us with peer-to-peer payments using Facebook is customer acquisition—a number of recipients of a payment from a Facebook friend will sign up for Moven at that point. We don't need to sell them on switching banks; it says to customer prospects, "Hey, this is a tool, you can pay for stuff, send money to friends via Facebook, get a real-time receipt on how you're using your money. It's similar to how potential customers think about opening a PayPal account versus a bank account—very different. Customers can use Moven as a replacement account; over time it can leverage a friend's score for decisions, help with a savings budget, and it will have more gamification elements.

Question: How is Moven's application viewed differently than a traditional mobile banking application?

King: When you come into the Moven application, you see your balance. But the home page is dedicated to your money and what's happening to your money instead of showing you a bunch of products. For example, "You've spent $100 more than you normally do, etc.; you can then analyze it. That gives people a connection with their money, combined with recommendations—for example, "Why don't you put the $200 more in a savings account?"

Question: What type of skills does an organization need to take advantage of this new approach?

King: At Moven, we have a data scientist who looks at where and what this data is showing us—potential partnerships, demand, distribution, but more interestingly, the person who heads up our customer experience who is working on connecting the dots is a behavioral psychologist. She is looking at the psychology of spend, the anxiety of money as an imperative, what is the control factor going to do—this is a very different skill set. Generation Y, for example, is much more self-reliant when it comes to retirement. They are not going to expect a pension and are going to do their planning much earlier. They'll be much more self-directed and will rely on tools. There are lots of opportunities in terms of what we can do based on how we see consumer behavior and data. Moven is working on referrals—word-of-mouth. These mechanisms are very important and a very simple thing.

SOCIAL BANKING IN EUROPE AND ASIA

Around the world we are seeing innovative use cases in the way financial services companies are engaging with social media to stay relevant with their customer base. Three compelling European examples include Erste Bank in Austria, mBank in Poland, and DenizBank in Turkey. All three have found a way to leverage Facebook to interact directly with its customers. In the case of Erste, it has set up a virtual branch where clients can chat and get information in a fun way 24/7. mBank in Poland can now deliver special offer to customers directly in their Facebook account, personalized based on their transaction history. DenizBank in Turkey makes money transfers available on Facebook.

These banks are all finding ways to become more of a consumer's digital financial life. Fidor Bank in Germany offers a terrific set of examples of this (see Figures 2.7 and 2.8). Not only are they integrated into social applications, but they understand that very quickly, consumers will have many assets of digital and social value that they will need to manage beyond the basics. Commonwealth Bank of Australia can also make peer-to-peer payments to Facebook friends using their mobile phone number and address, as well as request payments, check balances, and transfer money between accounts. In India, ICICI Bank gives its customers account information through Facebook. The Facebook application is actually hosted on the bank's servers and requires a debit card number and password before it can be accessed, all without leaving Facebook.[13]

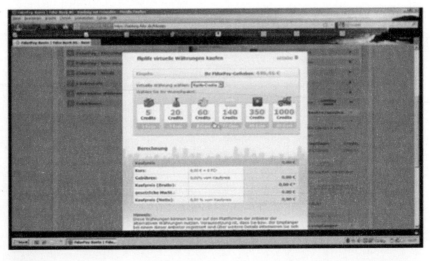

FIGURE 2.7   Fidor Bank Screen Shot of Virtual Credits It Manages for Its Customers
Source: Finovate Europe Conference.

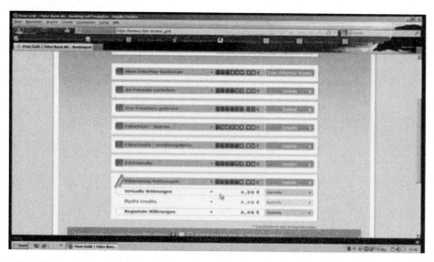

FIGURE 2.8   Fidor Bank's Interface to Manage a Customer's Digital Financial Value
Source: Finovate Europe Conference.

SOCIAL LOGIN, SHARING, AND TOP OF WALLET

We've already seen how many forward-looking virtual financial institutions are leveraging their customers' natural inclinations to use their social networking credentials as a way to log in and share information. Research from Gigya[14] reported that 52 percent of all logging and sharing preferences are with Facebook and skyrocket to nearly 89 percent of preferences when logins and sharing preferences occur at e-commerce sites, as Gigya's chart in Figure 2.9 demonstrates. Forty-one percent of consumers said they preferred using a social login to creating a new user account or using a guest account.[15]

There's clearly an opportunity for banks to take their customers' preferences to heart and offer the ability for their customers to log in any way they feel comfortable. While customer preferences may reflect a somewhat different preference when it comes to how they log in to their bank versus their retailer, it's clear that a substantial segment of the population is comfortable enough with privacy to go through a Facebook login process with their bank. Moven has mentioned upward of 40 percent of its customers log in using their Facebook credentials. Beyond logging in, we're now seeing institutions interested in becoming the payment button of choice, much like PayPal. It's not just Facebook, and it's not just social networks now interested in the payment button. It's companies such as Amazon that have already

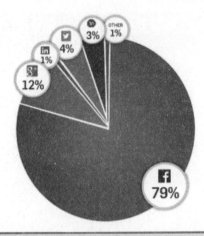

For online retailers Facebook is clearty the dominant identity provider, though Google/Google+ makes up a steable percentage of logins, which we believe will continue growting as Google Wallet gains traction in the vertical Additionally, Amazon is a new entrant in the space with Login with Amazon, and may quickly become a significant authentication player due to its ecommerce brand equity.

FIGURE 2.9   Facebook dominates social logins on third party Websites
Source: © Gigya. All rights reserved.

announced their intentions to bring their "one-click" payment enablement to other web sites. Why? The data, of course. These companies can see everything their customers are doing, even when they are not on their web site. It's a reality that many customers are likely to be comfortable logging in to a web site through Amazon or Facebook. Gigya research shows that many customer segments naturally favor convenience over privacy. What does that mean for retail banks, many of which derive a significant percentage of their revenue from payment card usage? Two things—first, advertising accuracy with Facebook and others is likely to go up, making them more important networks to leverage for marketing. More important, it will become increasingly important to allow a bank's credit or debit cards to be part of other payment "wallets" like Amazon or Facebook. These companies are also in a position to bring significant assets to industry security. One interesting thing to consider is how vast Facebook's database is on fraud behavior and how it very well might be in a position to underwrite payment fraud or other types of risk in the future.

PEER-TO-PEER LENDING: BLENDING SOCIAL AND BANKING

Social lending has been around far longer than formal financial institutions, but the Internet has given budding peer-to-peer lending companies an opportunity to acquire customers and grow loan originations at an unprecedented rate. U.S. peer-to-peer lending company Lending Club has over $2 billion in loans alone. In the United Kingdom, analysts project the peer-to-peer market to grow to over $2 billion by 2016.[16] The viral nature of social lending coupled with the Internet, a very-low-cost customer acquisition medium, will translate to double- and possibly triple-digit growth rates for the next few years as Internet penetration and consumer interest continue to fuel demand.

Peer-to-peer lending differs from financial institution lending in one important respect—by its very definition, it is not hierarchical. Interactions among borrowers and lenders often take on a much more personal, community-type feel. As such, more information flow takes place than in a typical banking transaction, which can make borrowing and lending a much more satisfying experience. There is a higher degree of individualism and control offered to individuals not available at a financial institution. Three drivers have spurred peer-to-peer lending growth:

1. *Personalization.* Consumers increasingly expect and crave tools that allow them to take more initiative in managing their finances. This trend began over 20 years ago with the advent of personal financial management software that empowered consumers to budget and track their personal finances, alert them to investments that may fit their criteria, and allow them to originate loans and move money. This trend has also manifested itself in the level of involvement some consumers would like to have with their specific lending and borrowing activities. Peer-to-peer lending can be a natural enabler for consumers to align their personal values and self-expression with their financial decisions, deciding who, what, and where to invest or borrow their money.

2. *Industry economics.* Peer-to-peer lending companies operate on efficiencies that are over 400 basis points lower than the traditional servicing costs carried by financial institutions. The transparency and usability of the Internet has made it challenging for financial institutions to differentiate themselves based on product, service, or personal affiliation. However, peer-to-peer lending companies will have to contend with marketplace growth and liquidity in order to become self-sustaining entities. They will also have to find ways to execute on bad debt collection in as low cost a manner as possible. For traditional financial institutions, the reliance on interest margin spread will require more use of the

Internet channel to seek out low-cost deposits and originate lending in as low cost a manner as possible to preserve net interest margins.

3. *Technology.* Account and identity verification have traditionally been an offline process. The emergence of online companies that leverage the Internet to pull eclectic bits of information for authentication and verification purposes has made the registration process much more consumer friendly. Many companies have exposed their services through application programming interfaces (APIs) that allow access to customer permissioned information. Other identification management companies ask users specific questions to validate their information, for example, "What color was the 1996 Honda Accord you owned?" or "Which one of the following people was related to you?" The emergence of Web 2.0/3.0 technologies has made the Internet much more interactive, and peer-to-peer lending companies have leveraged these interactive tools to create social communities that feel more connected to peer-to-peer lending marketplaces and the sharing of information. Consumers will continue to gravitate toward online lending models that offer greater degrees of personalization.

BEYOND THE HYPE: PARTNERING FOR THE FUTURE WITH PEER-TO-PEER LENDERS

There have been many media stories written about the disruptive nature of peer-to-peer lending and its perceived detrimental impact on the banking industry. The media usually take one of two positions. One position views banks as "middle men" that take too rich a spread of lending and borrowing transactions that occur, and welcomes technology companies as complete replacements for banks. The other position looks at technology companies as dangerous nonregulated entities that should not be in a position to offer financial services. Neither view is correct.

The truth is that the most powerful opportunities in the peer-to-peer lending space exist when banks and platform technology companies partner and leverage complementary strengths; most banks do not have the best user experience, nor do they have a breadth of unsecured lending products to offer. They are also often saddled with legacy technology that makes loan servicing more expensive. In the case of technology companies, most do not have a source of low-cost capital or access to a critical mass of customers needed to create an efficient marketplace. There is also a very strong social component that peer-to-peer lending companies have tapped into: the idea of putting money to work to help other individuals or small businesses directly.

Given that the consumer lending market has experienced significant consolidation over the past decade, many smaller banks have been left out and are no longer able to compete with the likes of a top 10 bank. Thus, for most banks and credit unions, the prospect of leveraging an online peer-to-peer marketplace to offer products not currently in their arsenal is highly relevant and appealing. The credit card market is a prime example of this consolidation, with over 80 percent of credit card originations held by the top 10 issuers. For mortgages and home equity loans, and to a lesser degree for student loans, the market is in the midst of a period of consolidation, with lenders aggressively striving to grow their origination volumes across all channels, including the Internet. Finally, the market for auto loans, personal loans, and small business loans remains largely fragmented (excluding the captive finance market, which accounts for over 40 percent of auto loans originated).

As partnering becomes more commonplace, we increasingly see banks offer their customers the financial products they're looking for, regardless of the bank's own specialization or origination. I've spoken with a number of banks that are working on active partnerships with various peer-to-peer players. As they see it, partnerships do not mean banks need to give up their customers. On the contrary, for the vast majority of banks, offering a new financial product that they couldn't offer to their customers before is all upside. It turns out that everyone wins, including 99 percent of the banking industry that do not have the business model, technology prowess, online expertise, or focus.

LENDING CLUB: A WIN-WIN FOR BANKS AND THEIR CUSTOMERS

In the U.S. peer-to-peer lending space, there is one company that continues to grow significantly and welcomes banks with open arms—Lending Club. I had the pleasure of speaking with Renaud Laplanche, CEO of Lending Club, to discuss his business and plans with the banking industry:

Question: Can you tell us a bit about the path you've decided to go down with the banking industry?

Laplanche: We spent quite a bit of time a couple of years ago, when we really had a choice between going down two paths, one being a very confrontational attitude toward the banking system and really competing head-to-head against the banks, and another path recognizing that we are transforming the banking industry but associating with banks through that transformation. We felt working with banks would be the better path for a couple of reasons:

First, I think banks are having a hard time delivering a great experience, transforming their business to a lower-cost business, like what's available online. Banks are struggling with operating cost and customer satisfaction, but they still have considerable access to low-cost capital and an installed base of customers, so we thought there would be a combination of what the banks do well and the assets the banks have with what we do well, which is operating at low cost and delivering a great experience. So that's one reason we thought we should partner with banks rather than trying to compete head-to-head.

The other reason is more defensive: many of the large banks are very powerful, they have representation in Washington, they're the biggest donors to political parties, and so linking the banks to our success—to the extent we're successful— would also be a good defensive move, rather than competing head-to-head against very powerful institutions.

Question: How did you think about partnering with banks?

Laplanche: The way we decided to build that partnership is really in two ways. First, there's a pretty obvious way to partner with banks, which is just to allow the banks to be a participant on our platform. We are a two-sided marketplace with borrowers on one side and investors on the other side. Investors can be a pretty broad range of entities, ranging from individual investors to financial advisers, pension funds, and banks. Banks can become an investor on the platform, and the banks right now have a lot of excess deposits and they are struggling to put these deposits to work in a way that makes sense in a very low yield environment. We are essentially offering banks the ability to invest on the platform, become one of the lenders and investors on the platform, and really buy assets in a way where they couldn't originate directly, and in that case you really end up with the best of both worlds, where you have Lending Club's low operating cost and great customer satisfaction and brand as a front end to the customer, and the banks' low cost of capital funding the loans. When you combine a low operating cost and a low capital cost, you get the maximum value at the lowest cost possible and can deliver capital that's more affordable to the consumer.

Question: What's in it for banks that want to do more than just becoming lenders or investors?

Laplanche: The first step, as I described, has been going on for about six to nine months. We now have seven community banks that are investing on the platform, but that does not involve the banks' customers; that just puts the bank's balance sheet to work and gives the banks access to assets. In a way, it's interesting for community banks not just in terms of yield but in terms of diversification—it's a way for a community bank to diversify geographically outside of their footprint. Some of the community banks might be able to lend to their customers in a small geographic footprint, but through our national origination platform, they might have access to a much broader base of customers—its yield-generating products in an asset class that they can know and can evaluate in terms of consumer lending and it is highly diversified. It's value for the banks and good value to us—very stable capital and great value for the customer because it's low cost of capital, low operating cost that really helps that lower our interest rates and make credit more affordable. So that's phase 1, and we're going to be doing more of it into the next year.

Then the second phase is becoming more interesting to us because it leverages a bank's existing customer base. If you look at the 8,000 banks in this country, only a handful of them have a consumer unsecured lending business, mostly major credit card issuers. Chase, Bank of America, Citibank, Capital One, Discover—they all have a lot of credit card loans on their books. Outside of that, you have a handful of banks that have a personal loan product, but that product has mostly gone away because it's harder to underwrite and it's not as profitable as a credit card, and the big banks have all moved to the credit card business. And really the other 7,980 banks can't do much in the way of unsecured lending, but they have a big customer base of customers with deposit accounts, mortgages, student loans, and many other products. So the play here is really to provide the ability for the banks to issue personal loans to their customers, powered by Lending Club.

Question: How have the banks responded to this?

Laplanche: We've been discussing this opportunity with several banks. We're going to launch by the first half of 2014 with two decent-size banks, and probably sometime in 2014 with one of the banks that has over a million customers with over $100 billion in assets. Again, for the banks, it's a way to have another product to cross-sell to their customers, and if they know their customers have a balance with Chase or Citi, why not try to recapture that balance in-house. But they can't do it because they don't currently have personal loan products. So we are providing the origination and servicing platform, and the bank would benefit from that additional product they can sell to their customers and we would share the revenue.

We're making the pie bigger; we're also taking marketing share and balances away from the largest credit card issuers. The only entities that really lose in that equation are the five or six large credit card issuers. Everyone else wins.

Question: Are there other benefits that accrue by operating as a platform?

Laplanche: Operating as a platform becomes very powerful because the banks might not be interested in 100 percent of the loans to their customers—they might have a credit policy or appetite that might be different from the other investors we have, so if we originate a range of loan grades from A to G, each corresponding to a risk bucket, the banks might be interested in the A and B grades because of their risk appetite, but we might have a couple of other credit hedge funds that want E, F, and G, and we might have a wealth management client from Switzerland interested in the C and D grades, and the platform is where we can get more of these funds rather than doing it directly.

The fundamental advantage we have is really a cost advantage because we have no branch, no physical cost structure, and because we have a mind-set of really solving problems with technology. We are really pushing automation as far as it can possibly go, and as a result, we are able to operate at a much lower cost than the banks.

We had a consultant come in and assess the precise cost advantage we have in the banking system and the answer he came up with was 425 basis points—and the usual operating expense of a bank is between 6 and 7 percent of the loan balance. So if you're charging 6 percent on the credit card, then 6 percent goes into the cost of originating and servicing those balances, Lending Club's cost is slightly under 2 percent. It would be really hard for the banks to replicate that.

Question: Aside from your cost advantage, are there other things you are doing that are contributing to the growth you're seeing at Lending Club?

Laplanche: We're also using technology to make the experience better. We measure the net promoter score (NPS) of our customers, and the NPS on the borrower's side is 72 percent, which is high by any standard but very high from a bank perspective, where the average is in the 20s and the credit card issuers are in the single digits, so I think the experience we deliver is considerably better than what the large banks have been delivering, and a lot of that is powered by technology and the ability to get to the answer you need for the customer.

Question: What else are you able to do that the banks have a hard time replicating?

Laplanche: It's really the lower interest rate, and second, convenience—not having to drive to a branch, and the fact that you don't have to fax or scan documents. To give you an example of how we make it easy for customers using technology to improve the experience—the primary way banks verify income or employment is by asking their customers to send in a copy of the their last three pay stubs, which is if you're like me, just finding that pay stub is challenging. And the process of scanning or faxing it—it's work. Our way of identifying income is to connect directly to payroll processors with ADP and Paychex, and we've built information connectivity that helps us essentially query their system and get an answer back in less than a second and with the authorization we get on the borrower, we get the employment history, the current employment situation, current position, and current salary, which helps increase the accuracy of the underwriting, but also helps lower our cost but also very much helps create a better experience.

Takeaways for Banks

It's clear that lenders that cannot partner to provide a streamlined and integrated user experience will do poorly with their online initiatives. Customers expect to see benefits from choosing the online channel such as the reduction or elimination of paper documents, the ability to track the status of their loan application in a comprehensive manner, faster processing and approval times resulting from streamlined back-office operations, and, ultimately, lower prices. Online borrowers are increasingly tech-savvy (particularly repeat borrowers) and value the Internet for the time and money they can save.

Perhaps the ultimate example of just how intensely personal online lending has become in some instances, customers increasingly view their financial activity as a means of financial self-expression. For these individuals, the personalization of online lending has increasingly meant the ability to choose who they borrow from, who they lend to, and what level of risk they should take in investing their money as their own lender. Peer-to-peer lenders have demonstrated that a growing consumer lending market exists in do-it-yourself-oriented lending, with the billions of dollars that are lent informally between families, business associates, and friends. There are clearly many opportunities for banks and peer-to-peer lending organizations to come together through integrated products that can open up new lending markets entirely.

Online lending is still fairly early on in its continuum, but the trends are clear. We will continue to see consumer empowerment in the financial services realm, which will present more opportunities for banks to creatively partner with peer-to-peer organizations. Loan securitizations will make their way to empowered consumers, who will eventually be able to buy and resell loans as investment vehicles on a secondary market. As such, there will be room for banks and nonbanks alike to offer online lending products, particularly when they are offered in an integrated fashion.

AN INVESTOR'S PERSPECTIVE ON SOCIAL BANKING AND THE EMERGENCE OF BITCOIN

Meyer "Micky" Malka has a unique vantage point to view some of the profound changes happening within the financial services industry. In 1998, Malka created an online digital brokerage operation Patagon with Wences Casares, his long-time business partner. Patagon became Latin America's first full-scale, Internet-based financial services portal. After expanding beyond Venezuela to the rest of South America and the United States, Patagon was sold to Banco for $750 million. In 2002, Malka cofounded Banco Lemon, a Brazilian retail bank that used the principles of microfinance to serve the underbanked. It was the largest private microfinance institution in Brazil when it was acquired in 2009 by Banco do Brasil, Latin America's largest bank. In 2011, he cofounded Banco Bracce, a merchant bank for the fast-growing midcap market in Brazil, and Lemon, a smart wallet app that allows individuals to manage their wallet on any phone. Aside from his involvement as a director with the Bitcoin foundation and MarcadoLibre, the largest online marketplace in Latin America, Micky serves as founder and partner of Ribbit Capital, and invests in companies that are in a position to radically change financial services as he has done as a long-time entrepreneur.

I sat down with Micky to get his thoughts on the banking industry and the largest trends he sees.

Question: What are some of the macro trends you see happening today in financial services?

Malka: A couple of things come to mind very quickly. The first is the need for a layer of trusted, transparent financial products. Banks right now are not very well liked by their customers. People don't walk around being proud of their banks like they used to—they don't wear the logos of the banks, they don't give them a five-star rating on their apps, and they're not happy with the service they get in general. And I believe there's an opportunity to build new financial brands, but the only way to do that means building trust, and that means you have to be transparent.

When you look at a typical phone any one of us have, what you have on your home screen is a search engine, which is transparent. You search for whatever you want and get answers—news, sports, etc. You choose what you like and you get the headlines you want to get in a clear transparent way, and you also have a clear way to write text or e-mail those news sources.

But when it comes to banking, it's gray. You never know how much interest you pay on your credit card, when your bill is coming, whether you prefer a loan or not, whether your next transaction is going to be declined or not, all these little things, you never simply know. I see a tremendous opportunity to innovate in financial services by matching this industry to the rest of the industries by the way we consume technology—that means being very transparent and building for mobile. It really means you can serve customers, you can communicate, you can be transparent with them, and end up building long-lasting brands and then create innovation. That's how I see the sequence of events. I think it will be easier than it has been over the last 20 years. Why? You know the channel, who's not addressing the channel, and what the consumer is not happy with. You used to have this nontransparent layer in financial banking, lending, or insurance. Now, information is available everywhere electronically; it's not an advantage as it once was for banks 15 years ago. They had their records and you received information once a month when you received your statement. At this point in time, anyone offering software as a service can extract real-time data—all the information that is needed—and that has leveled the playing field and made it more competitive.

When you think about what banks really do, they started as custodians, and only after that, they got in the business of lending against that money. Right now, their advantage is much more associated with regulatory hurdles. From a payment perspective, I believe you are better off in a very sophisticated encryption system and you are better off getting loans from underwriters.

Question: Are there certain core competencies that are necessary to have today if you are offering financial products?

Malka: Today, we have to be great users of data. Even in a bank like Chase, when you have an account for 15 years and want to get a mortgage, you still have to go through 500 pages. In theory, they have all the information they need digitized about your account. We don't consume products this way when we use Facebook or Google, so I think the big thing is that they shouldn't think product by product, but rather holistically serve customer needs. Third-party applications are going to be better at customizing experiences for subsegments and doing specific things. As a bank, you are better off doing what you do best—custody, legal/background checks and balance sheet lending.

As an example of how financial institutions should be thinking, if I as a customer want a car right now, I should be able to ask you how much will you lend me, rather than put in all the information you as my financial institution already have. In theory, you should already be able to offer me a loan on the spot. As my financial institution, you saw my last payroll deposit only 10 days ago. Nothing has changed, I'm not delinquent, and you know this because you've been monitoring me for the last five years. This type of experience has to be made possible if banks are to stay relevant.

Question: What changes are most important to make if you are leading a financial institution?

Malka: I would start by changing the product-centric culture of most organizations. I would look differently at segmentation, but not base everything on product and cross-sell. I would also ensure the institution uses all the data it now has access to as to—who our customers are, where they fit and draw opinions. I would also design everything starting with mobile, then desktop, then branch, and not the other way around because that's where you have no competitive advantage. I recall when I was leading a financial institution, I had an inherent conflict since I was stealing customers from my own branches, so it's important to set up the right incentive structure.

Question: Who would be the most compelling partnerships needed today for a bank to stay relevant with its customers?

Malka: Let's slice the company into functions that we do. Custody, payments, credits, lending, time deposit savings, and five to six more things—I would build the next 20 years' worth of product planning into an API-centric framework. I would not think of the guy running my back end, but the APIs, every single relationship runs through APIs—if a start-up wants to do car lending, we'll have an API for that—or if they want our balance sheet, if we can approve immediately, we'll take the balance sheet loan. This is about acquiring those who are building the next layer of better usability with customers.

You could decide your branch separately—create an API for "branches." With that mind-set, suddenly everything can become a branch. A bank could say, "I will approve any CVS [drugstore chain] franchisee because they will run appropriate risk checks on my customers and they are best drug store chain in the United States." If you were to take that model— fast-forward five years—you wouldn't interact with any bank channels anymore, you're interacting with new layers. That's where we'll go with banking.

Banks will be competing on trust, price, and speed of response, and in the end, banking will always have a social component, I don't think you just trust a system with your wealth. It will look very different than it does today; your banker may be part of your mobile application, but not the other way around.

If I am a smaller bank, this could be a way to compete with the larger banks. The customers for now and for the foreseeable future are waiting to trade in some of the established brands for more innovation, transparency, and effectiveness because they're not getting anything they're proud of from the brands.

Question: You are a big investor in Bitcoin-related companies. Tell us why and how banks might think about Bitcoin.

Malka: I describe Bitcoin as a protocol for transferring any time of value. It's like TCP/IP [Transmission Control Protocol/Internet

Protocol]—there are essentially five wrappers on top of it, such as e-mail and Web browsing. Bitcoin is a protocol—decentralized, on a trusted general ledger system, with a real-time response and fraud prevention. That is the basis, and you can tie any value to that protocol—properties, documents, stock certificates. We're just starting to see all of the possibilities. This is the first time in history we see the idea of a digital resource that can be considered scarce. You only need a fraction of this asset to tie all sorts of value to it—it is divisible by 100 million, so you can basically have 1/100,000,000 of a Bitcoin but you will never see more than 21 million coins. As more products are built on top of this protocol, we will continue to see the possibilities. Let me give you some examples of some of those possibilities. Right now, with the largest stock market in the world, you still need three days to settle a stock transaction. If you tie the stock to a Bitcoin, you settle in real time and it is irrevocable.

In Argentina, for example, when you buy or sell a real estate property, you need to exchange the money in front of a notary, but there are all kinds of issues: people were robbed, a cashier check takes 48 hours to clear, yet once you sign, you're done. Escrow services are very different than in the United States, and Bitcoin has come to solve for it—people actually buy Bitcoins, the seller gets a wallet of Bitcoins, on the spot when they transact, they know it's done and it can't be reversed, so you don't even need an escrow. Those are examples of things going on that are just happening and are happening more.

It was J. P. Morgan who said it best: "Gold is money and everything else is paper." That was the message and this was 1870-something. He would be out of business today. The world has turned into a paper-centric fiat machine and for a long time they weren't embracing this reality.

I feel the same way about Bitcoin—right now it's the same, money is government money, and everything else is whatever you want to call it—a toy. I think right now bankers are reacting—this is what I think—if you were Katherine Graham [ex-owner of the *Washington Post*] in 1990 and some 25-year-old kid from the company came to your office and told you that that something called the Internet would allow people to get the news on the computer and phone, would be easy to read, and that he thought it will affect paper and ads, most probably her reaction would be: "Get out of my office." And as much as they embraced it later on, they just sold the *Washington Post* for $250 million, something that was worth significantly more 20 years ago. I think that's exactly where we are with what the Bitcoin protocol is for money. This going to happen to the financial institutions that don't pay attention and underestimate the power of a protocol that is designed to create value better than anything that has ever been built, someone will end up buying a well-known brand for a quarter of the cost in a few years.

As a bank, the first thing I would do is embrace the Bitcoin protocol. There's not much you need to do more than embrace it at this time. If you are a custodian of people's wealth, start thinking about how would you custody this new asset. If you were a bank doing remittances, how would you use this? If you were providing escrow services, wills, merchant banking services, how would I do this? It isn't a matter of partnering at this point. The *Washington Post* would have been hanged if they had bought AOL at the time, but because they didn't embrace change, they didn't realize they'd have to sell big content instead of going to free content, and monetize ads online instead of allowing Yahoo and Google to take ads because they got in too late. That's my example.

As you build trust in a protocol, psychologically, it's a game of longevity—how long will it take for people to build trust—but every day, as more people jump into it, and more ideas come to mind, and you get more okays from regulators, it will continue to grow in value.

MESSAGE TO BANKS: BE A SMALLER PART OF A BIGGER PIE

In this chapter, we've heard from investors, entrepreneurs, virtual banks, and Facebook. Given that consumers will expect banking services to fit within any context or application they are accessing, perhaps the biggest message is to look at ways to partner and integrate with all those companies that are creating powerful consumer experiences. The smallest part of that overall experience may be the payment or the loan, but as a financial institution, you'll want to make sure you're partnered and integrated with everywhere you expect your customers to be, even if it's not on your channel. Table 2.1 outlines some of the common observations, insights, and takeaways that you may want to consider if you are in the financial services business.

TABLE 2.1   Common Observations in the Financial Services Business

A growing number of consumers will expect to:	Banks should therefore consider:
Interact with banking services through social media.	■ Take advantage of social media APIs for login. ■ Enable transactional capabilities through these channels. ■ Build peer-to-peer payment services linked to social networks. ■ Offer social banking/personal financial management such as Yodlee's Tandem products.
Engage bank based on context.	■ Partner with companies that produce popular applications offering one-click payments (e.g., Uber/Braintree). ■ Think about future custodial needs for managing customer's financial digital life, including Bitcoin.
Borrow and lend their money more directly.	■ Originate loan partnerships with peer-to-peer marketplaces. ■ Partner with peer-to-peer marketplaces like Lending Club—sell their originated loans to your customers.
Use mobile applications for a variety of different uses.	■ Offer services to other channels—tiny/all-mobile applications that could make use of financial services (real estate tools, car comparison tools, etc.).
Have more "one-click" experiences with payments.	■ Partner with Braintree/PayPal, Google, any institutions offering digital wallet capabilities to their customers—they often influence payment preference.
Consume banking services the same way they consume services on the Internet.	■ Create mobile/digital signature products that enable documents to be signed digitally.
Open bank accounts as easily as PayPal, Amazon, or Google.	■ Leverage mobile and new verification technologies to make on-boarding a better overall user experience.

NOTES

1. Harris Interactive, "The Harris Poll 2013 RQ Report," www
.harrisinteractive.com/vault/2013%20RQ%20Summary%20Report%
20FINAL.pdf. Accessed February 4, 2014.

2. Susan Ochs, "Full Frontal Banking," *American Banker,* www.americanbanker.com/bankthink/full-frontal-banking-1060578-1.html. Accessed July 15, 2013.

3. allthingsdigital.com, "Facebook to Test Its Own PayPal Competitor in Bid to Simplify Mobile Purchases," http://allthingsd.com/20130815/facebook-testing-out-paypal-competitor-in-bid-to-simplify-mobile-commerce-purchases/. Accessed August 15, 2013.

4. Jonathan Camhi, "How to Attract Generation Y Customers," *Bank Systems & Technology,* www.banktech.com/channels/how-to-attract-generation-y-customers/240153635. Accessed April 25, 2013.

5. Mobey Forum, Facebook presentation, San Francisco, April 16, 2013, www.mobeyforum.org/event/new-york-member-meeting/.

6. Sean Sposito, "AMEX Pushes Alerts to Cardholders' Facebook Pages," *American Banker,* http://cdn.americanbanker.com/issues/178_131/amex-pushes-alerts-to-cardholders-facebook-pages-1060473-1.html. Accessed July 9, 2013.

7. EFMA and Wipro Technologies, "The Global Retail Banking Digital Marketing Report 2013," www.wipro.com/Documents/the-global-retail-banking-digital-marketing-report-2013.pdf. Accessed November 12, 2013.

8. Matt Clinch, "Retail Banks' Worst Nightmare? Google," CNBC.com, www.cnbc.com/id/101127506. Accessed October 21, 2013.

9. Sarah Todd, "Bulgarian Bank Uses Gamification to Teach Customers Financial Literacy," *American Banker,* www.americanbanker.com/issues/178_218/bulgarian-bank-uses-gamification-to-teach-customers-financial-literacy-1063562-1.html. Accessed November 12, 2013.

10. "Third Time Lucky," *The Economist,* www.economist.com/news/finance-and-economics/21589471-banks-have-no-branches-are-making-surprising-resurgence-third-time-lucky. Accessed November 9, 2013.

11. Andril Degeler, "Mobile Social Banking Arrives in Russia," East-West Digital News, www.ewdn.com/2013/05/17/mobile-social-banking-arrives-in-russia/. Accessed May 17, 2013.

12. Michoel Ogince, "4 Startups Revolutionizing Social Commerce," *Mashable,* http://mashable.com/2012/06/04/startups-socialcommerce/?__hstc=34007934.5432921e5727d557c7ec2639d38c784f.1382851061746.1382851061746.1382851061746.1&__hssc=34007934.1.1382851061746&__hsfp=1197331964. Accessed June 4, 2012.

13. www.wipro.com/Documents/the-global-retail-banking-digital-marketing-report-2013.pdf.

14. http://blog.gigya.com/the-landscape-of-social-login-sharing-consumers-want-choice/.

15. Victor White, "The Landscape of Social Login & Sharing: Consumers Want Choice," *Gigya,* http://blog.gigya.com/the-landscape-of-social-login-sharing-consumers-want-choice/. Accessed February 4, 2014.

16. Elaine Moore, "Digital Finance Lending Set to Hit £1bn," *Financial Times,* http://www.ft.com/intl/cms/s/0/28bf596c-eafb-11e2-bfdb-00144 feabdc0.html#axzz2kevSFhcu. Accessed July 15, 2013.

CHAPTER 3

Connected Financial Commerce

Location-Based Services, Mobile Commerce, and Digital Wallets

"The interesting products out on the Internet today are not building new technologies. They're combining technologies. Instagram, for instance: photos plus geolocation plus filters. Foursquare: restaurant reviews plus check-ins plus geo."

—Jack Dorsey, Cofounder of Square and Twitter

We've talked about the effects of "mobile" and "social" on consumer behavior and how it is influencing financial services. The effects of location-based technologies will have a dramatic impact on how financial services will be delivered and the level of service you might come to expect from your financial services provider. We've discussed the powerful influence of the mobile phone and the higher level of expectations consumers have when shopping or managing money. With location-based services now such a normal part of a smartphone, it becomes a given for banks, consumers, retailers, and technology companies to work together to create more compelling customer experiences. How do banks benefit? They can better target their customers' specific preferences and maintain relevance with their customers by making it easy to use their services on other applications. Eventually, location-based services will be something that bank branches can leverage—knowing their customers' interests and needs as they walk into a branch. Similarly, retailers will have an opportunity to connect more deeply with their customers, help them navigate a store to find just what they're looking for, and serve up enticing offers depending on location and time of day.

There is a broad paradigm shift happening from offline to intelligent, connected devices that will completely change how we consume information, how we interact with friends, retailers, banks, and our community. The smartphone has brought the world online; social has created communities; now with location-based services and connectivity technologies like radio frequency identification (RFID), low-frequency Bluetooth, and near field communication (NFC), all devices will eventually be online and connected—from mobile phones, to tablets, TVs, game systems, even wearable items like watches. Even door locks, thermostats, and refrigerators share a similar fate, and most will be capable of facilitating commerce in some way. RFID sensors that can be embedded in almost anything have been thought to give birth to "the Internet of things," a world that connects billions of devices together. Accelerometers in phones, jewelry, clothing, and cameras will collect new forms of data and allow them to be used in some very powerful ways. An insurance company might collect information on someone's driving record and price insurance more efficiently. IHS, a research provider, estimates that "smart clothes" with sensors will jump to $605 million in sales in 2014.[1] The lines between online and offline are blurring so completely that it will be impossible to know what is considered e-commerce, m-commerce, or any other type of commerce; it will all just be considered commerce. The payments that will take place will not be specific to a device, but rather will continue to become a hidden, frictionless capability that will not require you to enter a number or go through a checkout process. It will give consumers a much richer, more secure, and convenient set of capabilities that will require banks to reimagine how they can fit their solutions into this new world. Since financial institutions will have insight into the context of a situation, knowing where a customer is and the type of device they're using, they'll be expected to tailor the financial experience to the precise device and moment that's best for the consumer. It starts by getting consumers enabled with products best for them and then figure out the best ways to use them.

No customer wakes up in the morning and says, "I want to find new ways of paying," or "I would love to apply for a loan today." The financial products are just enablers of consumers' life preferences. Consumers will increasingly say, "I'm hungry and want to order some food instantly." Connecting payments and financial transactions to the applications where consumers can have these types of experiences will create stronger relationships, and it will transform industries. In the past, a restaurant may not have made its hamburger until someone ordered and paid for it. Now, OpenTable, Yelp, PayPal, and many other companies are transforming the way businesses conduct their operations. As Brett King, author of *Bank 2.0*, says, "At end of day, banking and payments, it's not the place you go, it's something you do."

THE "LOCAL" DIGITAL WALLET

It has been a few years now that location-based services have been in smartphones, and we've certainly seen in the United States how Yelp, OpenTable, and Foursquare have seized the opportunity to connect small businesses to consumers. More than just listing services, they now connect consumers and businesses directly and facilitate the sale, often in advance of a consumer's stepping foot on premises. Are you in a city you don't know and feel like eating Chinese food? Use Yelp to find a highly rated restaurant, and if you have your credit card attached, order the food in advance to have it delivered or picked up. OpenTable provides a very strong tool for restaurants to manage their tables, a connected digital reservation book. The fact that consumers can now tap into this instant network to get a table or anything else within walking distance with a smartphone that is aware of your location has changed how commerce and, increasingly, banking can be done. Companies like Uber and Yelp are improving interaction, customer experience, and overall communications, which will be very hard for large companies to replicate on their own. And the fact is these companies are only just starting. Only 12 percent of restaurant reservations were booked online as recently as late 2012.[2] Once a critical mass of consumers put their cards on file with technology platforms providing localized services, these companies perform a digital wallet function, facilitating the sale with a simple smartphone.

THE NEW RETAIL EXPERIENCE

The concept of "showrooming" is fairly common today—consumers who browse store products and then end up purchasing online. However, "webrooming" is becoming equally common—the idea that consumers often browse first on the Internet but end up buying in-store. What we are seeing is the emergence of omnichannel commerce; consumers expect to be armed to the hilt with information that informs their purchasing decisions. A recent Accenture survey found a number of interesting statistics[3]:

- Seventy-two percent of respondents indicated they participated in "showrooming."
- Seventy-eight percent of respondents indicated they participated in "webrooming."

What's clear is that the future of shopping will rely much more on the Internet, and given that most interact with the Internet through their mobile phone, the mobile experience will be incredibly important. The same Accenture study found that when asked what they would most like to see added to new shopping experiences, 82 percent of consumers selected having access to current product availability as their top choice. Context is a larger theme we've been discussing that is expected in today's world of financial services. Scott Dunlap, managing director of 10th Dimension design labs, says, "Nothing makes more sense than a doughnut coupon right next to a gas station transaction. That's context— the most important thing you can offer to a consumer transaction." Part of a consumer's smartphone you have with you at all times; you can use the knowledge of your location to your advantage and trade your whereabouts in exchange for relevant deals and offers. If you've linked your credit card to Foursquare, and "checked in" to a retailer, you might just get some immediate offers tied to that credit card. What are the sorts of things we can expect retailers to do when interacting with consumers? Here are a few:

- *Free clerks from the register.* Imagine no longer confining cashiers to simply ring you up. If they instead can be free to help provide better service and allow you to checkout wherever you are in the store, it benefits everyone.
- *A higher order of tailored servicing.* Armed with a small tablet, retailers may have permissioned access to your size, your preferences, and wish lists. Knowing who you are and what you like can allow them to provide you with suggestions tailored to your unique preferences.
- *Product discovery and better researching.* Pointing your phone at the barcode of a retailer's product could provide you with all the information you've ever wanted to know—reviews, reliability, pricing, and how it might work for someone with your preferences.
- *Highly customized loyalty programs.* Knowing your preferred way of getting rewarded—cash back, loyalty points, special offers—can allow a retailer to service every one of its customers better. Loyalty is moving in a direction that tries to recognize every consumer uniquely based on their shopping patterns and individual preferences.
- *Better verification and authentication.* Imagine never having to take out your driver's license again and being identified by name. New services by PayPal and Square enable your face to show up on a merchant's device when you walk through the door (if user permissioned).
- *Frictionless checkout.* The days of waiting in line at the register, opening your wallet, and "checking out" will someday be a thing of the past, as new technologies instantly check you in.

RETAIL 2.0 AND ITS EFFECT ON PAYMENTS

As we have been discussing, there are quite a few technology companies that have leveraged location-based services and the power of their two-sided networks of businesses and consumers to spur commerce. The consumer value proposition has often been as simple as offering a one-click experience in exchange for consumers' keeping their credit card or other payment instruments on file. Uber, Yelp, and Open Table have all demonstrated that consumers are happy to keep their cards on file with multiple companies as long as they are providing a significant convenience. We've also seen the potential for Apple to enter the commerce space in a much larger way should it choose, with the hundreds of millions iTunes account holders (and payment cards) it already has on file. We've also discussed some of the larger technology companies' shift to a "mobile first" strategy that keeps them front and center with consumers when entering a physical retail store. The consumer experience had been thought of more narrowly, in the form of incremental improvements—a tap instead of a swipe, a click instead of entering a personal identification number (PIN), and so on. The larger issue is that payments haven't been thought about in a larger context of making the customer smarter. Connectivity technologies like near field communications (NFC) aren't valuable to the consumer or merchant if they only facilitate payments with a tap versus a swipe. The value has to come in very specialized offers, discounts, and promotions that take advantage of the individual preferences and attributes of customers. We are now seeing a few digital wallet providers that can do more than just make an easy checkout experience possible; they are literally making a consumer's wallet smarter. Next, we'll discuss some of the major providers of the digital wallet and what they are doing to help reshape the payments and commerce landscape.

The payments industry in particular has struggled in the past with connectivity technologies and how they might make the payment and shopping experience better for consumers. What has traditionally held the industry back has started with the relationship between mobile carriers and banks. Until recently, it was thought that point-of-sale (POS) systems would have to be replaced with those that have NFC connectivity, and all handsets would require secure chips to house consumer payment information.

That has given way to the realization that financial information can be secured in the cloud, or within software that does not reside on a secure element within the phone. That has given technology providers an opportunity to come in and offer platforms that can enable transactions without resorting to a massive overhaul of POS equipment.

The new experiences emerging in the retail world increasingly allow customers to bypass POS terminals, and instead utilize their phones to both discover relevant deals and pay. Often, these offers and payments platforms are run by technology companies that already have a customer's payment instruments on file. While banks have historically owned the point-of-sale terminals, the processing, or the way consumers have traditionally swiped cards at point-of-sale terminals, the next generation of customer experiences will be offered through smartphone applications. Consumers increasingly keep their cards on file with their favorite services, for example, Square, PayPal, Yelp, and Foursquare, and expect to be shown valuable offers through the mobile applications associated with these providers. Where does that leave card issuers and banks? And in this new world in which the traditional payment experiences have been subsumed by nonfinancial companies, how can card issuers and banks thrive? Banks become part of another company's experience, one that helps customers' reviews, real-time offers, and social media networks that may include reviews and recommendations from influential friends and family members. The ability to provide real-time information context has become incredibly powerful. These companies all leverage geolocation to surface things relevant to the consumer based on where they are. Companies include Google Places, Facebook Nearby, Foursquare, and Yelp. Delivering this information to help consumers make real-time decisions is very powerful and can become an important engagement tool for banks.

POS systems used to be systems where proprietary messages and communications took place, but with the growth of the Internet and Web services, there is no longer a need to have a monolithic device on every retail counter and behind every checkout experience. The world is moving toward devices that can process information through the Internet, and given the ease with which new companies can develop specialized applications for iPads and Android tablets, it's no wonder we're seeing a proliferation of next-generation cash registers that are leveraging tablets. While we saw the first major POS innovation in the form of plug-in dongles that could be attached to an iPhone or iPad, the next generation of POS systems will be portable devices that communicate directly with mobile phones and enable checkout from wherever someone is in the store. These register replacements can simply be paired to cash drawers and receipt printers through Bluetooth technology to allow retailers to move with their customers (see Figure 3.1).

Walk into any café to witness just how fast these hardware changes are occurring. In a span of 24 months, tablets and dongles have both dramatically influenced the commerce landscape for certain types of retailers. These changes are driving other enhancements at the point of sale, including sensors to track individual items of inventory and handheld bar scanners, all to better meet customer expectations.

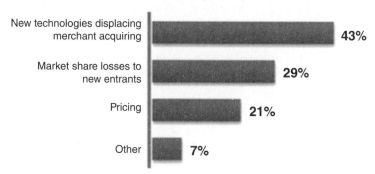

POS incumbents fear displacement

"What do you view as the biggest risk posed by new entrants to the merchant acquiring industry?"*

- New technologies displacing merchant acquiring — **43%**
- Market share losses to new entrants — **29%**
- Pricing — **21%**
- Other — **7%**

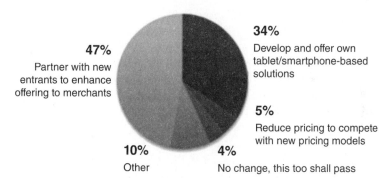

Incumbents show preference to partner with innovators to remain competitive

"What is your strategy to adapt to the new competitive environment?"*

47%
Partner with new entrants to enhance offering to merchants

34%
Develop and offer own tablet/smartphone-based solutions

5%
Reduce pricing to compete with new pricing models

10%
Other

4%
No change, this too shall pass

*Question posed to merchant acquirers, ISOs, and POS providers, N = 80

FIGURE 3.1 The Changing POS Landscape
Source: Goldman Sachs, ETA-GS Survey on New Entrants in Payments the incumbent perspective, January, 2013.

ENTREPRENEURS, DEVELOPERS, AND FINANCIAL SERVICES

Since tablets have become an important part of the of the POS landscape, it has given access and power to developers to build new software capabilities in the form of apps that can better help retailers attract consumers; plug in more deeply into a retailer's supply chain to help them manage inventory, offers, and sales; and use this information to better target consumers. Developers will play a very important role in connecting POS hardware and accounting systems together, and will be an important potential partner for financial services firms that are looking for ways to better help small businesses sell and provide accounting services. Look increasingly for disruptive start-ups that understand the value of creating and building on top of new operating systems specialized for retailers. In this new world, retailers can leverage complex, highly verticalized applications for their inventory, campaign management, or just about any service you can think of, just as a new specialized app can be downloaded for an individual.

CONTEXT BANKING: THE NEXT STEP

Sean Gilchrist is a longtime banker and the current managing director of digital at Lloyds Bank in the United Kingdom. I sat down with Sean to get a glimpse of how he is seeing some of these future technologies evolve and how he might think about how a financial institution can evolve with the times.

Question: Sean, what future areas are you seeing as opportunities for banks that leverage location-based services and future devices?

Gilchrist: The two big areas that I'm watching keenly, and have been the last two or three years, are what's going in with the technology developments in the auto business; they're doing some really interesting stuff. The other is the connected home, and all the electronics in the home are starting to connect up. Why am I interested from a bank point of view? If consumers are operating in a more connected-up way—if I'm a car driving along and I want to do my mobile banking, and I want to use my voice, I'll need to have an application to allow a customer to do that. Similarly, home automation is something that will be an opportunity. Voice and gesture will become a more important input device than the keyboard and mouse. We need to start thinking about how we build our banking experiences so you can operate through gestures and voice, and how we can take touch-screen and tablet banking and bring it into an even larger screen world.

The challenge as it relates to automobiles—if you think about driving a car, we think about where could that whole environment could go as the car becomes a connected device. One of the big providers of auto insurance is banks. Imagine when you get in a car, it's Sean who is driving and Sean is insured to drive this car. And if Sean has an accident, how can we use technology to facilitate the claims process instantly? We are starting to think about a much more integrated customer experience. If someone has a bad moment, a bank can work things out, and that's what a good insurance company can give you. We are looking at how we can join this up into our own processes to make this a reality.

LOW-ENERGY BLUETOOTH, HARDWARE, AND THE FUTURE OF COMMERCE

Recently, Apple rolled out new technology that has been receiving a lot of attention: low-energy Bluetooth. The attention it has been receiving is for good reason. Many of the communications technologies that have been discussed in the past have some large blocker, whether it be significant investment in new terminals, new adoption of handsets, or a requirement of a variety of actors from multiple industries to come together. Given Apple's significant power in the industry, its backing of a standard is all that is needed to pave the way toward ubiquity. As such, the latest release of its iBeacon could be transformative to the way mobile commerce could be done in the future. Beacons are small wireless sensors placed inside any physical space that transmits data to your iPhone using Bluetooth low energy (BLE; also known as Bluetooth 4.0 and Bluetooth Smart). iBeacon can run for up to two years on a single coin battery, and it comes with accelerometer, flash memory, a powerful ARM processor, and Bluetooth connectivity. More sensors can be added to iBeacon as needed.

Traditional location-based technologies, global positioning systems (GPS), or cell phone tower triangulation may get you close enough to your destination, but can never help you navigate within a store's aisles and look at specific shelves. This new level of location granularity, termed *hyperlocation* or *microlocation,* can have far-reaching effects for retailers.

We're already starting to see how we can go beyond just receiving offers for "checking in" at a particular location using Foursquare or another service. The iBeacon's low-energy Bluetooth technology works over shorter ranges than the traditional Bluetooth and has a much lower energy requirement on devices, which allows it to run continuously in the background on the equivalent of a small wristwatch battery. Using your smartphone in a store or branch environment could create a number of new opportunities for consumers, banks, and businesses. As you walk into a store or branch, you could get information on the latest offers or get a specialized coupon based on what you might have shared previously with the business.[4] You could certainly be greeted and treated in a much more personal manner. If you've been banking with an institution for the past 20 years, wouldn't it be nice to be given a much more personalized experience and be treated differently? New communications technologies like BLE can make this a reality. In terms of how future payment possibilities might work, imagine never having to take your phone out of your pocket. You have already been authenticated based on unlocking your mobile phone and confirmation that you're at a particular store. At that point, if your payment is already on file with a technology provider or merchant, you might not need to take out a card and swipe or even bump your phone against a sensor—BLE may already have already taken care of it.

iBEACON AND EASYPAY: THE FUTURE OF IN-STORE PAYMENTS?

If you have used Apple's EasyPay service within an Apple store, you just may have glimpsed the future of in-store payments. Over 500 million people have a credit card on file with iTunes, and as a result, Apple has the potential to create the most popular mobile shopping experience in the world, starting with its own stores. Once in an Apple store, the application will recognize your location and pop up a special menu for in-store use, including the EasyPay service (see Figure 3.2). This allows users to simply scan a barcode item and instantly pay for it using your mobile phone. The payment is then facilitated with the card you already have on file with iTunes after entering your iTunes account password. The purchase is then completed and you are issued a digital receipt. While there are still some frictions in this experience (opening the app and entering your iTunes password), this will very quickly fade away with iBeacon. Instant authentication technologies, such as the fingerprint scanner on the iPhone 5s, will no longer require you to enter information. This gives rise to a completely new in-store experience that does not require interacting with a store clerk or payment register. Not only does the user's phone know it is physically present in a retail location, the phone has been properly identified through the fingerprint and uses tokenized data in a secure way to ensure that the owner of the payment card is positively identified and connected with the device in their hand. Compare this process to the current approach of using signatures that are rarely checked, and it's clear that there are significant opportunities to not just create a more frictionless, user-friendly experience, but also to improve on the level of security and authentication in the process.

What is the missing piece that must happen to make this experience travel far beyond Apple stores to any retailer? If Apple simply links the

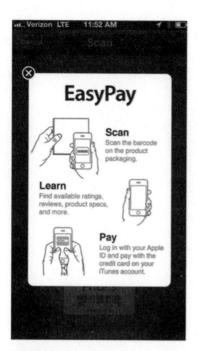

FIGURE 3.2   EasyPay
Source: Author's iPhone screen.

payment information it has on file to retailers that utilize iPads as POS terminals, which run on the latest Apple operating system, its merchants will have the ability to get paid. Consumers who gradually adopt the latest iPhone handsets with fingerprint authentication technology will be primary candidates to make frictionless "thumbprint" payments in the future. Outfitting a retailer with iBeacons could very well be incredibly cost effective as well; rather than embedding store inventory with RFID sensors, it could simply enable users to scan QR codes and show the security guard their digital receipt on the way out. It is also much larger range than NFC technologies, and given that most phones have Bluetooth and very few have NFC, it looks like Bluetooth could very well become a prevailing standard for retailers and banks alike. It also appears to be lower cost; a recent article looked at the cost of outfitting a Macy's department store with iBeacons and concluded that while iBeacons would cost the store $5,000, outfitting a store with NFC tags could cost up to $100,000.[5]

As financial institutions look at new ways of creating value from their physical locations—branches and automated teller machines (ATMs)—iBeacon could be a very powerful way to reconnect with customers and establish relationships. It also becomes increasingly apparent that no financial institution will have the opportunity to catch up with PayPal, Amazon, Google, or Apple when it comes to having payment accounts on file. It therefore becomes that much more important to continually find easy ways to connect a financial institution's capabilities to companies like Apple and its iTunes accounts, companies that have mass scale and reach and the ability to transform the way commerce and payments are done.

Apple's Passbook is another service that increasingly allows consumers to interact with their loyalty and payment cards, all from an application that acts as a keychain for stored credentials in the cloud. Passbook is a digital organizer that stores boarding passes, coupons, loyalty cards, and payment applications. Given that iPads are replacing cash registers at an increasingly high rate, it will be interesting to see how far they may go to facilitate commerce and payments directly, versus serving as a hardware and communications platform.

PAYPAL'S iBEACON: PROXIMITY AND CONTEXT

Apple isn't the only company that has come out with an iBeacon device leveraging the latest BLE standard. PayPal is betting that consumers will increasingly expect and desire instant, personalized experiences from their retailer. PayPal's iBeacon is a hardware device that plugs into any power source and acts like an in-store GPS system, leveraging BLE. Consumers who have opted in to be automatically checked in at stores of their choosing will provide information to PayPal merchants on who they are. If the PayPal application is running in the background, the mobile phone will vibrate as the consumer walks into the store, or they will hear a distinct sound. The merchant can then serve any number of offers the customer can take advantage of. Some of the interesting use cases PayPal has cited include refilling prescriptions automatically and having them paid for and ready for pickup at the pharmacy. Other use cases include offers that are targeted to the aisle the consumer happens to be in, for example, 15 percent off shaving cream in aisle 1, 25 percent off suntan lotion in aisle 2, and so on. The payment experience can simply be a hands-free checkout as the merchant identifies the consumer's picture that has appeared on the POS device. PayPal's integration into many existing and next-generation POS systems, such as Leaf, ShopKeep, and Micros, gives it a shot at becoming a more ubiquitous capability in the future. Its intent is to offer these capabilities as a platform to lure developers to build applications that could offer more valuable capabilities for PayPal's millions of merchants.

GOOGLE GLASS FOR FINANCES

If you're wondering what might come next after the mobile smartphone, Google Glass provides a good glimpse, and it might just provide some insight as to how financial institutions might leverage new technology and partnerships to offer compelling experiences to their customers (see Figure 3.3). Google's device runs on the Android operating system, and the device is shaped as a form of glasses. It has a small image that projects over the upper right lens, a five-megapixel forward-facing video/photo camera, rear-facing eyeball tracking sensors, 16 GHz of storage (similar to a normal smartphone), a horizontal touchpad running along the side of the right-hand frame, a cloud-based voice option, and approximately three to five hours of battery life. It is also Wi-Fi and Bluetooth enabled. What can you do when offering a device with a combination of voice commands, touch-based commands, and gestures like blinking and head tilting? It can provide a form of augmented reality. Imagine looking at a new car or house for sale and instantly getting the financing information on it or seeing how it will impact your overall budget and cash flow for the month. With Google Glass devices released to development partners and application programming interface (API) documentation, there will be many third-party developers that will reimagine what might be possible for consumers of financial services.

Intuit has been experimenting with Google Glass as a form factor for payments. The user would open up a payments application on Google Glass with the touchpad and then stare at a barcode on a tablet POS device. The user would then confirm the payment with a touch, and walk out of the store. Such use cases are very possible, but will still require work to become as simple and user friendly as a user's pulling out a credit card from his or her wallet.

FIGURE 3.3 Using Google Glass in a payments context

Google Glass can certainly make authenticating into your bank account a much easier process than entering a user ID and password. Voice authentication might allow you to instantly see your balance, transfer money, or make a payment. Fidelity Labs, a unit of Fidelity Investments, recently announced that it has an application that allows users to monitor stock quotes while wearing Google Glass.[6] Many other financial institutions are reviewing the possibilities of what the future of financial services could be like if consumers had a wearable portable computer continuously accessible. Certainly, just as we've seen a large leap in new use cases moving from the desktop computer to the mobile phone, this new form factor will surely offer new, convenient financial services of the future.

IN SEARCH OF THE DIGITAL WALLET

If you open your wallet now, chances are you'll find more than bank cards and cash notes, including receipts, loyalty cards, and coupons that far outnumber payment instruments. Therein lies much of the problem; digital wallets to date have largely been about paying differently, rather than creating a more valuable interaction and relationship with a customer. Mark Tack, VP of marketing at Vibes, explained:

> *One-in-three shoppers are using the non-payment side of the mobile wallet, and 85 percent of consumers would receive some benefit from the non-payment side of the mobile wallet. Yet, only 19 percent of smartphone users have noticed any retailers offering mobile wallet–specific coupons and/or loyalty cards.*[7]

What really is a digital wallet? Ideally, it must be something that makes using a leather wallet feel inferior in value. The broadest definition in the way I describe it refers to a service that helps consumers better manage their saving and spending habits and is accessible through the Internet. *Digital* refers to more than just viewing and using your plastic cards on a screen. It is the art of making everything in your wallet available in the cloud and accessible whenever and wherever you are, regardless of the device. It is really about accessing what you need through the Internet, whether that device happens to be a phone, wearable clothing, an Internet watch, or any other Internet-accessible device. *Wallet* refers to anything and everything that is in your wallet, or you *wish* were in your wallet—the right loyalty card at just the right time, the coupon you forgot to cut out of the circular, and so on. Often, people think a mobile phone is necessary to have a digital wallet, but think about how PayPal started. As long as you have access to the Internet, you can press a checkout button, log in with PayPal, and check out, all without having your wallet nearby. The digital wallet therefore is really a collision of the Internet, financial services, loyalty, and commerce. It enables payments at the point of sale, and should ideally surface just the right offer at the right time, redeemable when we decide to pay. It also enables payments online, at a kiosk or through any number of new devices that we'll see in the future. Getting the payment process right is now simply considered the price of entry.

The digital wallet that most people think of refers to everything someone can empty out of your back pocket and digitize—cards, loyalty programs, pictures, IDs, everything. The trick is to now make all of these items available for you when you need them, regardless of where you are, what you're doing, or the device that you have with you. It's taking that actual wallet in your back pocket, with all of its contents and associated behaviors, and integrating it into some type of digital device. Most often, that device is a mobile phone, though it doesn't necessarily need to be; it's simply a way to manage a user's increasingly digital financial and commerce life.

Today, digital wallets are starting to look a little less like one aggregate repository of all things useful and more about apps—individual services that provide a superior user experience for a very specific use case: Uber for taxis, AirBnB for rentals, and Fandango for movies. Others like LifeLock are allowing users to store all their information, but haven't yet introduced payments. Others like PayPal started with payments and are looking to move into other areas such as order on demand, offers, coupons, and loyalty. At this time, no digital wallets are truly life changing; they just aren't yet intuitive or ingenious enough. Just as we've evolved with the notion that an online experience and a mobile experience need to be very different and take advantage of time, place, location, and context, the mobile wallet will really have the "wow" effect when it can simply maximize our savings and truly help people better understand and better manage their day-to-day spending habits. Technology development for its own sake is never very compelling. It's when technology and business models focus on making a consumer experience significantly better that we see consumers begin to shift their behavior and subsequent industry transformations take place. The trick is to find digital wallet experiences that are compelling and explore partnering opportunities with the companies behind them. Following are some of the items that I believe will create a compelling experience for digital wallets and will ultimately make them far superior to the bulky leather item we have tucked away today.

Personal Financial Management

Imagine an instant alert as you go into an electronics store that tells you your electronics budget has $25 left for the month. That's a lot smarter than knowing your bank balance or having a "to-buy" list scribbled on a piece of paper in your wallet. Personal financial management companies like Yodlee and MoneyDesktop are helping people make decisions that can help them manage impulse buys.

Coupons

According to a recent study by First Data, consumers today demand a tailored experience that uses the information businesses have about them to their benefit. Globally, nearly half of consumers want businesses to get better at targeting ads and offers to them. Fifty-eight percent expect their bank to do a better job of considering their individual circumstances.[8] Wouldn't it be great to be able to take advantage of a coupon that you never would have seen had it not been delivered at just the right time and in the right context? As you walk by a café, knowing your next latte is free if you come inside now could strongly influence your decision. Companies like Groupon and ScoutMob are offering up digital coupons, accessible from any device. Other companies (e.g., Shopkick) offer you incentives if you "check in" at a particular store. Card-linked offers are becoming much more popular and user friendly—this refers to the linking of an offer to a credit card that will automatically rebate the reward in the form of cash back on the card. Companies such as Coupons.com, Cartera Commerce, Cardlytics, Womply, edo Interactive, and many others are tackling this area. Coupons.com recently rolled out its version of the service, which does not require participating merchants to change their point-of-sale systems—consumers simply link an offer to an existing credit card, swipe the card at the merchant and receive the benefit within a few days.

Shopping Tools

Comparison-shopping tools that engage consumers while they are in a retailer can help consumers and retailers alike. eBay's Red Laser allows bar code scans that give additional information on the product, such as reviews and pricing. Specialized versions can be leveraged for retailers that focus on the in-store experience versus pure shopping comparisons. Integration into a digital wallet allows consumers to scan UPC or 2D barcodes in a store to also get related content or additional inventory.

Loyalty and Prepaid

Do you know the balances available on the gift cards or prepaid cards in your wallet? Chances are that you may not, especially if you've already used some of those balances. Digitizing those cards and allowing a customer to view the actual balances on those cards can make them much more valuable. Like many people who patronize Starbucks, I cannot remember the last time I pulled out my wallet to pay there. I pay with the barcode housed within my passbook application, so I can be sure they will track me and provide me with a free drink on occasion.

Tickets and Passes

It used to be that using the phone with passes was difficult—the screen resolution and the lighting weren't always conducive to creating that frictionless experience that beat taking out your paper ticket to be scanned. However, that has changed, and one look at the airline check-in counter speaks volumes as you notice the number of people passing through simply holding their mobile phones to be scanned. The United States in general has been slower to adopt these methods given the traditional business challenges associated with two very strong, consolidated industries with entrenched agendas: mobile carriers and banks. However, the rise of two dominant mobile operating systems that provide relatively open platforms for passes has changed the adoption trajectory. Convenience wins the day with these items; applications that save people time and provide efficiency will continue to see strong adoption. According to Charaka Kithulegoda, CIO of ING Direct Canada:

> *Digital wallets will transform the payments ecosystem. Mobile ordering will have broad applications and relevance, but it is just one example of how nimble digital wallet competitors will leverage the latest mobile technology and the contextual relevance that mobile enables to compete on the basis of incremental value—just as mobile proximity payments adoption begins to accelerate. In 2014, we will see the rise of services like mobile ordering embedded in mobile digital wallet experiences. These services will remove friction from the commerce experience—for example, when lines and/ or time spent waiting for service are involved—and create value for consumers and a competitive advantage for merchants.*

As consumers are able to take advantage of money-saving opportunities and insights that help them with their everyday spending and saving, digital wallets will become increasingly valuable. As they do, it begs the question: should banks really create their own digital wallets or partner with those that do? As mentioned in earlier chapters, although there are opportunities to build wallet-like capabilities, they pale in comparison to the many technology companies that are creating highly compelling consumer experiences. Active partnering is the most important thing any financial institution could be doing right now, given the proliferation of wallet providers that offer largely complementary business models. Next, we'll discuss some of the major digital wallet players today and how the financial services industry might think of them.

THE WHO'S WHO OF DIGITAL WALLETS

Financial institutions, carriers, and retailers are all looking to own a piece of the digital wallet pie, and all three are critical in making the digital wallet a useful, seamless, everyday part of life for the consumer. In the case of financial institutions, payment instruments are simply not enough of a value to keep with a digital wallet. Rich data that can allow a retailer to identify a consumer simply by having a consumer's name and face show up on a screen, or the ability to instantly provide targeted offers that can be redeemed with the payment were never contemplated as part of a payment network (see Figure 3.4). As such, it has never been more important than it is today for banks to look at partnering with those companies that are providing a strong consumer value proposition that goes significantly beyond just facilitating a payment in a new way. While some credit card companies

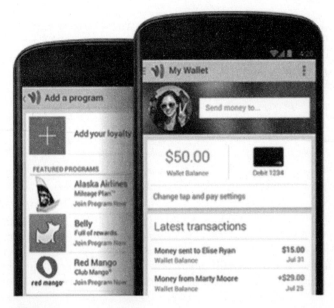

FIGURE 3.4   Digital Wallets
Source: Google.

and networks (American Express, MasterCard, and Visa) are creating their own digital wallets, there simply isn't a compelling enough consumer value proposition beyond facilitating payment. The companies that are beginning to provide a distinct and valuable consumer and merchant proposition are discussed below, including what each brings to the table, what's still required, and how banks might consider partnering with them.

Google

Google has had its trials and tribulations when it has come to its wallet. Originally, it had tied its technology to NFC, a standard that ultimately put it on a collision course with the major mobile carriers, which blocked its ability to actually offer contactless payments. In addition, very few customers had mobile phones with NFC technology in them, and most retailers haven't been looking to swap out their POS terminals for the specific reason of enabling cards (or mobile phones) to be tapped on a terminal versus swiped. However, in the past year, Google Wallet has made some very powerful breakthroughs that just might encourage retailers and consumers alike to consider it as a platform for commerce. Google Wallet has two types of usage modes: it's "Tap and Pay" capability, and "Google SingleTap™." The Tap and Pay capability now can emulate a passive contactless payment card, and as discussed in Chapter 1, through host card emulation, Google no longer needs payment information to reside on a secure chip in the phone, historically controlled by carriers. As a result, the Tap and Pay capability may become increasingly common, although it does not offer any special benefits other than to imitate the experience of tapping a contactless card on a terminal. The real interest is in Google SingleTap, where loyalty, special offers, and card information can be combined for consumer and merchant. The Google Wallet card, a MasterCard-branded payment instrument, has recently been released that will allow consumers using Google to spend the money instantly by using in stores wherever MasterCard is accepted or by withdrawing cash at ATMs. The card serves as an effective bridge between the wallet and a consumer's bank account, since any money received in the Google Wallet account can be accessed instantly with the card, instead of the time it would normally take to transfer the funds to a bank account. Part of the value Google Wallet and other digital wallets provide when at physical locations is the offering of instant notifications when you spend money (see Figure 3.5). These instant notifications can serve as an effective alerting mechanism to help you keep tabs on all of your transactions. One novel thing it does is allow users to instantly join new loyalty programs such as Avis, California Pizza Kitchen, and Walgreens, directly from the application. Users can also easily scan a new loyalty card into the wallet simply by taking

FIGURE 3.5   Google Wallet
Source: Google.

a picture of the bar code. For certain merchants, you can view your loyalty status and rewards point balance, and Google Now will notify you when you have a saved loyalty program nearby. Offers are another notable part of the Google Wallet experience. Google Wallet customers can obtain offers from a variety of Google properties in the Google Maps app, Google Search, Google+, or Google Offers, and they will be visible and redeemable in the Google Wallet app at checkout.

Part of the promise of the digital wallet will be how payments, offers, and coupons come together in a seamless way across multiple commerce channels. Google Wallet still has a largely separate payment proposition when it comes to payments and offers at the physical point of sale, but this will surely change in the months and years ahead and should drive continued adoption. As more consumers gravitate to Google Wallet, it will become an important partner to consider, one that could influence the financial instruments your customers use. As we discussed in Chapter 1, Discover enables its customers to load their cards directly into Google Wallet. Introducing Google Wallet directly from an online or mobile banking platform and enabling a payment card to be added could do much to help a bank retain mindshare with its customers as they use Google.

LifeLock (formerly Lemon Wallet)

LifeLock has some unique and compelling capabilities that are likely to make it increasingly valuable to customers. Adding a credit card to LifeLock is as easy as taking a photo of the card with your mobile phone (front and back). Its partnership with a company called BillGuard allows it to cull through all of a consumer's credit card transactions and help determine if they are suspicious or fraudulent. That is hugely valuable in the age of instant data and gives customers an additional level of comfort that the financial services industry has not yet provided. In addition, it is well integrated into Apple's Passbook and allows a consumer to instantly pull up any card they've added, whether it is their driver's license, loyalty card, or payment card. LifeLock has the lead in allowing consumers to digitize nearly everything in their wallet and present the digitized items in a clear and intuitive way. You can also scan, upload, or e-mail copies of receipts for archiving. Today, there aren't many places that are going to accept a copy of your card stored on your smartphone, but it can be very valuable if you need your health care plan number, driver's license number, or any of your card numbers—they are all stored in a handy location. Aside from the credit card transaction scanning service, some of the other premium services LifeLock provides include transaction sharing, exporting of data to CSV (Excel), Evernote, Dropbox, or Concur Timeline. How might banks think about partnering with LifeLock? If banks want to continue to be the center of a person's financial digital life, they might consider developing a cobranded "powered by LifeLock" capability in their mobile banking application. Banks have offered safety deposit boxes for hundreds of years; it's time to consider a virtual safety deposit box that can store valuable digitized information in the way LifeLock is offered. LifeLock's card-scanning technology is also quite impressive. Any bank that would like to make the experience of digitizing a wallet easy and convenient might consider partnering with LifeLock to add card-scanning technology to their mobile banking apps.

PayPal

PayPal can arguably be considered the original digital wallet. While a lot of media had focused on other providers of "mobile wallets" with NFC technology, PayPal's path has always been considered a cloud-based technology that allows consumers to access their PayPal account from any device as long as it's connected to the Internet. As mobile has become the most important way consumers access the Internet, PayPal has gravitated toward mobile experiences that allow consumers to interact directly with retailers of all types, both in-store and online. PayPal offers large merchants the ability to connect through the Discover network and leverage the same clearing and settlement capability it has today directly and through Discover's merchant acquirers. It offers a number of options in the market today, including "empty hands" functionality (typing in a mobile number and PIN at the

FIGURE 3.6 PayPal's Three-Pronged Approach to Point of Sale
Source: PayPal.

point of sale, or checking in with a mobile application in a store). While it is challenging to utilize legacy payment networks to create the rich future experience envisioned that combines payment facilitation, along with redemption of coupons and offers, those retailers that have gravitated directly to new POS systems with PayPal already integrated, or those that leverage PayPal's native application through their iPad or Android device can create some pretty compelling customer experiences (see Figure 3.6). PayPal's next-generation digital wallet is being designed to carry everything from traditional payment instruments to gift cards, loyalty cards, airline miles, offers, and coupons. How can banks consider partnering with PayPal? The company has shown receptivity to offering "Powered by PayPal" services to banks, allowing banks to incorporate PayPal services within mobile and online banking applications. There is a strong complementary opportunity for banks to partner with PayPal as the digital wallet becomes increasingly important. PayPal can help the banking industry by including a bank's payment card as a funding source in a newly created or existing PayPal account. In return, banks can help PayPal by helping with customer acquisition.

Carriers

In North America, carriers have historically been challenged in providing a digital wallet, since they tend to subsidize the cost of devices for consumers who are billed monthly for services. In most other countries, carriers do not subsidize the cost of handsets and therefore generally do not dictate what we see on their devices, they are largely top-up models. We have seen a North American conundrum in that we have AT&T, T-Mobile, Verizon, and Sprint, which all offer varying numbers of devices and operating systems. Currently, AT&T, Verizon, and T-Mobile are creating a joint venture called ISIS, a planned mobile payment network intended to create a standard solution for both retailers and consumers. This system will use smartphones with embedded NFC chips for contactless payments. Outside of payments, they're also working to introduce retailer-friendly value-added services.[9] As Russ Jones from Glenbrook Partners describes:

> *The basic Isis transaction emulates a passive contactless payment card. Contactless merchants, as with Google, don't have to do anything incremental to support the baseline ISIS transaction. If they can accept contactless cards, they're all set to be an ISIS merchant! But, as with Google Wallet, the real sizzle comes when the merchant integrates the POS environment with the ISIS Mobile Commerce Platform. This is the platform that provides access to (guess what?) coupons, offers, loyalty cards, tickets, and transit pass. Once again, two usage modes, one involves a sophisticated ("smart") transaction, the other involves a traditional payment-data-only ("basic") transaction.*

Unfortunately, ISIS appears to be the least likely to succeed among the various digital wallet providers for several reasons. First, banks balk at the idea of paying mobile carriers fees to have their cards digitized on the ISIS platform. Second, from a consumer value proposition standpoint, it's unclear what the consumer is able to do outside of make payments by tapping their mobile phone. The digital wallet hasn't yet proven to be smarter than a physical wallet, and the business model does not necessarily help retailers develop a stronger relationship with their customers that free them from traditional legacy POS devices. We will see how ISIS fares in the future, but this author is highly skeptical.

Retailers

Retailers certainly are not taking a passive approach to the digital wallet. Many are developing their own custom applications to help them better service their customers. Most see a digital wallet as an opportunity to better understand their customers and offer localized alerts that can be meaningful to their customers. Panda Express, a Chinese food chain has offered alerts on its Thai Chicken as a user is passing by. Historically, most of its customer did not take the time to swipe a separate loyalty card and a payment card to do a transaction. Now, with the mobile phone, the experience can be seamless and give the food chain a lot more information about its customers. Many, such as Walgreens, have taken steps to integrate with Apple's Passbook.

We have also seen some missteps from retailers as they attempt to create their own versions of a digital wallet, particularly when they are too focused on payment costs versus customer experience. The Safeway Fast Forward program is a good example. The value proposition is clear for the customer: pay using your Safeway Fast Forward card number and a self-assigned PIN for simpler checkout. However, to set up an account, the customer must provide a state-issued ID (driver's license) and Social Security number.[10] Most customers would not be willing to provide a retailer with the same information as their bank simply to pay another way.

In 2012, some large merchants came together in a coalition named Merchant Customer Exchange, or MCX. The organization is backed by some of the largest merchants in the United States, including Wal-Mart, Target, Best Buy, and 7-Eleven, which collectively process over $1 trillion in payments annually. The organization believes that by creating a retailer-led mobile commerce platform, they will ultimate be able to do three key things: better control the consumer experience at POS, better protect consumer data, and rebalance the payments ecosystem. As their CEO Dekkers Davidson has stated, "The value-to-cost ratio is out of whack."[11] The platform will initially be cloud based and rely on QR codes that can be scanned at the point of sale. Participating merchants will be able to add MCX capabilities to their own mobile apps via APIs and/or allow customers to purchase directly with an MCX app.

MCX ultimately has come together in reaction to two key things. First, retailers do not want to be locked into high interchange rates when they begin to move to the next generation of POS terminals. Second, merchants have been concerned about how digital wallet providers like ISIS and Google ultimately share their customer's data. Control of customer information remains a vital element for all participating retailers.

MCX has a few challenges ahead of it that might make it less likely to succeed. First, as a consortium of retailers that often compete to the death with each other, it is naturally a challenging environment for retailers to truly collaborate with respect to data and user experience. As my friend Kareem Al-Bassam at PayPal is fond of saying, "It's like having a Zebra, Lion, Monkey, and Wolf together in the same cage. Who knows how long that can truly last?" Second, it's objective of rebalancing the ecosystem is code for paying the financial services industry less interchange. Any organization that becomes too focused on cost reduction could prioritize cost over providing a highly compelling and frictionless customer experience.

While MCX has signaled that it would like to actively partner with the banking industry, I view the probability of true partnership with high skepticism, since MCX is largely formed to exercise business leverage over the banking industry.

Square Wallet

In Chapter 1, we discussed Square and the success it has in attracting small businesses with a very transparent, low-cost card processing proposition and easy registration process. As a result, more than 4 million merchants are now using its dongle to accept payments on tablets and mobile phones. It has processed so many Visa transactions that it is now considered a top 30 merchant. However, it has had less success attracting consumers thus far to its digital wallet. Consumers expect more than person-to-person payments in a digital wallet, they expect to shop at any retailer they choose. There are some terrific, user-friendly technologies included in the Square Wallet application, including a hands-free check-in experience and "face-pay." However, the most important ingredient, ubiquitous acceptance, isn't there yet. To date, Square Wallet is not generally accepted at larger retailers, but Square is starting to form processing relationships with larger companies. The value its wallet will bring to consumers will largely be a function of its ability to attract larger retailers to accept Square.

WHAT'S NEXT?

As the digital wallet becomes a reality, the services that stand the best chance of adoption are those that best integrate local, social, and mobile elements that make the digital wallet truly smarter than the physical wallet they carry around today. Similar to the digitization of the telephone, digital wallets started simply by using an easily adoptable "pay now" button. Value-added services will likely be critical in getting the user connected with benefits beyond simply swiping and paying. Helping customers simplify their digital lives by providing the offer, payment method, or insight at the right time in the right context will be the ultimate challenge and value. At the end of the day, the digital wallet must be something that slims down our workload, while becoming ever more convenient, intelligent, and relevant. Most providers of digital wallets are willing to partner with the banking industry and can benefit from banking partnerships. Those banks that opt to have a partner-friendly stance stand a better chance of staying top of mind with their customers and maintain relevance as retail commerce continues its metamorphosis.

NOTES

1. "Threads with Brains: How Sensor-Laden 'Smart Clothes' Are Trying to Change Lives," *Time,* November 11, 2013.
2. Glenn Collins, "OpenTable Bringing Restaurant Sites Mobile Booking," *New York Times,* http://dinersjournal.blogs.nytimes.com/2012/10/16/opentable-bringing-restaurant-sites-mobile-booking/?_r=0. Accessed February 4, 2014.
3. Accenture, "More US Shoppers Plan to Buy from Stores but Want the In-Store Shopping Experience to Match Convenience of Online, Accenture Study Finds," http://newsroom.accenture.com/news/more-us-shoppers-plan-to-buy-from-stores-but-want-the-in-store-shopping-experience-to-match-convenience-of-online-accenture-study-finds.htm. Accessed February 3, 2014.
4. Hari Gottipati, "With iBeacon, Apple Is Going to Dump on NFC and Embrace the Internet of Things," *GigaOM,* http://gigaom.com/2013/09/10/with-ibeacon-apple-is-going-to-dump-on-nfc-and-embrace-the-internet-of-things/. Accessed September 10, 2013.
5. Ibid.
6. Sean Sposito, "Fidelity Launches Google Glass App," *American Banker,* http://www.americanbanker.com/issues/178_155/fidelity-launches-google-glass-app-1061261-1.html. Accessed August 12, 2013.
7. Vibes, "Mobile Wallet Consumer Report," http://client.vibes.com/references/MobileWallet_ConsumerReport.pdf. Accessed February 6, 2014.
8. First Data, "First Data Global Study Reveals that Consumers Worldwide Seek the Same Technology Experience," http://www.firstdata.com/en_us/about-first-data/media/press-releases/06_19_13.html. Accessed June 19, 2013.
9. Christina White, "Thin Is In: The Future of Digital Wallets," SapientNitro, https://www.google.com/url?sa=t&rct=j&q=&esrc=s&source=web&cd=2&ved=0CDUQFjAB&url=http%3A%2F%2Fwww.sapient.com%2Fassets%2FImageDownloader%2F832%2F&ei=uiGZUoLYD9jioATKzIL4CQ&usg=AFQjCNEngVYbXidYrFaPtDp7pW0HV_Abbw&sig2=hAvQGYktJa6DMDERyF8mhA&bvm=bv.57155469,d.cGU. Accessed February 6, 2014.
10. Cherian Abraham, "MCX—Merchants Redux," Drop Labs, http://www.droplabs.co/?p=662.
11. CFBP payments panel, September 11, 2013.

CHAPTER 4

Innovating with Big Data and Open Platforms

Competing in a World of Unlimited Data and Storage

"Big data will spell the death of customer segmentation and force the marketer to understand each customer as an individual within 18 months or risk being left in the dust."

—Ginni Rometty, CEO, IBM

How does a financial institution compete in a world where data are instantly accessible to most and storage is virtually unlimited? More data and more archiving services won't necessarily help a financial institution serve its customers better unless the data can be leveraged in a unique way that brings insight to customers. Is your bank in the best position to come up with new and innovative uses of your data? If not, you might want to consider partnering with someone who can take new forms of data and make them valuable and insightful for your institution and for your customers. In this chapter, we'll talk about how financial institutions can get the most out of data and why data and an open platform often go hand in hand. We'll talk about some of the learnings PayPal had when opening its platform and how better use of data became one of the primary benefits as a result. Seventy-one percent of the industry is already using big data and analytics, up from 36 percent just two years ago, according to a survey by the University of Oxford and IBM's Institute of Business Value. In today's world, the probability of achieving the best data insights alone is very low, as so many financial technology companies develop core competencies in data procurement and analytics far better and faster than a financial institution. People are looking for signs that a financial institution really understands them and what they want. Consumers are also willing to share more personal information to get personalized services, according to a new customer survey conducted by Cisco. The Cisco Customer Experience Report found that 69 percent of U.S. customers would be willing to give their bank more personal information if it meant they could receive more personalized services, such as real-time financial advice and identity theft protection. Fifty-three percent of U.S. customers in the study indicated that they would be willing to provide their bank with a fingerprint for biometric authentication. The majority of U.S. customers in the survey (54 percent) did not think that their bank had enough information about them to deliver such personalized services. Cap Gemini recently released the results of a survey of 18,000 people and found that two-thirds of respondents identified with the statement, "My bank doesn't know me."

It's a very different world than the one we used to live in—the one in which it was hard imagine who knew more about a customer's financial situation than their bank. After all, the bank had all the customer data, spending and savings patterns, to itself. Customers today expect technology to do what branch managers may have done decades ago—look at their history, if they can afford things, and help them without overextending them. Using data, banks can better anticipate changing market conditions and customer preferences better than focus groups, and that will help them to deliver the kinds of personalized services that can create new markets and improve customer loyalty. However, even if financial institutions embrace data and partnerships as a way to make their offerings more valuable, the challenge still remains as to how easily they can integrate with providers to take advantage of their partner's offerings.

If you are an entrepreneur or developer looking at new ways to help your bank partners, data may very well be the first place you want to look. It could very well be the difference between helping a bank to stay relevant with its customers and going out of business. If you could help a bank make more loans than it otherwise would have, or if you can decrease the rate of declines by increasing a bank's underwriting prowess, it can be incredibly impactful. Wouldn't it be great to provide a customer with an instant line of credit knowing they are currently in a store ready to buy that new appliance? That's all possible with data. It's also possible to get more of the right financial products into the right hands through targeted direct marketing.

One very innovative company, Radius, has demonstrated how it has been able to help financial institutions establish much better sales conversion as a result of the specific types of data it is able to access. As demonstrated in the charts in Figures 4.1 and 4.2, Radius was able to help one major financial institution increase its sales by targeting businesses with a specific number of Yelp reviews and those who have various types of social

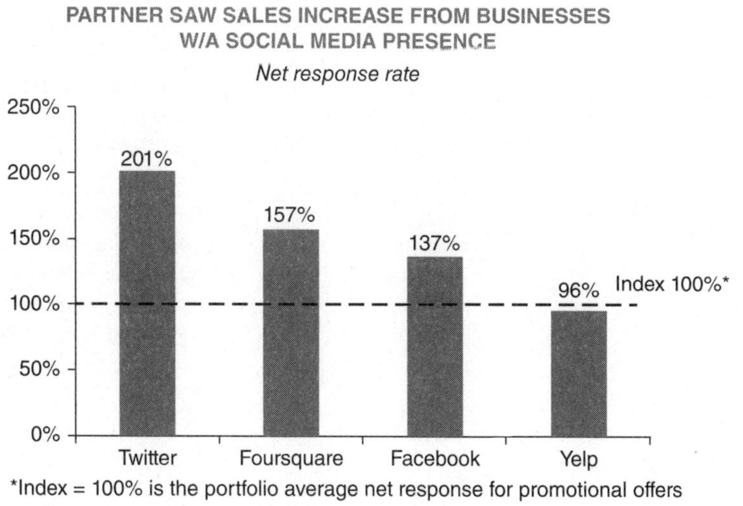
PARTNER SAW SALES INCREASE FROM BUSINESSES
W/A SOCIAL MEDIA PRESENCE
Net response rate
250%
200%
150%
100%
50%
0%
201%
157%
137%
96%
Index 100%*
Twitter
Foursquare
Facebook
Yelp
*Index = 100% is the portfolio average net response for promotional offers

FIGURE 4.1 Radius Helps Financial Institutions Get More Business by Focusing on Businesses with More Social Media Presence
Source: Radius.

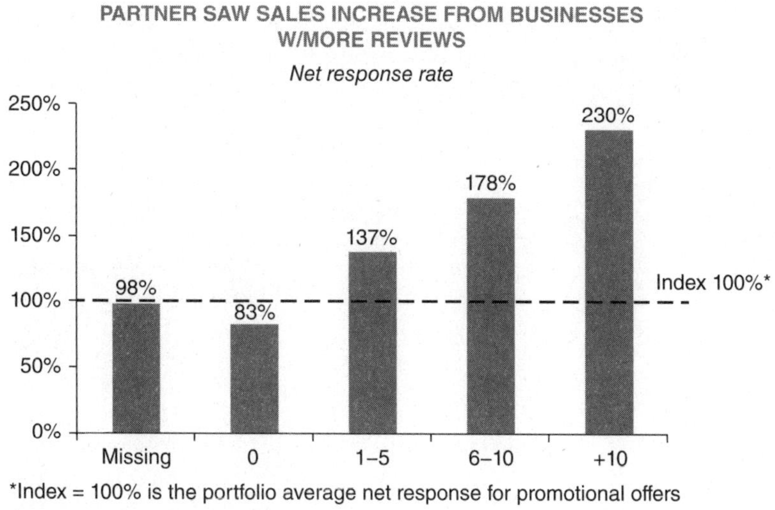
PARTNER SAW SALES INCREASE FROM BUSINESSES
W/MORE REVIEWS
Net response rate
250%
200%
150%
100%
50%
0%
98%
83%
137%
178%
230%
Index 100%*
Missing
0
1–5
6–10
+10
*Index = 100% is the portfolio average net response for promotional offers

FIGURE 4.2 Radius Helps Financial Institutions Achieve Higher Response Rates by Targeting Businesses with More Reviews
Source: Radius.

TABLE 4.1 Leveraging New Partners with New Data Elements and Insights Can Benefit Financial Institutions

	Historic Use of Data Led to Poor Results	New Solutions through Innovative Partners Can Be Impressive (e.g., Radius)
Direct Mail	Reliance on traditional providers and internal customer data. Stale data often result in low response rates and wasted marketing dollars.	Rely on partners who can normalize 30,000+ public and proprietary data sources. Significantly greater accuracy and net new records.
Industry Categorization	Reliance on Standard Industrial Classification (SIC), North American Industry Classification System (NAICS), and internal vertical categories for market segmentation, market research, and reporting. Information is too often determined upon the establishment of a business, and is not typically updated when a business pivots in its life span.	Utilizes new categories found on sources like Facebook, Google+, Yelp, Foursquare, and any other consumer-facing site that a business is listed on. Consumer-facing category trends that allow for more usability when crafting a pitch to an industry and specific business.
Underwriting and Risk Analysis	Banks rely on date business was established, business life span, DUNS number, Uniform Commercial Code, secured party data, revenue size, and head count. These data are limiting when evaluating the velocity of a business.	Offers predictive lifetime value for emerging businesses via Web and social assets, operational sophistication, digital foot traffic, online review ratings and popularity measures, and various other business activities. Alternative data sets can indicate a propensity for growth and are early indicators for Y/Y revenue increases.

	Historic Use of Data Led to Poor Results	New Solutions through Innovative Partners Can Be Impressive (e.g., Radius)
Account Management	Account data is housed and updated for businesses upon new inquiries and activity. Business information may change after last updates, wasting time and money on sales and marketing campaigns.	Allows for current account imports and bidirectional customer relationship management synchronization to ensure account data are as fresh as possible. New information is also appended to accounts to offer more insight to upsell conversations. Results in higher response rates in marketing and sales campaigns to current accounts. Overall increase in insight into the information, activity, and personality of a business.
Client Data and Analysis	Companies have traditionally relied on segment clusters from firm data and activity. Simplistic modeling regarding "who" the business is and "why" they have received a loan.	Identifies new attributes to current customer such as Web and social assets, advertising activity, and operational sophistication. Unique trends and attributes from current customers determine new criteria for more effective market segmentation and lead generation.

presence. Traditional data might not tell you that companies that have a strong Twitter presence are far more likely to sign up for a particular credit card product, but new companies like Radius can help financial institutions unearth data and make it highly insightful.

Table 4.1 illustrates even more how financial institutions can take advantage of new data to strengthen their business. Underwriting has received quite a bit of attention, since it is so directly impacted by data. New data can offer some predictive behaviors such as the potential lifetime value of an emerging business, when you take into consideration the various ratings it has received for its products and services and based on digital foot traffic. The same elements might be predictive of some consumer lending as well. The key takeaway here is that traditional firmographic information is not as good as data that are combined, appended, and segmented with publicly available online data, including social presence and activity, web site content, and media sources. As we move to an era where both customers and businesses expect one-to-one customization and marketing, it is incredibly important to use this type of data to target and build proxies for consumers' and businesses' persona and financial health and verifying if legacy data are accurate. Social data have become increasingly important when evaluating financial customers; they can identify businesses that have purchasing power and a propensity to buy. As an example of how these data can be very impactful, my friend Brett King, author of *Bank 2.0,* told me a story about doing some work with Deloitte in Poland, analyzing customer behavior. They found out that 45 percent of customers who applied for a credit card did so because of a change in employment due to a promotion or lost job. However, the loans were qualified based on current salary, so there was no way to differentiate which consumers were receiving a promotion and which were losing their jobs. In those situations, if you're trying to sell a credit card, some of the best information on data may very well be connected with a LinkedIn profile.

Companies that are able to offer a repository of many different normalized data sources for financial institutions to take advantage of can help keep banks current. For example, Dunn and Bradstreet (D&B) may be good for credit scoring or for navigating big company organization charts, but they infrequently update information and provide very limited data on small businesses. Yelp is great for retail businesses and reviews, but bad for medium-sized businesses and businesses located outside major metropolitan areas. Facebook and Foursquare are good for addresses and for relevant talking point from recent social activity, and Acxiom and Yellow Pages are good for business categorization, but all four are poor resources for identifying contact names and ownership. Only by utilizing a repository of many sources can banks uncover a holistic set of data on every small business and generate genuine insight that can influence and inform business strategy. To succeed long term, banks will need to arm themselves with technology that makes sense of the immense amount of available information, with the ultimate goal of engaging in more compelling sales conversations with more of the right prospects. What this means is that banks must differentiate themselves with data and insights that help them develop meaningful relationships with their prospects. Data provide an opportunity for banks to create much more of a digital dialogue with a customer and bring back some of the old-fashioned relationship banking. Data and behavior partnerships become very important. When you marry two sets of data to understand better than ever before, a bank can increase and maintain its relevance with customers. Solving this can ultimately provide data to consumers that give them insights into their own financial health and make it easier for people to have control over their money. That is a service in itself. For example, there are certainly there are many who would pay to have customized retirement plans and financial planning services offered digitally, if the data and insights offered were compelling enough.

THE RISE OF PLATFORM SERVICES

We've talked about the importance of connecting with new sources of data to form insights and the importance of partnering with data providers that have a competency in data and data analytics. Big data to many means a big need for integration to many systems. Banks today can't make the most of data without integrating together systems that can handle all of the disparate information coming in.

However, an equally important question is how banks can maximize the data and assets they already have. There are certainly many innovative entrepreneurs and companies that would love to leverage a bank's data to provide value, but often bank information technology (IT) executives will talk about the fact that much of the IT spend is invested in simply "running the bank," and there's a feeling that using the tools and technologies of the past is not going to make it in the future—innovations around making information real time, so that you can actually do something about liquidity risk management on the spot is just one example. Most recognize that the IT cost model in the banking industry is not sustainable. U.S. banks spend in the neighborhood of $300 billion to $400 billion on IT, which average 6 to 9 percent of revenue. The average for 24 different industries is closer to 2 to 4 percent. To underscore how big IT costs have become to banks, SAP is the largest enterprise software company on the planet, yet 10 to 20 banks have more software developers than SAP! For many larger banks, this has created a military industrial complex of banking and payments, in which pet projects and internal development continue even when they are to the bank's detriment. It's not a big surprise when one considers that Bank of America, Citibank, and Wells Fargo all have more developers than Microsoft and Oracle combined. It brings up an interesting question whether banks are actually IT companies in disguise. The prevalent product-centric cultures most banks have will eventually need to give way to customer-centric business models that require not new technology but new processes. Many are already moving in this direction. In fact, a recent IBM survey pointed out that customer analytics is what is driving most big data projects: 55 percent of their financial industry respondents surveyed pinpointed customer-centric projects as their top priority.[1]

These issues have given rise to platform services; the creation of standardized Web interfaces or application programming interfaces (APIs) that more seamlessly connect technology. With the ubiquity of the Internet and the advent of Web service technologies, it has become increasingly easier to connect platforms, technologies, and data. Increasingly, forward-looking financial institutions think of their future product road map as an API or interface to other applications rather than something that shows up on their online or mobile banking application. A loan might have more of a possibility of originating through Facebook, for example. If a financial institution makes it easier to connect financial services to companies that have already engaged their customers, there's a much higher likelihood that a financial institution can stay relevant and stay in business.

Platform services also help banks bring a myriad of best-in-class capabilities to their platform. We're seeing these trends happen in multiple industries. If banks turn a blind eye to platform services, they will continue to see many new sites that offer everything from personal financial management, such as Mint.com, to new savings applications such as SmartyPig.

In the retailing world, merchants are increasingly able to support multiple channels from a common infrastructure because everything is connected through the Internet, regardless of whether the merchant is utilizing a tablet, a mobile phone, or their inventory control system through a dedicated personal computer. More sophisticated software and logic will take advantage of real-time data, track item-level information, and offer dynamic pricing. As this happens, it becomes even easier to access customer relationship management (CRM) data across channels, provide predictive analytics, and take into account social trending data. Data and platform services thus become very connected, building upon each other and enabling institutions to offer more powerful customer capabilities.

APPLICATION PROGRAMMING INTERFACES (APIs) FOR ONLINE AND MOBILE COMMERCE

One of the history lessons we can learn from Silicon Valley companies is how many have managed to develop as platforms, by exposing their services directly to consumers through APIs (Facebook, Instagram, LinkedIn, Dropbox). All of these had both a direct-to-consumer experience and an API for developers. The API often brought more revenue and growth.

Recently, I had the pleasure to work with Deloitte's Center for Financial Services to evaluate some of the up-and-coming platform trends associated with payments and commerce. The group found that with the increasing proliferation of e-commerce, mobile commerce, and cloud-based wallets, banks could take quite a few lessons from commerce players who are already offering software developers sophisticated APIs to program payment acceptance and streamline customer experience. Robust open-platform APIs provide software developers with programmatic access to payment processors and card networks. These go far beyond traditional e-commerce gateway solutions.

Dwolla, an Iowa-based start-up, has engineered a closed-loop payment platform that links directly to consumer bank accounts instead of using credit card systems, which enables real-time automated clearinghouse (ACH) transfers and saves merchants interchange fees. Dwolla users can send, receive, and request funds from each other; share money through Facebook and Twitter; and buy goods and services through Web and mobile devices. There are no fees for transactions less than $10. For transactions over $10, Dwolla charges a flat $0.25 fee. Stripe, a venture capital (VC)-funded start-up, offers a simple, developer-friendly payment platform that lets entrepreneurs easily add payment services through a point-and-click interface and start taking payments in minutes. By bypassing the traditional sign-up process, Stripe acts as a merchant account for its providers, handling all payment card industry (PCI) compliance and merchant approvals. Stripe charges a standard 2.9 percent plus $0.30 per transaction with no setup or monthly fees. Look for innovative deals to take place with Stripe, such as Twitter, that could likely allow merchants to advertise and sell their goods through tweet advertisements, and have the payment processed through the likes of a Stripe.

Software developers are thus rapidly emerging as the new frontier of online and mobile commerce growth, and it is a harbinger of what we will surely see for most financial services as well. APIs targeted at the global developer community will unleash the next generation of innovative payment applications. Open APIs extend payment functionality integrated with multiple data sources and services and will continue to make their way into financial services.

COPING STRATEGIES FOR BANKS

Credit Agricole believes other banks will follow its lead or risk losing ground to outside parties that work entirely independently of banks. As they have said, "If we don't have enough applications to match the customers' needs, they're going to find them outside the bank."

Banks have a long, deep history in information and technology. By nature, banks are naturally in the digital and information business. There are two fundamental paradigm shifts that the financial services industry must accept to really stay relevant. First, the information they own on their customers is not the most important thing they own. Today, the digital world leverages an incredible amount of external information to understand behavior, as we have discussed. The second principle that is required is an embrace of the new ecosystem. Financial institutions have often thought about themselves in a vertically integrated way to protect their business by deliberately making it difficult for third parties to integrate to banks. Now, the way to innovate is to let third parties in—to build products and applications leveraging a bank's information. Innovation from within can never be enough; it must be done in a way that leverages talent, resources, and ideas externally, and to attract external talent to build and innovate on a bank's platform.

The classic bank might continue to own its accounts and customers end to end. These days, becoming a part of a larger ecosystem might mean that a transaction can originate with one bank and end with a nonbank. Authentication might start with Facebook and then end at a financial institution. There might be many third parties managing specific capabilities that go well beyond the "financial" part of any transaction. Certainly, to banks, a payment might seem to be the epicenter of a customer's purchasing experience. However, customers see the world very differently; they might engage in a broader shopping experience that involves digital coupons, ticketing, and loyalty that goes well beyond what a bank might be willing to provide. Yet in today's age, with the number of integration possibilities among providers of commerce and payment services, a bank may be a very small part of the overall experience. However, it is certainly better to be a small part of something big, than a small part of nothing at all, and that is the hard reality the banking industry must face. Consumers come to banks to do financial services transactions, yet most consumers really do not want to go to banks. I recall that the last time I stepped into my financial institution, it was only to get quarters to pay the parking meter. Customers want to conduct transactions from wherever they enjoy doing things, for example, in a shop or a stadium; banks need to go where their customers want to be. As such, it will continue to be incredibly important for financial institutions to look for ways to embed their transactions into a customer's life—not the other way around.

Beyond a mind-set shift, the challenge, of course, is that bank infrastructure is very large and very complex. Many banks have multiple platforms from merging, and once you layer on regulation and compliance, most will argue that any spare capacity that banks have leaves them with very little ability to innovate. The response to this, of course, is that the way through it is to develop an alternative model versus more of the same. If banks want to go faster and as nimble as newcomers, it requires a model predicated on partnerships. It also requires embracing a hard truth: which best-of-breed solutions do not exist internally. Banks need to get good at finding those best-of-breed solutions and become master jigsaw puzzle assemblers, creating an experience and developing a relationship that will entice customers with personalized services and capabilities that could never be done by one institution. Toyota is an interesting example; it owns the brand and the customer experience, but it certainly doesn't make or own anything—it assembles all the parts. Apple doesn't manufacture a single component, but they certainly own the design and user experience. Banks are at a point where several industries were several years ago; there's a standardized set of core processes and a traditional supply chain management working a certain way. Those ways will be disrupted in ways similar to publishing and music. Ultimately, the opportunity for banks will be to transform their models to outsource most elements of their business—from the back office to the middle office to the front office. Shared platform services can make this happen.

PAYPAL'S BOLD BET: UNLEASHING INNOVATION THROUGH AN OPEN PLATFORM

Scott Thompson served as president of PayPal from 2008 to 2012 and previously was PayPal's chief technology officer. While at PayPal, he helped scale the company through its most rapid growth years, from $1 billion in revenues to $4.4 billion in revenues, and established PayPal as the leading global online payment service. During this time period, Scott also unleashed the most significant wave of innovation in PayPal's 15-year history by opening up PayPal's platform. PayPal's open approach allowed it to appear on the Microsoft Xbox, smart TVs, gas station displays, and more. Digital goods in and of itself became a multibillion-dollar business simply from an API offering. Many established companies (Visa, MasterCard) followed suit with similar strategies. VC-funded start-ups (Dwolla, Stripe) also joined in on the heels of PayPal's announcements, offering their own fully integrated, highly customizable APIs that include software development kits, sample code, and virtual sandbox test environments, with diverse functionality and pricing models.

Scott currently serves as CEO of Shoprunner, a members-only service for online shoppers that provides some unique benefits across hundreds of online retailers. I sat down with Scott to glean some insight on what he learned from his PayPal experience and a few of the trends he sees happening over the next few years:

Question: Scott, you made a huge decision a few years ago to open PayPal's platform to the outside world. Why did you see the need to do this?

Thompson: The biggest problem that we had at the time was the number of opportunities that were available to us, given the core of what PayPal was for consumers and businesses. There were a number of areas where we wanted to innovate for our customers, and the reality was that there were never going to be enough people in PayPal to chase all the ideas that were out there.

The thinking at the time was: why not open this up like no other banking or payment system had done, and allow developers to innovate on top of the core PayPal wallet, account, and money movement capability.

It was not an insignificant bet on behalf of the organization. It had a lot of risk, and was a bit controversial when we did it. But, nonetheless, it was very clear that the failure would have been to limit innovation around the PayPal account to only those things we could do. Our customers needed a broad diversity of new initiatives and new capabilities that we just weren't going to be able to get to.

Question: Can you give some examples of what came out of this initiative—things you never had considered?

Thompson: There are probably dozens today. The one that I'm most familiar with and that I like a lot is with Kabbage, a small business lending company based in Atlanta. As an early adopter of the PayPal platform strategy, their core belief was that housed inside of the PayPal account was more data, and more insights into a small business's needs, than what you could otherwise get from conventional underwriting techniques, and if you could innovate on top of that data and those insights, you could actually make better underwriting decisions for lending than the banks could do, and you could make it continuously as you saw money move in and out of the PayPal account.

It turns out that it was a brilliant idea, and it was a fascinatingly good business to be building, but the best part of it all is, for the millions and millions of small businesses that use a PayPal account as their primary account—they can receive immediate access to working capital, without having to fill out forms, just because the data gives you the ability to understand the business dynamics that are currently under way. That is what the Kabbage guys were able to deliver. The usefulness of the account for those small businesses was exponentially more after the innovation took place.

All around the world—in Asia, where we attracted dozens and dozens of people to a meeting we had in Singapore; in Israel, where all kinds of people turned up that were developers— the number of great ideas that immediately surfaced was well beyond anything that I ever imagined. And by the way, if you're thinking about it from the PayPal perspective, it introduces a strategic competitiveness of that account by comparison to any other account that you might have in your life or business.

Question: Can you talk about some of the harder decisions/trade-offs you had to wrestle with moving in this direction?

Thompson: The biggest challenge was the historical mind-set around an account that has financial information in it. The PayPal account infrastructure was built and fortified and refortified. It is a very secure container of financial information, and a very secure method of moving money around, but it was hardened around the perimeter, so that nobody with criminal intent could get access to your account and move money, and it was years of building that fortification that secured that account.

Now, the minute you say you want to open the platform, what you could fundamentally be saying is you are putting everything at risk that you just spent years building, millions investing in, to allow a different audience access to the core financial information of a person or small business. Think about that conflict—that is no small thing. I think that is why no banks had ever done it before us. Because the mind-set is: "I can't, it's private" or "I can't, it's secure" or "I have to keep other people out of it at all costs."

We believed we could open our platform and maintain all of those necessary fundamentals of how you manage a financial account, and control it, and secure it and monitor it, all of those things even in an open environment. I think now after a few years, it has proven absolutely true—at its heart, you can open up some of the most sensitive and secure financial information in an open-platform world and still have ultimate control and security and privacy of that account for the individuals involved. It's a very tough problem to solve.

Question: What sort of advice would you give people who may be contemplating opening their platform?

Thompson: I think there are a lot of people talking like they want to—and in part, imitating selectively what we did and launched. It's not clear to me at the level we opened the platform that others are able to achieve that openness, at least in the near term. I think a lot are likely to come up short. Some may not have the technical depth, or they may have legacy issues with their applications and infrastructure that keep them from going all the way there, but certainly the business world wants to do more and more of this.

There were a lot of folks whose voice around this was, "We have to control the individuals who want to innovate on top of us—we have to know what they're doing, we have to approve it." The original thinking was that we were going to hire this enormous team of people to vet this stuff—not unlike what Apple does to vet its apps on its app store. But it wasn't going to be possible, not even imaginable, to build such a large team of people.

So my advice—you still have to have control, you certainly have to have discipline, you certainly can't open up a platform that has the sensitive data and information we're talking about and open it up in a willy-nilly way. But, at the same time, if you say, "I have to manage it the way I've always managed," then you are actually not opening up anything and not allowing anybody to innovate on top of you, because the weight that you'll put on everyone else will keep them from wanting to innovate on top of your platform. I think we ultimately got it right—you kind of have to let it go a little bit, but let it go in a risk-controlled way, because if you did something other than that and you had a security problem or a massive compromise, you would permanently impair you brand. We certainly had that risk at PayPal, but if you don't push the edges to let people innovate in ways where you are at least a little bit uncomfortable, then don't bother going through the exercise.

Question: Could there be developers that actually use PayPal's platform to compete against PayPal?

Thompson: There was no question that was another risk that we all saw: couldn't someone in a really interesting, expedited way create a better version of PayPal leveraging the pipes we built, exposed through the platform. Yes, no doubt about that, that is a risk, but then, the math on this says that can't possibly happen, and here's the reason why. We had a big lead in a number of places—the global nature of that business was a big lead, all of the licensing that we put in place in those markets, in the United States and around the world, all the payment pipes integrated into various banking and payment systems, and the uniqueness of the specifications of those banking systems—that was a strategic and competitive advantage. A person who says, "We can't open up a platform because someone will build something on top of us," is saying someone can replicate and improve all the hard work and the intellectual property we've built. That's true, but then if you do the platform right, you've got hundreds of other people that are making your business better, your account better, your payment system better; they're extending your lead through their innovation that you didn't have previously without them. So the new person that is building on top of you—they actually have to keep up with all that you're doing and all that everyone else is doing. That math doesn't work. It just doesn't work. Now, it's a risk because if none of the developers build something on your platform or they come but they don't build anything of value, then of course you're creating the nightmare scenario that you're describing. But that certainly wasn't the case, we opened it up so people could rapidly innovate on top of it and that actually resulted in the math problem that somebody sitting on top of us wasn't going to be able to replicate, and I think that's all part of the bet.

Question: If someone is seriously considering opening up their platform, what criteria should they consider?

Thompson: That's a good question, and several things come to mind. The first thing is when you start down the path of opening up, otherwise meaning building APIs, you quickly realize that everything wants to become a service, and even the smallest of things is begging to become a service, for others to consume this. I don't know if that is instinctively bad, but when you allow everything to become a service, and you allow everything to absorb that much incremental cost and that much incremental time, and you're creating the optionality in this core service that nobody will ever use, I would say that's a genuine waste of corporate assets. There is a need to be genuinely thoughtful of what you're opening up and what you're making available and how you do it, and it's not just "today we're a platform and we're going to build everything in the form of an API." The cost would just overwhelm you.

I think the second thing is—and this is the place where I ultimately got very comfortable—with your banking account, if you want to do something with that account, it's pretty routine that other people would say, "I need some form of paper statement about your account relationship with someone," so if you're looking at it from that perspective and you're saying the customer will ultimately provide all this information to somebody who's asking for it, but they're providing it in a slow, tedious, paper-based way that will add a tremendous amount of cost, then that begs to be opened up in the form of a service, doesn't it? If someone innovates on top of the platform and says, "You don't have to provide me with anything, you just need to check a box that authorizes me to have this data," from where I sit, that's the definition of "you should do it," right?

Conversely, if you look at it and say the small business or the consumer would never, ever, under any circumstances, say you could have the information about them, than I can't imagine a scenario in which you'd want to become a platform business. I just can't imagine that. Now, I don't know who fits into that, because that certainly wasn't us at PayPal. But if that's the business that you're in, then you sure as heck shouldn't be investing in a platform-oriented strategy, because you're going the wrong way with the assets that you have on your customer's behalf. I think that's the right way to look at it.

Question: What sort of skill sets does an organization need to run an open platform, and how is that different from the skill sets you need in a closed platform?

Thompson: Think about it this way: you're building an application or you're building a system, or you're building a set of features, whatever it is that you're doing, in the historical context of a business. It's then put in even further details; then it's handed off to an engineer, who builds it; and then it's given to somebody else in a quality assurance role to test it to make sure it's doing what it was intended to do. And that's how the vast majority of things have been built over the past 30 years.

Now, think about this in a platform business like what we were building at PayPal. What's the ultimate use case? Well, it's whatever the entrepreneur wants it to be, it's whatever the unique opportunity is to innovate off this platform. What is that? It's impossible to write it down because the person hasn't come yet and tried out what it is actually designed for. And so, all of a sudden, you're saying all of those people who used to think about it, and describe it and define it, and hand it off to an engineer—their role is very different now because they're not actually trying to do something specific, they're trying to do something that's actually very generic in nature, that has a lot of optionality and extensibility to it. And by the way, now the engineer is being given a specification that basically says, "Hey, I want to extend this service and I want it to be very flexible, but I don't know exactly what it's going to be."

So you end up having engineers that are just very talented from a product perspective but unconstrained from something that fits on an 8.5-by-11 sheet of paper, because you have no idea what that young kid in Israel or Singapore or anywhere in the world who's building something on top of your platform will try to make this thing do. So it actually turns your engineering organization for that part of the business almost upside down in terms of how they think about what they have to do, how they define what they have to do, how they prioritize what they have to do, and it's much more of this unconstrained "I have to build for future extensibility" than it is a specific product feature that someone in the business is asking me for. It's fascinating, and a challenging problem.

Question: When you look to the future, do you see more of the same [movement toward open platforms]? What other trends are you observing?

Thompson: No question, at its core, what we're describing now gets an exclamation point, and then another, and then another as we look forward over the next two to five years—no question. And not that it matters in this context, but the guys at Shoprunner are preparing in this way—we know we'll be operating outside the United States, and we know the day after that we're going to have a bigger business, and that extensibility is critical in how we build for the future because if you don't have it, you'll have a handicap that keeps you from competing in the future. The fun question to imagine is: how do these big enterprise businesses that have never done what we're talking about—how do they compete in the future when they don't have the capabilities that we're describing? That's going to be fun to watch. I'm not sure I have an answer for that.

The other big trends that seem to be happening (I can't do this in a general nature about a lot of subjects, just the space that we're in): if we were still in payments and financial services, and those sorts of things, I would say to you that I think the opportunity to disrupt the incumbents is bigger today than it has ever been. And it's just true in this country and every other country where there's a developed banking system. And, I think, there are all kinds of organizations, businesses, concepts, start-ups that are in the process of taking advantage of that big opportunity. As I said, it is bigger than it has ever been and it is bigger for a few reasons: What the banks complain about the most is increased regulatory oversight. That's true, but by and large it's an excuse because here's what else is going on: the customer demands more today than what most of these institutions are capable of giving them. They just demand more—more convenience, more immediacy, more everything—and I just don't see them being able to step up and do it in any meaningful way in the near term. We'll see; this will play out over the longer term.

The second thing that I think is vastly underwritten about is the ongoing demise of the internal technology organization in these businesses that maintains its own technology and data centers. Our business, Shoprunner, has been around for 3+ years and we don't own a server. Not one. For anything! Can you imagine that? We have a few desktops over there, but we don't own a server. Everything we have to compute, for storage, for all of that, is somewhere else. As the outside world would refer to it, "It's all out there in the cloud." We are never going to be an organization that has a data center that has a need for technology within the four walls of what we do. Isn't that fascinating? The pace at which we as a start-up can move without the legacy of having all that is accelerated even further. It will be fun to watch. For companies that are only a few years old, it's an exception when they own their technology in any way—it's truly the exception. And they're going to grow up and be very big companies with no need for a data center.

The third thing I know is true—and it is happening at a furious pace—is data and leveraging data in unique ways across so many businesses. If you are an organization that doesn't have deep insight that you can gain that describes who your customer is and how they behave and when they behave, if you are an organization that is not data capable, you lose. And it's probably worse than that because the playing field you're going to be in when you're competing against somebody who really knows how to use data is lopsided. We're in the early days and innings of this. What's the classic example: a legacy retailer that is trying to compete against Amazon. That's an unfair fight in almost any way! So data is a massive trend we're going to see.

I think the final point—and we saw this in a number of ways at PayPal, but it's coming in very fast—is the global nature of how all kinds of industries work today and the boundaries that used to exist are just fading away, and that person who is on the Internet can get access to anything regardless of where they live. Everything is becoming globally interoperable, for anything that you want or need in your life or your business or whatever it might be. It feels like underneath the headlines, there's a lot more there than people generally recognize, and it's going to change a lot of things about how we live and work in front of our eyes.

APP STORES FOR BANKS: WILL IT WORK?

On the heels of PayPal's open platform, we've seen larger financial institutions beginning to open their platform to developers to spur innovation. This new business model requires banks to incent developers to use their data, and to sustain the development and maintenance of the applications. It requires banks to think about serving another customer segment it has traditionally had no experience with: the developer. This model requires banks to no longer view themselves as creators of services but, rather, enablers and providers of a platform.

The results thus far have shown that there is room to come up with new and compelling experiences for bank customers leveraging data. It also demonstrates that when a bank needs more innovation, rather than hire an "innovations" leader, it might be far better to create an infrastructure that allows an exponential number of innovations leaders to build something interesting for the bank, without putting anyone on the payroll! Often, it takes more than two years for a financial services company to develop its own application, due to security and compliance considerations and the conventional IT process. Adopting a platform services and partner-friendly stance can potentially increase time to market significantly. You are, in a sense, leveraging IT resources other than your own that might allow an idea to move to multiple full-blown applications within a matter of months versus years. In addition, in this age where most consumers, particular those under 35, expect that there is always an application that will meet their particular needs, it can help a financial institution cater to its customers and move away from a one-size-fits-all approach. Let's take a look at what one large bank, Credit Agricole, has done in this way to spur innovation.

In January 2012, Credit Agricole introduced a financial application marketplace, called the CA Store, modeled on the way Apple, Google, and others have recruited outside developers (see Figure 4.3). Credit Agricole's business model includes financial incentives that encourage external developers to participate in the app store and its community of developers. It exposed a set of APIs that allow outside developers to build applications compatible with Credit Agricole that their bank customers can use. The APIs can be leveraged to provide solutions for access to account activity, money transfer, and connection with a financial advisory—all in the form of Web services.

Credit Agricole has established a community of external developers by allowing them to benefit from a financial model, paid based on client usage. The three principles Credit Agricole focused on to make the open platform successful were:

1. *Trust customers.* Rather than build products that Credit Agricole believed would be right for its customers, it asked its customers directly what they'd like to see next and offered developers the chance to build those products. This is an example of moving from a product-centric culture to a customer-centric culture. It has a fundamental shift in thinking that puts customers first and looks to prioritize and build services around their needs.
2. *Open the data model.* Credit Agricole knew that it not only had to expose its data but it also had to deliver a solution that generated revenue

FIGURE 4.3   Credit Agricole's App Store
Source: Finovate Conference 2013.

for the application developers. The more data are exposed to developers, the more the more valuable the solutions they can ultimately build. When launching its open data initiative, allowing geolocation information to be exposed (with the user's permission) could create valuable applications for customers, such as the ability to search for expenses by geographic area.

3. *Make the applications secure.* No innovation can happen without a secure platform. Credit Agricole still goes through a vetting process with developers and holds them to strict standards. Third-party developers never "see or know" any real customer data and cannot access it. Credit Agricole reviews the apps available in the CA Store at least every two weeks to confirm they have no malicious code.

As Bernard Larriviere, director of innovation for Credit Agricole, has said, "Applications designed by a banker look like what a banker can imagine. We needed to have the customer's point of view to make us think about another way of creating applications to meet customer needs."[2] One application was designed to notify customers of account overdrafts. Another makes a game out of saving money; customers get an award that is displayed on their Facebook page when they hit their savings goal. The CA Store already has attracted more than 50 outside companies and individuals who develop applications at the site, often based on the suggestions of consumers or of other banks. The developers are encouraged to contact customers who have posted ideas, so that they might participate in shaping the apps. While many of the applications might serve a very specific base of customers, it is still considered an important function and moves the bank closer to servicing customers in more of a one-to-one manner. Imagine an application for visually impaired customers that allows them to pick out the color contrast that fits their eyesight, or an application that allows you to choose a map display to more easily track what you have spent by location. Other ideas have led to games that can educate the youth market on personal savings. Imagine a child with a personal project he is saving for; there is now an application that can send alerts and share his savings accomplishments on social networks.

Credit Agricole's efforts have led it to some prestigious awards, including "Best of Show" at Finovate. As Jim Bruene, CEO of the Online Banking Report and Finovate, has said:

> *The willingness of a large and relatively conservative European retail bank to embrace outside developers is one of the more surprising innovations we've seen in Finovate's six-year history. Although Credit Agricole is a tad older than most presenters (founded in 1885), the bank's decision to build the first European*

LUMINOUS AND FNB: AN OPEN INNOVATION FRAMEWORK

Developing an app store and focusing on platform services is not the only way to solicit outside ideas. Simply finding opportunities to elicit suggestions from consumers and encourage entrepreneurs to brainstorm ideas for new apps and services can be very powerful. How can a bank take steps toward collaboration in this way? Some of the best innovations come through highly collaborative partnerships between the banking community and technology and start-up community. They may start as vendor relationships but can be cultivated and can turn into something very valuable, as we'll discuss.

In 2006, Luminous, a start-up technology company, approached the First National Bank of South Africa with an innovation to include an online accounting solution as an offering within FNB's Online Banking suite. At the time, this was particularly innovative from a number of different viewpoints. No bank globally had ever done this. Online accounting was still in its infancy, and cloud solutions were only just getting traction. So what became branded Instant Accounting was a giant leap of faith at the time. FNB believed in the innovation and also believed in the commitment from the Luminous team. It would have been possible for FNB to build this kind of offering in-house but the feeling was that the likelihood of success was far greater in partnering with a company that was highly focused on Instant Accounting. The bank itself has so many products that there was every chance it would get lost and not be driven to success if the same solution were built from inside the bank.

The key first step was getting a pilot under way, which was specifically built to be a market-ready pilot. This meant that as soon as the pilot had proven market readiness, then Instant Accounting could be turned on for all business banking customers. At the same time, a joint business case was developed with complete transparency. This meant that FNB and Luminous formed a joint view on what investment was required to make Instant Accounting work and what revenues were likely to be generated from Instant Accounting. The companies then agreed on how the investment and returns would be split, with a keen focus on investing in success rather than maximizing returns. FNB's key contractual requirement was a period of exclusivity so that FNB could be assured of first-mover advantage. For Luminous, the relationship gave it credibility in the market, which

(continued)

LUMINOUS AND FNB: *(Continued)*

made the period of exclusivity a good trade-off. The financial aspects of the agreement also tied all payments to success so that both FNB and Luminous had skin in the game. FNB asked that key members of the Luminous technical and call center support team actually sit inside the bank and gave Luminous desks within FNB's support centers. Operationally, Luminous's support team became highly integrated into the FNB operations, yet remained 100 percent focused on Instant Accounting.

Today, Instant Accounting has the major share of the online accounting market in South Africa, and FNB has come to be a leading player in a nonbanking vertical through partnering. The relationship with Luminous has also led to additional world and regional first products that have been incubated in a similar manner. These include Insights, Merchant Insights, Instant Financial Management (PFM solution), and BankFiling, which all play in the financial management space between FNB and its customers.

More recently, this relationship led to the creation of a brand new start-up called Matchi, which was founded in early 2013 and launched in November 2013. Matchi was founded as a matchmaking platform that brings innovators together with companies looking for innovations. Matchi decided to focus initially on banking innovations, and in the spirit of open innovation, Matchi provided FNB with a global platform to attract innovations at prototype maturity stage and beyond at a very low cost. The "prototype maturity stage and beyond" requirement meant that the innovation would have to have been implemented. It also helped Matchi avoid becoming a "suggestion" or complaints box. Matchi approached FNB and soon entered into a collaboration similar to their past working relationship. FNB and Matchi collaborated on a number of key aspects, including the business plan, web site design, digital marketing campaigns, and public relations. Matchi today offers services to over 25 global banks and is in a good position to help banks and technology companies collaborate, take advantage of new trendsand get to market faster. We will surely see more of these collaborative models develop as it becomes easier for banks and tech companies to leverage new tools to test concepts and ideas without incurring significant expense.

app store ranks right up there with the boldest start-up. And while there will be nonfinancial apps available, the clear focus will be on providing financial solutions the bank wouldn't be able to build themselves. The strategy also impresses as a way to foster collaboration between app developers/designers and the bank.

Credit Agricole's business model underpins how data and platform really come together. Customers of Credit Agricole are charged, but not for the applications—they are charged for the service of securing the data at €0.79 per month and only when an application is used. Customers can then use as many applications as they like in a given month. CA then passes the majority of the fee (minus a share for the bank) to the cooperative, which distributes total revenues among the developers based on the use of their individual applications. For the business model, Credit Agricole does charge customers—but not for the applications used. It charges for the service of securing the data, only €0.79 per month and only when an application is used.[3]

The approach of making widgets and applications available on banks has made its way to the United States. Yodlee, a leading financial technology provider to banks, offers an app store platform that banks can take advantage of, without requiring them to build their own. The app model can offer a real competitive opportunity. Many of Yodlee's bank customers are using their APIs today to build their own proprietary applications, powered by personal financial management data, to offer unique functionality to their customers as part of an integrated online/mobile banking experience. Yodlee believes banks will be running their own developer hack-a-thons and engaging more actively with outside creative experts to build new capabilities that create a truly differentiated customer experience. Because of the flexibility of their platform architecture, Yodlee makes it easier for banks to innovate, to build and deploy new applications, within a secure and compliant infrastructure. As Yodlee puts it, they are helping to break some of those shackles to empower a greater speed of innovation and agility for banks.

WHAT'S NEXT?

Two things become clear when speaking with banks and innovators alike. First, the banks that will be around in the next several years will be the ones that have found ways to interconnect their platforms with best-of-breed applications and partners. Second, bank data will only become valuable if it can be leveraged by third-party applications. These trends seem clear based on what we see today with consumer behavior. Consumers have voted with their mobile phones when it comes to accessing financial services. They expect personalized information at their fingertips. "Big data" has to translate into insightful, personalized data, and financial applications have to stay relevant for customers to use them. The *Wall Street Journal* reports that the number of banking institutions in the United States has dwindled to its lowest level since at least the Great Depression, as a sluggish economy, stubbornly low interest rates, and heightened regulation take their toll on the sector.[4] The way to combat that is through a much more personalized delivery of services, and that means focusing on opening up platforms and data models for external innovation. Brad Liemer, head of digital at Mechanics Bank, summed up the trends nicely in a recent posting on *American Banker:*

> As we move into this new era, the idea of profiting from glaring areas of friction disappears. The crux of the disruption argument is that banks are being dis-intermediated. But I think in many ways the industry, at least certain players, are responding, and in many ways reverse engineering the attacks to its foundation. In this new era of applications and partnerships driven by application programming interfaces, you can practically build a complete banking experience on the rails of Twilio, Stripe, and IFTTT ("If This, Then That"). The financial services revolution may not be televised, but it will certainly be driven by APIs. I digress.
>
> As much of traditional banking services become a utility, those that leverage personalized banking experiences for their profitable customer niche segments will thrive. As we move further into digital experience, the next decade will be even more incredibly disruptive than what we saw in the recent economic downturn. Banking is no longer something customers do. It's an experience they completely control. So where does that leave us, the bankers? We are moving away from a banking relationship defined by the goal of being a customer's primary financial institution to one where we focus on becoming their primary financial application. It's no longer about wallet share. It's about app-driven mindshare—as our customers reach into their pockets for their mobile device or use their glasses or other form of wearable technology and think about their financial relationship choices—before, during and after a financial moment of truth. So, what's in your app?

We've talked about data and platform services and some of the emerging business models that support the shift required to deliver financial services in today's environment. We've also discussed how incredibly important it is to partner with technology companies to get best-of-breed applications and to become more of an enabler of innovation versus a supplier of innovation. In Chapter 6, we'll discuss how new banking models will evolve in more detail and how banks can best prepare.

NOTES

1. Likhit Wagle, "What's Driving Financial Services? Think Big Data," *Forbes,* www.forbes.com/sites/ibm/2013/07/31/whats-driving-financial-services-think-big-data/. Accessed July 31, 2013.
2. Karen Epper Hoffman, "Open API for Bank Apps: Can Credit Agricole's Model Work Here?" *American Banker,* www.americanbanker.com/magazine/123_8/open-api-for-bank-apps-can-credit-agricoles-model-work-1060535-1.html. Accessed July 29, 2013.
3. Jennifer Belissent, "One Small Step for Credit Agricole, One Giant Leap for the Data Economy," *Forrester,* http://blogs.forrester.com/jennifer_belissent_phd/13-03-28-one_small_step_for_credit_agricole_one_giant_leap_for_the_data_economy. Accessed March 28, 2013.
4. Ryan Tracy, "Tally of U.S. Sinks to Record Low," *Wall Street Journal,* http://online.wsj.com/news/articles/SB10001424052702304579404579232343313671258. Accessed December 3, 2013.

CHAPTER 5

Math-Based Currencies

How Bitcoin May Prove Transformational to The Financial Services Industry

George Peabody
Glenbrook

"I'm a big fan of Bitcoin. . . . Regulation of money supply needs to be depoliticized."

—Al Gore, Former U.S. Vice President
and Nobel Peace Prize Recipient

[T]hese types of innovations [such as Bitcoin] may pose risks related to law enforcement and supervisory matters, there are also areas in which they may hold long-term promise, particularly if the innovations promote a faster, more secure and more efficient payment system.

—Ben Bernanke, in a letter to the chair of the
Senate Committee on Homeland Security and
Government Affairs, November 12, 2013

ENTERING THE AGE OF CONTEXT

In the fall of 2013, tech industry observer, blogger, and cloud computing advocate Robert Scoble and his coauthor Sal Israel published their book *The Age of Context*. Exposed to almost every Next New Thing from the minds of Silicon Valley entrepreneurs, think tanks, and enterprise-scale tech firms, Scoble in particular has had a front row seat to what's possible coming from the Valley, New York, Austin, Seattle, Boston, and other innovation hubs. Based on that exposure and their own experience, the authors identified five technologies, the union of which they believe will fundamentally change how we live, interact, market, sell, and navigate through our daily and transactional lives.

The five technologies are:

1. *Mobile devices and communications.* With well over 60 percent of us using smartphones in the United States and over 100 percent mobile penetration in almost all development markets, mobile devices are both the aggregation point for cloud-based services and apps, as well as a source of data to feed those, and other, cloud-based services. Mobile devices are the lenses through which activities, like light, are focused in both directions.

2. *Data, as in big data.* The recent ability to assemble enormous data sets and perform Bayesian analytics on them to discover unexpected correlations is at the core of Google's and Facebook's success. Less expansive data sets have given merchants the ability to mold marketing messages, even identify pregnancy (Target's target as it were), and financial institutions the ability to manage risk as well as reveal cross-selling opportunities.

3. *Social.* The relationships between people and the networks they belong to are powerful predictors of behavior, health, likes, and alliances.

4. *Geolocation.* With every cell phone equipped with a global positioning system (GPS), and that capability almost universally enabled, mobile network operators and an array of service providers are building behavioral models to predict travel patterns, shopping behavior, and more, with an eye to improving advertising efficiency.

5. *Sensors.* At an even more granular level (from 50,000 feet to 5 centimeters), sensors embedded in our smartphones, in wearable devices (Google Glass), and in our immediate environment will give us the ability to determine not only which building we are in but which checkout line we are standing in, which shelf of designer jeans we are examining, as well as tell a store clerk which of her customers has checked into the store for a pickup.

It is hard to argue with their position. We are already seeing the impact when even two of these technology trends are harnessed together. Smartphones (mobile) and motion detection devices (sensors) have combined to create a new class of fitness monitoring tools from the likes of Nike and Fitbit. When plugged into a new-model car, Travelers Insurance's IntelliDrive device can log a teen's driving behavior (data); produce weekly reports on speed, location (GPS), and distance; and even alert parents via text (mobile) when preset speed limits are exceeded. Even simple combinations are effective. My current favorite is from Google. Whenever I use Google Maps on my PC to find directions, that search is converted into a Google Now card on my Samsung Galaxy phone. With a couple of screen taps, the phone's navigation system and Maps app talk me to my destination.

In the hands of engineers and entrepreneurs, these tools are already raising the expectations for what's to come among consumers, retailers, major consumer packaged goods brands, and Internet giants like Google, Apple, Microsoft, Amazon, eBay/PayPal, and more. These tools will let merchants and service providers sell more and sell better.

From the 100,000-foot level, it's not hard to see that the interaction of these technologies will drive the environment that your future customers, account holders, consumers, and all of us as citizens will inhabit. You have to be building for that future. The elements are already in place, and those customers will expect you to deploy them for their benefit.

Drop down to the 50,000-foot level and you can see their relevance in action within today's payments industry. Some of these tools are already deployed by financial technology providers and their customers. IP geolocation, for example, and mobile data have been combined by early warning systems to improve fraud detection. Every mobile payments observer is watching the evolving impact of Square Register and Square Wallet, the combination of which allows a customer to tell, for example, the Square-using barista to "put that cappuccino on my tab" and for the barista to nod "yes" because the customer's picture is displayed by the Square Register app on the merchant's iPad screen.

Take it down to 25,000 feet and we can use these fundamental technologies to address specific use cases. For example, in combination, we can use them to generate stronger risk scores and authentication methods. We can ask powerful questions of each technology:

Mobile

- What is known about my device?
- How is my device configured?
- Am I using my device or is someone else?

Data

- What have I done in the past?
- How does that fit with what I'm doing now?

Social

- Who am I connected to?
- What is their reputation?

Geolocation
- What building am I in?
- Which direction am I going in?

Sensors
- Where am I standing?
- What am I looking at?
- What is my heart rate and temperature?

Now combine the answers. Knowing even half of the answers to these questions places the customer's transaction origination method, the location of that transaction's origination, the location of the merchant, and the profiles of the devices used to initiate that transaction into a crisp context that can improve both the security of the payment as well as sharpen the data gathering and delivery of consumer incentives. Contextual payments like these will wash away the decade's old distinction of "card present" and "card not present" payments.

Why is this discussion of contextual payments germane to math-based currencies (MBCs)? Because these upstart mechanisms for value transfer are arriving on the scene at the same time as Scoble and Israel's five technologies. Jump back to 100,000 feet and view MBCs as Scoble and Israel's sixth technology. As we've already seen, the first five tools used in even partial combination change what is possible for transactions of all kinds. The potential for MBCs in this larger technology context becomes apparent. The broad-scale innovation that the first five enable becomes the background in front of which innovations in money and value transfer will be played out. While tiny in volume and nascent in both business and deployment terms, MBCs are exciting entrepreneurs, engineers, investors, and a growing group of serious, experienced operators. MBCs promise to challenge almost everyone else who participates in electronic value today.

INTRO TO MATH-BASED CURRENCIES

If you follow the financial technology media at all, you're aware of Bitcoin. This MBC—a new way of representing and exchanging value using cryptography, a peer-to-peer network, and a public transaction ledger—continues to excite the imagination of techies, investor, speculators, and those worried about monetary stability.

In the spring of 2013, this "start-up" currency rose in value to nearly $250 and then fell to less than $100 in a matter of days. It had undergone a similar, smaller swing before and continues to oscillate. Between those swings in value, Bitcoin's cashlike attributes of partial anonymity and permanence—once you send bitcoin, you can't get it back unless the recipient agrees to return it—do make it somewhat useful for illegal transactions which, of course, has attracted media and regulatory attention. Add the concomitant fact that there is no central Bitcoin authority and this MBC has become fodder for no end of news coverage. Commentary has ranged from Paul Volcker's rather charming "I'm too old for this" to screeds on both sides of the central banking versus digital currency divide. In short, there's been a lot of noise.

But serial financial services entrepreneur and Bitcoin aficionado Wences Casares has it right: "Arguing about Bitcoin is like arguing over religion or politics." The right question is "what can we do with it?"

My goal in this chapter is to steer well away from both religion and politics, stick as closely to the facts as possible, and to suggest to you how the technological foundation of these MBCs could prove transformational for financial institutions.

WHY "MATH-BASED CURRENCIES"?

While Bitcoin is both the first and the most widely known and covered math-based currency, it is hardly the only one. There are a number of derivatives based on the Bitcoin algorithm designed for varying purposes. There are second-generation efforts like Ripple that are based on a different philosophy—Ripple Labs is the central authority—and offer broader capabilities such as built-in support for currency exchange functions. While different, they all use strong mathematical algorithms to prevent counterfeit currencies and fraudulent transactions. For that reason, I frequently refer to math-based currencies instead of only Bitcoin. Bitcoin certainly has the lead over the other approaches, but that's no guarantee it will be the only MBC in broad use. For that reason, throughout this chapter, I will refer to math-based currencies or MBCs whenever necessary.

MBCs Are a Reality

As with other Internet-based technologies, math-based currencies are already in the hands of an international group of techies, curious financial technology professionals, and, yes, even a few ne'er-do-wells. While the criminal element may attract the media and regulators, it's important that these concerns do not cloud your assessment of MBCs. Thus far, United States and most international regulators have applied existing regulations to

MBCs. So if they fall under the existing regulatory framework, that means use of MBCs may be an option for you.

Before taking a deeper dive into MBC use cases, let's start at the beginning and review some digital currency history.

HISTORY OF DIGITAL CURRENCIES

Digital money has been with us, off and on, for several decades. After all, what need could be more intuitively obvious than the ability to pay someone directly across a network like the Internet or within a walled garden like America Online (AOL) or CompuServe before it. Bits are certainly a lot easier to move than gold bars, bills, or bags of coins.

But failure stalked and captured earlier efforts like DigiCash, ecash, and others largely because of lack of trust in the currency operator, the conceptual leap it has required of skeptical potential financial institution customers, flawed economic models, or regulatory concerns.

Since those early efforts, the virtual money category evolved to answer the specific needs of low-value transactions within a game or online domain. Funded by payments cards or cash loaded at a physical location, this approach is more about user convenience when purchasing virtual goods—when you have to buy a herd of cows for Farmville—as well as the convenience and profit of the operator.

But between the friction of currency conversion and the strong attachment we have to government-issued currency, surrogate approaches have failed to fulfill the needs of open-loop Internet micro payments even as the economics of card-based payments stumble over that use case. Even Facebook's credits scheme has fallen back to an approach based on fiat currency because the vagaries of exchange rates across the planet made it unsatisfactory for millions of users who were never sure how much a credit would cost.

MATH-BASED CURRENCY CHARACTERISTICS

Math-based currencies are another matter entirely. With no central corporate or government issuer, distributed digital currencies are assuming a fascinating role in the evolution of money and value exchange. It is far too early to predict the fully expressed role of these experimental approaches toward the global exchange of value. However, we can predict the following outcomes:

- The evolving presence of MBCs will challenge regulators of almost every country concerned with the value of their own currencies, seigniorage revenues to their treasuries, and control of money laundering and terrorist financing. Given compliance with existing anti–money laundering and know your customer (KYC) requirements and better forensic tools should diminish the modest anonymity and utility of MBCs for criminals of all kinds. Since the Bitcoin block chain ledger is entirely out in the open, the actual flow of a transaction is unambiguous, only the owners of the wallets on either end are obscure.

- Math-based currencies will attract the interest and participation of a growing base of users. With uncertainty over national inflation rates, the condition of leading national banks, and sometimes a state's own central bank, a "flight to safety" in the form of MBCs, despite their novelty, has already taken place. While such "safety" is arguable—MBCs are still very new, after all—the value of one such currency, Bitcoin, has proven resilient despite occasional strong fluctuations.

- Math-based currencies will not go away. While government efforts to clamp down on their usage could affect their roles and valuation, MBCs open a range of opportunities and, once employed, user demand will keep them employed. Internet history demonstrates that once a tool is adopted on the Internet, it becomes part of the software developer's toolkit useful for new applications appealing to consumers and business. Because of that distributed, Internet-enabled nature, MBCs will be very hard to kill even if regulators decide to go after them.

- Digital cash, the ability to push payments across a network, is a good idea. Despite earlier failures, the Internet's need for digital cash remains. The application of card-based payment "rails" to Internet e-commerce transactions has produced an uneasy balance that continues to struggle with Internet technology's high rate of change and card-based economics. The explosion of mobile devices and a shift to mobile transactions has only exacerbated the tension between a system originally designed for point of sale transactions and our all-digital future.

BITCOIN: THE FIRST MBC

The math-based currency called Bitcoin is the catalyst for the current and expanding global interest in MBCs. Based on an elegant algorithm and possessing attributes of both currency and commodity, Bitcoin's emergence has struck a chord with the technically curious, the profit-driven, and financial technology entrepreneurs all over the globe.

Bitcoin's Brief History

Bitcoin has its own creation myth. Bitcoin was born in January 2009, a child attributed to one Satoshi Nakamoto, via a paper and software source code released onto the Internet. "Satoshi Nakamoto" is a pseudonym, the Japanese equivalent of "John Smith." He, or they, writes in flawless British English, is a master of cryptography, peer-to-peer communications, and has a deep understanding of money. Speculation over his, or their, identity is a cryptographer's parlor game (I spoke with two individuals in one week who suspected they knew who created Bitcoin). Since its release, Bitcoin's creator has made it clear he, or they, has gone on to other things, leaving behind a maturing phenomenon that continues to play itself out across the global Internet.

Satoshi has left a remarkable model for a digital currency. In many ways, it remains an experiment but, like most experiments, the knowledge that results has already improved Bitcoin itself as well as influenced the design and market development of other MBCs. A cadre of software developers, dedicated to both the open source software model and to the evolution of Bitcoin, lead the evolution of the Bitcoin protocol, teaching their cryptographically energized infant to crawl and walk. In the spring of 2014, Bitcoin's evolution is at the end of its beginning. Where it goes next will be exciting to watch and even better to participate in.

IS IT BITCOIN, BITCOIN, OR JUST BTC

The answer is all three. The capitalization conventions line up like this. When referring to the ecosystem using this method, the capitalized *Bitcoin* is used. The lowercase *bitcoin* refers to the currency itself. And the shorthand for the bitcoin currency is *BTC* just as *USD* is for the U.S. dollar.

Bitcoin Is a Powerful Concept

Bitcoin is an Internet phenomenon. Given its distributed nature and the fact that there is no central authority managing the bitcoin money supply, the new digital currency has fired the imagination of the media and, more important, a range of users for whom the currency has strong attraction (see Figure 5.1). Those who fear government devolution at worst or at least currency devaluation are attracted to bitcoin. Others are attracted to bitcoin as an alternative to gold or other precious metal commodities. Given the extent of quantitative easing by major central banks, there's skepticism over these deflated government currencies. Speculators look to make money on currency exchange fluctuation. And there are those who have learned through bitter experience that national currencies can go off the rails and have learned to move to other, more stable or appreciating currencies, to protect their assets. For some, frustrated by national currency controls that hinder currency conversion, bitcoin is assuming that role despite its novel, all-digital nature.

These are heady times for Bitcoin's backers as popular unease over government monetary policy in the United States and European Union (EU), never mind Cyprus and Argentina, has brought Bitcoin to the attention of a wider audience. The currency has been endorsed by mainstream luminaries like Al Gore and Internet celebrities like the Winklevoss twins.

For many, interest in Bitcoin and MBCs is hardly irrational. Even financial technology professionals and payments industry leaders are surprisingly bullish on the future of MBCs in general and the Bitcoin ecosystem in particular. A survey of these payment professionals conducted by Glenbrook Partners during the summer of 2013 found that 31 percent of the predominantly American respondents believe that Bitcoin will replace how money is moved in 10 years. While 27 percent thought Bitcoin will be forgotten in three years, the remaining 73 percent believe it will still be part of our thinking for a very long time. While the majority is uncertain of

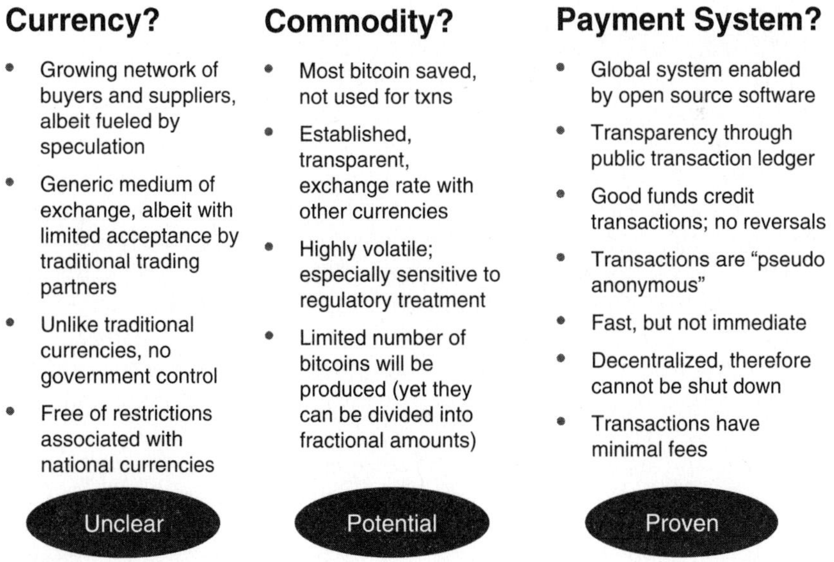

Currency?

- Growing network of buyers and suppliers, albeit fueled by speculation
- Generic medium of exchange, albeit with limited acceptance by traditional trading partners
- Unlike traditional currencies, no government control
- Free of restrictions associated with national currencies

Unclear

Commodity?

- Most bitcoin saved, not used for txns
- Established, transparent, exchange rate with other currencies
- Highly volatile; especially sensitive to regulatory treatment
- Limited number of bitcoins will be produced (yet they can be divided into fractional amounts)

Potential

Payment System?

- Global system enabled by open source software
- Transparency through public transaction ledger
- Good funds credit transactions; no reversals
- Transactions are "pseudo anonymous"
- Fast, but not immediate
- Decentralized, therefore cannot be shut down
- Transactions have minimal fees

Proven

FIGURE 5.1 What Is Bitcoin?
Source: Glenbrook Partners

Bitcoin's long-term role, it is astonishing that even a substantial minority believes that something so young, born in 2009 and just out of digital diapers in 2012, could challenge the today's world order of money movement.

HOW BITCOIN WORKS

The central feature of the Bitcoin ecosystem (see Figure 5.2) is a simple and familiar one, nothing more than a ledger that records all bitcoin transactions. At this level, Bitcoin is already well understood technology. We have used ledgers for centuries. Financial institutions, payment services providers like PayPal, and payments processors use ledgers, now managed by high-reliability databases, to make and record transactions. Nothing new there.

We protect those ledgers with high walls built of IT security technologies like firewalls as well as sophisticated business rules and practices that protect the proprietary data as well as the rents we pay to the ledger managers for keeping track of it all.

Bitcoin's ledger, called the block chain, performs a similar function, recording every bitcoin transaction since the very first block, the appropriately named Genesis Block, was generated. Where the similarity ends between PayPal's ledger, for example, and the block chain is in who has direct access to the ledger. While PayPal's ledger and that of every financial institution is surrounded by a technical and business moat, the Bitcoin ledger is completely transparent. Anyone can inspect it to see how a particular 0.025 BTC has been combined and subdivided since it first entered the block chain. The ledger is also permanent. The flow of value from the bitcoin transaction you made two months ago (hopefully not to a Silk Road imitator) will be publicly discoverable in 2019. And in 2123.

A copy of the Bitcoin block chain ledger exists on every computer running the Bitcoin algorithm. There are thousands of computers performing this task and communicating with each other over the Internet using its fundamental peer-to-peer architecture to connect, Napster-like, with other nearby peers. These computers validate and confirm bitcoin transactions, agreeing amongst each other that each and every transaction is unique. That's the basis of the mechanisms that prevents counterfeiting and dual spending.

Of course, the Bitcoin ledger needs something to track and record. That something, at least initially, is the bitcoin virtual currency itself. The currency is generated, and transactions are validated, through the same mathematical algorithm. What does that mean? It means every bitcoin is mathematically generated, using methods that assure the uniqueness of every bitcoin. Cryptographic methods protect access to a specific address where a bitcoin unit has been sent and resides.

A bitcoin is a very particular string of bits that exists only on the memory of a computer, on a hard drive, a thumb drive, or even as a long string of letters and numbers printed onto a piece of paper. A bitcoin is just data, very special data. And it's not a coin. It's a highly divisible unit.

Besides preventing counterfeit value and the double spending of bitcoin, that algorithm limits the total number of bitcoins that can ever be produced to 21 million. There were some 12.6 million bitcoins in existence in April 2014. Each bitcoin can be subdivided to eight decimal places; the smallest unit, 0.00000001, is called a satoshi, in honor of the Bitcoin designer. Bitcoins possess the attributes of both commodity and currency. The commodity character results from both the hard upper limit for bitcoin creation (21 million) and the fact that bitcoins are created through a computationally intensive process that is algorithmically throttled to create one one new block of bitcoins every eight to 10 minutes and no faster. This creates scarcity.

Perhaps the most controversial Bitcoin aspect is the fact that there is no Bitcoin, Inc. There is no Bitcoin central authority guiding bitcoin value exchange process or its supply. There is no 800 number to call if you want to dispute a transaction. Only the scheme's design and software, maintained by a collection of programmers who enhance what is open source software, guides its usage. In the truest sense, Bitcoin users have shifted from institutional trust to trust in the Bitcoin algorithm.

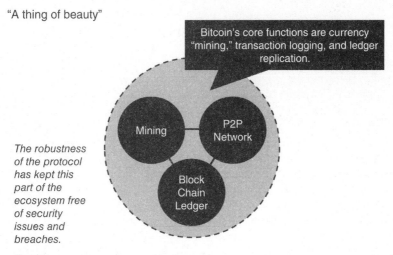

FIGURE 5.2 Bitcoin Ecosystem: Core
Source: Glenbrook Partners

Digging Bitcoin

Who creates new bitcoin and who processes bitcoin transactions? Bitcoin "miners" operate the computer systems that generate them. Mining is something of a misnomer in that all those computer systems aren't looking for something that already exists and requires refining. Miners compete to get lucky, all running the same Bitcoin protocol, as fast as they can, to "find" a numerical output that matches a very specific structure. The only way the Bitcoin software allows for that to happen is for every miner to run a routine, and it's the same routine on every miner's computer, over and over again in the hopes of finding the solution, that properly formatted value, before another miner produces a similar result.

To do this, miners all run the same software and run one straight-forward mathematical process called a hash (specifically the SHA-256 hash). Hashes are designed to take an input value and produce an output value that is wildly different from the input value. If you change the input value by one increment, the output value will be entirely different from the preceding value. This makes it impossible to take the output value and guess the input value (that's one reason why hashes are used so often in security applications.) What's fed into the hash algorithm is, in fact, another hash representing a collection of transactions that need validation, a Target value that raises or lowers the overall mining difficulty in order to keep the block production rate at one every 10 minutes or so, and a Nonce value that is changed every time the hash algorithm is run by the miner.

That process is run over and over again by the miner because the criteria for the creation of the next valid block in the block chain ledger are very specific. Right now, the "lucky" miner has to produce a value over 60 digits long that has 17 leading zeroes, and do that before another miner produces a similar solution.

Once that value is found, the miner is deemed to have found the next block and is rewarded by the algorithm—remember there's no Bitcoin, Inc.—with the next batch of bitcoins. To begin the validation process on the network that synchronizes the entire block chain, the miner who found and generated that properly formatted value advertises the values that produced the solution to adjacent miners on the peer-to-peer network. They, in turn, validate that those values produce identical results. Once that's done, the new block is thus confirmed and added to the block chain. As more miners validate the solution, the new block is created on other computers and the block chain's history is propagated across the network.

It's a computational race. Where once general-purpose computers were employed for bitcoin mining, second-generation hardware based on graphics processors increased performance considerably. These two approaches are now hugely obsolete. In the equivalent of a bitcoin mining arms race, a third generation of computing platform, in the form of 30-GHz application-specific integrated circuits (ASICs), has emerged to run the mining algorithm at far faster speeds. Bitcoin mining requires quite a lot of power. Some bitcoin mining operations, located in sophisticated data centers, are using highly advanced cooling methods simply to keep their power consumption down.

Why do miners mine? They're in it for the bitcoin they compete to generate, of course. Twenty-five bitcoin at $400 is a $10,000 win. But miners perform another critically important function. They provide transaction processing services. Every new bitcoin block contains the transaction history carried out during the prior 8 to 10 minutes. Every one of those transactions needs to be uniquely processed into a valid block and that block needs to be recreated on the block chain so that everyone is operating off of the same ledger. Miners are rewarded a small transaction fee of approximately five cents, a compensation rate that may drop in the months ahead.

It should be clear that Bitcoin is a mathematically strong system (see Figure 5.3). Within its operational domain, it works very well. More than one cryptographer has described Satoshi Nakamoto's design a "a thing of beauty." Others have called it "as important as the Internet." Bitcoin's combination of counterfeit-proof currency, Internet-based peer-to-peer

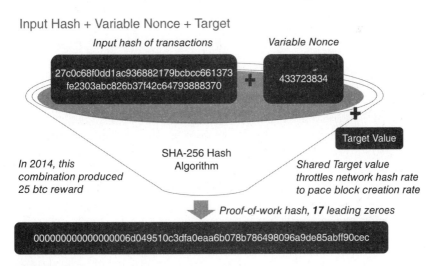

Input Hash + Variable Nonce + Target

Input hash of transactions

27c0c68f0dd1ac936882179bcbcc661373 fe2303abc826b37f42c64793888370

Variable Nonce

433723834

Target Value

In 2014, this combination produced 25 btc reward

SHA-256 Hash Algorithm

Shared Target value throttles network hash rate to pace block creation rate

Proof-of-work hash, **17** *leading zeroes*

000000000000000006d049510c3dfa0eaa6b078b786498096a9de85abff90cec

FIGURE 5.3 How Miners Find the Next Block
Source: Glenbrook Partners

communications, and the block chain ledger represents a substantial foundation on which to build value exchange applications that meet real needs. We're just at the beginning of applying those attributes to new uses.

Digital Push Payments

Unlike card-based payments and other bank-to-bank settlement systems, Bitcoin transactions behave like cash. Each transaction is irreversible. They cannot be repudiated. Once a bitcoin is transferred to a recipient's wallet, it can only be returned by the recipient. Again, there's no central authority to manage chargeback privileges, never mind the already fixed Bitcoin money supply. And, like physical cash, bitcoins are also somewhat anonymous, an attribute that is both overstated and yet of serious concern for law enforcement.

COUNTERFEITING NO MORE

Our recent experience with digital media—music and videos in particular—naturally makes us suspicious regarding the ease of duplication of any digital file. Between the block chain ledger and the use of public and private key cryptography, MBCs solve for that problem. Each bitcoin is unique. Bitcoin and other MBCs have effectively solved the counterfeit and double-spend problem that has challenged almost every currency throughout history. No successful counterfeits have been detected yet and, as time goes on, the level of difficulty increases.

In the case of Bitcoin, there is a concern regarding bad actors from the mining community. Should colluding Bitcoin miners control 40 percent or more of the Bitcoin computing base there is a risk they could create a fork in the block chain ledger. This fork would, temporarily, be construed as Bitcoin truth. But once the second fork was revealed, its advantages to the colluders would be very short lived. As soon as a second, spurious block chain was detected, confidence in the bitcoin currency and the block chain would evaporate. Further, the level of computational effort now required to perform such a hijack of the Bitcoin block chain ledger makes such an exploit both economically impractical and, while not impossible, technically very difficult.

MBCs Enable Programmable Money

A payments industry trend that is largely invisible to consumers and strikingly obvious to payments industry professionals is the embedding of payments into consumer and business transaction flows. Where once a payment was an explicit step—we write a check, swipe a card, or enter a card number into an online form—today, a payment may simply be a one-click process on a merchant's web site (Amazon) or the simple "put it on my tab" step of a smartphone-armed coffee shop customer (Square). Payments are becoming invisible, buried in wallets from the likes of Amazon, Square, Google, ISIS, and in apps from countless merchants.

Web and app-based software and services are, of course, the principal driver of the payment's submersion into the consumer's commerce experience. This trend will continue and could be accelerated by MBCs as they, unlike incumbent payment methods, are highly programmable simply because they, too, are software, unencumbered by card network rules and certification requirements.

How these currencies are employed is really up to the designer and programmer's imagination. As we will see, micropayments is a potential use case for making small payments for online goods and services. Bitcoin is already an easy way for me to leave a tip to a blogger for a post I admire. The automation of business-to-business (B2B) payments through MBC-based push payments is another application that could give international banking, with its complex and slow correspondent banking system, a true run for its money. Consider payments to online marketing affiliates or supply chain partners where the task of payment with its cost or scale has produced enough friction to limit the breadth of a marketplace. For example, a B2B payment application could be programmed to distribute the proceeds of a transaction as follows: "Of this $1 in clickstream revenue, send 30 percent to Affiliate A, 44 percent to Affiliate B, and send the remaining 26 percent to our company's bitcoin wallet address." MBCs could make such low-value transactions practical and cheap.

COMPLETING THE BITCOIN ECOSYSTEM

There are many in the Bitcoin ecosystem that, seeing MBCs as a new way of doing business, have elected to contribute to the building of this new approach via entrepreneurial activities (see Figure 5.4). Bitcoin "miners" use compute cycles to extract and create new bitcoins from the algorithmic ore. Others operate around the currency itself. Every currency needs a collection of payment services providers such as currency exchanges, merchant processors, and trading platforms to facilitate an individual currency's integration into the flow of global value exchange. Many entrepreneurs have jumped into this void to connect Bitcoin to the incumbent transaction and currency worlds. There are now 87 bitcoin exchanges serving 32 global currencies. California-based venture capitalists and a slowly growing set of cautious financial institutions have entered the scene to support the Bitcoin ecosystem.

Bitcoin Exchanges

Exchanges, cash-in services like ZipZap, and wallets, in particular, have been the focus of early entrepreneurial effort and the results have been, from both a business and a security point of view, mixed.

Exchanges are necessary simply to move value into and out of the bitcoin currency. Exchanges convert U.S. dollars, euros, and other currencies into and back from bitcoin. As a payment vehicle, Bitcoin is largely useless without practical currency exchange capability. For first-time Bitcoin participants, performing the currency exchange function is confusing at best. Most exchanges ask for one's banking information, an immediate stopper for many.

Using a cash-in facility is one way to begin. LocalBitcoins.com is a market maker that connects buyers and sellers. My nearest contact operates out of a Starbucks about 15 miles away from my office.

A number of exchange operations have cropped up and quickly perished from operational immaturity and undercapitalization. Multiple exchanges have been hacked via the standard toolkit of social engineering, phishing for malware delivery, and other tricks. Some of these breaches were childishly simple. While actually doing something with stolen bitcoin appears to be quite difficult, it's hard to be confident in such weak operations. A major currency exchange, Mt. Gox, has run afoul of both U.S. anti–money laundering regulations and litigation and, for a multitude of reasons, has since ceased operation.

These examples reflect the early evolutionary stage of the Bitcoin ecosystem. Better exchange operators to appear who view regulatory compliance and strong customer service as pillars of their business. Coinbase is one, backed by substantial, experienced venture capital. Circle, led by serial entrepreneur Jeremy Allaire and backed by similarly experienced top venture capital firms, is another entering the market has the characteristics we have looked for in the new entries into the Bitcoin marketplace, possessing a balanced focus on regulatory compliance and technology.

FINCEN's even-handed classification of miners selling bitcoin for profit and these currency exchanges as money transmitters should prove to be a very healthy stimulant to professionalizing the ecosystem. Acquisition of money transmittal licenses is a fiscally nontrivial activity, requiring $1 million and more in legal fees, licenses, and effort to cover the United States. If investment follows talent and has an ounce of prudence, then stronger operators should emerge, fueled by smarter money, to create a more reliable, secure services ecosystem around Bitcoin and other MBCs. That should give financial institutions and incumbent financial technology providers more reason to evaluate the MBC landscape.

Bitcoin Wallets—Where to Store Your BTC

The age-old problem of securing one's treasure has not been solved by Bitcoin. Because it is digital cash, protection of the bitcoin wallet is a concern. Both client-side software like mobile wallets and cloud-based wallets make tempting targets for thieves. The Age of Context technologies will help secure our bitcoin wallets as well as the Internet itself but, in the meantime, the use of Bitcoin will require thoughtful and thorough security measures.

Mobile Wallets Unlike account-based systems where authentication of the account holder to the account manager, that is, a consumer to a bank or merchant, access to one's mobile wallet is managed by software on the device because the wallet owner's bitcoin are there, too. The security requirement is primarily the necessity of identifying the wallet owner whenever the wallet app is "opened." A personal identification number (PIN) or password is typically the customer verification method. But as recent security flaws on Android devices (since repaired), mobile platforms, like PCs, are vulnerable targets so stronger, multifactor authentication is often used.

The ability to validate the owner via a fingerprint scan, voice print, or retina scan should become available within the next year as the FIDO Alliance and smartphone manufacturers bring fingerprint readers to market. Apple's iPhone 5S has a fingerprint reader built in. Samsung's latest Galaxy model does, too. With routine management of the biometric credential on the device and not in the cloud, it should prove useful to multiple smartphone-based applications like the bitcoin wallet.

Cloud-Based Wallets True authentication by a third-party controlling access to a resource is required for cloud-based wallets. That's the situation we all know from online banking, PayPal account access, and nearly other Web resource managed by ID and passwords. Bitcoin exchange Coinbase employs a second, independent app called Authy to generate a time-limited token value that the user then types into the Coinbase web page to gain account access.

Bitcoin wallets that store actual value make the limitations of the password-based security model even starker. Stronger, multifactor authentication is required, but it's still a generally inconvenient, one use-case-at-a-time affair. Given integration work, the FIDO Alliance approach should add strength to the authentication flow, demonstrating to the relying party in the cloud that the mobile device or its app (or both) was opened by the right finger or thumbprint.

Bitcoin Hardware Wallet   Today, neither the mobile wallet nor cloud-based wallets are foolproof. Both suffer from the same insecurity ills every other software-based financial application struggles against and in this case these techniques are attempting to protect the currency itself. A pair of Czech entrepreneurs have prototyped and are expected to ship their answer, a hardware-based wallet that stores private keys and signs transactions called the Trezor. A dedicated bit of hardware with two buttons and a tiny screen, the Trezor connects to the owner's computer via a USB cable and Trezor-enabled wallet software, currently the wallets from Multibit and Electrum. The inventors are encouraging other wallet developers to support the device by making an emulator available based on the very popular and low-cost Raspberry PI–based computer platform. The device costs 1 bitcoin and, no, you can't buy it unless you use bitcoin.

Bitcoin Vaults   For the ultimate in security, however, nothing beats getting bitcoin off of the Internet. Zip drives, thumb drives, and other means of storing bitcoins offline are the answer. Rumor has it that the Winklevoss twins, of Facebook "fame," have stored their bitcoin assets on zip drives locked in a bank vault.

A firm called Xapo was launched in March 2014 to provide secure electronic storage services for bitcoin owners that uses multiple physical and logical locations and encryption techniques to store its customers' bitcoin.

The ultimate in offline storage is, in fact, paper. A public and private key pair can be printed out and secured in a vault. Perhaps there's a new use for all of those empty safety deposit boxes in local bank branches after all.

Trading Platforms   While exchanges lean toward serving the needs of those using bitcoin as currency, trading platforms are optimized for those who find bitcoin's commodity characteristics attractive. For this constituency, a trading platform is required. These systems provide user accounts with which to hold or withdraw funds as well as the core capability to buy and sell currency in an active marketplace. While not requiring the millisecond trading speeds (or faster) of the largest stock exchanges, a currency-trading platform must operate at subsecond speeds, especially to support a currency as dynamic, and thinly traded, as bitcoin.

Atlanta's CoinX is an example. Founded and led by CEO Megan Burton, CoinX is a bitcoin trading platform that, at the time of writing, is still in its beta test stage. As a business, CoinX has a long way to go but its leadership is steeped in regulatory compliance, financial management, and banking security. Burton herself has a successful track record as a provider of security services to Fortune 1000 firms, an attribute lacked by most early Bitcoin founders.

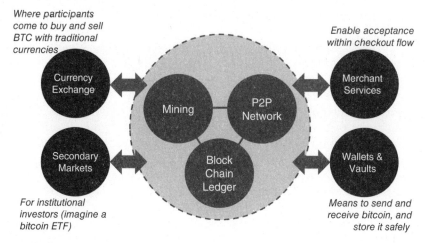

FIGURE 5.4 Bitcoin Ecosystem Enablers
Source: Glenbrook Partners

BITCOIN USE CASES IN PAYMENTS

As facilitators of value exchange, MBCs have, of course, multiple opportunities in the payments industry. Let's look at a few examples.

MBCs as Payment Rails

One of the immediate applications for Bitcoin and the MBCs that are emerging in its wake is its potential as a new set of payment rails. Rather than the incumbent card industry's reliance on the four-party model with its hierarchy of providers, authorization messages, and settlement steps that are necessary to complete a payment, Bitcoin and other MBCs promise a simpler cashlike process.

It's not quite that simple but it's not far off. Call it the two-and-a-half party model. There are, of course, the payer and the payee. The other half are payment service providers offering services such as currency exchanges, cash-in services to purchase bitcoins, trading desk, secure bitcoin storage (in a vault), and more.

Because Bitcoin is all about push payments between two end points, these facilitators of the Bitcoin ecosystem avoid most settlement risk. There's no authorization message and/or hours-long settlement lag. Once value is converted into BTC, transactions run over the peer-to-peer communication protocol that provides the payment rails. This works because every device, from the Internet Protocol's point of view, is a peer. (Despite our reliance on huge intermediaries like Google and Facebook, the Internet is fundamentally a peer-to-peer scheme.) Bitcoin and other digital currencies are simply using that Internet DNA and applying it to value exchange.

Putting aside the "bitcoin as store of value" discussion, banks and financial technology service providers should consider how these math-based payment rails could be employed. They have the potential to function as the currency equivalent of Esperanto, an intermediate lingua franca in the service of value exchange. As we'll see, international remittance is already an application for this approach and one that 61 percent of Glenbrook's survey respondents viewed as very important or critical. There are plenty of other use cases today and that number is growing as innovators explore new applications.

B2B Payments—The Known Counterparty

One of the simplest use cases but perhaps least obvious for MBCs as payment rails is in business-to-business payments. Yes, these are high-value transactions and it's unlikely CFOs and corporate treasury leadership will jump at the chance to save $50 on a $1 million payment. But over time, the advantages of immediate payment timed to the advantage of the sending firm may overcome corporate reticence. The expected lower cost (there will always be cost for security and fiscal controls) will only be a sweetener.

The limited number of participants in such a B2B payment scheme is one factor that could drive this use case. As known counterparties, both the sender and beneficiary could assure themselves of the soundness of the MBC method through careful pilots and the adaptation of existing security methods to the new rails. Unlike the multiday process required for an international payment via correspondent banking relationships, there is only an 8- to 10-minute time lag in a bitcoin transaction. The enterprise making the payment can hang on to its bitcoin-denominated funds until the last moment and then push the payment to the partner. Yes, currency arbitrage will be involved and that could be a good thing but the cash management aspects should prove especially compelling.

Bitcoin and Consumer Payments

Bitcoin's fit across all payments use cases is, of course, uneven. While MBCs have the potential to move value securely and cheaply, point of sale–level speed is not a leading attribute and that makes Bitcoin unsuitable across some important payment use cases.

As a push payment method, with cash as the physical analog, the expectation is that the transaction completes as fast as an in-person cash transaction. That is not the case.

Once a transaction occurs, the Bitcoin client sends a message that the transaction has occurred to its nearest peers on the Bitcoin network. Each of these immediately distributes the message on to its direct peers. This message about the transaction's existence is distributed globally in a matter of a few seconds over the Bitcoin peer-to-peer network. That's impressive but insufficient.

The time lag that really matters is the time it takes for the transaction to be written into the block chain, the public transaction ledger, to produce the validated evidence that the transaction has occurred. Having the transaction written into six copies of the block chain, a generally accepted level of transaction proof, requires more than the 8 or 10 minutes that, by algorithmic design, are needed to create the first block. That time limitation is a concern in a number of use cases.

Buy Me a Beer   For low-value transactions on high-margin goods or services, waiting for that 5- or 10-minute time period isn't a high-risk decision or merchant priority. The Pembury Tavern in Hackney, London, one of a four-location chain that accepts bitcoin, has a programmer owner who, having written his own point-of-sale (POS) system, added bitcoin support himself. The pub's POS terminal now displays the QR code representing the pub's public key, its target wallet. For that sale, the patron starts his bitcoin wallet app, snaps the QR code with his phone's camera from inside the app, and the bitcoins are on the way. (Notice the total absence of a POS payment terminal device in this transaction.) The barkeep serves up a pint once the transaction message reaches his system but without waiting for block chain confirmation on the assumption that even a fraud-inclined patron will be reluctant to leave a perfectly good pint of ale behind. By this same logic, a coffee shop would have little risk if it accepted Bitcoin because its costs are so low relative to its selling prices. Indeed, any location with very low chargeback rates could be a candidate for Bitcoin. McDonalds? Burger King?

E-Commerce and MBCs   Similarly, the block chain entry lag would not be an issue for an e-commerce merchant shipping physical goods given the more than adequate time lag between an online payment and actual shipment of a product or delivery of a subscription service. You simply wait for the money to arrive. Amazon's physical goods sales would have no risk.

Even Amazon's on-demand cloud-based movie rental business could be a candidate. The movie could begin streaming once the message about the transaction arrives. If the money doesn't show up within 10 minutes, the movie playback could be suspended until the problem's been addressed and the payment has been made. Why bother stealing the first ten minutes of a movie?

Getting Harder: Music and Video   A more problematic use case is a music download. Customers expect to get their music immediately. A 5- to 10-minute wait is not acceptable in a world where instant access to the catalog of iTunes or Amazon's MP3 music store is expected.

Challenges at the POS   Bitcoin's transaction speed shortcomings become more problematic in high-value POS transactions. A customer at Best Buy doesn't want to wait 10 minutes for transaction certainty before walking out the door with the new iPad or big-screen TV.

Improving Bitcoin Processes   Such challenging use cases can all be mitigated by stronger authentication and the assumption of risk. Bankers know how to mitigate such risks. The methods required to manage risk do add cost but they also provide opportunity for payment services providers. One of Glenbrook's Payments Principles is that "risk pays." While once it would have been difficult to market such services to elements of the Bitcoin community, committed to its "free" nature, that belief will run up against real world needs for risk mitigation. More important, for any MBC to succeed, usage matters. Financial technology providers and their established methods may find a market for their risk mitigation services around Bitcoin's core services.

Some consumers, accustomed to "zero liability" and the ability to charge back transactions, will struggle with the learning curve needed to safely conduct "push" transactions via MBCs. Education will be required. Experience certainly. Much better bitcoin wallet applications will be needed. Removing the complexity and mystery from bitcoin transactions is a task for creative user interface and process designers.

Improving the Bitcoin Protocol

Because of the programmability of the protocol itself and services around it, there is much that can be done to improve its current performance. The keepers of the protocol, the open source software leadership working on Bitcoin's evolution, have planned some significant improvements that expand the protocol to include information about the transaction itself. For incumbent payment providers and MBC companies alike, the availability of this metadata has much to do with consumer acceptance and uptake. Improvements under consideration include:

- *Merchant payment request.* When making a small purchase, the amount of bitcoin required for the payment could be as small as 0.00000001 BTC (this smallest of units is called a "satoshi"). Imagine the error rate on transaction values like 0.84268801 BTC if the consumer has to enter that value by hand on a smartphone screen. The Bitcoin protocol is adding a feature called PaymentRequest. The seller or merchant can communicate the amount of the transaction to the customer. The customer then simply approves the transaction and pushes the bitcoin payment to the merchant through her wallet app.
- *Merchant payment acknowledgement and receipting.* The companion message scheduled for inclusion in the next revision of the Bitcoin protocol is PaymentACK, a message from the merchant acknowledging receipt of payment.
- *PaymentACK then becomes the vehicle for a receipt.* If the merchant fails to deliver the promised good, the receipt can serve as a very public proof of payment that could be used by the buyer in a dispute. In this hyperconnected world of social media, merchants will have to manage their transactional reputation as well as their brand. Indeed, the two will become very publicly intertwined.
- *Merchant authentication.* For merchant-initiated transactions—please pay me—the customer has to be certain that the requester is, in fact, who they claim to be. Borrowing a well-understood technology, the payment request will be signed by a digital certificate issued by a central authority. For those Bitcoin zealots who mistrust any central authority, the use of digital certificates issued by a central authority is antithetical but it is the right choice, one indicating the maturation of the Bitcoin development leadership guiding the protocol's evolution. Financial institutions, especially those in the merchant acquiring business, could serve as trusted certificate authorities as they already do. Payment service providers like merchant processors could provide the same function.
- *Transaction descriptors.* A description field is being added to allow a merchant to communicate human readable, detailed information about the transaction itself, not unlike the item description field of today's consumer card payment statements. Fortunately, the Bitcoin description field will allow for far longer entries.
- *Easier subscriptions.* Because bitcoin transactions are push payments from the buyer to the seller, subscription-based publishers and merchants

have been reluctant to deploy bitcoin. Membership organizations are already using the card-on-file mechanism and preauthorized payments to charge recurring subscription payments to a consumer's card account. Bitcoin has to have similar capability. A reminder message facility is being added that takes the reminder burden off of the seller. Wallets could also be developed to respond, with payments, to those publishers with whom the buyer has a subscription plan or membership relationship.

Many of these improvements are, of course, already firmly established in the card payments space. It took decades for the card payment infrastructure to evolve to this point. Bitcoin is just getting started.

Programming Bitcoin for a Special Case: Online Micropayments

One of the uses cases for virtual currencies and a continued vexing problem for online services providers and publishers of digital content is the desire to sell access for transactions valued between one penny and five dollars. Think of buying an article at a journal you visit infrequently, connecting to a Wi-Fi network when you're traveling, or simply leaving a tip for a blogger whose work you appreciate.

The economics of using the card network for these transactions makes such transactions impractical because of the per transaction fee. Even transaction aggregation for a 24-hour period or a few days does not lower the transaction cost sufficiently to make it practical for infrequent sellers of sub-$1 services. What works for Apple's iTunes with its payment aggregation abilities won't work for the local newspaper or town blogger.

One idea is to use Bitcoin to meet this need. For example, a Wi-Fi network access operator would accept a small amount of bitcoin for payment. But Bitcoin won't work here because of the 5- to 10-minute time it takes to write the transaction to the ledger. The answer lies in the programmability of the Bitcoin protocol. A micropayment channel could be added to perform very fast micropayment transactions that draw on a prepaid Bitcoin purse as the source of funding. Like a closed-loop prepaid program designed just for micropayments, a modest balance in this bitcoin wallet could be used to pay for these minuscule transaction.

Another technical reason for this purse-based approach would be to avoid the high volume of traffic created by all of these tiny payment transactions as only the funding transaction would need to be written to the block chain ledger. Otherwise, that volume could degrade the Bitcoin P2P network's performance. Just like the box of coins I carry in my car for parking meters, we'd set aside a portion of a bitcoin for our very small ticket online purchases. A Bitcoin micropayments specialist could settle the transaction volume on a periodic basis.

In the meantime, bitcoin-denominated micropayments are taking place. Bitcoin browser extensions like KryptoKit's Bitcoin Wallet make it easy to send bitcoin to a blogger or a nonprofit. The recipient simply advertises its public key on its Web page and the Bitcoin wallet extension finds it and, when selected by the user, displays a simple screen that lets the user enter an amount to leave. It's quite straightforward. Start-up BitWall is taking this model to market specifically for publishers. Integrated with Bitcoin exchange CoinBase, BitWall is working to support the idea of accepting very small transactions for online content, especially those in the subdollar range. Taking Bitcoin directly is one option; however, because of its relationship with CoinBase's exchange functions, BitWall is expected to bring dollar-denominated micropayments to the publisher, no doubt for a higher cost.

Wallets

What's in it for a financial institution (FI)? Why not provide an automated top-up service that queries the wallet's balance and, once it reaches a preset low-balance condition, automatically tops up the account with a push payment? The FI may charge a modest fee for the top-up or make a little money on the exchange rate. In any case, its customer will no longer have to worry if she has the "coin" to connect to a public Wi-Fi network or get behind a publisher's paywall.

RIPPLE: THE SECOND MBC

Bitcoin was the first MBC out of the starting gate and we've seen that it suffers from shortcomings, many of which are addressable by protocol updates or external risk management. But other entrepreneurs and technologists have examined Satoshi Nakamoto's brilliant insights and decided to develop very different models.

Ripple, from Ripple Labs, is the leading and most highly evolved example. Ripple and Bitcoin both use math-based approaches to secure value transfer. Both have a hard upper limit on the number of possible currency units (21 million BTC, 100 billion XRP, the Ripple currency denominator). Both use a ledger to route and record transactions. Both have put the protocol development into the open source community. But there the similarities largely end.

Ripple Labs is a business. It intends to make money by increasing the value of XRP, 25 percent of which it plans to retain. As Ripple's utility grows and the demand for XRP grows with it, Ripple Labs will gradually sell its currency holdings. Ripple Labs is the architect and designer of the protocol. XRP is used less as a store of value and more as the carrier of value between nodes on the Ripple network.

Instead of a single, multi-gigabyte block chain containing the transactional history of every bitcoin ever created, the Ripple protocol uses a distributed database that is updated every 5 to 10 seconds and saved into a copy unique for that specific time slot. Once operating at full speed, the Ripple network will create over 6 million transaction snapshots per year. The Ripple ledger containing account and transaction records operates by consensus. Fraudulent transactions and the sources of those fraudulent transactions, the bad actors, are identified and, by consensus among sets of Ripple servers, eliminated or ignored. In effect, the Ripple protocol has an immune system against fraudulent activity.

The Ripple currency XRP has no counterparty. While XRP has real value, it is optimized to support the secure flow of bits over Ripple's value exchange rails. Gateways are expanding to connect multiple currencies to the Ripple network, a collection of transaction accounts. Unlike Bitcoin, Ripple allows transactions to flow across the network in any currency. The Ripple design includes distributed exchange capability that automates currency trades to support cross-currency payments. When a direct currency corridor is absent, Ripple employs XRP as an intermediary for value exchange.

The future, for both Ripple and Bitcoin, will be crafted by those who adopt and use these approaches. Bitcoin was placed into the hands of its global caretakers to see what happens as it matures. Ripple's design takes advantage of some lessons from early Bitcoin evolution to address functional shortcomings of its predecessor. Ripple is under far more directed guidance as well. While which model is right for financial institutions is not yet clear, Ripple's sophistication is without question and will deserve close examination.

MBC USE CASES IN BANKING

How can financial institutions take on MBCs and put them to work? This section examines a few other opportunities.

International Remittance Rails

The potential for MBCs in the international remittance business is squarely in the sights of multiple startups, from Circle Internet Financial to OpenCoin. That interest was confirmed by the Glenbrook's survey respondents, 61 percent of whom saw this application as very important or critical uses for Bitcoin.

Examples of Bitcoin's mainline use as a vehicle for international remittances are already in the market. For example, expense management company Expensify has added an interface supporting bitcoin transfers between its account holder and their independent contractors who perform project work. Other than providing the capability on its web site, Expensify has no involvement in the transaction. Remember, this is peer-to-peer payment with no need for an intermediary. And it is a very low cost transaction within the Bitcoin ecosystem. What it costs to convert bitcoin to and from the local fiat currency is another matter.

Note the distinction between "international remittance rails" and a Western Union or MoneyGram-level function. International remittance is about foreign exchange revenues and speed of transmitting funds to the beneficiary, requirements that MBCs certainly address. But the business of international remittance also hinges on a strong agent footprint in multiple locations and the ability to convert the electronic message back into cash. No MBC, in and of itself, can address that requirement.

That said, an MBC-based set of rails could help remitters manage their cash flow more efficiently and drop funds transmission costs while opening up possibilities for particular remittance corridors.

Bitcoin's impact on the foreign exchange market is infinitesimal compared to the nearly $4 trillion in daily spot or cash foreign exchange markets. From that perspective, there's only upside.

Interbank Settlement

As a new set of payment rails, Bitcoin could be put to use for interbank trading and settlement. As a peer-to-peer network, it could flatten the trading and settlement relationships within the international banking world itself. When every financial institution becomes an equal player on the same network, every financial institution has the reach of the largest money center banks.

Tiny Austrian software firm Bits of Proof is building Bitcoin applications that communicate to the IBM middleware that surrounds the core banking applications of some of the largest global financial institutions. The idea is to put each institution, as a full peer, onto the Bitcoin network.

This "peering" of financial institutions via a single flat value exchange web is the vision of Ripple Labs, designer of the Ripple network and its XRP math-based currency.

The inference here is, of course, the substitution of SWIFT-based functions with an MBC-based scheme. Serious examination of that opportunity by serious business teams is under way; a major investor in Circle Internet Financial is the former CEO of SWIFT.

Building Trust with MBCs

Programmers are adding features within and around Bitcoin that improve transactional trust. The Bitcoin protocol itself has trust at its foundation given the strength of its double spend protections that essentially prevent bitcoin counterfeiting. FIs have the opportunity to take their natural strengths, including KYC capabilities as well as institutional trust, and build revenue streams supporting Bitcoin or another MBC.

Card networks, based on payment authorization and subsequent settlement messages, include dispute resolution processes and chargeback mechanisms designed to protect the consumer. While chargebacks may prove challenging for merchants (or drive them crazy), the process provides a level of trust in the system without which the entire scheme could fail. While the costs may be distributed asymmetrically, the process works.

Bitcoin faces a considerable trust challenge. Leaving aside Bitcoin's novel nature and its struggle to get out from under its association with criminal activity, the very cashlike push aspect of Bitcoin transactions requires strong trust-building mechanisms to be in place, especially for transactions where the parties are separated by distance or there is a lag in delivery time. I don't want to send money to someone about whose trustworthiness I have doubts or no evidence whatsoever. Many early online buyers learned that lesson the hard way, sending money via PayPal to an eBay seller for an auction item and then never receiving it. Similarly, an online merchant selling physical goods for bitcoin or an international remittance transaction using bitcoin poses trust risks for the parties. In both cases, proof of receipt of funds to the recipient and not just a wallet address becomes important.

Automated escrow services are an answer. With these tools standing in the middle of the transaction, escrow service rules, agreed to by both sender and beneficiary, might require proof of payment to the beneficiary based on inspection of the PaymentRequest, transaction ID, and PaymentACK messages written to the block chain. Once these are in place, the escrow service would release the funds.

This trusted mediator role represents an opportunity for financial institutions and their partners. Despite the overhang of "too big to fail" controversies and the mortgage debacle, survey after survey continue to demonstrate that consumers trust FIs as stewards of their transactional lives. Financial institutions could offer escrow services of their own or utilize escrow services they have vetted as a feature of their consumer banking offering. Financial institutions could extend their certificate authority (CA) role to escrow service providers. As acquiring banks, they might serve as CAs for the merchants in their portfolio.

Because human intervention is so expensive, another approach is further automation of the process via a two of three transaction process. In these "N-of-N" transactions, if a dispute results, two of three parties may resolve the dispute by agreeing on what action to take. Of course, all participants must agree, beforehand, to such terms of what is, in effect, automated arbitration. The mediator does not take possession of the funds, just a role in directing their release or return.

Automating Transaction Policies

A hard focus on replacing existing functions with MBC-based technology severely limits what's actually possible. A growing proportion of Bitcoin-related discussion today looks beyond Bitcoin as currency or payment rails. The conversation has turned toward using the block chain as a public ledger supporting a range of asset types.

MBCs and the services providers using them could enable even more interesting services including the automation of transaction flows based on defined policies. For example, an online "oracle"—just a piece of software that examines policies and the state of required conditions—could manage the timing of an inheritance. The oracle would review both the beneficiary's birthday (is she over 21?) and the date of donor death (is he dead yet?). Almost any set of circumstances that requires validation of certain conditions for the exchange of value could benefit from these policy-based approaches. Crowdfunding without a Kickstarter is another example. Another could be the creation of an investment fund based on transparent policies. A policy might require a AA credit rating from two rating agencies and a bond that matures within six months and pays an average of 3 percent interest. The permutations are endless.

There is even discussion of using the Bitcoin block chain as a means of controlling property via cryptographic proof of ownership (see Figure 5.5). This "smart property" could be used as a collateral in a sale. Consider a borrower in need who sells his car to a lender while needing to continue to use the car. Via Age of Context technologies (a connected car) and a policy that includes a time limiting component (no late payments), the need for the lender to trust the borrower is reduced. Based on the policy and automation, the lender can turn off the car if the borrower doesn't make the payment. When the borrower makes the payment, the car can read proof of payment in the block chain and return to operation.

MBCs may be used to support uncollateralized lending, a person-to-person bond market or investment fund, all because of the transactional transparency the block chain or its equivalent confers.

Financial Services	Public Records	Private Records
Currency	Land titles	Contracts
Private equities	Vehicle registrations	Signatures
Public equities	Business license	Wills
Bonds	Incorporation/Dissolution records	Trusts
Derivatives/Futures	Passports	Escrows
Commodities	Birth/Death certificates	GPS trails
Mortgages/Loans	Health/Safety inspections	
Crowd funding	Court records	

FIGURE 5.5   Block Chain as Asset Register
Source: Glenbrook Partners

MOVING AHEAD WITH MBCs

It's all about partnering, of course. No one expects a financial institution to build its own Bitcoin tools.

What to Look For

1. *Strong, licensed exchanges.* Well-financed, highly available, low-cost, regulation-loving exchanges have to exist. And, for the most part, they are just coming on the scene now. CoinBase and Circle Internet Financial, founded by experienced entrepreneurs and backed by well-known venture capitalists and investors, are examples of the kind of business the MBC ecosystem requires.
2. For large institutions, lower Bitcoin volatility and faster settlement of Bitcoin to local currency could lower cost.
3. *Anti–money laundering and KYC expertise.* These operational skills are table stakes. While compliance skills were once a differentiator, they have to be part of the provider's DNA today. Money transmitter licenses have to be in place.

What to Look Out For

1. *Amateurish operation.* Waving a red flag at a bull is a good idea only if you're an experienced matador, and even then it's fringe behavior. Contravening long-standing money service business regulations or frustrating

consumer access to their money are flag-waving activities. Frustrating customers with poor customer service and extended system downtime erode confidence in the Bitcoin ecosystem. Fortunately, good operations —well-financed organizations, backed by experienced venture capital investors, and led by seasoned business people—are on the scene.

2. *Overregulation.* Internet history is replete with the tension between the potential for the technology and the need to regulate human behavior. Bitcoin and all MBCs are no different. Some have argued that Bitcoin transactions shouldn't be taxed. That obviously won't play. The risk to MBCs is that bad or incompetent actors will instigate an overreaction by government regulators or, worse, politicians unfamiliar with technology development and the power of existing regulations.

Fortunately, to date, U.S. government regulation of Bitcoin and other virtual currencies has been measured and appropriate. The U.S. FINCEN classification of exchanges as money transmitters was appropriate. The IRS decision to classify bitcoins as property, with all the capital gains tracking overhead that that entails,is awkward at best but it still recognizes the legitimacy of the approach. Square has received equal treatment from Florida's regulators over money service businesses. The German government has classified Bitcoin as a currency and, as result, it is entitled to equal treatment including strong regulation with minimum funding levels to assure operation.

China and Russia, however, have taken active measures to make using Bitcoin impractical (China) or illegal (Russia).

The bust and prosecution of the Silk Road operation and its founder has been a net positive for the Bitcoin ecosystem. Rather than plummeting in value, bitcoin value rose smartly after the bust and reached new pricing levels shortly thereafter. While new Silk Roads have come and gone, the connection between them and the huge potential of MBCs should modulate regulatory reaction.

Foreign currencies have always been a refuge for citizens living in fiscally uncertain times. The U.S. dollar has often served as just such a currency refuge. For example, citizens of Argentina have long used the dollar to hedge against the gyrations of their local currency. Once again, during 2013, Argentines have found themselves in that situation. Having survived the Argentine meltdown of 2001, Argentines are once again looking for safety. However, the government has imposed strict current controls, making legitimate foreign exchange into dollars or euros very difficult. That's left few options, forcing citizens to invest in far less fungible hard goods like automobiles and real estate as alternative store of value ploys. Bitcoin has emerged, among an admittedly small group, as an alternative currency to the peso. Real estate has changed hands using bitcoin as the currency. At least one real estate agent has advertised available rental property that can be rented for bitcoin through an online advertisement: "Rent studio in downtown Bariloche, lake view, accept bitcoins."

CONCLUSION

History has not been kind to those who have resisted the nearly inexorable force of Internet-connected technologies. The music industry is just one example. Ever since digital music became popular—and widely pirated—the music business has been fighting a rearguard action against the digitization of its product, all the while alienating many of its customers. There's been no easy answer to the problem. Except, of course, for Apple who shifted music publisher profits into hardware (iPod music players) and its own distribution system (iTunes).

One way to view MBCs is through that lens of recent history and the technical analogy of MP3, the digital music format that made music digital and rocked the music industry. MBCs are a bit like that. You can see them coming but what do you do about them?

First, don't ignore math-based currencies. And, unless these approaches are regulated into the shadows, don't think they will stay at the margins. Bitcoin or some other math-based currency, Ripple perhaps, has potential for banks, financial institutions, money transmitters, and many more. There's every likelihood multiple alternative MBCs will find useful, long-term roles. Once one or two major banks employ or connect to math-based currencies, many others will jump in. The combination of MBCs flexible and secure technical underpinnings with banking's regulatory and fiduciary position in the economy could be a perfect match.

However, it could be that math-based currencies become MP3-like kryptonite for the banking industry. As individuals and businesses start to use MBCs for an expanding range of use cases, beginning with providers solving small but useful problems, banks could fall further behind in their attempts to remain at the center of their customer's financial life. The answer will lie in smarter, faster, and more innovative partnering to gain access to the capabilities needed to cement those relationships. Now that the software ecosystem is so much broader than it was even five years ago, financial institutions have much better access to new services, including these emerging math-based currencies. Getting ready via education and market research will prepare you today for the next steps of internal pilot tests and market trials via partnerships.

No one can accuse financial institutions of rushing into taking the first mover advantage. Betting exclusively on the first mover position of Bitcoin may be risky. Maybe Ripple is a more bank friendly alternative. But in this Age of Context where remarkable combinations of technology will swiftly emerge, waiting too long to participate in this MBC-driven value exchange web could be detrimental.

By not moving, the banking industry continues to experience disintermediation, the disconnection of consumers from their banks for a variety of functions including payments. There are even companies making a bet that they can deliver better banking services than banks.

Moving money is one of the last functions to remain within the exclusive domain of financial institutions and their chartered partners. MBCs represent an alternative means of moving value. As that value exchange is such an essential function, financial institutions and their financial technology partners need to be ahead of the MBC phenomenon.

CHAPTER 6

The Smart Pipe

Models that Will Survive
the Next Generation

"The last buggy whip factory was no doubt a model of efficiency."
—Peter Drucker, Management Consultant

There is a growing belief in many developed markets that banking as a service or product has largely become a commodity and has been reduced to a "dumb pipe" that simply provides the "plumbing" to lend money, or move money from point A to point B. The traditional way of applying for a loan at a bank branch, or wiring money from one person to another, certainly is outdated with the proliferation of mobile, widely available information, and nonbank companies that provide significant customer convenience and delight. If the financial services industry does not spend more time developing new strategies to stay relevant, the best scenario for most banks might simply be to become the smartest, most efficient "dumb pipe." We've seen some revolutionary changes in the way many products are distributed around the world: music can now be purchased just one song at a time; newspapers and books are now delivered electronically; and, as we discussed, in Korea, food shopping can be done in a subway station and purchases delivered within an hour. There is no reason to think banking won't also go through a profound change in the way its services are delivered. That does not mean banks will necessarily be replaced, but it does mean that there will be some profound business model shifts that will need to occur to stay in business. In this chapter, we'll outline some of the perspectives on where and how the financial services industry might discover the next generation of viable models that will usher us into the twenty-second century.

THE PREPAID MODEL

Prepaid has been around for years, particularly in emerging markets, where the "spend as you go" approach works well, particularly in environments where prepaid phone cards are the norm. Traditionally, banks make money from a smaller number of large transactions; mobile companies often make their money from a large number of very small transactions. Since the bank model is based on float, deposits, and lending, it doesn't favor numerous transactions in small amounts compared to a mobile operator model, which bases its revenue model on usage. Banks have also traditionally overlooked prepaid models with the belief that they served unbanked customers that may not be profitable or creditworthy. Two things have happened that are making banks evaluate what prepaid might have to offer. First, recent regulation has set price controls on debit interchange fees, making it more difficult for banks to make money on debit card transactions. Second, we are now seeing many types of customers across income brackets gravitate to prepaid cards, no longer concerned about the need to write checks or have traditional bank accounts. Consumers are driving the shift from cash and checks to electronic payments, as preferences change from check writing to electronic bill payment and card payments. Prepaid cards favor these trends (see Figure 6.1). They still allow consumers to have direct deposit and the ability to access their accounts wherever major network brands (Visa, MasterCard, etc.) are accepted, but without the fees that usually accompany bank accounts. Consumers surveyed indicate that they generally like the fact that they cannot overspend with a prepaid card and do not have to worry about overdraft fees. For banks, prepaid cards are less costly to service—in some cases, as much as 40 percent cheaper.[1] With prepaid, credit checks and paper statements are not required. American Express has made some particularly large investments in this area with its Bluebird card, sold at Wal-Mart, with very few fees attached. Other large providers of prepaid include Green Dot and NetSpend, often positioned as a lower-cost alternative to a bank account that can cater to newly minted graduates, the unbanked, or unhappily banked consumers. Since these products are often sold in retail stores, they often enjoy a significant distribution advantage compared to traditional banking institutions. If you can make opening a financial account as simple as purchasing a card from a retail store and following instructions on a mobile phone and offer benefits similar to banking services, it can be a very compelling proposition.

How can banks take advantage of technology and consumer trends and get more involved with prepaid without losing their own customer base? It is inevitable that banks will lose some customers, and offering a simpler, lower-cost alternative to the traditional bank account is one way to

Feature	Bank Checking	General Purpose Prepaid
POS, ATM and digital transactions	☑	☑
Good funds model	☑	☑
Overdraft	☑	
Check-writing	☑	
Transaction fees	☑	☑
Bill payment	☑	☑
Paper statement	☑	
Online statement	☑	☑
Reload/Deposit	☑	☑
Employer direct deposit	☑	☑
KYC required	☑	☑
Credit check required	☑	
FDIC insurance	☑	☑

FIGURE 6.1   Many Traditional Banking Products Can Now Be Substituted with Prepaid Products
Source: Jim Bruene, Online Banker.

compete. Most financial institutions will need to partner with companies that are driving the next generation of powerful experiences in prepaid. This means that banks must consider becoming the very best account custodians for prepaid, even if it means leaving innovation and branding to others.

PREPAID NATION: REDEFINING WHAT A BANK CAN BE[2]

Matt Harris knows a thing or two about prepaid. He is an influential venture capitalist and thought leader in the financial services industry, who often invests in business models that can be considered disruptive to the banking industry, including prepaid. Currently he is a partner at Bain Capital Ventures, and he is also the cofounder and managing general partner of Village Ventures. Matt concentrates on the growing penetration of nonfinancial institutions into the financial services industry. Some of his key investments include BlueTarp, Consumer United, Dwolla, iSend, On Deck Capital, Simple, TxVia, and Zipmark. One of the opportunities Matt sees for the banking industry is prepaid. In the remainder of this section, Matt writes his perspective on where prepaid might take us.

* * *

Until recently, there were three types of payment cards, and each of them stayed pretty much in its place. Credit cards and debit cards were issued by banks, the former to provide transactional lending (pay later), and the latter to provide access to a current account (pay now). Prepaid cards, the new kid on the block, were still largely a gifting vehicle, but increasingly also included a general-use, open-loop reloadable version. These cards were a stored value account purchased either fully loaded or where value could be added through various load mechanisms (pay before).

But now that old triumvirate is crumbling. In particular, the prepaid card has rebelliously left its historical place as either a gift card or a card of last refuge for the underbanked, and has now entered the mainstream. This development poses many risks for community financial institutions, as the prepaid architecture gives rise to all sorts of entrepreneurial competition. That said, prepaid is also a significant opportunity to broaden product lines and modernize customer-facing applications without massive changes to core processing systems. How financial institutions grapple with, take advantage of, or succumb to prepaid may determine their relevance in the coming decades.

What do we mean by prepaid, and why is it so disruptive? The trade association for prepaid cards, the Network Branded Prepaid Card Association (NBPCA), defines prepaid cards as a "non-credit payment option,"[3] a classic example of the fallacy of defining something by what it is not. The organization does go on to usefully enumerate the largest categories of prepaid card: General Purpose Reloadable (GPR), Payroll, Incentive, Healthcare, Government Disbursement, and Gift. This inability to define prepaid is a general problem, and the NBPCA provides a version of the most common type of answer: It isn't a bank account, it isn't a credit card, and here's a list of examples of what it can be.

The problem with this definition and all of its variants is that they are quickly becoming dated. How is a prepaid account different from a bank account, when it comes with paper checks, automated teller machine (ATM) access, and Federal Deposit Insurance Corporation (FDIC) insurance? How is it different than a credit card now that companies like Insight Card Services and AccountNow offer hybrid products with a short-term lending component? These product distinctions (checking, savings, line of credit, credit card, etc.) have always been driven by regulators and bank technology vendors, not by consumer preferences in any event. The prepaid architecture is allowing them to collapse into a single account structure, with many diverse features, making the definition of prepaid as what it is not now impossible. And as the categories of prepaid multiply out from the six listed earlier, into Travel, Expense Management, Insurance, and Digital Content, among many others, defining prepaid by example becomes long-winded at best.

For the purposes of this chapter, there are two important characteristics of a prepaid card or account (in general, I will use prepaid card, but it's important to note that increasingly prepaid accounts won't need an accompanying card):

- Prepaid cards reduce the financial institution to the role of commodity utility, allowing an independent program manager to design and market the product, as well as manage customer interactions.
- Prepaid cards have limited transactional interaction with core banking systems, in that they create an account structure that sits atop a single pooled traditional debit account. Individual transactions hit against this intermediary account structure, which in most all cases is more modern, flexible, and feature-rich than a core banking system.

The combination of these two factors has allowed the prepaid card to be the primary vector by which entrepreneurial firms have entered the consumer financial services arena, threatening territory traditionally monopolized by banks and credit unions. These firms are redefining what can be offered to consumers and small businesses and, in doing so, shifting the basis of competition.

The latest wave of innovation in prepaid is focused on capturing the primary account for consumers, which had historically been a combination of a demand deposit account (DDA) and a savings account, almost always held by a "local" bank or credit union. Obviously, the term *local* when discussing financial services is fraught, given that the four largest banks control approximately 40 percent of household banking assets from central headquarters locations, but it has historically been the case that the majority of consumers chose their primary bank based on branch location, so if a Chase branch is the closest to your home or work, it is your "local" bank. Because of this dynamic, the consumer banking industry became largely a real estate play. The national banks went on a branch-building spree, aiming to become the bank of choice in the cities and larger towns, and truly local financial institutions took comfort in the knowledge that so long as they were a convenient option in their trading area, they would get their share of deposits.

Prior to the smartphone, it was difficult for any nonbank to challenge this physical reality except on the basis of offering high interest rates for savings accounts or CDs. It is telling that the latent threat to financial institutions was always Wal-Mart, and, in fact, prepaid partnerships with GreenDot and American Express enabled that latent threat to become very real. Wal-Mart always had the real estate, and the prepaid architecture has allowed them to offer financial products, with a geographic density far greater than any branch network. That said, Wal-Mart's customer base and brand positioning are such that the customers they are siphoning off from traditional financial institutions are generally the unbanked and underbanked. The graver threat, from a customer profitability perspective, are what are often called the "neo-banks"— nimble, entrepreneurial firms that are leveraging the prevalence of the smartphone to convince customers that physical proximity no longer matters.

Who are these neo-banks? The most public examples are Simple and Moven, but the prepaid architecture is so straightforward and flexible that many more are just launching or in formation. Perhaps the example that proves the point most dramatically is Card.com. Card.com has created prepaid debit cards that are as fully featured as most bank accounts, and are cobranded with dozens (heading towards hundreds) of micro-affiliates. Effectively, you can get a "bank account" that shows the world your affection for Gay Pride, Garfield the Cat, Frida Kahlo, or *The Walking Dead* television show, among many others. While it's easy to dismiss these as trivial, many banks had the same reaction when MBNA launched its affiliate model in the credit card industry, only to find itself thoroughly outflanked.

This proliferation of neo-banks has been enabled by technology. As mentioned, the core innovation that enables mainstream adoption of branchless banking is the smartphone, but there are companion technologies that are just as instrumental. The primary category of innovation is around account opening. Traditionally, account opening was almost entirely done in a branch, as much of it had to be done in person. Companies like Jumio and Andera have now enabled Web-based account opening, and even phone-only account opening, leveraging electronic signatures. Once the account is open, technology from Mitek and others enable mobile remote deposit capture, so that checks can be loaded into an account without a branch or even an ATM visit. One by one, the reasons to visit a branch are being demolished.

In the first instance, this seems largely like a threat to community financial institutions (FIs). Not only do you have the "big four" marketing into your base, but you have national branchless players trying to poach your customers. But let's imagine the possibilities whereby community FIs can leverage these trends and capabilities to their benefit. The fact is that most community FIs have been offering relatively plain vanilla products because they are dependent on their core system vendor to provide them functionality, and none of the large vendors are exactly dynamic. Community FIs need to consider ways they can leverage the flexibility of prepaid technology to innovate and move more quickly.

One opportunity is generational. The demographics of credit unions and local banks are not promising for the future; to be blunt, they skew old. Unless these financial institutions can survive as the bank of choice as the wealth and locus of banking activity moves from one generation to the next, they will become increasingly irrelevant. Prepaid is one weapon in that fight. It makes a perfect teen product, given its natural limits on overspending and the ability to add parental controls. It's useful for parents with children away at college, allowing them to load money for expenses as needed. In either of these instances, it becomes an opportunity to convert the child/recipient into a primary account owner over time. In particular, the community FI can leverage the relationship with the parent to offer credit to the next generation, with the parent as guarantor. At that stage of life, anyone who will offer credit becomes a student's best friend.

Another significant opportunity is within the small business segment within a community FI's trading area. Although there are some neo-banks now getting started to serve the small business population, no one has critical mass. These small companies are hard to reach, and frequently value their relationship with a local bank (or, less frequently, credit union) as a source of credit when needed. Small businesses have a variety of needs that prepaid can solve quite elegantly. More and more employers are offering health savings accounts (HSAs), based on prepaid technology, to their employees as an alternative to traditional health benefits. Prepaid cards can provide a less expensive alternative to paper checks for small businesses that employ the underbanked. Many industries that employ salespeople use prepaid cards as a sales incentive program; local banks are in a great position to provide this technology to small businesses. One area where prepaid has already started to make an inroad, largely driven by a PEX Card, is in the expense management area. This, too, is a product that could be logically distributed by community FIs.

If the community FI has both a solid consumer base and good relationship among the local small business community, there is an opportunity to capitalize on the opportunity presented by linking those two groups via prepaid. The economics of traditional debit, post Durbin, do not allow for bank-funded rewards programs to generate new accounts or create loyalty. That said, a community financial institution could leverage its relationships with local retailers to create a merchant-funded rewards program, which helps them to drive traffic to their stores and creates a distinctive product for the bank or credit union. Further along this theme, the FI could create a specialized gift card, leveraging Restricted Authorized Network

(RAN) technology to limit the spend on the card to local retailers. Again, a distinctive product for consumers that provides unique value to a financial institution's small business customers.

As has been articulated throughout this book, new innovations in financial services are both opportunities and threats for community financial institutions. Prepaid is a dramatic example of this important point. Small banks and credit unions have traditionally survived and thrived based on their local relationships and physical footprint; the prepaid architecture has unleashed the entrepreneurial energies of dozens of new and compelling branchless competitors, who challenge long-standing relationships and make geographic density irrelevant. Prepaid also provides a vector for innovation for community FIs themselves, enabling them to partner with entrepreneurs to create and offer cutting-edge products to local customers who otherwise would lack awareness or access to these innovations. It is critical to recognize that there is little time to ponder this issue; the competition is on the move, and the only question is: will local banks and credit unions be as well?

THE "UNDERBANKED" AND OPPORTUNITIES FOR INNOVATION

There are 70 million adults in the United States that are ultimately "unbanked" and "underbanked" and, on top of that, "unhappily" banked. The number of free checking accounts has gone down dramatically—less than 25 percent are free. In addition, the average bank fee has gone up to 20 percent a year, and the amount of overdraft fees in the past year reached $31 billion. Around the world, 2.5 billion people don't have bank accounts.[4] In the United States, we may see more people forgoing traditional bank accounts in favor of something simpler, more convenient, and less expensive.

A recent study by Tufts University indicated that underbanked individuals are likely to pay $4 per month more to access their own money than those with formal financial services access, and have a five times higher risk of paying fees with payroll cards.[5] It is expensive to be poor, but technology and business innovation are allowing institutions to offer traditionally underserved and even mainstream customers financial products that have traditionally cost them much more. As a result of new software platforms, retail partnerships, mobility, and prepaid cards, basic accounts can be serviced at a lower level and are morphing into full-service money management tools. The American Express Bluebird account now has over a dozen ways to load into an account and many ways to access it at low or no cost. These initiatives are democratizing access and expanding the opportunity for significantly more individuals and households to access basic financial services at a more reasonable cost.

Technology can better serve tens of millions of people in the United States and significantly more around the world. Banks have traditionally thought about those that do not have a bank account as poor, but the reality is that this growing population represents the new middle class. Most are working paycheck to paycheck, scarred by recession, and define their financial objectives as: spend wisely, avoid debt, and struggle to put some savings away. Roughly 45 percent of middle-class Americans making between $50,000 and $100,000 a year spend all or more of their income on expenses.

This large population has a lot of financial issues that a new generation of financial offerings can help with—particularly when it comes to saving time and money. Historically, paying bills, getting cash, and cashing a check have been incredibly time consuming—it is practically a part-time job and incredibly inconvenient. Going to a check-cashing location is not a fun experience and often not safe. For these consumers, if they miss a payment, they have been forced to send a money order at a cost of $10. American Express is starting to see people use their prepaid services differently; almost 40 percent are using their new Bluebird account with direct deposit and leveraging the mobile application to pay bills and manage their money.

Stockpile: An Example of Brokerage Innovation Through Partnering

My company, Stockpile, is a good example of how technology companies and banks can partner in ways that can offer new revenue models for banks, while significantly improving access to stock ownership for generations of consumers that historically have been excluded. Through its website at www.stockpile .com, Stockpile offers consumers a very low cost way to buy, sell, or gift their favorite stocks by the dollar. Imagine making it as easy to buy stock as it is to buy a book from Amazon: add $10 of Home Depot, $50 of Starbucks, and $40 of Berkshire Hathaway stock to a shopping cart, check out, and the stock is in your brokerage account that night. Or imagine giving a gift of stock as easily as sending money by PayPal: pick a company and dollar amount (e.g., $25 of Apple), pay by credit card, and e-mail it to family or a friend. The recipient clicks on the e-mail and signs up or signs in to get her stock.

Stockpile's services are also offered through APIs that banks, retailers, loyalty companies, and other third parties can use for their customers through the Stockpile platform. This enables third parties to forge a direct, enduring bond with their customers by tapping into the "pride of ownership" gene people have. Traditionally, this sort of service would have been cost prohibitive for a bank to offer. Stockpile's technology and business model innovations provide a terrific way for financial providers to reach their customers in a user-friendly and compliant way.

MONEYGRAM: AN EXAMPLE OF EXPANDING A BANK'S FOOTPRINT THROUGH PARTNERING

MoneyGram (MGI) has had relationships with many banks for years and offers a good example of how banks can expand their footprint and product arsenal through partnering. Globally, MGI has 327,000 agent relationships in over 200 countries. As financial institutions look at opportunities for expansion, MGI offers bank partners a very broad suite of products, including:

- Walk-in money transfers (globally)
- Walk-in bill payment (United States and Canada)
- Money orders (United States)
- Online money transfers via affiliate and virtual agency relationships (globally)
- Online bill payment (United States and Canada)
- Official checks (United States)
- Cash payout services (business to consumer)

Increasingly, MGI sees money transfer customers looking for tailored money transfer services, and its enhanced services can help a bank improve throughput and reduce costs. The inclusion of money transfer services into a bank's core range of product offerings brings new customers to the banks and directly onto banks' web sites.

For many banks the formal engagement process in engaging MGI starts with the traditional request for proposal (RFP) process. Key requirements commonly covered in the RFP process fall into four distinct buckets:

Network Coverage/Product Offerings	Integration with Key Banking Platforms
- MGI global coverage - Agent types by region - U.S. coverage - Channel options: Online coverage/ mobile options/Self Service Inc. kiosk and ATM - Consumer value proposition - Competitive pricing/servicing for consumers - Rewards offerings for consumers	- MGI ability to deliver a solution that can be seamlessly integrated into their core banking platforms - Integration with bank overall cash banking strategy and product suite - Single enrollment and ability to interact with banks' KYC (know your customer) processes - Integration into a single teller interface - Integration into a single customer transaction receipt

Agent Support	Regulatory
■ Compliance support	■ Compliance
■ Customer and agent support availability	■ Dodd-Frank
■ Marketing support	■ Fraud/Anti–money laundering management
■ Financials/Compensation	■ KYC processes/integration with banking processes
■ Daily settlement process (single cash drawer)	

Once a bank completes its due diligence of MoneyGram's offerings, discussions usually turn to key revenue, investment, and financing components, which include:

- Commission rates—generally ramps with volume.
- Marketing—a key part of the negotiation of any contract. In general, MoneyGram requests all its agents (including banks) to contribute to marketing based on a proportion of volume.
- A comprehensive rollout and support strategy with dedicated technical and account management resources during and after deployment.
- A dedicated account manager.

In the United States, mainstream banks have been slow to adopt the addition of core money transfer services into their mainstream consumer offerings; this has been particularly prevalent since the financial crisis in 2008. Prior to 2008, many banks were pursuing an aggressive acquisition strategy targeting the underserved/unbanked consumer. Following the economic crisis, many of these initiatives shut down, and only in the past couple of years have mainstream banks started to relook at the potential for targeting underserved consumers.

Many prepaid companies have utilized the MoneyGram Virtual Agency concept to embed MGI's core service offerings for money transfer and bill payment into their web sites or mobile apps. Over the past two years, MGI has seen interest from mainstream banks in incorporating offerings directly. Among core banking activities, service charges on deposit accounts have become a critical source of non–interest income for banks; however, these fees are also attracting increased scrutiny by legislators and regulators, and this strategically important source of revenue for banks is in decline. As a result, banks are actively engaging in reevaluating their consumer deposit pricing strategies and are searching for new revenue opportunities. In addition, banks are faced with the challenge of realigning their delivery channels to meet consumer demand and changing practices (e.g., driven by electronic payments via online/mobile).

One constant that is observed in numerous MGI bank relationships is the mandate to increase consumer cross-sell ratios. For many branch-dependent banks, the trend away from branch transactions reduces the number of opportunities for face-to-face sales. Creating new branch-based service opportunities is critical in leveraging these and other cross-sell opportunities.

Money movement services represent a significant channel to drive new cross-sales and transaction opportunities with consumers, and MGI has solutions to meet those objectives. While money movement options exist for retail bank customers, these are usually initiated by automated clearinghouse (ACH)-based wire transfer services. This is inefficient in many respects: (1) the sender is not in control of transfer timing, (2) unpredictable posting times of the transfer, (3) delivery of cash in emergency situations may be limited to branch hours of operation, and (4) the recipient must also have a bank account. A number of U.S. banks are now offering alternative financial services because they have found that upwards of 30 percent of their customer base are using these services already with other providers. Bringing these services in-house will enable these banks to capture new revenue streams while meeting the needs of their existing customer base.

As banks evaluate partnerships with MGI or others, they should consider the following:

- Ease of integration and strong approach to partnership.
- Working with a company that focuses on partnership versus a company that competes with the bank for their consumers.
- A provider who provides the core suite of product offerings via a single integration and focuses on managing the complexity of the remittance landscape on behalf of their partners, thereby allowing the bank to concentrate on giving their consumers great services.
- Revenue generation opportunities through new service offerings.
- Understand who are the current users of money transfers (banks may not be aware of the demographic changes occurring within their market footprint that are likely driving needs for international money transfer services).
- U.S. money transfer users have a variety of needs, from personal emergencies to routine recurring transfers and payments. Offering a range of solutions to meet these needs, including cash delivery in minutes and account-based money transfers, is critical to building consumer usage and awareness of money transfer services.

Partners like MGI have significant core competencies in ensuring global regulatory compliance with remittance rules, anti–money laundering and fraud management services. Their internal assets, databases, and transaction history are often best in class in managing the risks associated with the international remittance world. While banks share many of the same regulatory environments, MGI's focus on money movement enables the bank to concentrate on other banking-specific regulatory hurdles, for example, Dodd-Frank and its impact on "batch systems," which cannot comply easily.

INNOVATIVE WAYS TO EXPAND ACCESS—PAYNEARME

PayNearMe is another terrific example of a technology innovation that will allow more financial institutions to expand their network and drive new revenue in a very low-cost way. Operating branches and ATMs is simply too expensive for the vast majority of financial institutions. As a result, most banks are recalibrating their branch distribution strategy, and leveraging retail stores is a great alternative. The problem is, today, only the largest financial institutions can negotiate with national retailers to get a physical presence in their stores.

PayNearMe operates an electronic cash transaction network; think of it as a "Visa for remote cash transactions." On one side of this network are businesses that want to accept cash from consumers remotely. On the other side of the network are tens of thousands of retail locations such as 7-Eleven and Family Dollar stores where consumers can go to make a cash payment to those businesses.

When it comes to banks, there are two scenarios: either act like any other business on the network to collect payments—be it remote deposits or loan repayments—or banks can collect payments on behalf of their commercial clients such as utility agencies, government entities, property management groups, health care exchanges, and so on.

But why should banks bother with cash in this day and age? Because the Federal Deposit Insurance Corporation (FDIC) estimates that there are 68 million Americans in the underserved market. These consumers either prefer or have no choice but to pay with cash. Many of these underserved consumers currently pay their bills at walk-up windows and have to endure long lines, short hours, and not the safest conditions. It is no surprise that both consumers and merchants dislike these walk-up bill payment options because of the inefficiency inherent in the model. Alternatively, these consumers can purchase a money order and mail it to their auto lender, landlord, or utility. However, this option is costly for consumers, is not conducted in real time, and carries operational costs and risks for the merchant. Anytime there is a "card not present" payment, PayNearMe's payment network can add value because it offers simplicity, convenience, and assurance that the consumer's payment has gone through.

Given the regulatory upheaval of the past five years, most banks are re-evaluating their branch network operations as part of a larger review of their entire cost structure. Most retail banks have some subprime customers in their credit card or auto loan portfolios. When they need to make a payment, they simply come to the branch with cash or money order and pay the teller. It costs the bank somewhere between $10 and $60 to service such a transaction and offers little up-sell opportunity. As a result, the banks are more than happy to hand off this transactional business to PayNearMe and their retail partners. This allows the bank to run its branch network more efficiently, all the while offering consumers an expanded footprint to make cash payments. By offloading the transactional traffic from cash-paying credit customers, banks can attain more flexibility with the remaining branch assets.

How can banks partner with a company like PayNearMe? Generally, banks can get standard wholesale rates, which gives them the flexibility to define service fees, as well as determine if they want to pass them along or absorb them, based on what makes the most sense in the context of a given relationship. In return, the company asks for volume commitments. PayNearMe works with bank partners to devise the appropriate timeline for integration, beta testing with the bank's merchants, and ramp period to get to the full run rate.

HOW BANKS ARE PARTNERING FOR INNOVATION

Often, banks find it difficult to believe that many smaller companies have the compliance, security, and risk requirements in place to make a partnership work. The reality is that many smaller companies possess the technology and thought leadership necessary to comply with the intended spirit of many of these regulations and are more likely to come up with a solution to satisfy regulators.

Peter Aceto and Charaka Kithulegoda, CEO and CIO of ING DIRECT Canada, are terrific examples of this. They have continually outmaneuvered much larger financial institutions by maintaining an innovative culture and continually opening the door to partnerships with innovative models that can complement their capabilities. In the next section, Peter and Charaka discuss how they think about innovation in this context.

THE CEO-CIO RELATIONSHIP DRIVING THE INNOVATION OF ING DIRECT CANADA[6]

The world is not changing. It has changed. As recently as 18 months ago, bank executives had so-called control. We defined the rules of the game for consumers: "To bank with us, here's what we offer and here's how you do it."

But roles have since shifted. What consumers are now demanding is to make banking a compelling experience, consequently moving the power from the executive boardroom to the living room.

Today's consumers are telling us how, where, and when they want to bank. They are better informed, expect more, and have the voice to make a strong impact. And that is the biggest challenge and the greatest opportunity that lies ahead for the financial services industry.

Consider this: If you're sailing and there's no wind, it will be hard to gain momentum, perhaps to catch up on someone. But with the wind of change on your back, you have the opportunity to make hay if you can. For ING DIRECT, there couldn't be a more exciting time.

However, there is an important distinction to make. Yes, consumers want innovation, but not for the sake of change except rather to simplify their lives by making banking convenient. It is in that context that we use technology to enable a better customer experience, and faster than before.

We get very excited by technology. In fact, the entire senior leadership team—CEO, CIO, CFO, CMO, and COO—all clearly understand why technology as a core competency drives business success. However, we operate within a technology and business framework. If a technology does not simplify the customer experience, we temper our excitement and focus on what would.

It's not in the best interest of any organization, regardless of industry, to get caught up in technology trends. It's clear everyone is talking about mobile, social, cloud, and big data. But who knows what the next trend will be? And what do these buzzwords actually mean in the context of a business solution?

Meeting the needs of consumers isn't defined in research papers and trends, frankly. We chose to build on concepts and provide solutions. We tend to look at what has the most impact on our business and our customers. We search for issues and find technologies that fix them. In mobile, this means we provide services that offer immediacy and simplicity through a highly contextual experience. In social, this means choice, personalization, and control of consumer interactions with all touch points—as well as giving consumers transparent access to our employees and executives.

Consumers are demanding a deeper relationship, particularly when it comes to their hard-earned money! It's really not about content; it's about context. It's not about a transaction; it's about the experience. It's not about getting a mortgage; it's about buying a home.

Perhaps the clarity with which we see technology is rooted in our foundation. After all, ING DIRECT was built under principles to challenge, advocate for consumers, and simplify banking.

As a challenger in any marketplace, staying nimble and being able to quickly change and adapt to consumer preferences are key drivers of success. We always thought, and more so now, that the way our business thinks and the way it is organized need to reflect a rapidly changing environment. If we complicate matters, we lose our agility.

The culture and flat organizational structure of ING DIRECT have allowed us to make a big impact on the financial services industry. We're organized in a way that lets research and development happen without any amount of hierarchy. Decisions don't take a long time. Whether it's the lack of titles or the desire to not have silos, or the open office environment, our challenger culture empowers nearly 1,000 employees with the ability to investigate and experiment. In fact, much of our research and development takes place outside of the formal plans in what we categorize as "by the side of the desk" research. To have team members passionately and independently thinking about making the customer experience better and looking for innovations to deliver on our promise should undoubtedly be a leader's dream.

Whether the solutions we investigate involve payment options, biometrics, or the mobile or online experience, they are all designed to meet consumer needs and make banking easier. The fact is that banking can be confusing, complex, and can take up a lot of time. But it doesn't have to. So what a perfect environment to apply technology and empower consumers! Yes, empower consumers—a concept some of us welcome while others remain fearful of its inevitability.

With this dramatic shift, consumer expectations and behaviors continue to change, which can be problematic in a highly regulated environment such as the financial services industry. Technology is moving much faster than regulation. And regulation can significantly slow down the pace of change to meet new expectations. But that's exactly where the greatest opportunity lies.

People use rules and regulations as excuses not to innovate. It is in our nature to simply adhere to legal and compliance and avoid risk altogether. But those are areas we must challenge, too, in order for real innovation to happen in the financial services industry. We believe it can happen, and it is currently happening. Changes can absolutely be safe and secure. We can absolutely stay true to the spirit of the rule and the laws. But we must challenge the status quo, innovate, and keep the system safe and secure.

One of the greatest opportunities of innovation is in the area of security, particularly as it relates to consumers' banking needs. That is why banking, in our view, is the most exciting industry to be a part of in today's world because of its level of complexity. But that's where great partnerships are key. First, we believe in the partnership of a CEO and CIO and having a high level of trust and freedom to deliver on customer needs and business strategy through technology. We also believe in choosing the right external partners to help us move the strategy faster. We don't look for vendors—we chose strategic partners much the same way that we chose our employees. We hire for will and train for skill. We want culture fit and enthusiasm. We want partners who are visionaries and forward thinkers and who are willing to challenge us and meet our challenges whether they are a start-up or a large technology company.

To truly embrace partnership is important. To learn together, experiment together and benefit together. This idea requires openness, honesty, and trust. Traditional procurement processes miss this incredible part of the value chain in a partnership. For us, it is more about sharing the risk and the reward and less about driving a low-price partnership. We're aware this is unusual, but it is absolutely the way we approach partnerships, and it works. In fact, in our 16-year history, it is our large strategic technology partners that have been the quickest to adapt to our way of thinking. You would think that such organizations would want to partner with bigger financial institutions, but they repeatedly chose us, because we can get ideas to production faster. And we can in turn help them build proof points and become catalysts for other financial institutions. Sure, they will share our ideas with our competitors in time, but we will have had an 18- to 24-month head start.

We've experienced a tremendous amount of success because of our nimble culture. We began experimenting with biometrics 12 years ago and are close to providing the solution we feel is right for our customers, such as facial and voice recognition or fingerprint scanning. We were the first bank in Canada to sign a cloud services agreement, the first to release apps for all the major mobile platforms, and the first to introduce and enhance remote check deposit through mobile technologies.

With change comes incredible opportunity. And the competition is learning quickly. The task for all challengers is to not sit still. As the gap narrows, maintaining an entrepreneurial spirit is what we fight to keep. We have to master the art of acting smaller as we get bigger and move that much faster—all while continuing to empower the client by anticipating their needs, and interpreting them into features and functions that drive the right banking experience. It's a very exciting time!

A WHOLE NEW ERA[7]

Most senior leaders in banking and financial services today developed their industry knowledge in a completely different era. From the early 1980s until 2008, the industry enjoyed, with a few notable exceptions, steadily rising asset prices and steadily declining interest rates, all nicely clad in an era of general deregulation. The global financial crisis that began in 2008 wasn't just a bad year—it wasn't even the start of a rough patch—it was the start of a whole new era.

As the hangover from the crisis slowly eases, most asset prices have at least begun to recover, but interest rates are remaining stubbornly low, and we are now in a long period of re-regulation. The flood tide that floated the industry's boats in the prior era has become an ebb tide, and as Warren Buffett famously put it: "It's only when the tide goes out that you learn who's been swimming naked."

Even more profound than the changes within the banking industry are the changes that have been taking place outside of it. Throughout the prior era, financial institutions have gotten used to controlling the assets and the liabilities, controlling the platforms that moved money around the system and being the gatekeepers of asymmetrical information. But those days are over.

We live in an increasingly open source world, and consumers are more knowledgeable than ever. And they have also developed keen BS detection skills, which have multiplied exponentially with the rise of social media. They also have higher expectations than ever. They carry amazing technology around in their pockets, and they expect their financial tools to be as seamless as their Starbucks app.

The other huge difference between this era and the past is that bankers for the first time now need to contend with the threat of substitution. During the past eras, there was no real substitute for a licensed financial institution. Sure, we had large banks, small banks, savings banks, savings-and-loans, and credit unions, but they were all just slightly different flavors of the same basic thing. Now we have a dizzying array of choices in ways to save, borrow, invest, and move money, and not all of those choices are traditional financial institutions.

How Banks Can Compete in the Future

More than ever, banks today need to innovate new products, new business processes, and new revenue streams to stay competitive.

In 1995, Michael Treacy and Fred Wiersema wrote a book called *The Discipline of Market Leaders,* and in it, they broke down the three critical strategic domains of any business—Customer Intimacy, Product Leadership, and Operational Excellence. They argued that companies cannot really dominate in more than one. Now, none of these are exactly optional, but their recommendation was that companies should focus on truly mastering one of the domains and partner or subcontract with others in the areas where they can't dominate.

A few years later, Hagel and Singer from McKinsey & Company came to a similar conclusion in their *Harvard Business Review* piece, "Unbundling the Corporation." They even used very similar wording to describe Customer Relationship Management, Product Innovation, and Infrastructure Management, as seen in Table 5.1.

It's kind of a strengths-based leadership approach for companies—improve your weaknesses enough to prevent failure, but the only path to greatness is to focus on your strengths.

I believe that a financial service is a customer relationship management business. Many bankers probably agree with this, but if we're honest about the activities that get the most energy and attention, it really seems that most have taken an infrastructure management approach. Look at some of the descriptors for that strategy: "battle for scale," "a few big players dominate," "cost focused, "stresses standardization, predictability, and efficiency."

I would argue that very few banks to date have taken a product innovation approach, and I doubt that more than a handful are truly capable of being true innovation leaders—at least not in the vein of Mint, PayPal, Square, and other poster children for financial innovation.

TABLE 5.1 Unbundling the Corporation

	Product Innovation	Customer Relationship Management	Infrastructure Management
Economics	Early market entry enables premium prices and acquiring large marketing share; speed is key.	High cost of customer acquisition makes it imperative to gain large wallet share; economies of scope are key.	High fixed costs make large volumes essential to achieve low unit costs; economies of scales are key.
Competition	Battle for talent; low barriers to entry; many small players thrive.	Battle for scope; rapid consolidation; a few big players dominate.	Battle for scale; rapid consolidation; a few big players dominate.
Culture	Employee centered; coddling the creative stars.	Highly service oriented; customer-comes-first mentality.	Cost focused; stresses standardization, predictability, and efficiency.

Source: Adapted from Hagel and Singer, "Unbundling the Corporation" *Harvard Business Review*, March 1999.

I would also argue that most banks should take a customer relationship management approach, but this is not to say that banks and other financial institutions shouldn't innovate. I spend a significant part of my life advocating, encouraging, preaching, and cajoling bank leaders to place a higher priority on innovation. It's just that most cannot expect to create and commercialize the majority of new innovative products and services from within their own four walls. They absolutely should be innovating early and often, but with a much broader perspective that is more inclusive of outside partners.

Three Imperatives to Partner for Innovation

One of the ways banks can most effectively innovate new products and solutions will be to partner with FinTech entrepreneurs. In order to do this successfully, banks must do things a little differently than they do now.

1. *Think beyond vendor management.* Most FinTech entrepreneurs find it easier to develop complex new technology than it is to sell it to banks. Sales cycles of two years or longer are not uncommon, and the process tends to be more about managing risks and costs rather than testing and implementing new ideas. Risk management is a very important consideration, and any bank that would want to take too many shortcuts here will be quickly reminded of that by their regulators. Still, these risks need to be managed against the risk of falling behind by doing nothing.

   I still recall the words of a bank executive manager when presented with an opportunity to participate in the launch of a groundbreaking piece of new back-office technology. When told that they would be first to market with the product, he replied, "We don't do 'first.' Let someone else go first and make all the mistakes. This is four guys in a garage!" To his credit, he eventually allowed the team to win him over, and today those "four guys in a garage" have over $50 billion in assets under management using their product.

2. *Move from product development to customer development.* For too many financial institutions, new features and products come to market with a very internalized process. Quite often, the impetus is feedback from the sales team that sees a competitor launch a new product or feature that they don't have. The product team is tasked with creating a new product, and they ask the marketing department to create some selling points, and the marketing department wants a marketing requirements document, or something similar, listing features and benefits. Then, the finance department wants projections on how much this is going to cost, how much revenue it will generate and how it will disintermediate their existing products.

So what happens when the new product launch fails to meet expectations?

- The product teams complains that the sales team didn't know how to sell it.
- The sales team complains that they didn't have the right kind of marketing support.
- Marketing complains that the financial projections were unrealistic.

What's missing in this scenario? No one talked to the customer! Maybe, if you were lucky, you talked to a few if you had a beta test. But all the beta test did was prove that the product did what you said it would. It didn't prove that you solved a problem that your customers actually cared about or were willing to spend money on. It reminds me of one of the best live tweets I saw at a Finovate conference about a new product that was being launched on stage: "They're solving a problem no one has with technology no one wants."

So we have to move from product development to customer development, where we start with a deep knowledge of our customers' needs and wants and pain points. Only then can we think about features or products to meet these needs or opportunities, and then we can think about which external companies can best help us if we don't have the capabilities in-house.

3. *Create an environment where it's okay to fail.* Bankers are inherently risk avoidant. At best, they're risk managers. Bankers have to be right 99 percent of the time over the long run on lending decisions, but innovation is about taking risks and trying new things and learning from your failures until you get it right. The key to innovating successfully is to fail quickly and fail cheaply and fail in an environment that is firewalled from impacting customers and shareholders.

Successful entrepreneurs follow the Lean Startup ethos of "Build/ Measure/Learn" and make lots of iterations on their ideas as they learn more and more from their customers. *Good to Great* author Jim Collins calls this "firing bullets before cannonballs" in his book *Great by Choice.* Bankers can learn from this methodology as much as from the individual learnings, and they should embrace frequent use of prototypes, user panels, minimal viable products, and pilot testing. Partnering with the right entrepreneurs can speed up this process and bring in some much-needed external perspectives.

Banks should also embrace open innovation and work together when they are trying to solve larger problems. The Bank Innovators Council is a membership organization to help support, promote, and facilitate innovation within and among its member banks. The Council provides opportunities for members to pool their resources to develop and test new ideas outside of the day-to-day demands of their existing businesses, and in ways they could notdo alone.

We saw that FinTech entrepreneurs had a lot of ways to get support for innovation—venture capitalists, incubators, accelerators, and so on—but that banks were on their own. That may be fine for the handful that can afford their own dedicated innovation teams, but most banks can't afford that, and they certainly can't afford not to innovate.

A VENTURE CAPITALIST'S LOOK AT THE FUTURE OF BANKING

When looking at the future of banking, it often helps to seek out those venture capitalists that have done their fair share of investing in disruptive financial services ventures. Dana Stalder is a partner at Matrix Capital and former chief operating officer of PayPal. I sat down with Dana to glean some insight on what he's seeing and what trends might be on the horizon:

Question: Dana, what is your investment thesis when it comes to financial services?

Stalder: My theory is that innovation has come from new entrants and will continue to come from new entrants. In the process of that transition, the big will get bigger and the small will get squished out. Banks are going to become API [application programming interface] transactional services. Their value is going to be in sponsorship and the trust that comes with that sponsorship, and the reliability of these back-end services. There are certainly huge-scale advantages with that world.

Question: What is the competency they need to develop to support the next generation of virtual services?

Stalder: The most important thing, I think, is that banks need to think about themselves as being in the transaction business, not in the dollar arbitrage business, which is essentially what they have been in with credit and exchanges. I think the biggest issue is the technology stack behind these banks—technology will increasingly become important, in particular, exposing your technology stack to third parties. Modern-day Web companies think about the world in terms of services and programming interfaces, and that is not how modern banks think about their technology stack today.

Question: Can you give us an example?

Stalder: If I am a Fortune 100 company and I want to integrate my ERP [enterprise resource planning] system with my commercial bank's system to do foreign exchange calculations, money movement, these are big multimillion-dollar integrations. That is insane to me. As an example, HP's treasury group should be able to connect with JPMorgan's wholesale foreign exchange desk through a very simple set of restful APIs.

Question: Why has this been so difficult to achieve?

Stalder: The problem is—it is not that they don't have enough people in their technology departments; it's technical deficit. Technical deficit can consume enormous amounts of money and resources, and as old as these institutions are, they have a significant amount of deficit.

Question: What can financial institutions do from a skill set perspective to try to modernize?

Stalder: I'm sure there's not a CIO in any of the top banks who does not look at the Facebook developer platform or Stripe and say, "That's easy; I can build that in a month." The problem is actually they can't. It is not a question of technical complexity—it is 25-year-old engineers that have written all those platforms—I just think it's a new business model. Platform services is going to be a big part of our future, and you have to think about working with customers through these API services in a way they don't do today.

Question: What has made other institutions successful that offer platform services?

Stalder: Part of the reason why the Stripe platform has been so successful on a smaller scale is simply that it's easy to work with them; it's easy to on-board, it's easy to write to their APIs, and the documentation is so clean. It sounds so simple, but doing that is actually quite complicated. In a sense, it's being developer-centric, and that becomes your customer.

Question: Do you see new ways these tech companies can plug into banks to make banks more relevant?

Stalder: Here's the problem with developer services: everybody will eventually get there, but these transactional businesses will commoditize very quickly. It's a little bit like the web—another retailer is just a click away. It's the ultimate price competition. I know what everybody pays with just a bunch of clicks, and once you have people competing for wholesale banking services, and everybody has simple integration, it's all going to be about price, and that's going to be a big challenge, so is there a first-mover advantage? Yes, and I think there's a big scale advantage, too.

Question: What can a bank successfully do that Stripe or another API platform couldn't?

Stalder: It's a good question, not clear to me. At a minimum, they need to offer platform services so they're easy to work with. They need to commoditize Stripe, I guess, is the short answer. They need to offer services just so they can retain the customers that they spent so much money bringing in. What they can't do is let everyone pick off the transactional revenue.

Question: Where are traditional retail banking models going?

Stalder: The physical bank branch is a dying breed, and I think that's just going to continue. Today, I deposit my check from my smartphone. I don't think I've been into my bank like once in 10 years. The thing that kills me about banks—even the big guys, their digital experiences are awful—especially for bill payment at most large banks. I can go find 500 designers locally that could redesign in a week and make it a dramatically better experience. Now, I don't know if anyone would have the money or wherewithal to fix it.

Question: How about digital wallets?

Stalder: I'm not particularly bullish on any of the existing digital wallet solutions with the exception of Square. I look at this from the lens of consumer utility. How many of these have the "wow" factor? Google Wallet doesn't have the "wow" factor. PayPal doesn't have the "wow" factor. Square, in principle, has a wow factor—I don't have to take my phone or wallet out by standing in a retailer—but they have the challenge of no network; I can't use it anywhere. So I think the banks need to figure out how to design around that, and I've yet to see that. I look at, on average, one digital payment start-up a week. The optimal experience is: I never have to take anything out of my pocket, it knows that I'm there, it authenticates by my presence, it has a suite of loyalty experiences, the clerk knows my name, they know my history. Incentives are pushed to me, save me money, make my life easier, and it allows the merchant to deliver a better customer experience to me.

Question: What are the most interesting opportunities you're seeing now in financial technology?

Stalder: The phone changes everything. I've got a computer in my pocket, CPU, memory, screen—all the rules have changed in the last four years, which is probably why I'm more bullish on new entrants than existing because rate of innovation matters in cycles like this. So where is the opportunity? Square has built a surprisingly big business, definitely capitalized on the advent of the smartphone market. A lot of smartphones are doing things around loyalty and incentives, but they all seem to be siloed. I think they lack the amazing customer experience because they're not integrated with the point-of-sale payment system, and it therefore still requires work for consumers. If someone could take away the friction and knit together these things, that would be powerful.

Another big area is credit. There are new ways to think about underwriting through the use of machine learning and big data. Zest Finance is doing this in the subprime category, Wonga is doing this in the EU, and a bunch of people are going after small business lending, where it's easier to enter. Bigger margins mean more room for error and figuring this out, Ondeck, Wonga, Kabbage, Sofi are going after consumer lending. All of these are thinking about underwriting in novel ways and making better use of underwriting. There are a large number of companies that are getting big scale quickly, Lending Club included.

Question: How about banks?

Stalder: Banks have been in the business of using third-party tools. There will be new data providers. Lending Club is a marketplace; these things tend to have huge-scale advantages. It's very hard for an existing bank to come in and say, "We're going to do a credit marketplace," let alone so many regulatory challenges and competition with their existing business. There will be a lot of competition coming in credit!

All this is good for consumers. You can say high APR loans shouldn't exist, but access to credit isn't something that should just be made available to the top 40 percent of the U.S. population. So all the way down, starting with subprime, innovation starts where APRs are the highest and then works its way up the credit spectrum.

INVESTING IN YOUR ECOSYSTEM

Michael Strange,[8] CTO of Mitek, is no stranger to innovation and partnering in the arena. He currently is responsible for the many technology solutions that are allowing banks to evolve their financial services offerings through mobile—from remote deposit capture to identity verification products. Here, Michael discusses the importance of financial services companies' investing in their innovation ecosystems.

Successful financial institutions thrive on a complex set of third-party partnerships, including integration partners, network providers, and an array of others. These partnerships are central to the delivery of financial services in the United States, and therefore partner integration is one of the disciplines that are required to succeed. Vendors are often evaluated for a select role that they will play, and selected based on functional completeness and special skills, and ability to handle complexity, service levels, and cost. Many banking executives have internalized the fundamental concepts of "core" and "context," choosing to partner in areas where others have a better ability to deliver.

This relatively narrow approach to vendor management misses a core concept. Third-party partnerships are the best way for financial institutions, particularly larger ones, to innovate. Smaller organizations, with more "agile" methods, can often deliver out-of-the-box ideas very effectively, in their area of specialization. Innovation is one of the core disciplines that will differentiate financial institutions. As consumers are given more choices (including prepaid and alternative banking products), it will be important to deliver a rapidly evolving and increasingly modern consumer experience. Innovation is therefore one of the key "win themes" for 2014 and beyond. It is surprising, with this context, that many partner relationships are not designed to leverage agility and innovation.

I have personally negotiated over 1,000 contracts, both as supplier and buyer. My teams poured vast amounts of time into considering tiered pricing schedules, pricing caps, service levels, deliverables, project goals, schedule, impact on existing systems, change management issues, prerequisites, risks, return on investment, and total cost of ownership. We rarely talk about innovation. The vast majority of requests for proposals (RFPs) have hundreds or thousands of questions about features, functions, technology, process, service levels, and pricing. Most do not ask about how the partner could help the organization innovate.

So I propose a new strategy for partnerships. Determine the areas in which innovation is critical to your organization, and select partnerships that have the best opportunity to deliver continuous improvement in these areas. And then invest in these partnerships. There are four steps to delivering on this vision, as follows:

STEP 1: DESIGN YOUR INNOVATION ECOSYSTEM

Innovation can and should be intentional. We can and should plan and execute around it. The key is focus. First, determine the areas in which innovation is critical to the success of the company. I am not talking about soft goals like "quality" or "deliver value for our customers and shareholders." I am talking about hard-hitting goals like "drive a measurably different and compelling ATM user experience," or "leverage data better than any of our peers to manage deposit risk within bounds." Once you define the areas in which innovation is critical to your organization, you can map an optimal set of partners to those areas and define goals like these to govern the relationship.

STEP 2: INVEST

Each of your chosen partners brings unique capabilities, including breadth, integration, special skills, and operating leverage. In order to enable your partner to do this, you must invest. This may seem obvious but is often overlooked. You must invest in two areas to get results: expectations and data. Notice that investment, in this context, has nothing to do with money.

Invest by setting expectations. Explain your innovation ecosystem, why you created it, and their role it in. Reinforce that one of your expectations is rapid prototyping, which means that new and different ideas will be explored constantly. More important, you expect promising results (or failure) quickly. Either outcome is fine—speed is the key. Be prepared to see "rough" ideas and react to their potential. If you expect perfect, well-packaged solutions, then you slow down the engine.

Invest by sharing data. Partners will need to understand the goals, what has worked in the past, customer segmentation, usage trends, overview of current processes, risk categorization, and systems integration concerns. Most important, they will need data. If the goal is to improve the online banking experience, proactively share usage and

(*continued*)

INVESTING IN YOUR ECOSYSTEM (*Continued*)

abandonment data. If the goal is to improve processes, provide detailed data about current inefficiencies. If the goal is to attract the growing number of customers who prefer mobile, then share customer surveys and breakdown of the areas of likely improvement.

By investing through expectations and data, you are providing the tools needed to succeed. Also, you have created an environment in which all partners are, by definition, business intelligence partners. They provide, or analyze, key analytics data as part of their rapid-innovation program. Expect a collaborative, open, data-driven, but occasionally rough-around-the-edges experience.

STEP 3: CHALLENGE BY POSING TRADE-OFFS

As your partnerships grow and expand, based on rapid successes and rapid failures, challenge your relationships by asking partner input to key strategic trade-offs. Innovative partners should be expected to thoughtfully consider the environment in which their solutions are being implemented.

For example, imagine that you have a long-standing partnership with a mobile application development company that has delivered multiple iterations of mobile banking systems to your consumers, with positive reviews. As you bring them into the innovation ecosystem, you give them a challenge: "Analyze customer behavior and design new and innovative ways to reinforce that mobile banking can be the best way to manage your money with my bank." They propose a series of innovative features and a new look and feel to the mobile experience, making it even more streamlined. After careful testing, it is released, and the statistics show increased usage. This is great!

Now, as your relationship moves to the next level, give them a tougher challenge: "How can we deliver an even more modern and cool mobile experience, while reinforcing that we are a reputable bank?"

With each success, challenge the next level of innovation. I have found that some of the most actionable "breakthrough" ideas are created in response to difficult trade-offs, like the one above.

STEP 4: HOLD ACCOUNTABLE

If you are willing to share key data and structure an environment to reward innovation, expect results. Innovation can and should be measured and delivered, just like any feature or service level. Here are a few suggestions for ways in which you can hold partners accountable and be clear about how they will be supported:

> "If I shared customer segmentation and behavioral patterns for my customers, every month, what would you do with it?"

> "If I shared risk data, could you help me learn something new, no matter how small, every month?"

> "If I set up a collaborative working session to explore what drives customer behavior, what preparation would you do? How would you invest in the follow-up after the session?

These are the kinds of questions that should be asked of innovation partners.

STEP 5: MEASURE, MEASURE, MEASURE

Innovation can be measured, like any objective. Defined goals should be "SMART" like any operational objective. For innovation, I have found it effective to measure the process and the result. For example, one might measure an end objective, such as "increase mobile channel enrollment by 5 percent by October." The methods to achieve this goal can be iterative and may involve some very new and innovative ideas. In the end, measure the goal. At the same time, you can measure the process of innovation. For example, "try five or more techniques, one every week, choose one and drive implementation by end of fiscal year." This goal can be measured, too, and it addresses the rapid nature of your expectations.

In conclusion, financial institutions can and should rapidly innovate and differentiate, and should leverage partners to drive it. Many partners are smaller, simpler, and more nimble. Leverage this fact to your advantage, but organize to achieve your goals. By creating and investing in an innovation ecosystem, you can drive more innovation and more measurable results for the benefit of your customers and your shareholders.

TECHNOLOGY AS AN ENABLER AND PARTNER

We've discussed much about how new innovations are bringing about profound changes in the way financial services are distributed. Sometimes we can get so wrapped up in the new technology that we forget what we are solving for. People often talk about innovation and technology in the same sentence, but technology is not often the innovation, it's an enabler of innovation. Applied to financial institutions, it can be a fantastic enabler. The mobile phone can have profound effects, but if banks simply apply existing models to a new technology, there will be no innovation at all. Online banking had to be more powerful an innovation than simply moving someone away from telephone banking. Mobile banking must fulfill a fundamental need and convenience if it is to replace online banking, and if it is not, it will be driven by other players, not banks. If we look at all the big technology trends happening in Silicon Valley that can be enablers for banks, there are really three big things going on:

1. The ubiquity of social networks, which now can teach us more about customers and their day-to-day lives than ever before.
2. The rise of Internet-connected devices, from laptops to mobile/tablet to wearable devices. Lots of crazy new use cases and high customer expectations.
3. The proliferation of cloud services that allow new customer experiences to tap into a lot of back-end information.

Most innovative bank executives that I have interviewed have all told me how important true partnership is to the evolution of the bank. Charaka Kithulegoda, CIO of ING DIRECT Canada, tells me that the technology companies he works with cringe when he refers to them as a partner because they think you don't mean it, that you just want something. As he says it:

> To truly embrace partnership is important. Learn together, experiment together, and benefit together. This requires openness, honesty, and trust. Often, pure procurement processes miss this incredible part of the value chain in a partnership. Sometimes you want the cheapest price, but sometimes you need to find the best fit for a partner. Share the risk, share the reward. Makes sense but is seldom used in day-to-day business. We don't look for "vendors"—we are looking for strategic and technology partnerships. We want partners that are visionaries, are forward thinking and innovative.

WHAT THE NEXT 50 YEARS MIGHT HOLD

We've talked about the fact that in today's world, we live in a client-controlled environment. It's no longer about a transaction; it's about the experience. It's not about getting a mortgage; it's about buying a home. Some financial institutions are in alignment with these trends, but it all starts with how much focus is on the customer. The reason so many technology companies often come up with great financial experiences for customers is that they start with a maniacal focus on the customer.

How might we look past the most recent trends to those enduring changes that will fundamentally change how financial services are offered? There are a few long-term trends that appear to give us a glimpse of what we might see further into the future, discussed next.

Digital

Fifty years ago, two-thirds of Americans' wealth was in the form of demand deposits, and today it is less than one-third.[9] I've devoted a chapter of this book to math-based currencies, not because I believe that they will all survive, but because the protocol that it is built on will represent a seismic shift in the way data are transmitted. If we think of money as a digital representation of bits and bytes, we will surely see more of our own wealth—property, stocks, currency—all held in digital form. What does that mean for financial services institutions? They will not just be the custodian of physical assets, but they will need to be the custodian of a person's full digital financial life to stay relevant. The shift to digital will mean that banks need to focus their energy on safeguarding a consumer's identity above all else, and personal data will be the biggest treasure to protect.

Relationship Management

Today, most financial institutions originate their own loans, have their own information technology (IT) departments, and largely cross-sell their own products. If credit origination is increasingly done by nonbanks leveraging new data in new ways, it will be even more important for financial institutions to sell others' loans through their channels. It will increasingly become more important to manage relationships and identify best-of-breed partners and outside products and technology together in a way that creates a seamless experience for the customer. That's more easily said than done, but with the focus on integration services and platform versus product, successful banks will make the leap to what will likely be an enduring trend we will see. Trust will become even more important for banking, as data, sensors, and the ability to know more about customers will be possible. More banking will be done in the home or through mobile, in places where the consumer is most comfortable, and consumers will want to bring their bank or banker in only if they have a higher amount of trust. That trust will also be important because it's likely that the bank of the future may know more about you than you know about yourself. Similar to Amazon, where you may be presented with a recommendation for a product before you even realized you were looking for it, the number of demographic details combined with thoughtful analysis will offer all kinds of consumer behavior patterns, risk tolerances, and financial goals.

Platform and Identity Friendly

If you look at how Millennials engage with their phone, social media, and general information, it is often from their couch and in short bursts of attention at spontaneous intervals. As Millennials and subsequent generations grow up, managing finances might happen like most other things from the comfort of your couch or wherever you happen to be with your mobile phone. We've talked a lot about the need for banks to become master jigsaw puzzle assemblers, and this will be even more important in the future. We're now seeing the emergence of very discrete financial services capabilities that block by block can be assembled into a full-fledged financial services offering. Companies like Zopa, Lending Club, and Prosper will create better investment and borrowing opportunities as they better aggregate and exploit all the individual niche areas for credit. Simple and Moven have wonderfully intuitive designs that make it easy to manage, send, and receive money. Each of these best-of-breed financial technology companies will ultimately be bundled and provided by separate regulated bodies. Through APIs and Web services, customers will more easily be able to permission their bank to have specific information delivered instantly, whether it be for a new cell phone plan or an instant mortgage approval through a real estate application. Ultimate interoperability of services and reputational scoring systems could help assess credit in new ways. Imagine if we could take the eBay reputational scoring system, LinkedIn endorsements, Yelp ratings, and Amazon ratings, and combine them together to better evaluate the likeliness of a consumer or small business to fulfill their financial obligations.

THE FUTURE BANK BUNDLE: PLATFORM-RELATIONSHIP-UTILITY

Banking has always been about classic bundling of services—credit cards, savings accounts, checking accounts, home equity lines of credit, and the like. My experience as a banker, financial technology provider, industry analyst, and entrepreneur tell me that the future successful bank bundle will consist of three things:

1. Utility banking
2. Relationship banking
3. Platform services banking

Banks need to focus more on who they partner with and how than on product development. The economies of scale they have with respect to clearing, settling, and providing custody of funds must shift to technology that allows for learning of individual customer patterns, needs, and environment. Data become more of a focus. This requires turning knowledge of the customer into custom services, and a very entrepreneurial culture must be fostered. No longer will large-scale investments in proprietary networks make sense. In today's world, Bitcoin can reach far more customers more quickly than a bank could ever reach. If banks can make the shift to big data and identity management, they can become an ideal "smart pipe" utility to leverage as a platform. The services banks can then assemble on their platform will ultimately dictate the level of relationships they can build and nurture, and whether they are meeting the very unique needs of each of their customers.

The largest and most transformational step any financial institution can take is to focus on partnering with technology companies that are exhibiting signs of becoming major touch points for consumers. In partnering, we may not see traditional banks anymore, but a new array of banking services that promise to delight and capture consumers in the same way we have seen Google, Amazon, and Apple become such a part of one's everyday life.

NOTES

1. Jim Bruene, Online Banking Report, "New Opportunities with Prepaid Cards," August 2013.
2. Matt Harris, partner at Bain Capital, wrote "Prepaid Nation: Redefining What a Bank Can Be" for use with this book.
3. Network Branded Prepaid Card Association (NBPCA), "What Are Prepaid Cards?" www.nbpca.org/What-Are-Prepaid-Cards.aspx. Accessed February 7, 2014.
4. World Bank, "Who Are The unbanked?" http://siteresources.worldbank.org/EXTGLOBALFIN/Resources/8519638-1332259343991/world_bank3_Poster.pdf. Accessed February 7, 2014.

5. Bhaskar Charkravorti and Benjamin D. Mazzotta, "The Cost of Cash in the United States," The Institute for Business in the Global Context, The Fletcher School at Tufts University, September 2013.
6. Authored by Peter Aceto and Charaka Kithulegoda, CEO and CIO of ING DIRECT Canada, specifically for use with this book.
7. JP Nichols authored this section for the book.
8. Authored by Michael Strange, specifically for use with this book.
9. Dave Birch, "Leave Your Reputation with Your Banker," *Community Bank Insight,* posted by American Banker, July 25, 2013, www .cbinsight.com/leave-reputation-banker.html. Accessed July 25, 2013.

About the Author

Dan Schatt is a frequent industry speaker, financial technology adviser, and recognized expert in payments, mobile commerce, and retail financial services innovation. As the former general manager of financial innovations at PayPal from 2007 to 2013, his team led and executed PayPal's global initiatives with the banking and payments industry. His team's innovations included PayPal's first partnerships and product development with virtual currency and loyalty providers, PayPal's presence at the physical point of sale, and the Company's first cash products for the unbanked and underbanked. His team's work also led to hundreds of partnerships with the banking industry that have leveraged PayPal's open payments platform. He was cited by *Bank Innovation* magazine as one of the top innovators to watch in 2013, and received the A. R. Zipf Award for Payments System Innovation on behalf of PayPal in 2011 by the Western Payment Alliance in recognition of his national leadership in the payments industry.

Dan currently is on the founding executive team of Stockpile, Inc. and serves as chief commercial officer. His work focuses on the development of new business models and commercial partnerships that can increase global access to financial markets and transform stock into loyalty currency.Previously, he led the retail payments practice for market research firm Celent, covering emerging technologies impacting retail financial services, with a particular emphasis on mobile commerce, personal financial management, electronic cross-border and peer to peer payment systems. Prior to his role as industry analyst, he served as general manager of data services for Yodlee. Dan also worked as an investment banker for Salomon Smith Barney and held positions in Asia, Europe, and Africa with Citigroup. Prior to Citigroup, Dan managed payment and capital market infrastructure projects as country director of FSVC for Romania and the Republic of Moldova.

Dan has been widely quoted in the media, including the *New York Times, Wall Street Journal, Financial Times,* and *BusinessWeek,* and has also written articles for *American Banker* and *Bank Systems & Technology.* He has presented at national and international venues, including the United Nations Development Program Roundtable on Remittances, the World Bank/APEC Dialogue on Remittance Systems, NACHA, BAI, and the Internet Retailer conference.

Dan received a master of business administration and a master of international affairs from Columbia University.

Index

BY PAUL HORGAN

NOVELS
The Fault of Angels · The Habit of Empire · No Quarter Given
The Common Heart · Main Line West · Give Me Possession
A Lamp on the Plains · Memories of the Future · A Distant Trumpet
Far from Cibola · Whitewater
Mountain Standard Time
(containing *Main Line West, Far from Cibola*, and *The Common Heart*)
Mexico Bay

THE RICHARD NOVELS
Things As They Are · Everything to Live For · The Thin Mountain Air

OTHER FICTION
The Return of the Weed · The Saintmaker's Christmas Eve
Figures in a Landscape · Humble Powers · The Devil in the Desert
Toby and the Nighttime (juvenile) · One Red Rose for Christmas
The Peach Stone: *Stories from Four Decades*

HISTORY AND OTHER NONFICTION
Men of Arms (*juvenile*) · From the Royal City
New Mexico's Own Chronicle (*with Maurice Garland Fulton*)
Great River: The Rio Grande in North American History
The Centuries of Santa Fe · Rome Eternal · Citizen of New Salem
Conquistadors in North American History
Peter Hurd: *A Portrait Sketch from Life* · Songs After Lincoln
The Heroic Triad: *Essays in the Social Energies of
Three Southwestern Cultures* · Maurice Baring Restored
Encounters with Stravinsky: *A Personal Record* · Approaches to Writing
Lamy of Santa Fe: *His Life and Times*
Josiah Gregg and His Vision of the Early West
Of America East and West: *Selections from the Writings of Paul Horgan*
The Clerihews of Paul Horgan, *Drawings by Joseph Reed*
Under the Sangre de Cristo · A Writer's Eye: *Watercolors and Drawings*
A Certain Climate: *Essays in History, Arts, and Letters*

A CERTAIN CLIMATE

A

CERTAIN

CLIMATE

ESSAYS IN HISTORY,

ARTS, AND LETTERS

PAUL

HORGAN

Wesleyan University Press

Middletown, Connecticut

1988

Library of Congress Cataloging-in-Publication Data
Horgan, Paul, 1903–
A certain climate.
1. Arts, American.   2. Arts—Historiography.
3. Historiography.   I. Title.
NX503.H67   1988   700'.973   88–137
ISBN 0–8195–5202–x

All inquiries and permissions requests should be
addressed to the Publisher, Wesleyan University Press,
110 Mt. Vernon Street, Middletown, Connecticut 06457
Manufactured in the United States of America
First Edition

To

Victor Lloyd Butterfield

1904-1975

Contents

Author's Note

Most sources of quotations here are identified as they occur. Exceptions are Oscar Handlin's *This Was America,* to which I am gratefully indebted for views and events in the life of Father Antonio Grassi; and my own book *Great River: The Rio Grande in North American History,* from which I drew materials for the essay "Yankee Doodle: Models of Early American Style," enriching them with additions from other works named in their context.

For their various and generous services in the preparation of this volume I offer my thanks to Joseph W. Reed, Jeannette Hopkins, Cynthia Krupat, and in particular to the late Dean Martin I. J. Griffin, Jr. of Yale.

P. H.

Middletown, Connecticut

ONE

TOWARD

HISTORY

JOURNEY TO THE PAST

—AND RETURN

---

i. The Nature and Pleasure of History

Richard Hofstadter said, "Memory is the thread of personal identity, history of public identity." Or, as we might otherwise put it, history is man's collective biography, and though many scholars of the academy may quarrel with Emerson's biographical concept of history, that is another affair, conceived of in terms of individual lives instead of those abstract motivations whose study has also had its vogue among historical thinkers.

But particular approaches aside, let us reflect upon the notion that history dwells within two traditions—one, oral repetition on every level of intelligence, from rumor to gossip to eyewitness accounts; and two, a written text. The first is innocent. We ask nothing of it but to hear it. The second has pretensions, and these can be separated into two sets of values. One of these relates to the work of the literary artist, the other to that of the investigative artisan. Generally, the artist, in the very nature of his vision, must be left to himself; for he sees his subject first of all in a concept of form, and it is the form in which his vision is contained that gives it significance, in this, as in all other arts.

It is the artisans with which the academy, under immense pressures of the numbers of students seeking degrees in history, is obliged to concern itself. The result, as Henry Steele Commager remarked—I think, of Winston Churchill—is that the great historians are almost all self-taught. That is, the wonderful act, almost of transubstantiation, by which raw material becomes art is something which cannot be taught as a technique. What can be taught, in this connection, is the ideal itself, through which a talented young historian may be helped to discover in his own qualities those which, once recognized by him, he may develop and refine for himself. Historical writing that is not literature is subject to oblivion—unless, of course, it may belong to that category of material called the primary source. But it is obviously not this category with which we are dealing here. It is the act of literature—not the urgency of topic or drift of culture or power of events alone—that keeps individual books alive. It seems to be the trend today to judge the value of a work more by its subject, and the author's attitude, than by the degree of art involved, and, as of history, so also of the contemporary novel, the drama, the poem.

What we are talking about is the double nature of the act of recording human life, which is the purpose of both the historian and the artist. The historian is traditionally associated with the pursuit and retention of fact. He is sworn by his professional ethic to objectivity. He therefore devotes great effort and time to amassing evidence to verify his report that will convince anyone who does not possess his studied knowledge.

In itself, however, the virtue of objectivity is not enough to create a record which will endure beyond the capricious span of public interest in his subject. Something more is wanted. This is the literary power raised to the degree sought by the artist. Fact is always interesting, but it takes more than fact to keep alive a subject that would fade away but for the historian's addition of the other gift which keeps memory memorable—and that is a power of reconstructive imagination equal to a power of methodical research.

Not to forget, either, that the inventive literary artist needs his aspect, too, of the double nature of the art—and that is the sense of actuality, to which we shall return later. Here it is that the very nature of the literary gift comes into confluence with the gift of critically assimilating information for the purpose of recovering the past. And therefore, we take the risk of claiming that the historian, in addition to his *objectivity*, must call into play the sort of *subjectivity* identified as intuition. We shall return to this, too, as we proceed. For now, let us suggest that it is intuitive understanding which will allow him to revive the past, not only with factual certainty, but with a sense of the passion that must always be seen in human affairs, individual or collective. It is a writer with just such a gift who tells us, whether in history or the other arts, more about the nature and action of man than any dispassionate observer.

If literature and its intuitions become allies of history, so, too, must all the arts and the sciences; for these, as modes of expression, are in effect the vocabulary of intuition. No act of thought or projection of knowledge is necessarily isolated from any other. Our ideal broadens—we seek the polymath, at least in spirit, if not in universal accomplishment. Leonardos and Oppenheimers are scarce—but their wonderful love and projection of understanding as both private connoisseurs and historical achievers offer us at least an ideal to consider and measure by. Even in its very subdivisions, history requires the breadth we speak of. Political history, biography, cultural and social history, to name a few of the more obvious, all demand that the historian, if he be interested in a specialty, see it not in its isolation but in its relevance to the widest human experience. The collective purpose of man's autobiography imposes on us the ideal that we express it through the collective intellectual means of the polymath.

Here is the opportunity not for narrowing the appeal of history by formidable displays of special knowledge, but for widening its appeal to readers through diversity of perception. Scholarship has its own pure ideal to which everyone pays high respect. But at times it carries with it an exclusiveness that seems to disdain the general reader, however intelligent he may turn out to be. A quite artificial set of oppositions has arisen as between what is patronizingly called popular history on the one hand and what is with an excited tremor of exclusive delight called scholarly history on the other. The difference often appears to lie in the variations of apparatus between the two, and here, also, seem to rest the opposing concepts of history as an art and history as a science. In the English-language world, oddly, it is only in America that it is disreputable in the academy for an historian to be comprehensible by the large public. It is an unhappy reflection, perhaps, of that snobbery which invariably accompanies any colonialism—in this case an intellectual colonialism migrating from nineteenth-century Teutonic systems of historiography. It may seem apposite to quote here, perhaps with more of a smile than he wore as he wrote it, a passage by Carl Jung in his book *Memories, Dreams, Reflections*: "Loneliness does not come from having no people about one, but from being unable to communicate the things that seem important to oneself. . . . If a man knows more than others, he becomes lonely. But loneliness is not necessarily inimical to companionship, for no one is more sensitive to companionship than the lonely man. . . ."

Here we are again, face to face with the unnecessarily self-conscious modern problem of "how to communicate." Surely even the most severe of historians hopes to be read, and be understood—in brief, to communicate. If it is not too frivolous a notion, perhaps we might say that a great quality for the ideal historian is that he must possess a low threshold of boredom—at all costs he must write in such a way as to save himself from being bored either by his own material or his own manner.

Frivolity aside, let us say with all respect that every intellectual or artistic maker (I use Igor Stravinsky's proud and simple word for artist) hopes to enter into the kingdom of his own vision—the kingdom where his vision will prevail— the vision which has the power to capture meaning and give it form; for it is only by means of aesthetic form that he will convey his total vision to others.

ii. The Historian and His Proper Subject

To speak from the experience of a novelist who has written history and an historian who sees no quarrel among the various forms of literary or other artistic truth, I must deal candidly with an aspect of historical writing which is primarily aesthetic, and that is the historian's relation—his primal response—to his subject.

Any student can be told to go to work on a given assignment, and if he is a good student, he can give us a creditable paper, based on diligence, technical orthodoxy (with its own tyrannies), and perhaps a legalistic tendency to argue an inference. But the true historian cannot work on assignment, he cannot in fact proceed at all unless his subject attacks him not only in the galleries of a knowledgeable mind but in the unaccountable labyrinths of the viscera. That is where his pang of recognition seems to occur—that sense of his born vocation in relation to a given subject. Lacking this, we may of course be given a respectable work. With it, given technical skills, we may well be given not only a worthy work of history, but a masterpiece of literature.

It is of vital importance that the historian find resonances of many kinds within himself as he responds to his subject. At first he may be charmed with the mere procedures of his task. An opinion of his may suddenly find some support in an incident of the past, and he may have the notion that he has found a subject. He may weigh it and, as it were, taste it for some time, while revolving about it in a kind of intellectual nuptial dance. If he is lucky, the matter will increase its hold upon him, until he can manage to look ahead without dismay to years of study, travel, investigation, and the rest, to provide him with the substance of his interest. But there is always a dire possibility: his subject may seem to grow into vast significance, until it comes in danger of losing its proper dimension in the scheme of his knowledge.

If all this process is merely cerebral, it is likely that the historian, in projecting his undertaking before attacking it, will wear himself and his subject out in the onerous effort of convincing himself first, before he sets out to convince anyone else. If so, and if again he is lucky, he may awaken in time to the true state of affairs and undergo a dismal period when his beloved subject suddenly seems trivial, when his hours of thought seem in retrospect to betray a lack of real sophistication on his part, and he may find his self-confidence badly shaken. I am sure many writers have had such experiences. It is an odd thing how, despite the first excitement, some preliminary notes set down with perfect faith in their vitality will die when looked at later; and how others will live, burgeon, take on a wonderful relevance to everything in one's life and thought, and eventually come to something.

But the narrow escapes, however painful, are valuable: and we think of Gibbon, who after lengthy and majestic intentions and preparations suddenly saw a certain subject for what it was, and awoke from it, so to speak, and thus left open the way before him to the marvel of his real lifework, while the rest of us were thus narrowly spared a history of the Helvetian Revolution which, had he gone ahead with it, must surely have foreshortened and—who knows?—possibly closed away from us forever the *Decline and Fall*.

Now this sort of sudden halt, after hopeful and serious considerations, is much less likely to happen to the writer whose subject seeks him, rather than the other way round. It must break over him like a revelation, and, again, it is impossible not to refer to the universally known moment when Gibbon, seated in the church of the Zoccolanti at the hour of vespers above the ruins of the Forum, knew with a power of revelation surely physical in its immediate effect that in his great Roman subject he had found the work of his life, whatever time must pass until he could undertake and finish it.

We have other testimony about how to know when a subject, or an idea, really reaches you—the poet Housman said, "Experience has taught me, when I am shaving of a morning, to keep watch over my thoughts, because, if a line of poetry strays into my memory, my skin bristles so that the razor ceases to act." Others have cited the strike of certainty as arriving at the solar plexus, when the impact of intuition as to theme and meaning, and the concept of the enclosing and releasing design, and the sense of tone—style and texture—all manifest themselves together. The whole work and its major implications exist for the first time in the vision of a few seconds, essentially complete. All then that remains is the time it takes for the research, and the writing—perhaps five years, perhaps ten, perhaps a lifetime—years of marvelous industry and utterly satisfying absorption. Some of the rewards are, of course, famous for their inverted claim to immortality, such as that bestowed upon Gibbon by a mini-minded royal personage with the greeting, "Scribble, scribble, scribble, eh, Mr. Gibbon?"

Grand dimension can, of course, tempt the historical maker to become addicted to the chase rather than to the capture. Extended research has its own intoxications, and the desire for completeness, the definitive, the utterly non-improvable, can, through the years of a major undertaking, come to seem like the chief purpose, instead of the apprenticeship, of an achievement. The moment must come when, whatever the intoxications of the process and the deep and loving respect for the subject, the historian must draw a line and say, "I will not cross it. If I do, I may never finish." Lord Acton has one of his grand phrases for what is wanted at such a moment—he calls upon himself to observe "a resolved limitation." We thank him for it, and the illustrious example behind it. To his precept we may perhaps suggest an appendage. It is this: that research extended beyond a sensible period can in time smother the most essential of the elements in the historian's makeup, that is, his imagination, his grasp of the whole, his projection of form. For it is idle to suppose that any human production of any virtue or interest can be produced without the animating energy of the imagination—the very action of which initially found for the historian the subject that evoked its special response in his innermost resonance.

iii. Imagination and Technique

The imagination has three great functions: (1) to originate; (2) to re-create; and (3) to relate diverse elements of life to each other.

It is easy to see in all three of these the basic anatomy of talent, whether in art, science, politics, or philosophy. It is the maker's problem and challenge to move from imagination to expression, and it is here that artistry enters the process and with it the values of literature. These, of course, are diffuse, and sometimes lamentably subject to fashion, but of the artist's equipment surely the historian can refine to his use the faculties of vision, and the dramatic, the auditory, and, in certain situations, by transfer, the tactile senses that serve the artist so intimately. As an artist cannot give us convincingly any account of his life he himself has not intensely observed, so the historian must know physical proximity to his subject and its settings—its objects, its ambiance, the atmosphere of its culture, before he can possess the life he must re-create. His task is not merely to assemble and to prove: he must enter into and animate the facts without betraying the truth. This is the artist's share in the historian's mission.

The historian who is not also a competent connoisseur and aesthete, as well as a thinker who may be politically, economically, militarily, psychologically, or scientifically oriented, is insufficiently equipped. The mind of the merely materialistic fact collector is, like the moon, lighted from only one side. Evidence provided by the arts is the most direct means by which we achieve entry into the *spirit* and *style* of the past; and any treatment that does not essentially grasp that spirit and penetrate that style is sure to be incomplete as history and inadequate as literature.

Cultural history and political history cannot be separated; for in both, it is the presence of man in his time that we peruse; and in the historian's own life, these elements, though he may not think much about it, are not distinct from each other. Versatility is not distracting—it is an enriching capacity that should be cultivated. One art will predominate in an individual's capacity to exercise several; but all will enrich the predominant one. Goethe accompanied his account of his journey in Italy with watercolors and drawings which he made along the way. He attempted to describe in drawing as well as in writing. He was no great draftsman, but that he saw in the double faculty was important. The animation, visual intensity, and sense of actuality in his writing surely owed much to his embrace of experience through a second medium.

Then, given command of the approaches to history, and even at times in spite of error or incomplete information, it is the *way* in which the historian sets them forth that elevates a work of historical writing into literature, or not. Many great classics of history, corrected in various detail by later scholars, remain valid works of historical literature simply because of their power of imagination and splendor of style.

Fashions change in historical techniques as in any other intellectual systems or structures. I suppose the whole debate implied by the background of our subject would not even exist were it not for the systematic zeal of the Germanic historians of the nineteenth century who sought to bring history into the sciences by methodology—that overdressed word. But we cannot ever forget that most of the world's masterpieces of historical writing antedate the invocation of this scientific attitude, and even as it was being posed, Carlyle was making his claim for history as an art.

Methodology by itself is never enough. All the possible technical mastery will not alone create an enduring work in the written medium. Its permanent value, as well as its immediate authority, can be made certain only if accompanied by such nonmethodical qualities as empathy, narrative gift, dramatic sense, intuitive intimation of human character, regard for fresh precision in statement and for beauty of language. Precepts from the fictive art occur to us again and again as we read or write history: Henry James with his cry, "Dramatize, dramatize!" and Dickens with his "make me *see!*" Perhaps Berenson summed it all up neatly when he said, "History is an art which must take cognizance of the known facts."

Here I offer a small passage that might be called "The Itch of General Pershing's Nose." I do so in reference to our incessant search for the animating detail. Cumulations of animating detail will never take the place of the subject at large: but without animating detail the subject at large can sink into dullness. When, during World War I, General Pershing stepped upon the soil of France from his transport, and with a keen professional eye gazed about at the logistical apparatus on the pier, the attending officials, all the machinery of a great adventure waiting for him on a grey French day, his nose itched, and with a forefinger he vigorously rubbed it just below the nostrils. How trivial! Yet how human! For me, at least, through such a detail, for a tiny instant of common sensation, the eminent general and I feel something together. Only a living creature can itch. It is a living man—life itself—we seek to restore. Any detail that may help in this act of resurrection is of value.

Nobody wrote this detail down—it came to my sight through the medium of one of the most marvelous instruments of historical reference ever created: the motion-picture camera. In an old newsreel of the disembarkation in France I saw the general rub his itch, and I found the little incident somehow a fine detail to note as part of the solemn occasion when the words "Lafayette, we are here" are said to have been uttered.

I plead again, as I have elsewhere, for the establishment of a great central depository of factual news film, indexed and catalogued down to the smallest analytic degree, where historians may see in actual motion certain persons they may write about, observe their mannerisms, the heft of their bodies, the characteristics of movement, and hear how they spoke. From all such avenues of access to personalities of the more or less immediate past derive impressions otherwise obtainable only in life itself. Scattered collections of this sort exist, but already much priceless film material has crumbled away forever. Daily editing and filming of the unceasing increase of film footage must be undertaken. The film, from almost the start of our century, is the incomparable witness to events. What would we have done hitherto without newspapers and gazettes as sources? How can we henceforth enliven our subjects without recourse to the animated journalism of both silent and sound film? The cost of such a film archive would be immense—but what would a real civilization not pay to keep the living image of the past?

In respect to method, we have all felt the constrictions of scholarly apparatus, and some of us, I imagine, long to be free of them; but this is of course impossible so long as we must substantiate material, or statement, or even opinion. Ultimately, in the use of apparatus, much depends on the reader for whom the historian may be writing, and such a consideration may determine the degree of visibility, to the reader, of technique. There are some historical writers, of course, who revel in the ceremonies of pedantry—indeed, the famous musicologist, and my lifelong friend, Nicolas Slonimsky, once cried out to me in the highest gaiety, "I adore pedantry!" But too often we encounter, say, footnotes which, in adding supplementary information, belong in the body of the text; and the presence of such information at the bottom of the page instead of above seems often to be a sign of laziness or of an inability to manage a comprehensive sentence.

The air of the learned afterthought is a personal indulgence that shows little regard for literary control, or mercy for the reader who would prefer not to be distracted. Who could resist citing here, if only for his own pleasure, the echoing perspectives of our present subject set up through rhetorical arcades in issue number 173 of *The Rambler*:

"The general reproach with which ignorance revenges the superciliousness of learning," trumpeted Dr. Johnson, "is that of pedantry; a censure which every man incurs, who has at any time the misfortune to talk to those who cannot understand him"—how this must reflect Dr. Johnson's own relentless elevation—"and by which," he goes on, "the modest and timorous are sometimes frightened from the display of their own acquisitions, and the exertion of their powers. . . . All discourse of which others cannot partake"—and of course there is a silent dialogue between the historian and his reader, at whatever level—"is not only," says *The Rambler*, "an irksome usurpation of the time devoted to pleasure and entertainment, but, what never fails to excite very keen resentment, an insolent assertion of superiority, and a triumph over less enlightened understandings. The pedant is, therefore, not only heard with weariness, but malignity; and those who conceive themselves insulted by his knowledge, never fail to tell with acrimony how injudiciously it was exerted. . . ."

The old Thunderer may specifically be referring to

speech, but his views may surely be applied to writing. If pedantry may be reread as a term for earned authority, rather than mismangement of that authority, perhaps we could say that the degree to which pedantry, factuality, accuracy, intuition, the sense of design, and the humble and loving execution of the written sentence are brought together in equal play is a measure of the dimensions of the complete historian.

One final factor in technique and style may be cited here, and that is the ability of the historian to deal with significant affairs of any period in language whose tone is close to the vernacular of his time, and which is yet used fastidiously enough to achieve the air of the classic. In our day we are too often tempted by various trade jargons in the writing of history, or by the vogue words of the moment. But cant expressions lose their inner illumination very fast. If we use them for our intraprofessional satisfaction today, we do so in peril of tomorrow's indifference or derision. Great history has been written in the raciest and most personal tone. Scholars I know who command Latin with thoroughness and delight assure me that what I detect in translations of Tacitus is of course even more to be felt in the original, and that is, his delightful regard for the rhythms, the pungencies, the immediacies, of ordinary speech.

How directly he conveyed his personality! He was indeed a racy historian, with such a digestible way of presenting inflexible fact, such a narrative gift, such an appealing conviction that what he has to record is of universal interest, and therefore that it deserves to be recorded in a form which will live a life of its own—that is, the life of a work of art. The adaptation of the thoughtless knacks of ordinary speech to written form is no easy matter. It is not simply a matter of the transcription of the common speech or of echoes of its simple styles. If we think so, all we have to do to be abashed in this notion is to listen to a tape recording of even a most literate extemporaneous speaker and compare it with what he writes. Between these two means there is a world of difference in the employment of all the literary elements.

Much of our present production in written history seems to show small care for the transformation of the fugitive common idiom into timeless rhetoric. We do not commonly teach the mechanics of the art of writing any more in any intensive way. When we consider the ancient art of rhetoric, so eagerly studied by Tacitus, and its classical and empowering heritage, we discover uneasily certain implications for education toward expression as we know it now in our country. We lack a *tradition* of how to write, speak, and even read. Americans tend to improvise a style, no matter what the occasion. We are individualists in this as in so much else. Lively in opinion, better informed now than ever before, the garrulous citizen-democrat thinks more about what he has to say than how to say it. One is reminded of our national faith that anyone who can write a "good" letter can just as readily write a serious novel or a sensible book review. Our fiction, our criticism, and, alas, much of our historical writing reflect this folk belief. We should heed Anthony Trollope's recommendation concerning prime attributes for a good writer. Suggesting that "some man of letters" undertake the task of writing a history of English prose fiction, he specified one "who shall at the same time be indefatigable and light-handed. . . ." It goes without saying that he took correctness for granted. Let it be noted that correctness need not suppress freshness or originality of thought or text.

iv. Form, Spirit, and Intuition

One of the most famous, and in my view, one of the most masterly opening sentences in a work of history is this: "The archangel loved heights."

It is, of course, Henry Adams's opening statement in his *Mont-Saint-Michel and Chartres.* Fortunate the author whose opening sentence contains the seed of his whole book!

In a stroke of magnificent comprehensiveness, Adams gives us a rich atmospheric suggestion of the form that is to follow. The statement is pure in relation to the subject of the medieval mystery in civilization; it is pure in its relation to the style of the period Adams is writing about; it is fresh and enduring as a concept of projected feeling; and it makes plain at the very outset the point of view of the writer, for in speaking of the archangel as a sentient reality who is at home in great altitudes, he gives us all sorts of subtle entries into many meanings—that in the time of history when archangels were positively visualized, their habits must thus be known; and that heights may be taken literally as well as metaphorically in theological terms; and that architecturally Michael himself may be seen crowning his temple; and that in giving him distinct personality, Adams serves notice to us that he is paying respects, even if with an exquisite restrained irony, to the beliefs he is about to examine.

Thus, in a single opening sentence of four words, the seed of an entire book is planted in our thought, and as its form unfolds, we stir with the aesthetic pleasure of encountering a perfect fulfillment in form of ideas, impressions, opinions, descriptions which brought together less beautifully would remain scattered, and thus bereft of their common meaning. It is in this sense that the solution of form for a work of history, or any art, is probably the most important of the many important aesthetic acts that must be brought to bear.

Design itself becomes a reference—to information, to a point of view, to a flow of proper proportion between the parts, and to the just placing of emphasis. These are clearly the acts of the artist. Adams himself is quoted by Ernest Samuels as writing in a letter to John LaFarge, "The historian must be an artist. He must know how to develop the leading ideas of the subject he has chosen, how to keep the thread of the narrative always in hand, how to subordinate details, and how to accentuate principles. . . . The most difficult thing for me," he said, "is to vary the length of my sentences so as to relieve the attention. In the struggle to do this," he concludes, "I have sometimes found myself doing very clumsy things."

It is a consoling passage, not only for our general thesis, but for the failures of the day as we get on with our job. It is also edifying to know that even so fastidious, so remote, so skeptical a man, was not above consciously trying to hold the reader's attention. Devoted to truth in fact, he could present it only through literary power in the hope of communicating his vision.

Carlyle, in his essay on history, made a fine sequence about the nature of historical form, from its simplest to its most complicated state. "A talent for history may be said to be born with us as our chief inheritance. In a certain sense all men are historians. . . . Our very speech is curiously historical. Most men, you may observe, speak only to narrate. . . . Thus, as we *do* nothing but enact history, we *say* little but to recite it. . . . Narrative is linear. Action is solid. . . . The artist in history may be distinguished from the artisan in history . . . artisans [are] . . . men who labor mechanically in a department [meaning *portion*] without eye for the whole; not feeling that there *is* a whole: and [artists are] men who inform and ennoble the humblest *department* with an *idea of the whole*, and habitually know that only in the whole is the partial to be truly discerned."

Within successful literary form, the sense of character finds its best representations. Here the art of the literary intuition—the novelist's or the dramatist's, the poet's or the historian's—can come into powerful play. All the evidence and documentation for what a personage of the past may have done is incomplete unless there is some sense of who he was who did it, and why, compelled by his nature in response to circumstance. It is the sort of estimate which the artist-historian makes more often than the recording-historian, as we might call Carlyle's artisan. I am moved by what E. M. Forster wrote more or less in this connection in his piece on

Gibbon, who, he says, was "a historian who realizes that it is impossible, through reading alone, to interpret the past. Nor is emotion enough. The historian," said Forster, "must have a third quality as well: some conception of how men who are *not* historians behave. Otherwise he will move in a world of the dead. He can only gain that conception through personal experience, and he can only use his personal experiences when he is a genius. . . ."

We are returning closer and closer, as we think of form, and speak of the importance of narrative, and reflect on the importance of suggestive atmosphere, to intuition and its indispensable place in our task. The spirit of a work will often rest most deeply in its author's point of view, and try as he may to suppress his point of view, he will fail: if it appear not in his words, it will glance out at us from between his lines. This being so, it were better for his point of view to be established by his natural capacities of understanding and his own resonance of character than according to any schematic system of belief or judgment. The play of ideas that he sets in motion will create tension between the ideas of the historical period under discussion and the ideas of the author.

If he has undertaken a work of some amplitude, he must face two hazards or challenges, the first a matter of discipline, the second a matter of the spirit.

Firstly, then, he will have the hazard of sustaining the airy structure of those tensions of ideas I have mentioned, and of keeping them alive in the daily excitement of his imaginative conviction over the period of years required for the completion of his work: and it is my belief that the daily revival of that excited conviction will be possible only if, *before* he has started, he has projected a form, a design, for his work so beautiful and just that as he advances it toward completion bit by bit he will feel in every daily encounter the same pristine lift that accompanied his primal conception.

Secondly, he must admit to himself that the mystery that lies at the heart of literature must be related to love—love of subject, love of the act of work, love of the human mind and its desire to be informed, love of the responsive understanding which may await his work. While many of these aspects of the task call upon intellectual resources that must be as highly developed and refined as possible, there is, then, something beyond these more valuable—indeed, indispensable. In her collection of medieval Latin lyrics, Helen Waddell said, again of the exemplary master to whom we turn so often, "Tacitus, beyond all historians, has the humanity that means the gift of divination; he had pierced to the secret spring. . . ."

v. Raw Material and the Sense of Actuality

Ideally, the secret spring must become our habitat if we are to lead others there through history. If we are to aspire to success in translating our inmost responses to history, which are often formless, however powerful, into such form as will allow others to join us in our own vision, we must take the raw materials, of whatever sort—documentation, geographical observation, aesthetic and cultural visitations—through the crucible fires of our own achieved awareness.

In such a refining process there is some danger that all may turn to ash, and so we may lose the spark of life in those raw records upon which we would build our own presentations of past epochs. Without conscious care, and the taste bred by years of reading and weighing inwardly the true significance of past lives, individual and collective, we may be led astray from the suitable uses of feeling into the exclusive uses of scholarly components.

And when none but these latter survive on our pages, every virtue may remain but one—and that is the essential one for life—the sense of things in their own truth, completed by ours, based on our acquired later information. We seek the truth of how life went in its own time—seeking its shadow, we attempt to restore its substance. There exists, too, the corresponding danger of leaping at attractive conclusions made persuasive to us by our emotions alone. Everything about *such* conclusions may be splendid, with one fatal exception: they may be wrong.

Neither emotion nor information is a substitute for the other. Both must supplement each other in just proportion, and both must serve that sense of the real which is our most valuable form of credit.

In an essay called "The Consolations of History," E. M. Forster—once again I trust him—declared, "The sense of actuality . . . sleeps forever in most historians." Is is a strong statement, and it raises an uneasy question: Of what value is any history which does not restore to us a sense of the actual?

We all know the piercing sense of life which we are given by primary source materials—letters, diaries, eyewitness accounts, and the rest. Even at their most artless they have power to move us according to our own degree of sensibility to life itself. But the writing of history is not devoted merely to collecting and publishing original raw materials. We put the weight of our whole structures upon them—but it is the design we bring to our structures that in the end represents our whole achievement.

The historian's great challenge is, therefore, to keep alive as he draws from them the very actualities of that once urgent concern which impelled someone to record in immediate, or raw, form, the acts of his days. The historian's sense of actuality is achieved by a feeling for humanity that has been finely honed from the very beginning of his studies, indeed, of his independent life as a receptive human being, child or adult. Then when he comes into possession of the raw, direct evidences of the past, he will really feel in them the perfectly conscious emotions of the original participants or observers, as well as find the suitable framework, crafted from subsequent knowledge, in which to present those evidences.

If we long to know anything at all, we long to know "how it was," not merely "what it was," in any given situation. Our own interest in reaching the sense of *being there*—whenever or wherever—our sense of participating in, of living with, the time before our own, is surely what impels the historian on his way. As I have elsewhere stated, one's hope is "to produce a sense of the historical experience, rather than a bare record." For the bare record already exists in scattered elements, and we cannot compete in basic authenticity with what we find in archives and other raw sources. The best we can do is respect them absolutely—and find the often unconscious overall design within which their first once urgent daily concern was committed to record. So as we apply the original materials we strive to protect in them the flow of their original life, not only to illuminate our projects, but for their own sake as lingering signs of that which passes.

John Aubrey said of his own reportings that they were like fragments of a shipwreck "that after the Revolution of so many Years and Governments have escaped the Teeth of Time and (which is more dangerous) the Hands of mistaken Zeale. So that the retriving [*sic*] of these forgotten Things from Oblivion in some sort resembles the Art of a Conjuror, who makes those walke and appeare that have layen in their graves many hundreds of yeares: and to represent as it were to the eie, the places, Customes and Fashions, that were of old Times."

It is the empathetic responses of the artist and the true teacher—and both of these time and again give us the same insights—that help to bridge the gap between raw material and significance in form. Here it would be a luxury to enter upon an orgy of citation and quotation—yet, in a state of hilarity, astonishment, or enchantment before marvels, how can we not quote favorite passages from such as Aubrey, the Duc de Saint-Simon, John James Audubon, William Bartram, Marshal Coulaincourt, Bernál Diáz del Castillo, or whomever?

As I am weak, I yield to quote a trifle from a favorite book which often travels with me, *The Life and Times of Anthony à Wood* in the elegant little Oxford World's Classics selection. Flipping at random, because I love the imperishable old wretch, I find him reporting that, on a certain day in 1664, the weather was so hot that poultry died of the heat in Abingdon market. What on earth does that matter, you might say. And of course, by itself it doesn't matter at all, after three hundred-odd years, except as a curiosity such as our darting author is full of. But if I had to treat historically an affair of serious consequence as of that same day and place, I would think that chickens dying of the heat—in England, of all places—would lend a certain air of actuality to my total picture.

It is for us to be as specific as the past, if we cannot hope to be as comprehensive. I am, further, content if the past also arranges to provide the marvelous. Some raw materials can forever be read for their own power to delight us, and nothing is without its power of reminder or analogy.

Now, is it possible to propose a "law" or even a "principle" about this matter of the conversion of raw material into a finished thing? With all diffidence, let me hazard this: There are two general intellectual tastes in all of us—one is for the abstract, with its lovely orderly austerities of pure thought, which propose patterns related mostly to subjective life; the other is the love of human experience in all its objective, and disorderly, variety. The one satisfies a wonderful capacity and instinct of the mind; but abstractions either end with themselves or lead to other abstractions, and tend to concern only the individual thinker. Perhaps we may say that he will be interested in the raw material of life only as it feeds his self-fulfilling speculations.

On the other hand, man's collective experience, with its fantastic range of intimate reminders of our own private condition, in which there is nothing new and yet in which everything is amazing through its very likeness to life as we know it, is everyone's concern, whether observed through Plutarch or the anchor man of the evening news on television. Nothing could be farther from abstraction than what man has endured, created, observed, recorded, died for, or triumphed over.

Perhaps, then, we might say that, in the rhetoric of history, a final value is this: Historical writing that remains tethered to raw material even though methodically organized and factually respectable, but no more than this, may well miss the whole truth through lack of full human perception; whereas, historical writing that is faithful to fact while transmuting it by means of design and artistry may produce a sense of actuality and the whole truth, because its supports rest in both the past—the past of unalterable fact—and the present—the present as represented by the historian's developed and embracing sensibility. Our sense of the abstract surely serves in helping us to arrive at form; while our sense of common life, however disparate its details, may bring us to imaginative re-creation within our resolved form.

vi. The Metaphor and Mystery of the Journey

Fact of course is not synonymous with metaphor; but meaning does emerge from metaphor, or whatever sort of analogy may enliven metaphor. Truly realized in appropriate form, any given period or condition of man can be seen as the metaphor of mankind's estate at large. Achievement of this— as Carlyle had told us earlier—is the mark of the artist who deals with facts; and it is surely one of the governing fascinations attached to the writing and the reading of man's collective biography.

In his essay "History and Fiction," G. M. Trevelyan said, "History starts from this astonishing proposition—that there is no difference in degree of reality between past and present. Lady Jane Grey was once as actual as anyone in this room . . . we are all food for history. Not one century, not even the twentieth, is more real than another. That is the most obtrusive and hackneyed, and yet the most mysterious, of facts. It is the common ground of all religions, all philosophies, all poetry. . . . There is nothing that more divides civilized man from semi-savage man"—and for my part I might insert, the artist in historical writing from the artisan—"than to be conscious of our forefathers as they really were . . . truth is the criterion of historical study; but its impelling motive is poetic. Its poetry consists in its being true. Work that out and you will get a synthesis of the scientific and literary views of history."

The task, so proposed, calls for humility in the face of the visible truth and also before the undoubted but unseen mystery which lies at the heart of literature. The best we can do about the whole matter is to meditate upon what can be formulated, and to search our answers as hard as we do our questions. There will always be the temptation to fit a formula over ideas or circumstances possibly alien to it. In the last lines of his *To the Finland Station*, Edmund Wilson has a warning to the historian who would sacrifice historical values to the pressures of *any* dogma. He must remain on guard against such schematic solutions, and, says Wilson, "to accomplish such a task will require of us an unsleeping adaptive exercise of reason and instinct combined."

To penetrate the depths of the past, and to find familiar the places and circumstances the farther one travels back, and see with the eye of the imagination that which is true because once it existed—this is the first half of our journey in time.

The other half of our journey in time is our return from the past, bringing what we have seen, bearing in honor whatever truth we have found, and remaining humble before the mystery which abides; for with all the method in the world, and all the cumulated facts, and notes, and proper cognizances and discriminations amidst the modish views prevalent in our own times, there must always remain that which cannot be explained: the artist's inmost relation to his work. There are as many explanations for wisdom as there are wise men and women. In man's progress in knowledge there abides some intuition that is proper to every stage of life, from childhood with its great longing stare, to youth's hard conviction, to the old man's acceptance of the word "perhaps."

I might do worse than end these remarks of exploration by quoting some lines from what Walter de la Mare called a "dandling rhyme" when he included it in his magical collection of poetry entitled *Come Hither*.

For this dandling folk song seems to me to suggest by way of parable man's eternal interest in his past and his inescapable return to the present; and in these anonymous old English lines, if you will accept their lightness and sweetness, you will know perhaps one more illustration of the beguiling and mysterious nature of history itself as we try, step by step, to unfold it:

> *This is the key of the kingdom—*
> *In that kingdom there is a city;*
> *In that city there is a town;*
> *In that town there is a street;*
> *In that street there winds a lane;*
> *In that lane there is a yard;*
> *In that yard there is a house;*
> *In that house there waits a room;*
> *In that room an empty bed;*
> *And on that bed a basket—*
> *A basket of sweet flowers:*
> > *Of flowers, of flowers:*
> > *A basket of sweet flowers.*

And now the return:

> *Flowers in a basket,*
> *Basket on the bed;*
> *Bed in the chamber;*
> *Chamber in the house;*
> *House in the weedy yard;*
> *Yard in the winding lane;*
> *Lane in the broad street;*
> *Street in the high town;*
> *Town in the city;*
> *City in the kingdom—*
> *This is the key of the kingdom—*
>   *Of the kingdom this is the key.*

YANKEE DOODLE:

EARLY MODELS OF

AMERICAN STYLE

---

i

How few ventured, in how brief a time, across the lower half of North America, from coast to coast, to implant their lives and create the outlines of the continental nation in the name of the individual American, and in honor of a new order of society. Yet the few were to become the many in a matter of decades, when the independent national identity was secured by the Revolution. As the American pioneer west took root, made living places, planted institutions, worked toward amenity of private spirit and public association, all such expressions came to be through the individual work of men and women obliged to use their personal skills of mind and craft, however rude the materials at hand and far away the origins of their social memory. By and large, continental America was handmade.

ii

As the individual felt equal to the vast wilderness, so he was able to get on with the job of turning a continent into a neighborhood. Men who knew how to use themselves against the wilds made a close community, whenever they consented to congregate. Out of their congregation would emerge the expressions through which they would originate, and bequeath, the earlier styles of their national character. It was a character derived from the eastern seaboard meld of the old New Englanders, the Dutch and Swedes of the Delaware, the Germans of Pennsylvania, the ultra-Appalachian mountaineers, the Huguenots of the Carolinas—all reinforced by later waves of immigration from abroad.

In an absurd, immemorial suspicion, the first venturers who remade the continent gave any later comer a hard time until he was able to prove himself in frontier terms of physical prowess. The habit sometimes showed itself in a comic hostility that masked a process of sharp appraisal. Who are you? was always the first question. The new population, in its noncoherent form, demanded that each member be, in effect, an independent unit of society in himself, until grounds for acceptance were established between him and his prospective fellow-citizens. It was a process that called forth improvised traits of social demeanor. A British observer in 1772 found that "the natives of these provinces [reveal] a shrewdness and penetration not generally observable in the mother country . . . even beyond the bounds of propriety." In the advance against the wilderness, judgment upon the newcomer was suspended until he could earn acceptance in the occupations and diversions of the initiated. Hazing sometimes went to the limit of test and danger. Dimly its perpetrators wanted to make a stranger prove that he could take care of himself or, if need be, do his part for the common safety in situations of peril.

But further—the attitude was so exaggerated, so prepos-terously more than itself, that it suggested some obscure but grinding necessity to enlarge and insist upon all the masculine attributes that were taken for granted in most other environments. It seemed as though a predominantly male society like that of the frontier was obliged to accen-tuate its maleness to make an outsize virtue of it, and so to preserve in extended boyhood the secrets and discoveries of essential virility which in the boy's first awareness of them assumed such proud, obsessive, and exciting value. In some of its social expressions the early frontier west resembled a vast boys' club whose members dealt with puzzling perils and uncertainties by shouting them down under incanta-tions of prowess. Echoes of such primitive clamor still sound in today's popular culture and its notion of the "West."

iii

From the first the frontiersman saw himself as a new breed of cat, and said so, and behaved accordingly, in cut-ting himself off from the past. Whenever he saw that he was regarded as rude and coarse he at once acted more coarsely and rudely. He jeered at any of his fellows who might retain any hint of the manners and tastes of the Atlantic East, or of England. His patriotism was real, but he pounded eastern or foreign visitors into exhaustion with his defiant assertion of it. Yankee Doodle, the patriot's image, was a figure in a piercing little song—but he was more.

He was a reality who made actual appearances among frontier crowds, when some fellow felt like dressing up in red-striped trousers, a blue swallow-tailed coat, and a tall beaver hat with a band of stars, to remind himself and all others of what an American looked like. He was regarded without local surprise or question. Any man had a sanction for self-worthy oddity. John James Audubon saw a man in New Orleans on the levee wearing a flop-brimmed hat, a bright green coat, wide yellow nankeen pantaloons, a pink vest, and a frilled shirt. In his open shirt was a bunch of magnolias from which the head of a live baby alligator lolled to and fro. He carried a loud silk umbrella in one hand, and with the other a cage of brightly feathered birds. Stalking grandly, he was singing "My Love Is but a Lassie Yet," in a Scottish accent; but when he talked his speech was native American. He was a one-man drama, and his observers let him be in his dream of democratic individualism that was haunted by his passion—arising from buried discontents dimly recognized by all—his passion to be distinguished among his kind, in any way he desired. He would be happy at any time to defend it with his muscle.

Wildcats? Such a man could lick his weight in wildcats, and so stated with truculence and often. He would cry that he was a blacksnake, the longest, slickest, wiliest of all. He was a weasel, clever to steal whatever he craved. He was a raccoon, a tornado, an earth-screamer, a river at flood, a gamecock, he said. He used a pine tree for a toothpick and he drank a lake if he was thirsty. He was cocked on a hair trigger and it was death merely to look at him in a certain way. Choose gun, knife, or bare hands with thumbs to gouge out eyes—it was all the same to him.

Slick as a whistle, he could resort to aggressive humility, which was perhaps less to be trusted than open rancor. It suggested envy, embracing private schemes to take what was wanted. Many a frontiersman could manage his face with a technique of shrewdness. It was the poker face, and it could conceal a teeming mind or one empty and at a loss. If a man felt ignorant, he did well to conceal his feeling; and in any case, aside from Dr. Franklin, who knew *everything*? If men believed in equality, then what one man did not know was just as good as what another did not know. Out of tact, knowledge had better be as carefully concealed as ignorance. It sometimes seemed to detached observers that democratic citizens—including candidates—either dealt exactly with small matters, or vaguely with large ones, but with few thoughts in between.

Like all generations, those of the early republic went in for rages of belief which seemed to enlighten the people by giving them thin authority in obscure affairs, which they could display with challenging flourishes. (We have our equivalents today, filtered out of Moscow, Vienna, and California.) A most empowering popular science was phrenology and its offshoots, which appeared to offer a penetrating key to human capacities and natures. It was a period accomplishment to know with finality the secrets of personality by a glance and a touch upon the skull. Gravely accepted at the time, such an imported diagnostic fashion gave tone to the society.

But there were local notions of fantasy that really caught something of the society's likeness. A lyric note has always been heard amidst the American clamor. Davy Crockett passed from life into legend before his death, and was quoted in a body of literature written upon his heels. One time, out hunting, when the sun rose, he lighted his pipe from it, shouldered his bear, and walked home "introducin' people to the fresh daylight with a piece of sunlight in my pocket." The expression held something of the blitheness, the sweet fresh primality, the sense of outset, as at dawn, of the early nation.

Confidence dwelt in such a large view, and reflected the trust with which Americans moved alone through solitudes. When they met one another they fell into easy, immediate fellowship, a habit they would never lose, except in metropolitan concentrates where weary competitiveness now induces the world's most hideous public manners. Despite dangers inherent in wild nature, Audubon said, "so little risk do travellers run in the United States that no one ever dreams of any to be encountered on the road." In the 1830s a German traveler, one Francis J. Grund, nearing the Mississippi on horseback, found himself at dinnertime miles away from any public refreshment. Only a lonely farmhouse stood near. He paused, thinking of buying a meal there, but then saw that the farmer and his wife were about to set out for the next market town. Herr Grund then made as if to pass by; but the farmer and his wife dismounted, took him in, prepared dinner, declining payment. "Oh," said the farmer, "I assure you . . . I never suffer myself or my wife to be *troubled* either by strangers or friends; we merely discharge our duty. Lucy!" he added, to a buxom girl who was playing with a pretty child, "you will see that the gentleman wants nothing." With which the farmer and his wife went off on their errand.

iv

In a national habit, strangers, when they met, talked, and the talk sooner or later got around to it—who ought to be thrown out of office, and why, and who was going to be elected. Early elections were incorruptibly visible. In 1843 a prairie expedition set about electing their officers "to regulate and conduct their proceedings." The New Orleans journalist Matthew C. Field watched the process. "The candidates stood up in a row before the constituents, and at a given signal they wheeled about and marched off, while the general mass *broke* after them 'lickety-split,' each man forming in behind his favorite, so that every candidate flourished a sort of tail of his own, and the man with the longest tail was elected."

As to politics, every American was an expert. He knew this was true, for he *was* the government, on the prairie or in the capital. To make him so, his forebears had fought and died; and to keep him so, he would fight and die himself. He saw himself as the people at large, and the people embodied in himself, and liberty was their theme. "In this country," wryly declared the French royalist Montluzon, who inspected it in 1816–17, "where the word liberty is never omitted in conversation, there is the greatest tyranny

[*34*

of opinion; that is, of political opinion, for that is the only kind that seems important." What this royalist authoritarian failed to note was the important condition that the opinion in the end was not that of a single controlling individual or class of individuals, but that of a majority of all individuals who controlled. An art of contributive living was at birth; and as it would govern the destinies of all, so it took the energies of all, in the guardianship of man himself, who was the proper heart of the matter of life.

When the Americans revealed this fact, and the world heard them talk about it, they were listened to with an awakened sense of recognition. Tocqueville was a witness: "The political debates of a democratic people, however small it may be, have a degree of breadth that often renders them attractive to mankind. All men are interested by them because they treat of *man*, who is everywhere the same." America seemed to stand not only for equality of opportunity, but to be also the land of mankind's second chance. To the degree that Americans were interested in each other, the world was interested in them, and listened to them talk.

And how they talked, in an inexhaustible outpouring. With sharp opinions ready, they spoke their pieces freely.

"Eloqence is, in fact, after gold, their highest ideal," observed Father Giovanni Antonio Grassi, S.J., an Italian priest who gazed at the Americans during his years as president of Georgetown College from 1810 to 1815.* He went on to say that New World orators paid less mind to the inner values of a speech than they did to its manner. They knew their success with a public waiting to be violently edified rested upon florid metaphor (often gorgeously mixed), elegant vocabulary, grand periods. Indeed, the American orator confessed that he was impatient of "a vulgar and sterile state of facts," declared Father Grassi: "A people who have fresh and lively feeling will always relish oratory," and, accord-

---

*See "The Father President," pp. 93–106.

ingly, the oratory of the frontier was "free, lofty, agitating, grand, impassioned."

It was a people's art; and like a people's art it had a curious double spirit. It both derided and imitated the richness of more aristocratic or better-educated models of expression. It was aware of the idiom of an elite in whom all elevated expression was reposed by older societies, and rejected it in the name of a whole population who shared equally the joys and powers of making utterances that could sound splendiferous, whatever on earth they might mean.

Much frontier oratory in its inflation took to kidding on the level. The inflation was conscious and was often meant to be comic—and yet at the same time it hoped to intoxicate with its reminders of large acts, projected fantasies of patriotism, and a new and self-conscious historical spirit. For metaphor it drew on the marvels of the unfolding continent—the might of Niagara, the sweep of the prairies, the noble rise of the Rockies, the blaze of Western starlight, the arc of heaven that embraced America in the end from coast to coast, and endlessly the scowling American eagle who dwelt on pinnacles and crags, and soared in freedom above the restraints of earth. Like all the arts of the people, their oratory expressed desire, character, and style. If there was vulgarity in its expression, there was also pathos; for what showed plain was the violent dancing of a spirit that must assert or be lost.

As the country—its land, political purpose, and united energy—was new, so must its common means of expression—language itself—attempt the new. Within the old forms of English, the people laid down new rules and made up new words. Inventing his character, and adopting wilderness ways through which he had to achieve physical victory, the American needed fresh styles through which to express the conditions and demands of his new life. By about 1815 he had a new dialect that was a distinct tangent of the mother tongue.

Much of its vocabulary was consciously fantastic. Anyone was privileged to coin vivid, homely, and extravagant locutions, and might even become a virtuoso of the process. The frontier talked the raw materials of a new literature. Politics, work, daily character, competitive community in shrewd masquerade stimulated the vigorous flow of new speech expressions. Those that had a real spark of aptness, a truth in their color, passed into current use. It was a language that sought understanding at the level of least education. As such it reflected a general distrust of studied correctness, and in the beginning it even disdained formal recognition of different social levels. "Our dictionary," noted Crèvecoeur before the nineteenth century, "is short on words of dignity and names of honor." But it was not long until the frontier granted unofficial titles of distinction to anyone whose calling or whose knack of impersonation seemed to demand them—judge, general, colonel, major, doctor, reverend, along with "gentleman" and "sir," bestowed at all stages of society from top to bottom. "Sir," in particular, was, in effect, a kind of punctuation in discourse, and in 1842 it drove Charles Dickens to distraction as he heard our citizens in dialogue. He recorded a wearying conversation between two gentlemen—one in a straw hat, the other in a brown hat.

Straw Hat: I reckon that's Judge Jefferson, ain't it?
Brown Hat: Yes, sir.
Straw Hat: Warm weather, Judge.
Brown Hat: Yes, sir.
Straw Hat: There was a snap of cold, last week.
Brown Hat: Yes, sir.
Straw Hat: Yes, sir.

And so on through an endless exchange of banalities of assertion and inquiry. Indeed, Dickens pinned down the insatiable American appetite for personal information. One citizen he encountered "never spoke otherwise than interrogatively. He was an embodied inquiry. . . ."

Tocqueville found American speech full of abstract terms which enlarged and obscured the thoughts they were meant to convey, and he concluded that democratic nations preferred obscurity to labor—the labor of speaking and writing correctly and clearly. His observation again caught something of the character of a people working out a vast experiment in equality. Make it *sound* grand, and you *are* grand. In 1837 the British sailor-novelist Captain Frederick Marryat noted an exchange in Congress during which splendor triumphed over language. A member speaks:

"What the Honourable Gentleman has just asserted I consider catamount to a denial."

"I presume," replied the opponent, "that the Honourable Gentleman means tantamount."

"No, sir, I do not mean tantamount. I am not so ignorant of our language not to be aware that catamount and tantamount are anonymous."

Roar, then, and inconvenient truth or painful accuracy may be stilled. Keep it loose, and you are not committed. Generalize, and you are delivered from the concrete, which in terms of your own life may be hard and graceless. To the untutored ear, the accents of education sounded fancy. So, without education, adopt the fanciness, and you will sound educated. Upon such traits much comic character was based—the itinerant evangelist, the courtly blackface in the minstrel show, the windy swindler, the country lawyer, the quack doctor with his wagon pharmacy. . . .

Primitive American humor rested less on inherent wit or sharp observation of human failings than on rough drolleries full of exaggerated usage for its own sake. The people mocked refinements they did not possess. The speech became noisy and profuse. It conveyed sounds of smacking and thumping and poking and digging and clapping and sawing and sucking and cracking and slicing and chopping and exclaiming and hushing. It stuck in extra syllables for elegance and comic surprise. It repeated in the same word the sounds of dental consonants that gave a jerky, droll effect. It made comedy out of mouth-widening vowels and speech-yodels whose effect depended upon a swallowed *L*: heard simply as vocables, the gobble of the North American turkey.

To throw fits into someone was to cornuck him. To mean huge was to say monstropolous. A total abstainer from alcohol abstained teetotaciously. An angelic character was angeliferous. Someone who wanted to flee skedaddled, which meant that he absquatulated. Something complete was bodaciously so. To defeat or overcome was to ramsquaddle and to obliterate was to obflisticate. A strong man was a screamer, and an important one a ripstaver. If a fellow took off his clothes, he shucked himself buck naked. If there was a kettle of meat and vegetable stew for supper, it was known as burgoo. To cheat someone, or deceive with false love, was to honeyfogle. . . . It took only a few such words salted through an otherwise conventional passage of speech or writing to change its character into something new in effect. The effect was that of imaginative enlargement of experience, rather than of precise record.

Yet if the native speech could evoke rough, hilarious, or absurd experience, it could also summon forward much of the accidental beauty that pervaded the memories of the westering people. It was Audubon, again, who noted a lovely usage that made a picture of countless frontier encampments: firelight, he said, "is named in some parts of the country, forest light. . . ." In both the grotesque and the lyrical lay predictions of the national literature that was to come.

With the open secret of the whopping lie, the frontier made its own first conscious literature. Competitions of tall tales were held in which people tried to create their own myths. Boasts of prowess, marvels of animal origin or incarnation, farces of anthropomorphism, fabulous reversals of the natural order, minglings of Indian, immigrant, and huntsman's lore—these were the typical raw materials for the made-up stories with which their improvisors in camp hoped to entertain and stun each other. As such narratives dealt high-handedly with the mysteries of nature, they were in great contrast to the mythologies of all Indians, who stood in awe before the elements; and as they celebrated the rebellious triumphs or howling humiliations of man alone in a fantastic world, they were opposed to the decorousness of spirit of even earlier adventurers in the desert and mountain West—the Spaniards.

v

How, out of the phantasms of the frontier muse, would something like a broader literature emerge? In his 1891 essay "American National Literature" Walt Whitman tried to envisage what would yet be.

The American character shows, he said, "three prevailing personal traits . . . good nature, decorum, and intelligence. Essentially these lead the inherent list of the high average personal and born and bred qualities of the young fellows through the United States, as any observer can find out for himself. . . ." Well and good, and "a national literature is, of course, in one sense, a great mirror or reflector." But, he adds, "there must be something before—something to reflect," implying that from its long early history there was nothing of the United States to reflect. Yet, "I should say now, since the Secession War, there has been, and today unquestionably exists, that something."

Previously, however humbly, literature came to the service of the people. It was a service required of all the arts in early America. "Nothing," declared Dr. Franklin, "nothing is good or beautiful but in the measure that it is useful: yet all things have a utility under particular circumstances. Thus, poetry, painting, music (and the stages of their embodiment) are all necessary and proper gratifications of a refined state of society, but objectionable at an earlier period, since their cultivation would make a taste for their enjoyment precede its means."

But Benjamin Franklin was looking east, not west, and thinking of opera houses, theatres, museums, and palaces in the cities of Europe. He saw that utility must be a determining value for the handmade arts of a forming democracy; but having little of the creative temperament, he forgot that the arts would never wait for ideal conditions or a refinement of society to bring them forth. Even as the frontier took its westward course, they came forth because it was in their nature never to be denied; and as they appeared in the context of democracy, the arts spoke both to the people and for them. Theatre, music, crafts, were expressive parts of an all-enclosing spirit.

By river and road, troupes of theatre players followed the settlers. Floating along waterways, actors rehearsed in costume on deck to the astonishment of people working in riverside fields or traveling along towpaths.

In the actors' hampers were stuffed the wrinkled habiliments of their repertoire—the blacks of Hamlet, the stripes of Yankee Doodle, the crowns and swords and ermine and velvet for Richard III, plumes for Pizarro. Towns were far between and the theatre company was ready to play wherever anyone could attend—a cluster of huts on a riverbank, a clearing in a forest, a short street of rough-hewn cabins. In such places the play was given out-of-doors, with no curtain, and, for scenery, only what adjacent woods provided. A space between thickets served as stage, with real trees instead of painted wings from behind which the actors could enter. Scene and location were affirmed, in Elizabethan style, by the spoken text. Tallow candles held in potatoes made footlights, unless the settlement was too poor to spare these, and then the lights were made out of old linen rag wicks burning in pans of fat. If not even these were to be had, then the play was given in the dark, and imaginary life rode forth on the voices of actors unseen but speaking with doubled intensity to pierce their listeners who sat on benches or on the ground. But perhaps the moon was out, and then, silvered in common magic, the forest, the spectators, were united in a creation of spirit as powerful as it was mysterious, as desirable as it was rare, and as poignant as it was fugitive—a little point of light shining one night in the deep continental darkness.

A recurring figure in plays improvised within a strict convention was the rube who for four acts served as the dupe of clever, rich, educated, city men, such as lawyers, bankers, or land speculators; and who in act five turned upon them with a blinking innocence that got the best of them in the end. He raised the people by impersonating someone laughably lower than their lowest specimen who yet overcame the rich and clever.

And there were plays of early American history—*The Arab Chief and the Pirate of the East* (1834), which recalled the Barbary wars; dramas in which Washington appeared; adaptations of Cooper's novels. But the most popular native theme was the Indian. Both in the theatres of the east and the very clearings at woods edges where the people had killed Indians and known killings by Indians, Indian plays were acted in such profusion that a suffering critic declared that they had become "perfect nuisances." Such dramas presented the tragedy of the Indian, recalling promises made by white men and broken. In *Metamora, Or the Last of the Wampanoags*, written by John August Stone in 1829, and played for decades by Edwin Forrest, the Indian hero ends the play with an apostrophe to the soldiers who have felled him:

"My curses on you, white men! May the great spirit curse you when he speaks in his war voice from the clouds! Murderers! . . . May your graves and the graves of your children be in the path the red man shall trace! and may the wolf and the panther howl over your fleshless bones, fit banquet for the destroyers! Spirits of the grave, I come! But the curse of Metamora stays with the white man! I die!" [Falls and dies.]

Theatre meant spectacle. Music made community. Whether joining together for religious, political, social, or working occasions, Americans made music at first as an essentially communal expression. Yet already in the late eighteenth century William Billings brought a new formal excitement into the prevailing worship-music of Puritan psalms sung in unison. In primitive imitation of the high contrapuntal style, he arranged the sacred songs in harmonies for part singing. When he published a collection of them in 1794 he gave them the general title *The Continental Harmony*—drawing upon the nationalistic connotation under which Washington's armies had fought, and the Congress had made its declarations, and the society had enlarged its self-image before its physical realization. His new pieces, arranged for four-part singing, were, he declared, "Twenty times as powerful as the old slow tunes. . . ."

The frontier made up relatively few new songs. Appalachian and savannah and prairie songs were mostly modifications of old expressions developed long before in the British Isles and Africa, and were often simple corruptions of these. But they were augmented by beauties of tonal expression which Western life produced in its work. On the crystal rivers, when a flatboat or keelboat came to a bend, a boatman sounded a warning on a horn, lofting a vagrant tune that drifted on the water and was lost in the trees. An early poem caught the sound:

> *O, boatman, wind that horn again,*
> *For never did the listening ear*
> *Upon its lambent bosom bear*
> *So wild, so soft, so sweet a strain!*

In the golden mists of river perspective such as we see in the paintings of George Caleb Bingham, the boatman's horn made a signal of wonder, nostalgia, and the stir of going over America, much as the sound of railroad whistles would do in later times. . . .

As American life became as civic as rural, and more polite than rude, grand musical societies with serious purpose were founded in the cities to produce works of Bach, Haydn, Handel, Mozart, Dr. Thomas Arne, and Sir Henry Bishop. The Revolution, with its achievement of independence through martial valor, was followed by the appearance of native composers. Francis Hopkinson of Philadelphia came forward as the first sophisticated American composer, producing songs that echoed the manner of Dr. Arne, and yet reflected the simple sweetness of morning light. His works for harpsichord were given in proper concerts. For stylish audiences, a company came now and then to present French opera in New York, Philadelphia, and New Orleans, and soon there were attempts to shape dialogue-and-ballad operas on native subjects.

In a more popular vein, the fife became the rage. Its shrillness and panic legerity suggested the state of the national feeling. With little stinging scales it challenged the conservatism of the past, forcing an animated vision of a future as brisk and insistent as its voice. If a fifer went traveling, his instrument provided a walking skirl to keep him company and to announce him when he arrived at inns, fairs, or parties, where, being asked or no, he would oblige with solo airs and tweedling songs. His clean, hard, direct style told his hearers of themselves.

vi

A clean, hard style could be traced also in the knacks and crafts of the inland settler. One such man bragged that "with only hickory withes and a jack-knife he could make a very good wagon."

In such a statement lay the seed of the arts and crafts—the "practical arts," as they were called—in early America. Dr.

Franklin's concern for the marriage of beauty and utility was unconsciously answered by men and women who in successive settlements were obliged by scarcity of materials and remote overland trade to equip and ornament their daily lives with objects of their own making. It was natural that in a democracy the arts were, first of all, functional. If the conditions of their lives denied to the settlers access to the fine arts, there was also in the crotchety plainness of the people a hint that the fine arts were suspect. Puritan bleakness was partly responsible for such a view. But another and overriding sense had effect also.

This was the democratic suspicion that the fine arts had always been identified with aristocratic patronage. Palaces crammed with splendors, artists appointed to court, prestige and expense attached to the work of master-artists—such airs of luxury seemed highfalutin, and to partake of them called for a whole world of experience, education, and allusion in which the democrat could only feel at a disadvantage. In their gnarled self-respect the people must earn their own evolvement of fine art and its usages.

In the pattern of ordinary social development the settlers would have climbed through slow generations toward a flowering of refined art based on their utilitarian creations.

But there were two reasons why such a sequence was not necessary. First, the settlers were not socially primitive people, but people civilized in various degrees taking new land with a new social idea. Second, to their new idea of man, and to a new land in which to realize it, there was soon added a third newness which swept the first two along at an amazing rate of development. Historical time itself seemed to be triggered into a "fast forward" phase. In a foreshortened view, the completion of the design creating the continental nation was accelerated by a revolution in practical science.

This was the discovery and spreading use of technological methods: many new means of making corporate life closer, and individual life easier, so that united to his fellows the individual man was to be relatively free from toil. The frontiering and encompassing of the American continent took place during the early decades of the world revolution in technology.

The era of scattered localisms which had made the first statements of the American style drew to an end, for with the growth of the machine culture came a national unity of utility, taste, and information. The governing aspects of collective life were shared through transcontinental syndication of all expressions of style.

vii

The era of handmade America was over.

PREFACE TO

AN UNWRITTEN BOOK

Because of its mere citations instead of examinations in depth of aspects of our popular culture, I must think of this essay as a sort of preface to an unwritten book. Given time and extent, the book might turn out to be a study of how local character, sectionalism, in various parts of our country, once valid if often naïve culturally, had to give way under machine technics to a certain commonality of attitude, taste, and character. It happens that my lifetime has overlaid the final phases of this change from the many regional or sectional styles to a nationalism whose advent we can attribute to new devices of immediate communication. Here we can scarcely describe them, let alone offer a richly furnished judgment of their effect. But I have observed whereof I speak, and so inevitably my preface takes on at times an autobiographical character—that of a witness.

Ever since the immense event of the rapid overtaking of the great West by the established Atlantic society, there was deep response in feeling that more than a geographical triumph was accomplished. Distance and the unknown carried mystery, as always; but there was in addition an element of projected imagination that made "West"—the idea—quite as important as "West"—the territory and material opportunity. "West" was adventure, was romance, was independence, was a new dimension of selfhood; but it was more—it was health. The prairies, the Rockies, the ultimate Pacific shore, all carried connotations of cure of one or another sort.

Josiah Gregg, nearly dead in Missouri in his finicky and depressed youth, was sent to the prairies with a Santa Fe trading caravan in 1831 by his family physician, for a last chance to come back to life. When the wagons started west from Independence, Kansas, he had to be lifted into one of them on a litter. Within two weeks he was riding a horse, and by the time he reached Santa Fe after six weeks he was entirely well. In time, he became a kind of Humboldt of the prairies and desert West, and his book, *The Commerce of the Prairies*, published in 1844, the first to describe the Westward experience in full detail and finished form, remains a classic. Forty years later a gifted but debilitated, bereaved young New Yorker went west as a tenderfoot and returned as a man two-fisted enough to become a police commissioner and a president of the United States. In the 1880s the Vicar General of the Archdiocese of Santa Fe reported to the Vatican that "this territory will be, in time, when better known, the great sanitarium of the United States . . . weak persons will find here security to life, and undoubted benefit for the health."

And indeed the Western tradition entered another phase when the climate of the high plains and lower Rockies was medically adjudged beneficial for tubercular invalids. Because my father was one of these, he took his family from New York State to New Mexico in 1915, to settle at Albuquerque. My second view of an American style came into focus there, after a first vision of the world had come to me on the shores of Lake Erie.

New Mexico presented the most clear picture of the laminated history of the Southwest, with its first components the Pueblo Indians, its second the Mexican Americans, and its third the Anglo-Americans—alike those who survived from pioneer settlement and those new immigrants who, like my family, came for climate, and those others who followed the railroad across the continent and for whatever reason stopped to help with the formation of a town somewhere along the line.

Along the line—what a different matter from remaining to live at a fixed point of origin like New York or Chicago or Los Angeles, where the great railroad system both started from and returned to. It was an eloquent statement of the difference when you recognized that the most interesting event of every day in Albuquerque was going to the railroad station to see the California Limited of the Santa Fe Line arrive, pause for thirty minutes while traveling celebrities strolled (I remember Douglas Fairbanks and Mary Pickford), and then depart into the perspective, which was both diagramed and activated by the parallel tracks. Gazing after the train filled the mind with thoughts and images of far away, before a return to the local reality. This reality was like nothing else, and what dominated all was the splendor of the landscape in its vast scale, its earth features, its colors, its immensity of sky, its rarity of air, and its spacious light.

It was impossible not to collect contrasts between East and West.

In the urban East, landscape seemed to withdraw; you could not see it without going to some effort. In every Western town of that time the open country in its vastness could be seen at the end of every street—the desert was there, the mountain in its degree of blue which measured its distance away, the huge encompassing sky. Eastern winters were grey and sometimes as dark as ink over hillocks of snow which lasted for months in city streets. Western desert winters were matters of gold light on yellow sweeps, with occasional blizzards whose evidence often vanished within hours under the sun. In the East, all marvels were man-made, on a scale intimate enough to be bought or rented, visited or inhabited, in man's dimension. In the desert West, all marvels were natural ones on a scale so grand as to make man's survival there an historical triumph. If the East was largely industrial, the West was a kingdom of raw materials, animal husbandry on a broad range, and organized pursuit of health. Sizable fortunes were made out of such concerns, and various amenities survived importation from the East and beyond. Even as the frontier was in its last phase, it was considered desirable for gentlemen of means, or pretensions, or both, to have their shirts sent from New Mexico to Chicago to be properly starched and ironed, and with the railroad came the certainty of Chesapeake Bay oysters on beds of ice.

But in general, as life thinned out going Westward, the manner of it grew less formal, until time and riches brought into being at the extreme of the continent the California patio habits of the heliophile, his relaxed cult of the body accompanied at large by a kindly incuriosity of mind.

The sophisticated East was represented by an audience society. In the West, for a great length of time, members of the society had to perform for themselves what their own experiences could celebrate locally. Amenity and cultural wealth, in the East, came together in complement. In the West, neither was notably prevalent so long as the local character preserved itself. In one aspect of the culture, sports in the East early became those of the machine—motorcar gymkhanas, motorboat races (the fragile little shells of the boats were called hydroplanes), airplane regattas with the first double-winged Curtiss flying machines unconsciously being rehearsed for military use; while in the West, sports stayed close to the animals of the open country—cattle, and the horses of the cowboys who rode herd on them. The Eastern style of life had old foreign cultural roots; the Western, a condition curiously echoed in many ways that recalled the earliest human terms of survival on the land anywhere.

The contrast seemed to suggest to many a condition of exile, and so did the resettlement of phthisical invalids. The theme was poignantly, indeed angrily, dealt with by an American artist of beautiful gifts. Miss Willa Cather, of whom I first heard from her sister Elsie, who taught me freshman English in the Albuquerque High School. In a number of early works, Willa Cather posed the pathos, the tragedy, of the higher culture, in the person of a great artist, against the uncomprehending society of the frontier West and its philistine mentality. If Miss Cather's portraits of her exiles seemed to lack full sympathy for helpless states of un-informed life, and to risk seeming overfastidious, the fact remains that great contrasts in cultural ways naturally call forth personal choices—or, at least, should afford the oppor-tunity to choose.

In Miss Cather's story "The Sculptor's Funeral," a distin-guished artist's body is brought home for burial in the poor town of his origin—Sand City, somewhere in the West. He had risen from its gritty life to eminence in Boston of a sort which brings to mind such an American sculptor as Augus-tus Saint-Gaudens. The young pupil who brings his body home to the bereaved family in "this borderland between ruffianism and civilisation," that "bitter, dead little western town"—the young pupil shudders at the complacent igno-rance, even the mockery, that underlie the local view of Sand City's only eminent son. In another story, "A Death in the Desert," Miss Cather has an exquisite singer, who also has gone to fame in the great world, now dying of her lungs back home "like a rat in a hole, out of her own world, and she can't fall back into ours"—though she had come in a last hope for a cure. The same story contains seeds for the later novel *The Song of the Lark*, about a wondrously gifted girl who rises from a little Colorado railroad town (marvelously described) to the opera houses of the world, an escapee from her birthright of exile. Bitterest of all, the story "A Wagner Matinee" gives us the visit home to Boston of a once-cultivated woman who has married a Westerner and has moved from Boston to exile and hardship—physical and spiritual—on a little ranch out West. How she has starved during all those years on the ranch for what she hears once again, now, in her withered middle age, when the great Boston Orchestra plays a Wagner program in Symphony Hall! When the concert is over, she remains in a daze in her chair while the hall and stage go empty. The narrator, her nephew, speaks to her. ". . . She burst into tears and sobbed pleadingly. 'I don't want to go, Clark. I don't want to go!'" The nephew understands. For her, he reflects, "Just outside the door of the concert hall lay the black pond with the cattle-tracked bluffs; naked as a tower, the crook-backed ash seedlings where the dishcloths hung to dry; the gaunt, molting turkeys picking up refuse about the kitchen door." In such early fiction, Miss Cather touched on three determining themes of the West (though of course there were others of a more inspiriting nature)—the cultural exile, the all-powerful railroads, the act of going west to get well, or die.

As these pervaded her early work, they may have reflected her own sense of deracination in her girlhood after the removal of her family from Virginia, with its old traditions, to a raw Nebraska. Later, to be sure, she fell in love with the open land, wrote fondly of those (usually European immigrants) who made their lives there, and in many a lyric passage she described the Western earth through nostalgic vision. Rude limitations became humble beauties, and behind these lay something more wonderful. This was the prehistoric life of the cave and mesa Indians whose civilization left such noble monuments as the cliff dwellings of the Southwest with their superb artifacts. But if Miss Cather's view softened as she attained her own great eminence far beyond the West, there were still to be seen various evidences of a culturally deprived population striving to fulfill for itself various impulses toward aesthetic expression and enjoyment and self-celebration common to all men at whatever level of taste.

I remember some of these at their most primitive in the Southwest of my boyhood. The art of painting, before the migration of artists of talent to Santa Fe and Taos, was represented locally by store-window artists who painted to order, by formula, on pieces of shirt cardboard, at brilliant speed, and in slickest pigment, lurid landscapes for parlor and kitchen. A gifted few of these itinerant artists could paint with both hands at one time, while sidewalk locals watched and marveled. Their works could be had for an average of fifty cents each.

Lacking museums, the earlier outlands people flocked to see, in a local undertaking parlor, a huge painting of Christ at Gethsemane, which was shown in surroundings hushed not only by the subject (one which all knew and understood well) but also by dense black velvet hangings that extended the night of agony into the room, while soft light was focused on the Bible scene. Most wonderful of all, an electric star glimmered in the sky through a pinhole made in the canvas. For a fee, lines of viewers could advance to enter a reverent and aesthetic experience until the painting—it was on tour—moved on to its next engagement. Music and theatre were most commonly available through traveling revival meetings, which set up their tents on vacant lots and filled the lust-laden summer nights with percussive hymns and the drama of visible conversion, under the acid glare of Coleman lanterns. Yet music of fame occasionally stepped off the sumptuous transcontinental Limited trains for a single concert, and Miss Cather's exiles could once again hear such artists as Paderewski, Tetrazzini, Schumann-Heink, Lillian Nordica, Jan Kubelik. Too, dramatic troupes came through with their tent shows and their primitive plays whose predominant theme was the triumph of the redwigged small-town hick over the fast-talking city slicker. Literature was often the duty of the local editor, who had read Mark Twain and saw himself as a similar wag, or a tubercular invalid from the East with a gasping talent for sardonic remarks in his own occasional little half column on the editorial page. One such whom I remember used the pseudonym "T. B. Crabb." As for architecture, dwellings were mostly humble frame houses, while public buildings, of masonry, reflected aspirations, much diluted, in reference to either the beaux arts or Richardsonian style.

It is easy, and not illuminating, to see all such primitive manifestations only in comic terms. Their real point is that, as they were characteristic of any removed society, they were allied to unself-conscious folk traditions. Perhaps there was an expectation that, if ever superseded by a national style, their degree of cultural sophistication might rise. We suspend the point for the moment.

Of the indigenous arts, it was the rodeo that spoke for the population at large, when hardy and skillful men showed at great danger and chance their mastery of the animals that supported their living and gave their culture its predominant tone.

Though, to be sure, widely scattered, there were a few islands of sophisticated taste and even elegance. An occasional great house stood isolated on the plains at the center of a vast ranch; and in it might be seen a collection of master paintings, and an impressive library in English and French bindings, and pieces of sculpture by such as Canova and Thorwaldsen, and important visitors who arrived by private railroad car on the nearest rail line. Such exoticism would persist for perhaps one generation only, and then the great possessions would be dispersed, the unlikely mansion worn down by the hot light of the sky and sandstorms stretching across entire states.

But if the intensely local was suggested by all such expressions, it was not for the most part self-conscious in any conspicuous way. Then, however, came the force of the great depression in the 1930s that brought a self-awareness to the various distinct parts of the nation through a study of each state by writers and artists in need of employment—an assignment asked of them by a wise and compassionate government through the Works Progress Administration. One of its great results was the series of WPA American Guide Books, which in both the making and the later reading gave each state and region of the nation a clearer idea of itself than it had ever known before.

The effect of this, and of the immediacy of grave human suffering, was to bring to intensified consciousness, discussion, and criticism, both social and aesthetic, the idea of regionalism—a word that suddenly came into wide usage.

My sketchy citation of those aspects of regionalism which I knew by accident—those of the Southwest—could be correspondingly itemized for any other of the distinct regions of the country—the Northeast, the South, the Middle West, the Pacific Coast. Each originally had its localism that was unself-consciously evolved out of natural conditions. This is not to claim that the naïve, just because it was regional, had to be preserved for its own sake. But it is to say that a living expression of a sectional character, or local folkism, had an honest character that met its doom when it began to be meretriciously exploited.

Because the impulse of art is universal, artists in all forms of work have always recorded their homage to where they lived. Where they lived was largely determined by accident. One always deals with what one knows through natural association in whatever degree of honest response.

In this there is a kernel of the notion that to elevate regionalism per se into an artistic virtue is somewhat beside the point, and even more so, when the vogue for organized regionalism, wherever in the land, became pervasive. For then the idea of the corporate regional self became self-conscious, and what followed was all too often a burlesque of the original style, as a common nostalgia promised to become convertible into commercial advantage. Tourism must follow.

Traffic-borne tourism helped to show the way to intellectual tourism, or at least to an organized exploitation of the study of the "folk." Stereotypes were set in entertainment. The local flavor was marketed, and soon enough the question must be asked, How long can a social or historical frontier last? It is innocent enough for people to organize celebrations of their collective character, however crudely, but what won't be of much use is to set up systems of classification of interpreters possessing genuine gifts as artists or scholars by lumping them as regionalists, as though some inherent virtue accompanied the designation. The point is that the true artist always rises above "region"—that is to say, his material. I have never seen a statement by a truly gifted artist which admitted to his being a "regionalist," no matter how firmly he has been assigned the classification by those who make their livings by detecting patterns in accidents and symbols in intuitions, which is to say, the sort of critic whose vocation requires certain conveniences. Perhaps all one can finally say on the subject is that the minute regionalism "sees" itself it disappears, and a counterfeit takes its place, with every likelihood of a long and commercially profitable run.

Oddly commingled, the American nineteenth-century tradition of gentility, which persisted for so long, and the eager awakening to the regional as matter for exploitation, both in the end succumbed to a force greater than either. Folkways when corrupted by commerce lose first their validity. Gentility when faced with a vast increase in the means of transmitting culture loses first its tradition of high style. Where commerce and wealth are great enough, and population dense enough, and mechanical ingenuity lively enough, the communal behavior and perception are delegated to surrogate means. With the passing of American gentility went the European models on which it was generally based and which American Puritanism sterilized morally.

When, during the 1914 war, America discovered the world four and a half centuries after the world discovered America, many restraints of convention and even law vanished, evidently forever; and very soon afterward, the powerful energy of the established material motive, combined with the fast and often brilliant development of technology, started the headlong trend toward the dishuman in cultural regard and scale.

The authentically regional was engulfed by the national, and the genteel by the unlimited vulgarism which gave public instead of private employment to the extreme vernacular. Technical means of communication were of course the vehicle by which this came about, in a cultural revolution of astonishing power and velocity. As had happened before, historical coincidence brought together at the same moment a change of style and the means of widely distributing it. This one began with the movie film, went on to radio, which caught on very fast, and these started to create a national standard—a substandard—of taste which for commercial purposes seemed to impose a character on the population instead of draw one from it.

Sound recording played an immense part in the process, as did motor travel on a transcontinental scale, and the climax arrived with television in its instantaneous and simultaneous transmission of vision and sound across any boundaries that once might have preserved local character, manners, values, for whatever they were once worth.

Yet previously, too, there had always been a need for American art to rise above the homely, to let the emerging nation ennoble its ideals visibly and intellectually. America's early architecture, its Greek Revival houses, all the references to the classical established in barely cleared forest lands, and even the machine vernacular (as John Kouwen-hoven has so beautifully demonstrated) with its cast-iron business façades and ornamented industrial engines, reached for the high aesthetic. But this was the work of a cultivated few. How in an age of machine popularism could the native cultural habits come to expression en masse, in broadly pervasive forms?

Was the life-material itself too spiritually meager? Are its current exploiters too ignorant of, or indifferent to, all cultural heritage? Is America now really without a past? But the act and meaning of human life anywhere are always illimitably potential for the artist who remains indifferent to any vision not his own. Was the American creative consciousness too strangled by the national popular speech, which confused democracy with the sort of illiteracy assumed for fear of giving offense through noticeably educated idiom?

Before an American aesthetic revolution could arrive at an orderly realization, in which diversity could be sought in the highest cultural terms, the question became irrelevant; for the finally democratic common denominator was forced into being by technology wedded to commerce. Given two or three more generations, the United States maker of taste might have found heroic forms beyond those demanded by the material imperative of our defined national motive of commercial ambition, before which, in deference to individualism unrestrained by a tradition of style, all has given way, including political probity. The great leveler brought swiftly and too soon the commercial necessity of new forms, from the grotesquely attention-getting advertisement to the short-lived skyscrapers, which were built to accommodate crowds in narrow and therefore tall space, and were always being outgrown, torn down, and replaced taller still. Perhaps through the machine a leveling of the arts to a national new folkism is in process, as against the old local vision free of demands of mass comprehension and commercial expediency. No tyranny is more powerful than that of common taste when it has two things to make it pervasive—a commercial purpose, and a mechanical means of transmission to an entire public.

In means of communication, then, and in physical forms alike, and consequently in habits of behavior, common reference, and opinion, centralization seems to have come to govern the American popular expression. For the better? Here is our suspended point of some pages ago: not better in general quality, only more sophisticated in technical means.

Industrial or commercial convenience, not individual human choice, always now decides. Metropolitan increase requires in cities that people live in hives. We now have an imposed neighborliness. It is one distributed to us by engineering means in infinite replication without regard to individual interest or preference among the general population drawn to it by the pathetic tyrannies of gainful employment. And even in nonmetropolitan areas, where the older order of separate houses still prevails, what now enters the house, by way of information, idea, and consequent belief, comes through a vastly syndicated electronic or graphic means created by technics. The imposed culture leaves no one alone.

To be commercially successful, most forms of expression now gratify not the highest, or even the average, but the lowest standard of emotional, intellectual, and aesthetic adventure. The central sin of the aggressive society is competitiveness, with its indignities and vulgarities meanly motivated by material ends. On a private scale, this leads to the cheapening of ethical and aesthetic standards, not only of the present but of the future, through its inescapable influence on children, who have appetite but no critical judgment. In the national character, it leads to schematic expediency in domestic politics, with a huge part of the electorate, as now, shamefully indifferent to the exercise of the franchise; and conceivably, in foreign policy, it leads to war.

Man's view of himself is all-revealing, as he strives to achieve the ends of survival along with comfort and a position of esteem. It is impossible to overestimate the lowering effect upon this view of two particularly pervasive modern cultural forces, in their degree peculiarly American.

The first of these is the deforming of the human aspect by the general comic-cartoon style, either to entertain or to sell: by representing persons as grotesque or revoltingly whimsical or subhuman, the cartoon, animated or still, cajoles the viewer into feeling superior. It is a visual vulgate which reassures him. Made to feel superior, he is an easier mark for whatever persuasive idea is thus offered to him. The comic strip, the movie cartoon, the canned greeting card, the social exhortation, the flattery of distortion, violence as a joke, provide image and sentiment so impersonal that they even suggest a hidden desperation at the state of man's condition. We have in recent years seen millions of little round lapel buttons with a smile painted on them in three childish strokes. Why must we be incessantly reminded to smile? Are we inherently so savage that this precaution is nervously needed? Perhaps man's discontent is all too clear to him today, and perhaps he must do his utmost to deny it, in order to live with it.

The second of the two powerful forces of persuasion and education today is the craft of advertising, which all too often goes beyond its only legitimate purpose, and that is to meet, rather than create, a need. Advertising, with bland contempt for common intelligence, sees truth as a merely relative and adjustable value. One television commercial has a sternly reassuring man on camera, dressed like a financier, a character which he represents, who is trying to convince us for his own commercial purposes. Hear what he says:

"This is not just an *ad*—it is a *fact*."

There is a sort of wild innocence, if not a bloodless cynicism, in this tacit admission that advertising is not factual, even as it pretends to be. The ethical squalor of this, so widely unrecognized, may tell us much by analogy about why a vast malaise has come over our country. The young people almost alone have recognized it—though in their repudiations of it they have sometimes resorted to measures hurtful to themselves and others. The cheerful acquiescence of the public in the organized dishonesty of most advertising—and its purposeful offspring "public relations," with all too few honorable exceptions—are symptoms of the ethically unsatisfying nature of much of our technological life. To be sure, in earlier generations, it was not unknown for a gullible public to be cozened by sharpers. The medicine show, with its spielers, its snake oil, its guttering torches, its "free entertainment"—played upon susceptibilities as old as the art of bartering. But the reach was limited and the swindle did not create manners.

If we view today's equivalent nationally, and dismiss it by saying that it is all passing nonsense, lasting only a half minute or so on TV or in an eye-flicked printed sales pitch, and thus without enduring effect, we delude ourselves. For the aggregate of those minutes makes a formidable total, especially through incessant repetition. As a result, without our conscious consent, we become used to it as a style is formed, or a habit of thought is formed, and, consequently, behavior is affected, and with it the future.

So persuaded are we of the authority of technology, and its ability to make mechanical miracles, that we see the whole future in its terms. The future is now a fad instead of a responsibility.

I suppose, as of now, that the best we can do is to say, if technology means the ultimate expression of the material motive in cultural terms essentially undifferentiated anywhere in the land, that our escape may come only through a direct reversal of our material imperative in human affairs. Perhaps the escape from the blandly synthetic—the imposed culture—may lie only in the renewed pursuit of a higher humanism by which to celebrate the individual body and soul of man among his like-constituted fellows, each of whom is unique. This implies a spiritual rehabilitation which once might have been secured by a common comprehension of the divine. Lacking a general agreement nowadays on the terms of that, perhaps we have to command the technics to perform only their proper function, that is, service, instead of delegating to them that mastery of human life in even its *im*material aspects to which we have been more and more subjected. It is a purpose worth pursuing for the sake of all the positive splendors of our land, and of our founding principles, and of our best institutions, and of the respect owed to the best in our people.

There may be a ray of hope in some recent words of Sir Peter Medawar, who as a medical scientist did not incriminate technology, but only its misuse. "Insofar," he said, "as any weapon can be blamed for any crime, science, and technology *are* responsible for our present predicament. But they offer the only possible means of escaping the misfortunes for which they are responsible . . . an entirely new technology is required, one founded on ecology in much the same way as medicine is founded on physiology. If this new technology is accepted, I shall be completely confident of our ability to put and keep our house in order."

Dr. Medawar was referring to the physical environment. Is it apposite at this point to report that the optimistic Santa Fe Vicar General of 1883 could now see a tawny envelope of polluted air over Albuquerque, and more layers of the same at the desert junction of his state with three others? Still: may we hope that the other—the nonphysical—aspects of our environment may be reclaimed through a long-term proper use of the very technology that made pervasive an imposed culture—one which falls below the best nature of our people?

We have come a long way around from the idea of local American popular cultures and the often naïve but genuine expressions of their many different styles. But the contrasts which once existed in concrete regional circumstance have been succeeded by others. Serious contrasts now exist between the abstract early idealism of the nation and its erosion in our time through an unworthy exploitation of technology. It was an idealism resting upon a hope for a people to be enlightened through common control of their own character and condition. How much of this can be recovered? That issue itself, now, is what transcends our present practice in any sense whatever.

THE HARMONY OF

THINGS UNLIKE

Whenever I think how little I know and how much there is to be known, I always think of a fancy that came to me one day while on a long walk with a friend who, though a brilliant painter, was not limited in his interests to the art in which he made his career. It was instructive and rewarding for someone like myself to have had the friendship of a true polymath, that is, one who was interested and effective in more than one subject. Committed by talent to art, he was also deeply interested in science; and in his scientifically speculative hours, he found pleasures akin to the aesthetic.

The creative artist's ultimate problem is the solution of form. It is a problem of which I have heard scientists also speak. The perfect achievement of a vessel to contain precisely the appropriate amount of substance—this represents the solution of a problem in form, and in the arts it is the power of design which gives us satisfaction, as in the sciences it is the exquisite meeting of the concept with its demonstration which scientists, in a usage that always delights me, characterize as having "elegance."

The criterion of precise suitability is common to both art

and science, and my friend the painter—it was Peter Hurd—
taught me many a lesson in this regard. On the long walk I
speak of, when one day we were idling along a small river
that runs through his ranch in New Mexico, something he
said about knowledge, and its confined applications, and
also its illimitable dimensions, made me say, "I would give
much to be the absolute master of any one subject, great or
small."

He quickly made me aware of the responsibilities of such
a wish, for seeking knowledge of one matter, he said, must
also require exhaustive study of all related other matters.

His reply made me change my statement. Looking at the
ground, with its tangle of growths, I said, "Yes, then, think
of what it would be to separate a cubic foot of this earth,
and to find out everything that could be learned about it
and all its components in any relationship. If I were master
of the knowledge that pertains in any way to this tiny fragment of the land, I must extend my learning of some things
I already know, and then I must enter into discoveries far
beyond my present knowledge." It seemed to me I might
spend a lifetime exhausting all there was to know about my
cubic foot of earth.

I thought of a wonderful watercolor drawing by the German master Albrecht Dürer—a little paper about twenty
inches high by fifteen inches wide—which he called "The
Great Piece of Turf." He drew it in 1503. It is an examination, drawn from almost eye level at the ground, of all that
he could see that grew out of a clump of turf whose clotted
roots under the cut of the surface and whose green growths
above are drawn with masterly precision. Single strands of
grass rise in clear relief against larger leaves behind, and in
optical terms this is an exposition of my hypothetical clump
of earth. The drawing is of course a masterpiece of drafts-
manship and application of color and arranged design. But
it is much more than this—though until recently it has been

the modern fashion to require nothing further than these nonobjective values of a work of art. The Dürer drawing is a human document of a man's immense delight in the solution of a complicated problem, and it is also a piece of eloquent testimony of the same man's profound respect for the works of God in nature. Dürer was a deeply devout man who was endlessly studious in the concerns of his craft, and his devotion and his study came together to bring their separate values to create the wholeness of his statement about the piece of turf. He studied his plants so well that as he drew them he reproduced their identity, and we recognize, among other growths and grasses, the dandelion, the yarrow, the plantain, and the pimpernel.

To see them as he did, he must have used that child's vision which all true artists possess, so that each discovery is made with primal innocence at every turn of observation or experience; and when to such innocence of eye is added a perfection of craft, such as only a mature artist could command, then a great work must result, with two general effects, the first of these being private to the artist in his sense of fulfillment of his vision, and the other being the fresh experience received by the beholder.

Now to the information of the piece of turf that Dürer gave to us in 1503, add suggestions of what else there is to know about that separated bit of earth, and you must wonder, among many other things, about the chemistry of the soil, and the physics of color and light and warmth, the secrets of mineral structure, the cycles of seeding, growth, decay; the effect of the presence or absence of moisture and the interaction between sky and earth; the mystery of transpiration; the beneficent or harmful properties of plants in human use—their value in the making of artifacts or dyes; their uses as food by animal or insect life. Your thought goes under the floor of the turf to the creatures who live in the moist darkness below, and their orders of classification.

You could discover matters of interest about roots and their functions in feeding their productions, and also in binding the clod, and from the small clod your notion takes flight to the vastness of watersheds and the act of runoff and the part played against the ravages of erosion by the binding not merely of clods but of whole mountainsides through vegetation. Runoff turns into rivers, and the great piece of turf takes you from its tiny unity with a meadow to the great dimensions of a journey to the sea. The physical information to be had from the lump of earth has no end. And then you consider what the spiritual implications of this material object may be, and you think about creation, and—according to your sense of it—you pray.

And, too, your thought will go to the poetry written about aspects of nature. What poets have celebrated its grasses and flowers? What other painters besides Dürer? How have they done it? Without any fatuous literalism, what is to be learned from the "Pastoral" Symphony of Beethoven about man's response to the common and intimate wonders of nature? If you take either my cubic lump of earth or Dürer's "Great Piece of Turf" as a subject for exhaustive study, the chances are you will be exhausted before the subject can be. And in doing so, you will think of the unity and the relevance of every departmented or systematized fragment of man's general awareness.

Our witness for the moment is still Albrecht Dürer of Nuremberg. In 1512 or 1513 he composed an essay to introduce his writings on the art of painting and drawing. Concerning himself with the principles of his own craft, his spirit was still very much that of a polymath. In his style as teacher, he wrote:

". . . we should all gladly learn, for the more we know, so much the more do we resemble the likeness of God who verily knoweth all things. . . . Nature hath implanted in us the desire of knowing all things, thereby to discern a truth of all things."

Having so posed for us a grand general principle, our master then measures our poor humanity against it:

"But our dull wit," he resumes, "our dull wit cannot come unto such perfectness of all art, truth, and wisdom. Yet we are not therefore shut out from all arts ... much learning is not evil to a man, though some be stiffly set against it, saying that art puffeth up."

It was, in his day, perhaps a serious indictment, but Master Albrecht has a sweeping reply for it which holds good now:

"Were that so," he says, "then none were prouder than God who hath formed all arts. But that cannot be, for God is perfect in goodness." Both his logic and his theology refute the assault upon learning. Dürer can continue:

"The more, therefore, a man learneth so much the better doth he become, and so much the more love doth he win for the arts and for things exalted ... some may learn somewhat of all the arts, but"—reasonably he views how men are made with differences—"but that is not given to every man. Nevertheless there is no rational man so dull but that he may learn the one thing towards which his fancy draweth him most strongly. Hence no man is excused from learning something."

Since my own professional experience has largely been limited to the practice of an art—the art of writing—I find my own affinity with Dürer's reflections through the artist's apprehensions. But what is true of someone working in one craft may well in principle be true of one working in another; and I would plead that any man concerned with any expression of his gained knowledge—let me specify music, for example—can vastly profit by lifting his vision now and then away from his immediate vocation and examining and seeking experience in modes of expression of secondary professional interest to him. If he develops his sensibilities widely enough he will find certainly that his primary pursuit will be directly enriched by his secondary. Indeed, he will often discover that wonderful analogies of style and fulfillment come to him within his own cross-cultural experience.

I cannot help thinking of examples to illustrate the drift of my argument. Nobody needs to be reminded of Leonardo da Vinci and Michelangelo in this connection, but they were not so exceptional that illustrations end with them. Many men of letters have been able and interesting draftsmen or painters. The drawings of Victor Hugo are astonishing ideographs for the very spirit of the Gothic romanticism that informed his atmospheric novels. John Ruskin, studying the materials of art history in Italy and elsewhere, made watercolor or wash drawings very close in feeling, as witnesses of his vision, to the texture of his prose style. Eugène Delacroix, as his wonderful *Journal* shows, commanded a literary style which if cultivated would have made him an important writer as well as a great painter. Richard Wagner had so many sides to his nature and his talent that literature and music and management of people played equally important roles in his career, and his duality led his wretched friend Von Bülow (whose wife he stole) to declare that Wagner had the full face of Faust and the profile of Mephistopheles. And of course mention of those widely treated characters of drama reminds us that their most notable interpreter, Goethe, was an aristocrat among polymaths, with his modes of writing, reaching from the novel to the incomparable lyric poem to the epic drama; and his watercolors, through which he captured for himself the emotions that visited him on beholding the landscapes of Italy; and his collections of scientific apparatus; and his libraries full of philosophic clutter; and his adventures in statecraft.

Of all the pleasures of the varied sensibility I should think the greatest would be the arrival at a sense of harmony between man's various capabilities; and through such a sense of harmony to discern the marvelous tendency of life to show itself in a mysterious unity, the more one enters into its diverse components with curiosity, respect, and delight. As Dürer said, "A real harmony linketh together things unlike."

If I call in a couple of illustrations of my notion out of my own experience, I do so in all modesty, and I excuse myself by reflecting that if it were the experience of someone else I were referring to, it would equally well support my subject. I therefore feel impersonal as I cite these examples.

The first has to do with the pleasure I take from making drawings, which I have done all my life. Mostly I do them for fun, but, at times, the act of drawing what I see has a useful purpose, in the preparation of certain kinds of writing.

It has long been my habit to make drawings in India ink and watercolor of places and objects as notes for books dealing with historical subjects. Traveling in pursuit of the backgrounds of my subjects, my purpose is to make a record of what I see, as clearly as I can set it down. Now whether my drawings show to other people what I saw is not my main concern—though I am always gratified when they seem to recognize what I saw and drew. My main concern is to possess a graphic note of a place which later on will show me not only what I saw but remind me of how I felt when I saw it—and it is in the revival of this feeling that the value of my preparatory drawings exists for me. No photograph would give me this feeling—though it might show me what I had looked at. But when I take a photograph I do not become involved directly with my subject. In making a drawing I do become involved directly with my subject, through my concentrated effort to re-create it on the spot with whatever sensibility and skill I may command. Excitement attends the process, and something of this excitement returns to me later—even long later—when I look at the drawings as notes for my writing. And when I treat the same subject in words, I think the words are more true and more interesting as a result of the process I have described.

If you permit one last bit of supporting evidence for the value of the broad view of a personal culture, not only for its own sake, but for the sometimes useful results of the interaction of the varied interests of the polymath, I'll offer another example related to my own work, which after all is the only field of which I can speak with firm knowledge.

A generation ago I published a book of almost a half-million words, which dealt with the history of the Rio Grande. The great length of the river (almost two thousand miles) its extraordinary variety of cultures through the ages, reaching from the pre-Columbian to the present, the marvelous variety of its landscape, from the perpetual snowfields of the Rocky Mountains to the semitropical littoral of the Gulf of Mexico—all seemed to me to call for a full treatment and a noble design, if I could manage these.

The first problem was perhaps the hardest—how to begin the book. I wanted to find some way to find a literary suggestion for the physical beginnings of a river; how such a significant river—indeed, how any river—comes out of amorphous beginnings, that is to say, out of the moisture that is drawn from the sea to the sky through evaporation, is then let down upon the earth as precipitation, and then finds a beginning on earth for its career of going ever lower, through natural channels, and calling into its volume tributaries from other channels, until, constantly reinforced and enlarged by the entry of waters going the same way, it proceeds as a river to its ultimate resolution in its return to the sea.

Simply stated, I wanted to find a way to suggest how out of nothing, something came, which grew, and developed, and went splendidly on its way through a great variety of theme and development.

I searched other literary works to find an analogy—found none. I composed many written sketches for the opening and failed. And then, in an echo of the notion of a theme and its development, I thought of musical form, and, in musical form, the greatest illustration of the derivation of something mighty out of the most mysterious hint of nothingness was the opening of the Ninth Symphony of Beethoven.

I found a copy of the score and read it as I listened again and again to a recording of the work, and I said to myself that here was the noble model for my design.

I set to work writing my text with the score of the Ninth Symphony open before me, and I did so in full humility and trepidation. Now, of course, I was not out to contrive a simple-minded imitation, but to read constantly in Beethoven's wonderful development of his form how the first single statement became multiple through the arrival of added voices, themes and intensities; and I thought of the nothingness—that is, the practical impalpability of the act of evaporation—from which came the first drops of water on the earth to make a river, the trickle of melt off a snow ledge that fell into a declivity which soon became a system of tributaries bringing more moisture, until with the additions arising from an organic form in nature—a watershed with its drainage—a river came to be and to increase its might as it flowed.

The sheer cheek of telling about this is not to invoke indecent comparison in degree or value between my glorious model and my production, but only to indicate what a fool a man would be if he knew where to learn from his great forebears and failed to do so. In this case, to do so required a response out of my experience as a listener in another art than the one I practice, however I can, as a writer.

If I am in this far as a shameless name-dropper—Beethoven indeed!—I can perhaps only let momentum carry me even farther, and risk telling about certain results of my raid on the Ninth Symphony.

When the book was published, among its early readers were two friends who knew nothing of my process of work in this instance. One is now director of one of the nation's most vital and important museums, the other is a composer and scholar in music. Quite independently, each said to me, "The opening of your book is like the opening of the Ninth Symphony." Surely no aspiring cultural pluralist—to coin a regrettable phrase—ever had more direct confirmation of his course.

Let me finish with a simple resolution of all this by suggesting that even the devoted specialist must only enhance his vision, capacity, and achievement if he bears upon life with a wide-angle lens, as it were, and if he listens as keenly to intuitions as he does to demonstrated proofs, and if he lets his observations range far beyond his own field into other fields of man's expression, the better to realize in himself not only his vision of his work, but his fullness as a man.

To bring a sense of this fullness nearer, in the analogy of music, let me approach my conclusion with a picture of musical glory in a time of youth—a youth for which we may feel a dear and blithe affinity.

In September 1853, Clara Schumann wrote in her diary: "This month introduced to us a wonderful person, Brahms, a composer from Hamburg—twenty years old. Here again is one of those who comes as if sent straight from God. He played us sonatas, scherzos, et cetera, of his own, all of them showing exuberant imagination, depth of feeling, and mastery of form. Robert says that there was nothing that he could tell him to take away or to add. It is really moving to see him sitting at the piano, with his interesting young face which becomes transfigured when he plays, his beautiful hands, which overcome the greatest difficulties with perfect ease (his things are very difficult), and in addition these remarkable compositions . . . what he played to us is so masterly that one cannot but think that the good God sent him into the world ready-made. He has a great future before him, for he will first find the true field for his genius when he begins to write for the orchestra. Robert says there is nothing to wish except that heaven may preserve his health."

In the energy of this passage the statement that is the most revealing about the young artist is that in which Clara Schumann speaks of his "exuberant imagination, depth of feeling, and mastery of form." The major elements of artistic expression are here. It is these very attributes that can be enriched by study in as many fields of art and learning—which is to say, intuition and intellection—as possible. Talent is inherent, and nothing can insert it into anyone. But cultivation of talent is within the reach of all who possess it.

I will end with another quotation which seems to me to crown all our discussion here of the lovely possibility of interaction between many expressions of life, even to achieving Dürer's "Harmony of Things Unlike." It comes from Montaigne, who said:

"Every man carries in himself the entire form of the human state."

TWO

AFTER-IMAGES

WILLA CATHER'S

INCALCULABLE

DISTANCE

i

The land was open range and there was almost no fencing. As we drove further and further out into the country, I felt a good deal as if we had come to the end of everything—it was a kind of erasure of personality.

This was Willa Sibert Cather telling in 1913 of her first sight of the flat lands of Nebraska in 1883. She was then a child of nine, coming with her family from the leafy valleys of Virginia to a new home on the prairies. She had been "thrown into a country as bare as a piece of sheet iron." Her father told her to show grit in a new country, and she tried to, but she was undone by the song of meadowlarks that

every now and then flew up and sang a few splendid notes and dropped down into the grass again. That reminded me of something—I don't know what, but my one purpose in life just then [at nine] was not to cry, and every time they did it, I tried not to go under.

It is an easy game too often played in our age of pop psychology to fix one childhood experience or trait as the determinant of a whole life; but here, surely, we may see something of Willa Cather's enduring character: her eye for the fact, her clarity in stating what she saw, her susceptibility to the lyric expressions of nature, her deep store of the nostalgic impressions needed by every artist, and her courage in self-discipline.

In any case, we know from her early novels how she came to love that very land of its immigrant people in their universal simplicities. As with her particular, deep-running awareness she entered into such lives, Willa Cather time and again gave arresting glimpses of their world, once she had with the advance from childhood come to see, and to feel, from a distance, its beauties and its troubles. In her felicity of word and vision, she is a great artist of *place*.

From *One of Ours*, a novel whose first half is laid in the prairies, we take some quick views which are conveyed to us through the days of young Claude Wheeler:

When he came up the hill like this, toward the house with its lighted windows, something always clutched at his heart. He both loved and hated to come home. He was always disappointed, and yet he always felt the rightness of returning to his own place.

And again:

The sun had dropped low, and the two boys, as Mrs Wheeler watched them from the kitchen window, seemed to be walking beside a prairie fire.

And again:

His body felt light in the scented wind, and he listened drowsily to the larks, singing in dried weed and sunflower stalks. At this season their song is almost painful to hear, it is so sweet. He sometimes thought of this walk long afterward: it was memorable to him, though he could not say why.

But perhaps we can, if we remember the nine-year-old who tried not to cry when the larks sang to her homesickness.

Such examples are abundant. Every book by Willa Cather is alive with them. Some of the most memorable are in *Lucy Gayheart* and *My Mortal Enemy* (both are small masterpieces generally misunderstood), and *A Lost Lady* and *The Professor's House*—another magnificent novel whose form is often regretted by unimaginative teachers and critics. But no example of Miss Cather's painterly evocation of surrounding life which makes her people so believable in their times and places seems to me more memorable as scene and prose than a certain passage in the story "Two Friends" from the book of stories *Obscure Destinies*, when the narrator remembers a scene from her girlhood:

The road, just in front of the sidewalk where I sat and played jacks, would be ankle-deep in dust, and seemed to drink up the moonlight like folds of velvet. It drank up sound, too: muffled the wagon wheels and hoof-beats; lay soft and meek like the last residuum of material things—the soft bottom resting-place. Nothing in the world, not snow mountains or blue seas, is so beautiful in moonlight as the soft, dry summer roads in a farming country, roads where the white dust falls back from the slow wagon wheel.

Any list of foregrounds—we say foregrounds rather than backgrounds because the scene is always so closely woven into the very presences who enact her stories—any such list significant to Miss Cather's characters must mention the mysterious and primal splendors of the cliff dwellings of

prehistoric Southwestern Pueblo people that occur importantly in her work. The Mesa Verde of Colorado early
captivated her with its evidence of a deep and purely self-
sufficient past, and in suitable variations it gave extraordinary dimension to her novels *The Song of the Lark* and *The
Professor's House*, and (the first appearance of the scene,
done entirely from imaginative reading) the little story
called "The Enchanted Bluff," which appeared in a magazine in 1909 before she had first gone to the Southwest.

There the landscape gave her the vastness of an outer dimension in a country grander than that of her early prairies.
Yet, at first, she felt once again that "unreasoning fear of
being swallowed up by the distance." But soon she felt the
human tug of small-town life amidst the vast abstraction;
and visions of both Western space and small community
returned in her later books.

Her eye is not only for the open country and the small
community. Many of her cityscapes are memorable, as in
such novels and stories as *The Song of the Lark* (Chicago
and New York), *My Mortal Enemy* (which has vistas of
Madison Square like early photographs by Stieglitz), *A Lost
Lady* (Denver), and the New York prima-donna stories in
Youth and the Bright Medusa. In many of these there are
reflections of the period taste, the open-air vision and glistening atmosphere, of the French Impressionists. In all her
place-painting, Willa Cather, drawing on the riches of her
visual worlds, saw in them not only inherent beauties, but
also their hold on her people—a hold often tyrannical and
imprisoning, from which, whether through larger inner vision, or actual physical action, there must come removal:
escape, deliverance, a release into distance: or death, physical or metaphorical, will follow. It is this larger element of
awareness behind all her place-pictures that relieves them
of softness or sentimentality—that merely pictorial statement which when unattached to character has so little

value—though in much fictional writing it is widely admired by innocent readers who congratulate authors on their "descriptions."

ii

So from her physical worlds, Willa Cather early began to create for herself a dimension of her life that she had to reach no matter what local limitations in her younger days might have done to restrain her leap of mind. It was a world-mind she sought. If this was not commonly available in the Nebraska of her youth, she reached for its evidences as they could be studied and reimagined from afar.

While still a student at the University of Nebraska she ardently created her own local center of reference to the world of culture that lay beyond the prairie horizon. She was the provincial connoisseur who closely followed reviews and criticism of the arts that appeared in newspapers, magazines, and books from important centers of the higher culture, foreign and domestic. The very names of great, distant writers, actors, painters, singers, composers were of essential comfort to her. It is not likely that Nebraska in general was at that time deeply concerned with what went on in the theatres, opera houses, galleries, and literary workings of New York, London, or Paris. But such matters were the breath of life to the brilliant student at Lincoln, and it was not long before she became the critical correspondent on highly diverse matters of art for the local press.

Chicago was the lodestone to aspiring talents in the upper frontier region and the Middle West. Willa Cather was aware, as a young discoverer, even at a distance, of the concert and theatre performances, the opera, the growing museums, and that sense of artistic independence of New York's cultural primacy, which Chicago always splendidly declared; and in time she traveled to attend Chicago performances by the Metropolitan Opera Company and to see plays acted by fabled performers. From years of hungry reading about her subjects in order to report on them, she was well prepared, on encountering some of them later, to meet them with firm authority, even if it had been largely acquired through vicarious experience.

In 1896 she moved to Pittsburgh to assume teaching tasks and editorial work. This move brought her closer to New York and—more significant—to Europe. In due time—1902—she found Europe itself, and forever after, her vision held a deeper perspective, an informed criterion, in life and art. After publishing her second novel, *O Pioneers* (1913), she first saw the American Southwest. Her brother, to whom she was close, was a young trainman in Arizona, and on visits to him, and to New Mexico, she came to know other Americas. Finally, settling in New York, she became a fastidious and discerning inhabitant of the world of arts and artists, the latter chiefly among musicians, and among singers, chiefly singers at the opera. New England for summers, Canada for excursions into history and other climates, were pendant to her New York life.

But if she was at home in all such places that she understood with so fine an eye for detail and so deep an intuition of atmosphere, she was also their inhabitant in inner dimension: for the evidences of the different climates of life that beckoned to her gave a versatile power to her art as a writer. As we have seen, the very landscape of each place became part of her vision and richly affected her prose expression. The local lives subject to their respective places extended the range of her responses to the infinitely variant terms of human aspiration, with its constant, often secret call to that desire which might lie beyond the immediate grasp. In the discerning appetite of her early career for those achievements that lift mankind above the ordinary run of life—"Oh Lord!," as Jules Laforgue exclaimed, "how *daily* life is!"— Willa Cather was rehearsing an aspect of her vision which comes plain again and again in her novels and stories.

[*84*

iii

In her short novel *Lucy Gayheart*, Willa Cather has her heroine looking forward from her revisited hometown on the Platte River to the next evening, when she would be returning to her rented room in Chicago. She was going to hear a great singer's song recital in the city. "In a few hours," says the novel, leading us to the phrase that seems both to enclose and extend the determining concept that runs like a precious vein throughout the controlled passion of Willa Cather's life and work, "one could cover that incalculable distance; from the wintry country and homely neighbors, to the city where the air trembled like a tuning fork with unimaginable possibilities."

So short a tale, so small a journey, and yet so "incalculable" a distance between the mundane binding of life and the utmost freedom and exaltation! The distance is incalculable because finally it has an interior dimension. It is aspiration. It is humility before the greatest of human works. It is delight so keen in the established justice of a truly achieved work of art that no pang is too much to suffer if only it can be felt. Let the homely neighborhood commitments do their best to frustrate the desire to travel that distance. They will do so in vain. The desire is greater than its passive foes. It will prevail, or if it fail, as it does in the story "A Wagner Matinee," it does so even while passionately affirming its values. It prevailed in imagination when Willa Cather created for her provincial newspapers the atmosphere and knowledge of the cultivated world elsewhere. It prevailed in actuality when later she had closed the distance and was able to hear music, to see paintings, to watch famous actors, and to write her books.

The obvious quality of distance is physical—the distance measurable between two points. More important for Willa Cather's artistry and her grasp of the passions of human life is a moral distance—the span between ignorance and awareness; between hope and bitter denial; between the civilization within a soul and whatever corroding condition would work to destroy it in hatred or, worse, indifference.

"We like a writer," stated Willa Cather, "much as we like individuals; for what he is, simply, underneath his accomplishments. Oftener than not, it is for some moral quality, some ideal which he himself cherishes, though it may be little discernible in his behavior in the world. It is the light behind his books, and it is the living quality of his sentences." But it may not invariably be ingratiating—the intimate energy which we sometimes feel is often what appeals, even when it is unconventional.

Bruno Walter said Mahler "was likely to regard the world with the absent-minded glance of the creative artist. . . . Like many a creative artist he was likely to forget man while loving humanity." One thinks of Beethoven and possibly Brahms. Walter's observation may be applicable to composers of music and their concern with the essence of the created abstraction. It cannot always be quite so neatly true of the literary artist who must be not only concretely communicative, but also keenly observant of the individual human life upon which to erect those intimate commonalities that in literature seem so uniquely our separate recognitions.

And yet—perhaps through her love of music—there *is* something in Willa Cather of the musician's detachment: the nerve of the abstract; the endistancing of the immediate in search of the ultimate. The ultimate is an incalculable distance away, yet it can be confronted. It is the first-rate of any sort, seen from afar, to which escape from the mediocre, the banal, the local and limited satisfactions rooted in the familiar is vitally necessary. The discovery can be found in many forms—music, art, place, character, a whole way of life: pure expression at its most intense; aspiration unimpeded by petty cautions, and, perhaps, even duties. Accordingly, Miss Cather, as we have seen, began her search for her own inner as well as outer distance in her early life, until she finally found it in the writing of her novels and stories; and again and again she made that same search the deep concern of her fictional people.

In *Lucy Gayheart* we read of the little town and its setting: "The tides that raced through the open world never came here. There was never anything to make one leap beyond oneself or to carry one away. One's mind got stuffy, like the houses." Lucy herself desired the unknown distance: "How often she had run out on a spring morning, into the orchard, down the street, in pursuit of something she could not see, but knew!"

This was not Bovaryism—Emma was after material fashions and satisfactions. Lucy Gayheart, and Willa Cather, were beckoned by the moral distance. When Miss Cather made her first European journey, in 1902, at the age of twenty-eight, the result was "great imaginative experience." But what was important about it was what she brought to it on her own. Already she owned through study and imagination much of European culture. It was a long leap geographically, but not in inner distance, when in Paris she found a pictorial model for so much she worked to express:

Just before I began *The Professor's House* I had seen, in Paris, an exhibition of the old and modern Dutch paintings. In many of them the scene presented a living-room warmly furnished, or a kitchen full of food and coppers. But in most of the interiors, there was a square window, through which one saw the masts of ships, or a stretch of grey sea. The feeling . . . that one got through those square windows was remarkable, and gave me a sense of the fleets of Dutch ships that ply quietly on all waters of the globe—to Java, [and farther].

Here again is that opening into the distance, whether in fact or metaphor, for which Willa Cather had her own particular square window of consciousness. For her the incalculable distance reached not only forward toward the risk

of unfamiliar action, but also deeply into the human inheritance, which could enfold like a mantle and give re-
assurance to those able to clothe themselves in it. While she
was unsurpassed in her lyric if restrained passion for the
American scene at its humblest—the farms, the small towns
smothered under their great snows or wilted under their
great heat waves—she was not limited to Emerson's view
when he said that "our day of dependence, our long apprenticeship to the learning of other lands, draws to a close."
Always, for her, the immediate foreground was given greater
interest by the contributive nearness of mother cultures in
lands abroad. Thus her love of opera, Wagner especially,
French painting, Latin literature, the manner and dress of
old well-seasoned societies in long-mellowed cities of the Old
World. If she looked deeply into North American history,
it was to celebrate character and atmosphere among the
French in seventeenth-century Quebec (*Shadows on the
Rock*), and the French and Mexican in nineteenth-century
New Mexico (*Death Comes for the Archbishop*). For novel-
istic purposes, the bridge in one direction—old world to
new—was made by immigrants with their cultural roots
harking back in the other direction. For her, the inner life
was without seam. It was this seamless fabric that rescued
her from the limitations of the common events of the day,
wherever they may have occurred.

In many of her fictional persons, that space of inner freedom in taste and reference took differing definitions. For
herself, in one instance it took the form of a living contact
with a remnant out of her literary experience. At Aix-les-
Bains, she says in her essay "A Chance Encounter," she met
an ancient lady who was the niece of Flaubert. The old lady
offered Miss Cather a keepsake of the famous uncle. But
Miss Cather said, "The things of her uncle that were valuable to me I already had, and had had for years. It rather
hurt me that she should think I wanted any material reminder of her or of Flaubert."

So, no collector of souvenirs, she distanced herself from the material, the mundane, even at the cost of a small emotional rudeness in the face of innocent pride. It was as if she must escape, in this little comedy of mistaken civility, the dailiness of life, and implant in her art, again and again, her vision of that escape in the creatures of her contained and impassioned creation.

One of her people whom she seemed most to love is Tom Outland in *The Professor's House*. He typified the natural yet sensitive man of the open country—perhaps rather like that brother who moved farther west in her girlhood. In the novel, when Tom enters a room, "one seemed to catch glimpses of an unusual background behind his shoulders," and, to be sure, he turns out to be the discoverer of "The Blue Mesa" (for which read Mesa Verde) and its preserved marvels of a civilization poignantly long lost.

It is a sort of declaration of honor that Willa Cather, having formulated her own distance so eloquently, was yet able to see and love so eloquently the origins, in their modest localism, that she had so briskly left behind. Lucy Gayheart, talking with her Chicago music teacher as he extols small-town life, says to him:

You think so because you live in a city. Family life in a little town is pretty deadly. It's being planted in the earth, like one of your carrots there. I'd rather be pulled up and thrown away.

But oh, we reflect, the greys: life is never simple. The novelist goes on to say of Lucy:

She loved her little town, but it was a heart-broken love, like loving the dead who cannot answer back. . . .

iv

Willa Cather was of her time, as all true artists are of their times. They cannot help but be so, no matter what the origins of their beliefs and styles. And yet, of her time, as she was, it was never in the way of prevailing modes—those treacherous, often blaring causes and voices which season after season seem both timely and eternal, but which actually are as fugitive as the newspapers and the critical orthodoxies of the day, and which are not necessarily of enduring aesthetic interest, whatever other values they may possess. The intellectual slang of a given period, with its reigning critical modishness, is rarely capable of enclosing aesthetic judgment. In the early 1930s, criticism was heavily weighted by commitment to social activism, which then meant fashionable Marxism. *Lucy Gayheart,* published in 1935, had no political concern with either the left or the right. It was a work of art reflecting an individual vision, not fugitive conformity to a soulless orthodoxy that was the passport of the time to a certain intellectualistic respectability. In consequence, the book was demolished by the reviewers, who had the professional priorities of their consciences all mixed up. Secondhand insights still, all too often, affect the art of criticism.

Writing amidst the atmosphere, the facts, of her time, Willa Cather reflected some of these quite naturally as elements of that integument of believability which is necessary to any body of life. But what makes the effect of her work abide, as in the case of any work of art, is not primarily the matter, but the quality and style of expression in which it is presented. She was a true artist of prose, and it is her prose that breathes with the life of her characters, near and far in her own experience. Every artist has a vision reaching farther than his art can express. Who has ever fully realized for others his design and feeling? But without that reach in the inmost nature of those inherited works that we regard as our greatest, their makers could never have approached as nearly as they managed to do.

For a last glimpse of Willa Cather's use of the prosaic to

express the innermost nature of a sympathetic human being, we make this summary:

One time when Lucy Gayheart was a girl of thirteen, workmen came to pave the sidewalk in front of her small-town family house. After the cement-workers were done that evening, she went, when she thought no one was looking, to the still wet cement and "ran over those wet slabs—one, two, three, and then out into the weeds beside the road," leaving three footprints in the fresh cement, which would soon harden, to retain its triple intaglio. Then suddenly she saw, standing nearby, a young man who later, all his life, wanted to marry her but never did, because of a tragic misunderstanding. Long afterward, she drowned in an accident on ice that was thawing. A few days after her funeral, the man who loved her but never held her, went, after all those years, to her old family house, which is closed and abandoned for disposal. He is taken by thought. "What was a man's home town, anyway, but the place where he has had disappointments and had learned to bear them?"—so he mused.

Now we come to the closing of this affecting novel—a conclusion that stands as the resolution of our theme, and also as a breath-taking summary of a particular human creature—Lucy Gayheart, the girl who tried to reach for her own incalculable distance, had failed, and had come home.

"As he was leaving the Gayhearts'," the now middle-aged man, who had once hoped for Lucy in his life, came upon the worn old slabs of pavement. The book ends with these words:

He paused mechanically on the sidewalk, as he had done so many thousand times, to look at the three light footprints, running away.

THE FATHER

PRESIDENT

If he should look out through the tall, narrow windows of his first sentence, the Very Reverend Father President of 1814 would be able to see his second.

"The college," he wrote in his flying script, whose down strokes were heavy, while the lighter lines whipped upward, "is an extensive and most convenient edifice. It commands one of the most delightful prospects in the United States, and its situation for health is exceeded by none. The garden and court where the students recreate are very airy and spacious."

He was writing the text of the college catalogue, and the claims he made were intended to attract and reassure parents in the early years of his residence at Georgetown in the District of Columbia. Proceeding, he could look farther in his prospectus, to an educational advantage available at the time to no other institution of higher learning. This was the United States Congress as the philosophical voice of that still-young marvel of the political world: the American democracy that learned men crossed the ocean to examine.

The Father President went on to say of Georgetown in 1814:

"Among the many other advantages which it enjoys, its contiguity to the city of Washington, the seat of the federal government, is not the least considerable, as the students have occasionally an opportunity of hearing the debates in Congress, it being only a pleasant walk from the college to the capitol."

Even greater claims had accompanied the foundation of the college in 1788. It was to be a place where "an undivided Attention may be given to the Cultivation of Virtue and Literary Improvement," and where "a System of Discipline may be introduced and preserved incompatible with Indolence and Inattention in the Professor, or with incorrigible habits of Immorality in the Student." In fact, "the Benefit of this Establishment should be as General as the Attainment of its Object is desirable." Moreover, a breadth of charity must prevail, for "Agreeably to the liberal Principle of our Constitution, the Seminary will be open to Students of every Religious Profession." From the very beginning, many years before the Father President's arrival, an august intention had accompanied the foundation of the college by Archbishop John Carroll, who wrote in his proposals of establishment: "On this academy is built all my hope of permanency and success to our holy religion in the United States."

The Father President—his name was Giovanni Antonio Grassi—had called upon Archbishop Carroll in Baltimore to pay his respects on arriving in the United States in October 1810. He was assigned to the Georgetown academy and two years later was appointed president. He had already discovered what a difference there was between the ideal and the real at Georgetown.

The college had not prospered, despite its great purposes. There were ten boarding students, and these with a handful of day scholars added up to "nothing," said the Father President, "but a crew of blackguard youths and boys." He had to admit that he found himself in a "melancholy situation, compelled to be a sorrowful spectator of the miserable state of this college." There was much work to do and he fell upon it with all his uncommon energy.

On assuming the presidency, he was thirty-seven years old, and was described as "a man of elegant manners and polished address, learned and able." He was of medium height. His short-cropped cap of hair and arched eyebrows were of auburn color. He had an intent gaze in his large, clear, hazel eyes—the gaze of a man drawn by life's evidence all about him. His color was ruddy and his wide mouth and generous chin suggested even in repose a pleasant nature.

If his movement expressed his qualities of mind, he moved rapidly, with precision, grace, and economy. An Italian, he was born in Bergamo in 1775. At the age of twenty-four, moved by a dedication to a cause that seemed all but lost in 1799, he entered the novitiate of the Society of Jesus at Colorno in northern Italy.

Almost everywhere in the world the Society was banned, having been dissolved in 1773 by Pope Clement XIV. Civil and religious governments refused organized status or canonical existence to the Jesuits everywhere but in Russia. There, under the patronage of Tsar Paul I (son of Catherine the Great), the refugee Father General of the Society guarded for the future the live spark of the intellectual and spiritual tradition of the followers of Ignatius Loyola. Italian novices were sent to Russia for their training, and there went young Grassi.

ii

His ability—the style of his mind and energy—was quickly recognized. While still in his twenties he was ordained and became the rector of the College of Nobles at Polocz. Though in exile in Russia, the Society kept its gaze upon the larger world and searched for work where it needed doing. Father Grassi was chosen to accompany a mission to

Astrakhan on the shores of the Caspian Sea, and fell at once to the study of Armenian.

Early in 1805 his plans were changed for him. He was called to St. Petersburg, where the Father General assigned him to a mission preparing to make its way to China. There was no assurance that once arrived at Pekin the missioners would be received with good will or even in safety. But with two companions of his order, Father Grassi plunged into his preparations, and in mid-winter, dressed in Russian furs, he set out in a train of three sledges for Sweden. It was the beginning of a fantastic effort to reach China.

The reverend travelers took full sets of vestments, and sacred vessels; small religious images and objects to use as gifts; secular clothing for risky environments and the white-stocked habit of their Society for places where they might openly live in their profession; medicines; letters of recommendation; and—for Father Grassi, who was scientifically inclined—various mathematical instruments and systems of apparatus to demonstrate physics and astronomy. They crossed Finland, and the Gulf of Bothnia, and got to Sweden, and after many delays succeeded in proceeding to Copenhagen. There they took ship for London, planning to sail on for the Orient.

But despite cordialities from enlightened noblemen and courtesies from continental diplomats, the missioners were frustrated in every effort to take passage for China. The East India Company, which controlled British shipping for the Orient trade, refused to have commerce with Jesuits. To be at least partway on their course, they finally sailed for Lisbon, where they hoped to be granted passage for Macao or Canton in a Portuguese ship. Here again, they were denied what they required, and two years passed in Lisbon, until the missioners obeyed orders from their Father General in Russia to return to England, to escape a threatened French invasion of Portugal.

They settled at Stonyhurst College in England, a haven

of their Society. There they awaited further orders, but none came for years, and they worked as they could. Father Grassi pursued his scientific learning. He studied English. He observed much about the administration of an educational institution. And then, once again—and for the last time—China seemed to call. On 10 April 1810, the stalled missioners received a letter from the Father General ordering them to return to Russia, where they were to arrange for a journey overland, across independent Tartary, to China. They prepared to go; but for Father Grassi, in any case, the five-year attempt to reach China was at an end. New special orders reached him at Stonyhurst. Under obedience, he proceeded to Liverpool, and on board the North Atlantic packet ship *Leda* he sailed in August 1810 for America, taking with him what was described as his "fine collection of philosophical instruments."

He has already told us with a sigh what he found on his arrival at Georgetown. But he was a cultivated man, and such a man always does honor to the traditions of his vocation and his place, both. He could only give his best. Finding little learned enterprise in his new environment, he set to work, with the aid of a Jesuit lay brother, to construct models out of wood to demonstrate the Copernican system, the movement of the planets, and the diurnal and annual movements of the earth. He devised a terrestrial globe. In a room in the original building of the academy, built in 1788, which had been visited with stately courtesy by General Washington, he set up a small museum for the display of his apparatus.

These, the common necessities of his own intellectual life, were at once the marvel of the time, not only for the rascally student body, but also for visitors. Members of Congress came. Commodore David Porter came. Commodore Stephen Decatur came, and presented to the museum a fragment of his flagship.

Education, abstract in its philosophical character, had

also its visible virtues, some of which could be demonstrated. It was not long until astonished students under Father Grassi's hand heard themselves performing for the college visitors a dialogue on the Copernican system composed by their mentor. He prepared them to perform chemical experiments for the public, and rehearsed them for flights of elocution on the "vicissitudes of the seasons." For himself, he took pleasure in calculating eclipses and determining the altitudes of the sun, and noting the results in his diary, where in October 1812 he recorded also that for supper the "boys eat their possum, which lives in the woods, and is found only in America."

iii

By then he was the Father President, and had forty-two resident students in the college and seven day students. Year by year the enrollment figures steadily climbed. Archbishop Carroll visited the institution when he could; once he gave a special dinner as a treat to the boys, for which the total bill was fifteen dollars and eleven cents, and he declared in December 1815 that "Mr Grassi has revived the college of Ge.Town, which has received great improvement in the number of students and course of studies."

The Father President's labors and their results were for a time shadowed by war, for the British, pursuing their land campaign in the War of 1812, maneuvered their forces near Bladensburg, northeast of Washington, in August 1814, and, on the twenty-fourth, defeated raw United States troops there. At the college a number of students were remaining for the summer vacation. Late in the day they saw American soldiers retreating through Georgetown, and when night fell they looked through the college windows to see the sky over Washington break into firelight. The British were burning the Capitol. Soon afterward, the invaders put the torch to the Executive Mansion, the Treasury building, the Navy Yard, and shipping anchored in the Potomac. Someone said the firelight was so bright that those at the college could read by it.

When day broke the collegians saw British troops at work in Washington, and prepared themselves for the sack of Georgetown. Sacred vessels and plate were hidden and prayers arose in the chapel. Presently the enemy was seen to withdraw; thanksgiving was offered; and a week later, with a dissertation by the Father President and the singing of the *veni Creator*, the college opened its next regular session on schedule. Present were five priests, two scholastics, sixty-five students, and twelve servants. The students wore the traditional Georgetown uniform of a coat and pantaloons of blue cloth with large yellow buttons, and a waistcoat of red kerseymere.

And now, by a turn of events full of joy for the Society of Jesus, Father Grassi was in a position to proceed with a step of great importance to the college. Hitherto he could not conduct it officially as a property of the Jesuits, since their Society had no canonical existence under the ban of Clement XIV. Under this condition, in which local rather than general values must obtain, the long view seemed foreshortened. Subject to chance, local opinion, and vagary, the college must have found it difficult to claim for a still modest institution any kinship with the grand academic communities of an older world.

But now, in the summer of 1814, not long before the British lit up the skies of Washington, a far-reaching change of climate occurred in the philosophic cosmos of the Vatican. Pope Pius VII, reversing the decree of his predecessor, restored the freedom, the integrity, and the open gesture of the Society of Jesus throughout the world. It was a gain of great dimensions for Jesuits everywhere, with powerful effect in all possible local significance wherever the fellows of Saint Ignatius awaited their restoration. To the Father President of Georgetown it meant, among other, and perhaps more general, things, the occasion for identifying the college as a Jesuit institution in honor and vitality—with justification now of seeking official sanction for the granting of degrees under academic respectability.

He lost no time.

The first enrolled student of Georgetown was now a member of Congress—William Gaston. After suitable advisements and draftings, he presented to the House in January 1815, "the Petition of the President and Directors of the College of Georgetown . . . to be invested with authority and power to confer the usual academical honors on those who by their proficiency in the Liberal Arts may be judged deserving of such distinctions. . . ." Thirty-three days later, on 1 March 1815, President James Madison signed an act sent to him by the Congress which gave full powers to the college. It was also the day on which peace was ratified between Great Britain and the United States. The year held another act of momentous satisfaction for the Father President. On December 27 he wrote in his diary, "I was made a citizen at the Court in Washington," and by now, of course, he was John Anthony Grassi.

For the rest, the world was moving fast, and marvels were freshly at hand to be examined. At the Navy Yard a certain Mr. Rose showed the Father President and a group from the college an apparatus of "perpetual motion" and "explained in what it consisted." Students were given excursions on the Potomac in steamboats, daring the experience first known ten years before by Robert Fulton with his *Clermont* on the Hudson. On one outing, they went as far as Mount Vernon, had a picnic on the shore below the famous old house, were "kindly received by Colonel Washington, walked in the garden, saw the vault in which the General's remains lie," and sailed upstream again at four o'clock to arrive home five hours later. The use of the steamer cost five dollars for the day. Another expedition ran aground, and the Father President had to wait and wonder for his boys until midnight.

But still, all believed that such outings demonstrated "that travel by steamboat was practicable, rapid and safe."

Current wonders awaiting disclosure in other elements were also examined. Father Wallace, who taught mathematics, natural philosophy, and chemistry, assembled his class out-of-doors on the Feast of St. Ignatius in 1816 and "sent off a balloon." If it carried no passengers—though in 1783 at Annonay in France a balloon had carried aloft the first creatures to be lifted skyward, which were a sheep, a cock, and a duck—Father Wallace's balloon was watched with such interest along its whole course that, he was pleased to discover, "it led to no little correspondence." It must seem that the arts of learning were contagious under John Anthony Grassi.

His own duties were various and demanding. In addition to his presidency, he served the office of Superior of his Society in the United States, and he also went about on horseback to carry his priestly offices to the surrounding countryside. He often said Mass at the Alexandria Mission, where Madam Custis, General Washington's adopted daughter, heard him and gave him "two pictures for the church." The Lees and the Fitzgeralds received him, and when occasion required he took the Last Sacraments to their slaves, whose condition made him reflective. "The sad clang of servile chains," he said, "may yet often be heard beneath the sun of Liberty."

iv

All that he saw of life in the United States was of interest to him, and much of it was surprising. How utterly wrong was the general European idea of America, he said. He remembered that "many Europeans imagine that a large proportion of the inhabitants of America are civilized aboriginal Indians," which of course was preposterous, when the population was almost entirely derived from European stock—

the English, the Irish, the German, the French. And yet life in America was like life nowhere else, and he gazed upon it in fascination.

He saw no palaces like those in Italy, for example, in which many families lived. Here there was one family to a house, which was usually built of wood. The rooms were simple and clean, without any hint of "Italian magnificence," but instead had plain mahogany furniture and few pictures. There were no courtyards or plazas with fountains. He thought the "arts of ornamentation" were held in little esteem, though he recognized that Benjamin West and John Trumbull were not only accomplished American painters but much admired ones. American interest ran to mechanical inventions, which by machine did the work for which there were not enough hands. In a society busy with trade and the desire for money, it was, he thought, "not surprising that the flowers of poetic genius fail to flourish." He saw that there was "no lack of gifted men," but he believed they remained more satisfied with "a wide acquaintance with many subjects than a profound knowledge of any single field." He had to add that the educated ear was often astonished at the confident and decisive views uttered by poorly informed citizens.

He examined the New Englanders, and though he refused to think their practices characteristic of all the Americans, he had to recognize that Yankees, as he heard them called, were regarded "as the most knavish and capable of the most ingenious impositions," as they took their trading ventures everywhere. Though he found American behavior "generally civil," certain niceties were wanting in manners. His fellow-citizens thought nothing of knifing away at their fingernails or combing their hair in public, or lounging about with their feet on another chair or "propped up high against the wall." It was sad, but he must admit that though newspapers were everywhere, and edifying literature was available, the "most popular reading" was to be found in "novels which serve to deprave hearts and minds"—indeed, novels were read in "incredible quantities."

It was hard to believe, but Americans gambled and got drunk more often than Italians, with consequences which he must declare to be "fatal to individuals and to entire families." Dancing was the most general entertainment. The Father President observed that "the mania for jumping about in this manner was not less powerful than in France itself." He never saw such luxury as that available to any American. Why, they dressed as well in the country as in the city, and he concluded that the cost of "a holiday garment" was "no index of the condition" of the wearer. But if there was a veneer of well-being it did not in the end hide the waste that was "common in this country." Fortunately, bread was abundant. "Those who are not lazy will not be poor," he decided, "and will not beg in public." He was glad to observe that "civil order and tranquillity" were generally well maintained. There was "much show of piety"— this despite "indifference to sect ... everyone reads his Bible and in New England they will not permit a traveller or allow a messenger to continue his journey on a Sunday," which seemed absurd to a cultivated Mediterranean spirit.

Education, he saw, was "far from neglected," though it was mainly sought "to maintain status or to earn a fortune." Everyone reached for education, and families made sacrifices so that their young might rise. There seemed to be two general curricula: one of elegant learning for those destined for law or medicine—the professions; the other of simple value to those promised to agriculture or trade who would require little beyond arithmetic and a pinch of writing.

He deplored that the American youth, on reaching a certain age, became "impatient with suggestions," and, determined to have his way, sometimes descended to "insubordination and violent revolts against superiors." He must conclude that "such uprisings" were "not unusual in American colleges," and he shook his head over riots that only recently had occurred "in Princeton in New Jersey and in William and Mary in Virginia, where the students broke windows, chairs, furniture, and everything that came to their hands, and were at the point of destroying the very buildings." How could such infractions come about? He shrugged. "Since the people who preside over such places gave small attention to morals and deportment, and concerned themselves only with the injection of a little knowledge into the students," it need not have surprised anyone when the students should "bring themselves to certain excesses of behavior." These, to be sure, were "condemned by honest Americans." On the whole matter, the Father President resolved in conclusion: "The observers of American customs have always deplored the fact that the fathers, especially in the south, yield sadly and foolishly to their children whom they seem unable to contradict and whose capricious wishes they do not restrain."

Meanwhile, his college prospered. At commencement in 1817 the first baccalaureate degrees were conferred—two of them, which were received by brothers, Charles and George Dinnies. A few weeks later the Father President, on an ecclesiastical mission for the Archbishop of Baltimore, sailed for Rome. He had lively plans awaiting his return to the Potomac.

But when he reached Rome, he was informed by the Father General, who had returned from Russian sanctuary, that he was to remain in Rome. The disappointment must have been keen, and later, for a little while, it even seemed possible that he would, after all, resume his presidency at Georgetown. But in the end, reasons of health made a sea voyage precarious for him (he had always suffered excruciatingly at sea) and for his remaining thirty years of life he lived, and worked—for it would always be certain that he would work, as always, with imaginative high spirits—in Italy.

One of his useful concerns was to bring knowledge of his transatlantic country to the Old World. A confrere wrote that Father Grassi was "doing much good in Rome correcting misconceptions about America." Father Grassi, in fact, lost no time in writing and publishing, a year after his departure from the college, a book which, briefly, became famous, and which still engages scholars. He called it *Various Advices on the Present State of the Republic of the United States in North America*. In four years it had three editions. He wrote it "to give Europeans a better idea of America. They had the wrong idea entirely," he said in a letter to the Archbishop of Baltimore.

His other late concerns included duties as Rector of the College of the Propaganda Fide at Rome; confessor to the King and Queen of Sardinia, to whose palace he used to walk instead of riding in the coach sent for him, and rector of the College of Nobles in Turin. He lived a rich life to a full age, and died in December 1849 at seventy-four.

v

As his college prospered and grew, he became known as "the second founder of Georgetown"—Archbishop Carroll being the first. To the Father President, they said, Georgetown owed "its first great impulse and thorough organization." What was more, "probably no other ecclesiastic of the day enjoyed in greater measure the esteem and confidence of the hierarchy" in America. Indeed, old Bishop Flaget of Louisville nominated him for the throne of the new diocese of Detroit. Everyone he dealt with seemed to feel the creative bounty of his nature.

It is good to think why.

He believed in man's power to achieve inspiriting ends under the blessing of good intentions. From the beginning it did not seem implausible to him that two small structures, with ten young "blackguards" for pupils, should contain under God's grace the viable seed of an institution worthy to rank one day with the proper universities of the world. Possum suppers, unruly wretches, and all, he proceeded on the assumption that, given time, the difference between his struggling academy and the universities of Europe would be one only of degree, not of kind.

MAURICE BARING

RECONSIDERED

"Rien de trop!"
—*The favourite maxim of LaFontaine,
according to Maurice Baring*

"Everything about him . . . gave one the impression of
centuries and hidden stores of pent-up civilization."
—*Maurice Baring, describing Altamura
in "The Coat Without Seam"*

i

The Honorable Maurice Baring was born in 1874, a younger
son of the first Lord Revelstoke. The Barings, like the
Rothschilds, were prominent in international finance, and
members of the family made careers in public affairs. He
grew up in a world of great country houses, and town houses
in London; of grand social style under Queen Victoria and
King Edward; of opulence in the externals of life; of casual
and habitual contact with royalty and its fringes; and of
rigid adherence to a code of manners which seemed at times
a conspiracy to maintain the visible structure of the upper
class at the expense of individuals—both those within it and
those without it.

Baring's world was defined for him by a succession of

nannies and governesses, tutors at Eton, Cambridge, and Oxford, highly placed aunts and uncles and cousins, some of them gifted with intellectual as well as social interests. From his Lutheran clergyman ancestor emerged bankers, cabinet officers, and diplomats. Brilliant marriages produced an easy, thoughtless, conventional grace for the Barings, in a world where nobody seemed to work. People went from house to house on visits, and from capital to capital, where everyone knew everyone else, lived on gossip, much of it penetrating and true, and where all kept alive a formal fabric of society behind which every variation of infidelity was arranged, with every effect of joy or sorrow. At all costs convention was preserved, with all its faces of power, wealth, privilege, and high style glistening in the afternoon light of the Victorian and Edwardian heydays.

In one of Baring's novels, a great lady "divided people into those you know and those you didn't know." She derived much of her attitude from the heritage of the eighteenth century, with, as he put it, "its horror of enthusiasm." The same peeress saw the Eton-Harrow match as "one of the most sacred festivals of a well-spent life," and this hint of busy complacency suggests the society in its grand decline.

It was not just the world you'd think of in which to breed an artist of sensibility and justice. But Baring was fortunate in his father, who had charm and imagination, if no professional talents, and he must have given encouragement to his son's first revelations of these qualities. Lord Revelstoke was spoken of as "a good humanist," who knew Latin and was fluent in French, German, and Spanish.

One day he gave Maurice Baring a present that he never forgot, as an artist never forgets something that has powers for his work. Walking down a path in the park of his country house in Devon with his son, Lord Revelstoke said, "This is your path; I give it to you and the gate at the end." Delight in possession was crowned by a leap of the imagination. "It was the inclusion of the little iron gate at the end," wrote Baring, "which made that present poignantly perfect." It was a gate through which he could forever go.

He was an intensely imaginative child—and he remained a responsively imaginative man and writer. Childhood, for such an individual as he, gave him his most memorable idea of happiness, and as he grew away from its occasions, he yet retained, as an artist, the child's acuity of feeling and observation—with the addition, not always happy, of mature meanings necessarily unknown to the child.

In a poem written in middle life he saw boyhood as a long dream of happiness, and leaving it he spoke of "crossing the Stream." We can only think of the Styx, and wonder why he equated the departure from boyhood with a crossing into the realm of the shades. But imaginative children live with burning intensity and if he was never so happy ever after, he brought with him into this work childhood's primal sharpness of feeling and the immediacy of response to experience that gave him his power as an artist in maturity, who reaches us still with the sense of life complete.

There was much light-hearted tradition all about as he grew up. Puns were a family tradition—he remembered the delight of all at the answer of a shooting guest at his father's country house when asked if he had shot any duck. "Not even," replied the guest, "not even a mallard imaginaire." His own wit, which a friend called "fantastic and unaccountable," was nurtured by polite family prankishness with jokes, riddles, allusions, literary games with fashionable verse forms such as the triolet. He carried his wit into action. One time as a small boy he asked an ancient aunt to give him an antique onyx ring with a pig engraved on it.

She said, "You shall have it when you are older."

An hour later he went back to her room and said, "I am older now. Can I have the ring?"

She gave it to him.

His appealing sense of fantasy, then, governed the reality

of time in such a small episode as this; and his vocation was forecast early in the nursery atmospheres and occupations which were his daily pleasure. The family governess was a remarkable Frenchwoman whom the children called Chérie. To her, Maurice Baring owed a lifelong debt in the development of his affinity, and thus his sensibility, for the life of the imagination and many of its great embodiments in works of literature. Chérie—though, as he said, she was not a literary person—had a love of literature which she communicated by reading aloud to her small charges. He reciprocated by composing a story to her, "La Princesse Myosotis et Le Prince Muguet, par O.M.G. (Reine de Beauté), Illustré par M.B. (Son Mari)." The illustrations are done in pencil and watercolor. Any gift for Chérie surely could not be purchased—must be made by hand, and so return her loving achievement to her from one whose imagination she had helped to release. One time she brought Maurice Baring a toy theatre from Paris. It became France to him—he called it quite solemnly the Théâtre Français—and its toy characters made a population for his mind that must ever afterward have held meaning for him as he regarded the real world and traced its patterns in his books—a Harlequin, a Columbine, a king and a queen, many princesses, a coarse ruffian with black eyebrows, a masked hangman, and various peasants, officers, papal halberdiers, and loutish gendarmes with heavy mustaches. Many children have toy theatres and make up plays and stories—but most outgrow them. The destined artist among the generality of child-artists never does. The mystery and delight of creative expression lives on with him as he leaves childhood, and for Maurice Baring the slowly discovered real world always bore something of those early trials of the imagination and helped to animate his mature work and vision.

When, after Eton, where he haunted the library and devoured books as other boys devour sweets and sticky messes, he entered Trinity College, Cambridge, he impressed an older student as "an unremarkable youth, shy and shambling, with prominent blue eyes, and nothing to say for himself. . . . He sat on the edge of his chair, only uttering from time to time an abrupt high dry cackling laugh, between a neigh and a crow." But very shortly, he was discovered to be "a most amusing companion, with a genius for nonsense in word and deed." Sir Edward Marsh wrote this impression years later. He remembered that Baring's humor "was the most ridiculous thing in the world," and supported the remark with an anecdote of how Baring on buying postage stamps in the post office at Florence "sniffed them with an air of suspicion. '*Sono freschi?*,' he asked."

Such a talent for caprice had its first formal literary expression at the end of Baring's first year at Cambridge, when, said Sir Edward Marsh, "he brought out an elegant little daily called the *Cambridge ABC* in four numbers, with a beautiful cover by Aubrey Beardsley. . . . Three quarters of it was written by the editor. The feature was a charming series of *Immortal Stories for Children*, exhibiting the triumph of Evil over Good." He felt his path into writing by way of youthful perversity made innocent by the ridiculous.

He was always as ready to enact his absurdities as to write them. His rooms at Oxford, later, were above a chemist's shop, and he enjoyed it when he would "slip down and pose as an assistant," prescribing plausible remedies for customers, with a professional air. Once, on a moving train he could not fit "a new and expensive overcoat into his suitcase," and solved the difficulty by throwing the coat out the window without interrupting his stream of conversation. He once used a British battleship and its appurtenances, including the sea, as comic props. It was his habit to spend several weeks a year aboard H.M. ships, and throughout the fleet his nickname was "Uncle." After lunching on board with the admiral commanding, Baring, going ashore, deliberately stepped into the sea instead of into the admiral's barge.

It was a sort of prank available only to a member of the privileged classes, who by association and blood had the use of the Royal Navy for farce as well as defense, free to cause bother and inconvenience and perhaps expense for the lightest purposes.

His comic style took him to any limits, and sometimes, we uneasily think, somewhat beyond, to amuse friends. Lady Diana Cooper said that he would set fire to "his sparse hair and it would fizzle a little and go out, and he would light it again with a match till it was all singed off, but his scalp never burnt, and he laughed uproariously as I did. . . . Next day he sent me a telegram every two or three hours." But his gaiety was not always so self-punishing, and his humor often called forth responses in kind. One day, while playing tennis with Sarah Bernhardt—a circumstance remarkable enough in itself—he drove a tennis ball directly to her and it struck her in the bosom. At once she "died" in her best tragic manner—eyes rolled up out of sight, terminal sighs—while she was lowered to the lawn by horrified bystanders. And then silence, long enough to impress, followed by an immediate recovery.

His verbal comedy anticipated something of the style of Ronald Firbank and Saki. Attending the first night of Madame Bernhardt in *L'Aiglon* (17 March 1900), he wrote that "the theatre was paved with beaten celebrities." After a visit to the Château of Coutances, with its aisles, avenues, canals, and ponds, he said the park "was inhabited by exiled peacocks and discredited white pheasants." G. K. Chesterton said "the levities of Maurice Baring were worthy of some fantastic *macaroni* or *incroyable* of the eighteenth century."

If his comedy enlivened his personality and his friends, it was not simply a superficial accomplishment but a true strain of his versatile character. In 1903 he wrote somewhat heatedly to a solemn friend: "I think that the existence of merely frivolous people who are bent on amusement is a necessary element in this grey world, and that Helen of Troy, Mary Stuart, Ninon de L'Enclos, Diane de Poitiers, Petronius Arbiter and Charles II are equally necessary in the scheme of things as St. Paul, Thomas Aquinas, John Knox, Pym and Lady Jane Grey."

ii

Along with his sense of comedy, whether in the frivolous act or the parodistic vein (which presupposes a serious knowledge of the matter in hand) Baring held a considerable store of learning in the lightest possible grasp—except for any branch of mathematics, for, noted the London *Times*, "He had extraordinary incapacity to deal with figures." In the face of the tasks of study he had been a wildly irreverent schoolboy, yet without visible effort he became one of the most deeply cultivated men of his time. Monsignor Ronald Knox, who knew him and all his works, said, "There are . . . certain rare intellects which aspire to a sublime ignorance in vain. They cannot choose but learn." Baring's nature, he went on, "was one which constantly absorbed, as it constantly exuded, something which (for want of a less abused word) you can only label 'culture.'" Baring himself hit off this sort of character in one of his novels, as he described a certain Wilfred Abbey, "who seemed never to have read, nor to read anything at all, as if a well-educated man knew all that was necessary without reading a book. He could always cap a quotation, and never missed an allusion. He seemed to have absorbed his culture from the air. . . ."

Literature and reality were for him the same. Looking out over Rome one day from the Janiculum, he spoke of memories "from Macaulay"—and in the lightness of the reference he caught the sustaining power of literature to create reality, so that an artist's words once read become part of our own truth and of our own qualifying memory. As for Rome, its beauty entered into him "like a poison," he said, and "the delicious poison ran through my veins and the eternal charm sunk deep."

Places held him as people did, and he responded to their spirit with his own particular reflex—which was to produce his response in art. The sitting room of Count Bencken-dorff's house at Sosnofka in Russia was his "favorite room in all the world" and in all his life, he said, and "at its big table I painted innumerable water colours, and wrote four plays in verse, two plays in prose, three long books in prose, besides translating a book of Leonardo da Vinci and writing endless letters and newspaper articles. . . ." The versatility hinted at in this animated statement actually went farther. He loved music, could play at the piano scandalous imper-sonations of great composers, was adept at musical jokes, and was happy with musical people, like Donald Tovey and Ethel Smyth. Of his swift understanding of her music, Dame Ethel Smyth said, "He always knew what one was aiming at," and though he could not read music, his pianistic par-odies were accomplished enough to deceive Tovey.

He grew up during the period when Wagner was a cause and a battle cry, a prophet or a false god, and he described at the time the odd double effect that the Wagnerian sounds still carry. He spoke of a "quality of slowness and hypnotic mesmerism. . . . At its worst it is like the noise people make by rubbing the rim of a glass of water; at its best it is some-thing very mysteriously beautiful." Both ecstasy and op-pression came with it, and "the feeling of being suffocated, like laughing gas."

Personal discovery of the great artists and their work be-came in Baring's books as in his life a dominant power, and few novelists have made more real the private experience of an awakening to the sound, the humanizing force, of liter-ature and music. Beethoven, Heine, Tennyson, Swinburne, Schubert, the Russian poets, novelists, and playwrights, all "happen" to his fictional characters as they did to him in life, as cataclysmic events after which they are never again the same. For him, the arts were not mere pastime or entertainment—they were profoundly effectual encounters in his own growth and discovery.

iii

As a young man in London cramming for examinations for the diplomatic service, he made friends with various literary men of his time, besides his natural company of acquaintances in the interlocked circles of the great families of his class, whose members, wherever he went in the world, seemed to have representatives who governed and set tone and provided the comforts of recognition and the reassurances of familiar style.

"His genius for languages," remarked a close friend, "was greater than a natural gift," for he "could think and create in the mind of the language rather than translate it into words." Perhaps like a character in his novel *The Lonely Lady of Dulwich*, he "spoke most languages and was silent in none." In his opening page of *Have You Anything to Declare?*, he referred to the literatures that had been his lifetime "baggage," and mentioned the Sanskrit, and Hebrew, Greek, Latin, French, Italian, German, Spanish, Scandinavian, Chinese, Arabic, and Persian. Oddly, he did not list English and Russian language and literature, but these may by their very familiarity to him have slipped his mind.

Already mobile in thought, through his mastery of foreign literatures, he was to be for all his active life a great traveler. In the most offhand manner possible, he would set out for Rome, Paris, Malta, Seville, Lisbon, Constantinople, Vienna, Berlin, St. Petersburg, or Mukden with the ease of one who was at home in any land or language. Even in time of war, he gave the air of an experienced itinerant who composed himself in movement. In his diary of the 1914 war he wrote, "A Frenchman sitting next to us in the train whom I knew said, '*Il y a seulement quatorze personnes qui voyagent en temps de guerre et on est sûr de les recontrer. Vous êtes l'une des quatorze.*'"

His gift of generosity and outgoing love of people, friends or strangers, high or low, was a proper attribute for such a traveler. And yet about his ease of response to the incidental moment, place, or person of life, there was in spite of its light civility a deeper value. He put his finger on it in a letter from St. Petersburg, in 1914, when he wrote, "I see how I may be superficially influenceable and influenced, but my inside *kernel* is very independent, very difficult to influence, and it takes a long time to form."

To a lady of the Russian Imperial Court whom he knew in Petersburg, Baring seemed "to be rather a freak." But then she found that he had "wonderful insight," in fact, "almost uncanny," and if he was "sometimes absurd," he was again "and even always very lovable." He had the gift of continuity in human relations, for, she said, "one always met with him again as though one had only parted yesterday."

If we try to call alive the essential energy that his contemporaries found in him, we could do no better, I think, than to quote a friend who was asked whom he considered a man of genius in his generation. It was Herbert Asquith, later to be Prime Minister of Great Britain, who replied, "For genius in the sense of spontaneous, dynamic intelligence, I have no doubt that I would say Maurice Baring."

iv

Let us now look a little more closely at the literary work of this personality, who was so observant of the universally human under the particular and transient style of his time.

He was a votary of a vocation all but vanished—that is, a writer accomplished and expressive in all literary forms, from poetry to drama, journalism to the novel, the critical essay to the learned literary spoof. With so much to cover, we have little opportunity to do justice to all these, and I shall give most of my attention to his pastiches and his novels, in which, I think, his most expressive work is to be found. But a word or two along the rest of the line will be useful in developing a view of his quality.

In 1904 he gave up what began as a career in diplomacy after holding junior posts in Paris (". . . having such fun here now," he wrote from the British Embassy in 1900), Copenhagen, and Rome, and went as a reporter for the *Morning Post* to cover the Russo-Japanese War. His journey to war took him across Russia, and the whole episode was significant for him chiefly because it introduced him to the Russian people, whose language he had been studying for five years. His war reports are full of a clear light and a warm heart—"Bless you," wrote Vernon Lee, "for your courage of being capable of horror and pity and yet no sentimentalist, and for your passionate desire for good understanding between the nations." The life of every day glistens in his dispatches, and his zest for the arresting detail in man and his ways turns up again and again. But nothing in his early career as a journalist exceeded his interest in a discovery he made on the way to the theatre of war: his first dispatch came from Moscow and it introduced the art of Anton Chekhov to the general English world, for he saw a performance of *Uncle Vania* at the art theatre and immediately knew he had come into communion with a new literary vision. His review of the performance is the first chapter in his collected volume of reports and impressions called *With the Russians in Manchuria*. The pieces in general skillfully demonstrate his idea of his task: "The essence of journalism," he said, "is sensation captured on the wing."

In 1914 he came to war again, this time as a volunteer officer attached to the headquarters of the British Royal Flying Corps, in the command of General Trenchard. Baring's calm in the face of unfamiliar military details led straight to comic improvisation, which the royal service bore with fortitude. Going out to France, he found it impossible to cope with the wrap puttees that were regulation for officers and men. Anyone who has ever tried to roll these up from the ankle with spiral precision must sympathize when Baring discarded his and, instead, acquired and wore a pair of long pale gaiters. The regulars of his service frowned upon these, and he thought to improve matters by switching to the black gaiters worn by sailors, but they, too, were all wrong. In the end, it was General Trenchard himself who instructed his new staff officer in how to roll the wrap puttees about his calves.

Baring remained with Trenchard until the end and later spoke of him "in the highest terms" to Arnold Bennett. Lord Trenchard returned the compliment even more extravagantly.

v

The theatre deeply engaged him, both as an observer and as a playwright. He delighted in great stage effects and persons. In particular, Sarah Bernhardt, Eleanora Duse, and Feodor Chaliapin were objects of his fascinated worship. In essays and novels he tried with remarkable success to arrest on the printed page the exalting impact of their evanescent art. He caught the majesty of Chaliapin (who once told him he wanted to act in Shakespeare), and one feels that he admired Duse to the farthest limits of thought—but that he adored Bernhardt with both mind and heart. His monument to her consists of a biography (1933) and many pieces scattered through his essays and novels. She figures as Anais Dorzan in *Darby and Joan,* and she appears as Madame Lapara in *C* and other novels, always with electrifying effect upon the persons within the book—an effect conveyed so convincingly that the reader, too, is brought to feel it.

It was inevitable that he should write plays—ambitious, full-length pieces, meant to be acted. He wrote also many short and witty parodies and pastiches in dramatic form, but these were clearly meant only for the page and the eye. The earliest of his serious plays belong to a genre which, once respectable, now raises qualms, for they were poetic dramas, written in blank verse, full of studied archaisms, operatic situations, lost gallantries, oversignificant incantations, and the rest.

He had somewhat better fortune with drawing-room comedies set in his own period and written in the almost telegraphic dialogue that he used in his fiction. Several of these plays had productions in respectable art theatres, but none succeeded, and what is probably his best play, *His Majesty's Embassy*, has never been produced at all—professionally, anyhow.

Max Beerbohm reviewed Baring's play *The Grey Stocking* on 6 June 1908, and came to the conclusion that this playwright was an "adramatist"—that is, one who deals not with heightened life such as we generally associate with theatre— "heroes, villains, buffoons . . . people who are either doing or suffering either tremendous or funny things," but, rather, was one who dealt "merely in humdrum and you and me." To be an adramatist, Beerbohm said, the playwright must be "very much an athlete" if he is to bring enough energy into his non-happenings. *The Grey Stocking* gave Beerbohm the impression that Baring was "very athletic by nature," but that he had "not trained" quite hard enough. Beerbohm came to the play "on the lookout for things happening; and the fact that nothing happened rather bothered me," he decided. He ended his review with the statement that "Mr. Baring gives us deliciously clever sketches of his characters; but he does not give us the full, deep portraits that are needed."

Another play, *The Green Elephant*, offers an entirely different tone and energy. It is designed after French farce— rapid entrances and exits, wildly involved plot, confusions, lies, intrigues of love and crime concerning jewels stolen at a weekend party in a country house—all laid on with a bare-faced air of plausibility which is naïvely theatrical. The play's action has rather the air of children acting—"being" and "declaring"—things patently unbelievable, and believed only through a conspiracy of politeness. If his earlier play was formless, this one is overplotted and too rigidly formalized.

In *A Double Game*, it is atmosphere that seems to consume the author's available vitality at the expense of other values. It is a play of the revolutionary movement of 1907 in Russia. While it has some dramatic tension, and certainly suggests Baring's love of the Russians and knowledge of their style, the "Russianism" of it seems synthetic, and the end is a finale in the manner of Chekhov, with a pistol shot and suicide offstage. Again, the individual characters merely seem to have lines to speak, without the inner resonance of life that would make them into genuine creations. Baring's feeling for the place and time of the play are better—indeed wonderfully—brought to page in *The Puppet Show of Memory* where he describes the vast funeral procession in Moscow of the veterinary surgeon Baumann, who was a victim of shooting in the streets during political demonstrations. A hundred thousand men marched with the coffin, which was covered by a scarlet pall, and hushedly sang revolutionary songs, expressing "the commonplaceness of all that is determined and unflinching, mingled with an accent of weary pathos." He never forgot the impression of the moment, but in his play he caught little of its spirit.

In *His Majesty's Embassy*, Baring used materials he knew well, combining the schoolboy antics of junior diplomatic clerks with a hopeless love affair at ambassadorial level. The play conjures up, out of insistent trivia of the daily diplomatic round, but with the tyrannical and reckless power of all secrets, the central love story, an affair between the British ambassador to Rome and the wife of a passionate nonentity in the Italian Diplomatic Corps. The story is made of heartbreak and helplessness, and convention protects itself, and the train guard blows his whistle, and on goes the current, sweeping into separate channels the lives that long to come together, however disastrous the brink of the falls waiting ahead. Of this play the London *Times* said that it was a "fragment of English life as alive as it is unique;" and we have a hint that in any but a commercially controlled theatre Baring might eventually have achieved recognition as a playwright, for Shaw wrote to Dame Ethel Smyth that "it was really a calamity that the theatre was incapable of him." If this was an extravagant statement, it is of interest for the flat placement it makes of where the incapability lay. To Baring himself Shaw wrote, "I do not see why the dickens you should not go regularly into the trade of play-writing," and after reading *His Majesty's Embassy*, Shaw told him that the play was "quite a miraculous success," and ended up saying that "if it were attractively cast, anything might happen." It is difficult not to be impressed by such a judgment from the supreme, and supremely skeptical, professional of the twentieth-century English-speaking theatre. Henri Bernstein (the French playwright who dominated the popular dramatic stage of Paris after Sardou), whatever his claim to literary sagacity, had a right to an opinion about box-office values, and he said to Baring after a production of Baring's second play, "What will you do with all the money you'll make?" The play closed at once. But if he failed in the theatres of the West End of London, Baring left evidence in his published plays of how delicately he could lay back the layers of convention to reveal the passions that society both generated and concealed.

Perhaps it was Vernon Lee who gave the most plausible clue about why Baring's writings for the stage never made their way. "You have, dear Maurice," she wrote, "a quite peculiar, great and enchanting gift . . . how to define . . . ? It is a gift of the love-duet; of giving in metaphors, and lyric flights and pathetic snatches, the equivalent of the deepest unspoken feeling. . . ." And here it is: the theatre cannot very effectively deal with "unspoken feeling." Its very effect depends on feelings, and all the suggestions they contain, quite openly spoken.

It was to be the novel in which Baring's particular nuance could linger between the lines, where the real values always linger in significant fiction, which would release his whole talent and give it the long breath, the unconstricted range, which it required for full expression.

vi

He wrote poetry from his boyhood onward. At Eton in 1891 he had printed for himself a small volume called *Pastels and Other Rhymes*, containing verses seriously intended, which inevitably, in the tone of a responsive schoolboy, echoed the current styles of Wilde, Morris, and the Pre-Raphaelite vission. A booklet of prose, *Damozel Blanche and Other Fairy Tales*, printed for him in the same year, was also consciously literary, as its title suggests.

His poetry had only a few themes—the same ones that informed his novels. These were nostalgia, death, love recognized but unrealizable, honor, God's mysterious way, and power. Over much of the verse lingers an air of weekendish polite accomplishment, conventional and pallidly felicitous. But the best of it holds real emotion, contained in formal rhymes, stanzas, and meters, yet with an effect of inner freedom that is particularly his own—possibly the metaphor for his life as well as for his art.

His best poetry is to be found in a handful of sonnets; in several long elegies for friends lost in war (written in a flowingly effective form of ode with irregular lines and deliberately simple rhymes that summon up feeling through the effects of ordinary literate speech); and in a small group of translations of Russian lyrics that survive as English poetry while scholars praise them as successful equivalents of Russian originals. Poetry was not Baring's major achievement—and yet his love of the act of poetry, his ingenuousness which was so intuitive as to lie far beyond sophistication, and his vulnerability to true feeling, all entitle him to inclusion among the lesser spirits who have so loved the English language and voice that their proper element can be said to be that of poetry, however small their contributions to the great stream of English verse may be. Valuable as he is as a poet in his best poems, it is in his best novels that his poetic gift most truly rests plain; for what his poems celebrate under strict metrical governance finds its best presence as it hovers insubstantially behind the lines of his prose. He was one of those artists in literature whose quality comes into view not at once but only after a long time and many pages in its presence. The brief lyric and even the funerary panegyric of several pages do not allow this emergence its full opportunity.

To be versatile was his necessity, summoned forth to permit illustration of his many responses to the external terms of life, each demanding its characteristic style or medium. So the literary act required him to compose essays and criticism, impressions and prose sketches, which he gathered in various volumes. His most notable work in literary study is his small book *An Outline of Russian Literature*, written for the Home University Library series. Along with the thin volume by Lytton Strachey on French literature, done for the same series, Baring's book on the Russians is a model of its kind.

His own prose was never better than in this brief survey, and his most personal responses set off by his excellent knowledge of the literature he discusses, whose masterpieces he read in the original language, come through at their most intuitive and penetrating. He had a strong affinity for the Russian vision of the literary art, and time and again as he discusses Pushkin or Lermontov or Tolstoy he makes you think of aspects of his own imaginative works. We are assured that he knew the Russian language perfectly, with an instinctive power far beyond all the grammatical apparatus.

By 1899, on the evidence of his Russian exercise notebook (now in the Beinecke Rare Book and Manuscript Library at Yale), he was already studying Russian. Sir Edward Marsh later said that "Russians used to appeal to him on points of their own grammar." He lived like a native of many literatures, and out of his love of these, and touched by the compunction for life from which he so often diverted notice by his cheerful idiocies of behavior and his literary pranks, he moved in the final phase of his work toward the creation of his own unmistakable style.

vii

The last categories of his abundant production—he published almost fifty books—whose air and substance I shall try to suggest are two: the first, his literary jokes; the second, his major novels.

When I say literary jokes I do not mean to suggest offhand japes or mockeries. On the contrary, Baring's literary jokes are to be taken with respect for all the ingenuity, the extended and expert knowledge, and the special sense of fun, out of which they are made. Informally, in correspondence and in sustained exchanges with companion spirits, he always enjoyed literary games. One of these was a contest to remember the first lines of Shakespeare's plays. He played it with one of his dearest friends, Lady Diana Cooper. Both of them, noted Arnold Bennett, were "very good at this." Literature could have its meaning for him as a playful as well as a serious genre, and he kept alive into maturity the schoolboy's genius for historical travesty, sublimely wrong-headed construction, and inventive misunderstanding. Much British humor is built upon these foundations; and Baring refined the use of them in a delicious set of nonsense inventions published first in three separate volumes as *Diminutive Dramas, Dead Letters,* and *Lost Diaries,* which he later collected in one volume under the title *Unreliable History.*

Typically in these pieces—they run to perhaps six or eight pages each—he took a famous historical or literary situation or set of characters and treated them in the accents of the modern social condition. The colloquial is imposed on the classical, the suburban upon the historically august, the irreverent upon the sacrosanct; and the results, informed with all the range and penetration of Baring's knowledge, are hilarious to the degree in which the reader shares Baring's culture and all its allusions. To amuse friends who would receive the joke, he wrote satires in French on eminent English social figures after the styles of Flaubert, Bourget, Maupassant. His lifelong delight in sportive play with great subjects of history and letters, playing with translations, committing impersonations of all styles and periods and characters, is not really just parody or pastiche, but something beyond these, for they all draw upon wide learning. His jokes are often profound jokes, and, further, they reflect the general notion of life that runs through his work in whatever literary form. He gave himself in his humor as fully as he did in his more serious efforts.

Monsignor Knox said Maurice Baring's jokes rested on genuine learning. Even as we revere these credentials, we must remember that Baring himself said, "The word research is not even remotely applicable here, for in my case it means the hazy memories of a distant education indolently received."

His pleasure in trifling with literature, as differentiated from making it, was illustrated by the play of variations throughout his life in collecting excerpts, *pensées*, felicitous scraps of writing brought together in a small harvest of intellectual pleasures referring to literary styles. The particular Baring aspect of the earliest of such little collections is that all its small literary pieces were written by him in the manner of other authors, classical or modern, and presented with no clue to their actual origin. If they were imitations, they were also serious, and were meant to call up resonances of recognition in an experienced reader, yet without re-warding him with identifications. In 1916 a small book appeared under the title *Translations (Found in a Common-place Book)*, "Edited by S. C., and published at Oxford by B. H. Blackwell." Translations? But no sources are given, and in a prefatory "Note" we read, "The editor of these translations has not been able to trace the originals even in the rare cases where the author states the language from which the translations are made." So the private joke sol-emnly extends to the posture of scholarship. In 1925 Heine-mann published the same text, but now with significant ad-ditions—not only with nine more pieces, bringing the total to thirty-eight, but also, at last, with presumed original texts from which the "translations" were made. Each English piece was faced by its suppositious source in another lan-guage. And here the joke went into a further dimension, for in the small book, now called *Translations Ancient and Modern, (With Originals)*, his "fictitious translations of imaginary originals," as he said, "from ancient or modern language on any subjects," were supplied with their imag-inary sources by various distinguished literary friends, in-cluding Monsignor Ronald Knox for the Latin and Greek, André Maurois for the French, Prince D. S. Mirsky for the Russian, Mario Praz for the Italian, and others for the Swedish and the Spanish.

This sipping of many literary flavors and vintages was a continuing delight to him, and it had further printed dem-onstration. In 1928 he published through Heinemann a small volume called *Algae: An Anthology of Phrases*, and in 1930, privately printed for him by the Cambridge Univer-sity Press, another gathering of "Algae" with the designa-tion "Second Series." The little excerpts come from liter-atures in English, Greek, Italian, French, German, Spanish, Latin, and Russian and are printed in the original lan-guages, without either translation or commentary, and all are real, as against the earlier impersonations. His fabrications and his selections from actual writings eventually led to a late work, the anthology *Have You Anything to Declare?*, but with the addition of his own commentary and, in the case of certain actual translations, with alternate versions. In most of these "commonplace" books he gave a full page to each text, however small, so that it stood an island of printed letters in a sea of white space. If the process was extravagant, it was not wasteful, if the purpose of the selection was to be fulfilled—the chance to reflect without distraction on each small passage until its particular resonance could sound in the inner ear for us, as it did for him.

Such undertakings bring Maurice Baring's highly sophisticated fancy close to us. Precious, learned, delicate, painstaking for the sake of keeping the fraud plausible, where fraud was intended, they were characteristic of his literary atmosphere and the friends who inhabited it with him. If this sort of thing had been all, there would have been no career to reconsider—only attractive and appreciative wisps of reference to him in other people's memoirs, in which he would be seen as a witty and expert amateur at the art of carving cameos. But along with the exercise of the informed amusements of his early life he was also becoming a professional journalist who dealt with the coarse world of war; and when he was ready to become a novelist, he was master of a greater reach than his early diversions suggested. In time he became far more concerned with grasping life itself in his writing than with pursuing scholarly and private references to its echoes. Of course, his erudite gaiety persisted, and when he published his various sketches in "unreliable history," he was confronting us with a straight face, while hoping to make us laugh.

There is no point in being pedantic about all this aspect of Baring's multifarious talent, but it is of interest to note that his inspired triflings with solemn matters for the most part had the added interest of good scholarship. This scholarship was not an affectation—was not boned up for the occasion. It was simply his by nature, and when he wanted to be funny about heavy affairs, he had what he needed in his head. For what it may be worth as incidental satisfaction, let me quote what Ronald Knox wrote about Baring's classical learning as it bore upon his managed nonsense.

"More than half of the 'Diminutive Dramas,' more than a third of the 'Dead Letters,' and a quarter of the 'Lost Diaries,' have a classical setting. Nor do I think he was ever better inspired than when he thus played on the eternal themes in Greek or Latin dress. . . . The utter simplicity of the décor suited his genius. And I never remember discovering," concluded the Monsignor, "a single lapse of scholarship in the whole of the three volumes. . . ."

We pause respectfully at this. But we have another word that lets us recover, for it makes just the right point, when Vernon Lee says of Baring's comic writing, "What a wonderful and particular thing this kind of English funniness is. . . ."

viii

Turning now to Maurice Baring's novels, let us try to get at their general tone. He wanted them to sound like real life, and yet as an artist he must deal in arrangement and invention. But he took out a sort of double insurance as a novelist when he had someone say in one of his books, "Such extraordinary things do happen. Nothing is too extraordinary to happen." And again, when he said. "Then one of those curious small coincidences happened which are so frequent in real life, of which writers of fiction fight shy, although they are not afraid of the grand ones. . . ." And again, "Things happen that no writer would dare to invent." And finally, "The French put things so well—so clearly. They are not afraid of platitudes." Thus, anything, from the most amazing to the most familiar, is prepared for; and what gives it interest first of all is the simplicity, like the vision of a child, through which his stories take their course. The child's sense

[*128*

of first clear view was, of course, governed by the adult experience of consequences and values, but the uncomplicated vision which struck lightly and directly to the heart of whatever matter was consistently Baring's way.

Historical tradition, the living breath of the great past, plays a part in his novels, sometimes through minor characters and allusions by the way; but they help to create a fabric of social and historical continuity that offers support in plausibility and richness of conviction. It substantiates the amplitude of the world in which one of Baring's leading characters lives when he meets in France two old maiden ladies who "seemed to be the living ghosts of prerevolutionary Versailles," for "the mother of one of them had been born seventeen years before the revolution . . . and she herself remembered Napoleon at *Trianon* and the *Cent Jours* and the Battle of Waterloo with perfect distinctness. . . . The mother of the eldest [*sic*] remembered seeing the Dauphin playing in the gardens of Versailles." Another of Baring's novels opens with the words, "Henry Clifford was born in the year that Byron died." The past is not lost, but lives in its transmitted reference and effect, and the people in Baring's novels bring it with them.

They bring, too, the world of cultivated taste. He is one of few novelists who can have his characters discuss ideas, art, literature, and music as vital matters, and keep these within the frame of the life of the book, and make them seem natural interests without which the book would lose dimension. To use himself completely as an artist he must use his culture. "I think he was," wrote Monsignor Knox, "in the literary sense of the word, a humanist. He went largely, no doubt, to the romantics for his inspiration. But there was a restraint about everything he wrote which is utterly classical. I do not say he owed it to the reading of the classics; it may have been due to something in his own nature; but it made the classics congenial to him . . . with a sure instinct, he breathed the airs of them."

So the romantic in him was drawn to dramatic patterns of emotional energy, and the classic in him strove to suppress or enclose these within the boundaries of pure simplicity. We might say of him what he said of Henry James, that he made a "divination of what is going on under the mask of convention, prosperity, fashion and extravagance." One of Baring's ruling interests and achievements was to illustrate the complex within the simple. In his essay on Eugene Onegin in *An Outline of Russian Literature*, Baring gave us another quotation to turn upon himself. ". . . The scenes are as clear as the shapes in a crystal; nothing is blurred; there are no hesitating notes; nothing *à peu près*; every stroke come off; the nail is hit on the head every time, only so easily that you don't notice the strokes, and all labour escapes notice. The poem arrests attention as a story, and it delights the intelligence with its wit, its digressions, its brilliance. . . . And when the occasion demands it, the style passes in easy transition to serious or tender tones." If Baring did not reach Pushkin's degree of achievement, he clearly held as an ideal in kind the quality of the Russian poet. What's more, the very plot of Baring's novel *C*, which, along with *Cat's Cradle* and *The Coat Without Seam*, is one of his three most considerable novels, could have been strongly influenced by *Eugene Onegin*.

Of all twentieth-century novelists in English, he is the most successful at giving us a sense of the power of society, of the worldly world—and that is a real world, no matter what various fashions may do to the novel as they come and go. Sometimes it seems to us that he wrote only one novel, and that all his separate ones are like great chapters in which we continuously meet the same people from one novel to the next.

Meeting these people so often we can imagine them writing letters to each other, so real do they seem. With few external strokes of portraiture or characterization, Baring brings them into our awareness by two means. The first is his habit of telling us all about them in an accent of gossip, and the second is to let them talk to each other extensively once they are placed in their scenes.

If we sometimes wonder where all the pages and pages of flat-voiced trivia and gossip and social detail are taking us, we soon realize that we are witnessing the build-up of distinct lives in their world. The air of gossip in the general establishment constitutes the *donnée*. Once past it, the action can take over, and the general tone then arises from our feeling about what happens. We soon see how important are the fragments of information when we understand that they are needed in order to make the big changes and events, when they come in the novels, as powerful and meaningful as they would be in real life, which also mostly has its days and years of trifles. When Baring seems to be chattering rapidly and carelessly, he is really making lives entire, including the trivial as well as the large.

His novels are generally built around the chronicle of a complete life. His typical ones carry the central character from infancy to death, and in doing so traverse both outer and inner worlds. *C*, a novel of some three hundred thousand words, takes Caryl Bramsley (the title is the initial of his first name, the nickname by which he was always known) through his discoveries in the act of maturing, enlightenment through literature, music, and art, and love, sorrow, passion, and futility, faith and death. All through this novel, as in many of his others, is woven the pathos of the absolutely certain young people who are at the mercy of the absolutely forgetful experienced elders. The strongest themes are those of love and of that inner need for a purpose or at least a grasp in life that answers more than simple material requirements. It is the total architecture of a life that interests him rather than its high-keyed details or moments. He is a novelist with a long view and an enclosing faith. *Cat's Cradle*, his other extremely long novel, is a detailed chronicle of the whole life of an Englishwoman who marries without love to please her father, betrays her husband in intention but remains with him through duty when he falls ill or pretends to, and finally, widowed, claims her love by stealing him from another, younger, woman, and pays bitterly for such an act of theft when she comes to see herself as she really is. *The Coat Without Seam* is a lifelong narrative of a young man who, born to the upper classes, though in poverty, is obsessed with the idea that he is patronized and despised by others of his world, and who through his resentment loses chance upon chance for proper advancement and even fulfillment of love, and who dies in war knowing that his worldly existence is of little importance next to the immortal life of his soul.

The lesser novels play variations on such themes, and several of them suggest in their very titles—*Passing By, Overlooked, The Lonely Lady of Dulwich, Comfortless Memory*—the ingrained melancholy, a sense of detached loss, a hurt regard of life without the sense of consolation through its commonizing touch, that linger between the lines of all of Baring's fiction. He seemed often to be the victim of a pang of intuition which must always have implications beyond the moment. One day he watched the brilliant young officer son of Count Benckendorff set out for Manchuria and the war. Baring said, "He looked so radiantly young and adventurous, when he started, that we were all of us afraid that he would never come back." The artist, here, feels so keenly that he not only feels the first meaning of what he observes, but also its second, and quite opposite, one—life makes him think of death, happiness of grief, goodness of evil.

If all his novels are love stories, they are all unhappy ones. All his lovers are star-crossed, and this arises, we feel, less out of a storyteller's dramatic necessity than out of an unshakable view of life. Love is the worst thing that can happen, and at the same time it is the only thing worth wanting.

Its pursuit begins in tremulous, bated breathings of hope and intention:

" 'Goodbye,' said C. 'May I come again?'

" 'Yes,' said Beatrice, 'please come again.'

"And that little minute seemed again to take them farther, to open the door a little wider, and like all partings, even the happiest, it had a slight shiver lent by the shadow of death, but it seemed so slight that it was almost like a blessing. . . ." It is a tiny fragment, hardly a scene, and yet within it we seem to embrace the full cycle of creature life, which must start in hope and desire, and can only end in death and dissolution, and all is the more poignant because we know much about life that the young lovers do not yet know. He understands love like a Tolstoy.

ix

To consider the matter of Maurice Baring's style, let us listen to what he said about it: "In the art of writing, and in fact all the arts, the best style is that where there is no style, or rather [where] we no longer notice the style, so appropriate and inevitable, so easy the thing said, sung, or done is made to appear. . . ."

It is one of the two official attitudes about the act of art, the other attitude being that which loves for their own sake the gestures of virtuosity. As an argument it can never be solved, since great artists have worked under both attitudes. Who would sacrifice the rich texture of Shakespeare? And who would change the unadorned line of Racine? Style is, simply, the sympathetic resonance of a given temperament to intellectual or emotional stimulus.

It was Maurice Baring's whole temperament that led him to adopt the tone of a cultivated and sympathetically intelligent man talking gossip rapidly, in a level voice, with never a hesitation to choose between ways to say things, but simply running on to capture a sense of life because life—

any life—is so important to catch before it is gone. Behind the offhand manner, of course, lies a fine sense of the organization of material, of design, but this must be concealed.

Vernon Lee wrote to him to thank him for his "bony, dry style," which she called "a blessing after so much lusciousness—(sleepy pears with wasps hidden in them)." When his fiction was translated into French, it was remarked that "his clear, unaccented style" seemed "in some ways to read as well, if not better, than in the original," and Princesse Marthe Bibesco noted that the French writers whom he most admired were Racine, La Fontaine, and Stendhal. "That dry little style," said Vernon Lee of C, "which looks as if it weren't one at all, is quite right. . . ." And she said again that he had "somehow, and perhaps by this very thinness of texture, contrived to give an extraordinary sense of passion, rather like what music gives. . . ."

Finally, in respect to the tone, the effect, of Maurice Baring's writing, we must apply to him one of his literary judgments made upon someone else. In *An Outline of Russian Literature*, speaking of Krylov, he said that Krylov had "the talisman which defies criticism, baffles analysis, and defeats time: namely, charm."

x

One strand of the threads that made up his biography had recurrent power as an element in his novels. Ethel Smyth said to him one day in 1900, when they were out bicycling, that he would eventually become a Catholic. A long time afterward, he recalled that at that moment, though he would ask nothing better, "nothing was more impossible."

But one of those tiny seeds had been planted without ulterior purpose which in time could grow to an overarching design, and after many years, and much soul-searching, as evidenced by the exposition of conversion in his novels, Baring was received into the Church and came into possession of the ultimate reality for which he had long been looking. It is Baring's triumph that, in a literary world generally oriented to skepticism, he is able to make religion a matter of reality and importance in his writing. It is for his characters and in the fabric of his world a reality in respect to social condition, a reality in culture, and a reality in what is most significant of all, private conviction. His manners as a Catholic apologist are better than those of other English literary men of his persuasion. He is never bantering or patronizing, like Chesterton, or rude, impatient, and contemptuous like Evelyn Waugh, or glumly rebellious, like Graham Greene. He is always delicately respectful of explanations of life that differ from his own; and in fact he is scrupulous to echo the skeptical world's case against the Catholic church.

Baring's own gradual religious experience led François Mauriac to say, "What I most admire about Baring's work is the sense he gives you of the penetration of grace." Of his own conversion to the Catholic church, Maurice Baring said—and it was all he ever said about it—it was "the only action of my life I am quite sure I have never regretted." If the statement has the air of a defense, it was perhaps called forth by the sort of remark Vernon Lee, in the fierce candor of her emancipation, made to him. She was bored, she said, by "the everlasting theology" which got into his books. Had he made a vow, she wondered, and she thought so, a vow to provide "so much theology for every glass of vodka!"

xi

There remained with him something of the serene amateur, which seems characteristic of much in the British genius. You think of Byron, and the Sitwells, and even, supremely, of Shakespeare, as against the less original, more formal, more surely professional men of letters on the continent, and in other, more coherent, careers in English. Sometimes he was little more than clever, as when someone in society or in a club is admired for saying a number of "good things."

If he was at times careless, he was careless about mechanical detail and trivial repetition. Professionalism interested him less than life. His range was limited but what he saw he saw and felt deeply, and if he was not an original thinker, it was fortunate that he need not be such in order to write enduring novels, since distilled feeling is of more importance to the artist than intellectual acuity.

The history of Maurice Baring's literary position is interesting, even if typical in many ways of the traditional treatment of important writers in the period immediately following their death. Having achieved a uniform collected edition put out during the thirties by Heinemann, he could not today see a volume of it remaining in print. Ten of his books were translated into French, and one—*Daphne Adeane*—went through twenty-three printings in the edition of the Librairie Stock. Others were translated into Italian, Dutch, Swedish, Hungarian, Czech, Spanish, and German, and several titles were included in the Tauchnitz editions. Serious studies of his work were made in England, France, Germany, and the Argentine. After reading *C*, André Maurois wrote that since reading Tolstoy, Proust, and certain novels by E. M. Forster, he had not known such pleasure from a book. In 1949 he was given a stylish accolade by Max Beerbohm, who, calling him "the brilliant, the greatly gifted Maurice Baring," published a deliciously pointed parody of his fictional manner in a new edition of *A Christmas Garland* (1949).* The memoirs of the time give us frequent references to him and his work, with delighted fondness for the one and critical respect for the other. And yet few of his books are in print, though new editions of *C* and *The Puppet Show of Memory* have appeared (1986, 1987), and the Home University Library edition of *An Outline of Russian Literature* and a related treatise called *Landmarks of Russian Literature* have never disappeared.

*He had already appeared in various Beerbohm drawings of public figures.

But there is a small and active underground, so to speak, devoted to his work. Wherever in the world you find civilized company, you are certain to find people who collect his books, read them over many times, receive rewarding impressions of continuing life from his vision of humanity, and hand his pages on to others who have not yet discovered them. There are signs that a new generation has taken to reading and discussing him. A large collection of his letters is now being gathered and edited, to be followed by a full biography. A general restoration of Maurice Baring as a contributor to the continuing stream of literature in English seems not far off.

xii

So long as he was able, he lived in his small house at Rottingdean, by the sea, facing across to France, surrounded by books and mementos. The house—like his small earlier place in Chelsea—was, as Lady Diana Cooper saw, "arranged in the taste of his young days, with the same William Morris wallpaper of spraying olive-branches, with water colours of Italy and Switzerland and a grand piano." He loved to play and sing pieces from the operas of Gilbert and Sullivan, though without notes. He kept in view "faded photographs of Sarah Bernhardt, famous beauties, Russians, Danes, literary Frenchmen and women." In his house he had a private chapel, where Mass was frequently said. Friends were constantly by him. Lady Diana came every week to see him—especially when, during the 1930s, he began to suffer progressively from a malaise which had occasioned many visits to doctors. Even before the 1914 war, when they went out together and he was performing his fooleries to amuse her, Lady Diana noticed that he did so with trembling hands—"they always trembled," she said. It must have been an ominous signal. For another decade it did not seem to signify anything serious, but in the 1920s, as he supped or laughed less or resisted the lighted candles "at any grand

London ball," she noted that as "we ate our quail and drank our champagne together," his hands were still "trembling," while "he wrote verses on the back of menu-cards." They were verses to her—her beauty, grace, wit, and beguiling presence.

In the mid-thirties he was "trembling more than he used to. He did not speak of anxiety." But one day as she was trying to help him into his overcoat, he said to her, "I'm becoming paralysed. I'm sure I am." She felt it to be true, she said later, and could not bring herself to exclaim, "Nonsense!" He—everyone—knew the truth soon enough. He was suffering from Parkinson's disease—*paralysis agitans*. At Rottingdean with the help of a faithful nurse he spent his time in simple awareness of each day. If he could no longer handle a pen, he could still dictate typed notes, and if he could not easily move about, he had other ways of knowing and continuing with life. "Crocuses are out here in the garden, so I'm told, and snowdrops, and the birds sing quite beautifully in the early morning." He could hear them, since he slept hardly at all during the nights. "Don't think I claim to have learnt anything at Eton," he told someone through a dictated note. "I don't, except the art of enjoying life, which is something."

He enjoyed it most, perhaps, when Lady Diana was able to come to him at Rottingdean. She might find him sitting in the garden, or, later, bedridden. "He did not yearn for death," she saw, "though every day was racking and his nights were without rest. His valiance was never daunted." One of his daily amusements was to listen to his blue parakeet, whose name was Dempsey, as it sat on his head and chattered privately into his ear. Maurice Baring listened fixedly, and repeated to Lady Diana the "perfect sense" which, he said, the unintelligible bird spoke. He translated for her from bird-talk "whole lines in the Chinese tradition: 'The pear-blossom floats on the sad waters where alone I sit....'" It was an hilariously solemn extension of his earlier joy in parody, even, as she saw, how he "was enduring with saintly fortitude a slow and merciless overthrow."

During the month of July in what came to be called the "invasion summer" of 1940, she saw him at Rottingdean and he was "half the size he used to be." Dempsey was still talking to him. Two weeks later she found him "in high spirits today, owing, he said, to being in acute pain. . . . The visit passed in a flash. We both felt so gay, sipping sherry, and nibbling chocolates, and arguing about the Pope." The bombing raids from Nazi Germany were now incessant. The home artillery on the high chalk cliffs near his house spoke night and day. In mid-August Lady Diana thought, in an exquisite and loving phrase, that "he had best take his last patience" far removed from the explosions of war, and go to Scotland, to his kinswoman, Laura, Lady Lovat, who was waiting to keep him at Beaufort Castle.

There went Lady Diana to see him, for the last time, in the winter of 1942–43. It moved her dearly to see him in such "patience"—a person "so near to one's heart and still alive and alert." She said he was "playful all his life and to the end—playful as snow, weightless as it dances down. . . . Newman said there were angels in disguise; some get canonised, some, like Maurice, don't." She saw that "he was in the centre of the Faith he proclaimed." So she left him, with what feeling we know through her words.

At Beaufort Castle, at Beauly, in Inverness-shire, he was cared for by the family of his cousin. It was well that he had moved, for his house at Rottingdean was later demolished by Nazi bombing. Bedridden, he must surely have been killed in the attack.

Lady Lovat has left a memoir of that time. It is a further record of grace under difficulty. "From all angles," she wrote, "life beat down on him and through him; he lived with a fierce intensity and a perfect resignation at one and the same time. . . . His thought at times seemed to travel as swiftly as light, nor could it always be expressed in speech. . . .

Others have known Maurice's enormous erudition," observed Lady Lovat, "of the wit and brilliance of his conversation, but perhaps I knew him best in the last five and a half years of his life as a lover of small children, of unimportant and neglected people, of minor episodes in the pot-pourri of wartime life, of fantastic nonsense and laughter and gaiety, so far flung despite so much suffering that at times one followed him with difficulty. I also knew his stark understanding of sorrows great or small. . . ." Another wrote of him as the "incomparable friend" who had "the grace of innocence," and another said, "In such fortitude as his there surely is something given that pays the ransom of the world. . . ."

One time during his last vigil days, his cousin said to him, "You are tired."

He replied, "I am never tired. Sit near me. It is so strange. I cannot say a prayer these days—not a single prayer."

"So unnecessary," replied Lady Lovat, "—so many are saying your name to God—night and day."

"Tell them to *shout* it," he exclaimed in the high comic style that did not desert him even in the hour.

In December 1945 he developed pneumonia. There were to be only a few more days. In his discomfort he took joy from listening to recordings of Beethoven's Symphony in A, and the Schubert Piano Quintet in A Major (*Die Forelle*), and various poems of Heine, read out to him by his cousin. Though as always he remained reticent about great things, those near him were moved by the sense of unearthly peace within him.

A friend said to him, "It is a miracle to us all that your inner peace is never disturbed."

Having within him his knowledge of God's peace as "a matter of tremendous fact," he answered, "How could it be?"

He died an hour before midnight on 14 December 1945. The *Magnificat* was said over him immediately by a friend, an Air Force chaplain from a nearby RAF base. His last book of favorite fragments was the anthology of literature extracts, with commentary, entitled *Have You Anything to Declare?*

The last lines of that late book convey something of his sense of the life beyond his own mortal nature, and the expectation of his own humble and anonymous immortality. These are the lines:

"Et à l'heure de ma mort soyez le refuge de mon âme étonée et recevez-la dans le sein de votre miséricorde. . . ."

(And in the hour of my death be the refuge of my shaken soul and receive it in the bosom of your mercy. . . .)

HENRIETTE WYETH:

SCENES FROM

A PAINTER'S LIFE

i

Born in 1907, Henriette Wyeth was the first of the five children of the painter Newell Convers Wyeth and his wife, Carolyn. The family was a wellspring of talent. Three of the young became painters—Henriette, Carolyn, and Andrew. Another, Ann, a composer, later turned to painting. Another, Nathaniel, matured as an innovative technological engineer. As all five grew into independence they married painters or writers, and many of their children in turn were artists. Convers Wyeth, the father and grandfather, needing for himself a profusion of aesthetic and intellectual experience, bestowed upon his children an enfolding world of the arts, with its compelling disciplines that would nourish the teeming family apprentices with the sustenance they needed most.

In Chadds Ford, Pennsylvania, the family's large brick house stood on a gentle hill among trees. Wyeth's barn-size studio rose separate and higher up, with a grand view of the Brandywine Valley through its great window. Here he worked all daylight hours, mainly on illustrations to classic writings for children, with which he richly educated the imaginations of several generations through his robust, dramatic, and emotionally free pictures full of beauty and power on their own account as pure painting—an evaluation only recently coming into favor with critics and collectors. Here, too, he executed his mural paintings in heroic scale, and in his rare hours of retreat from commissions he produced those easel paintings, all too few, which delved deeply into his private, often nostalgic, sometimes dream-born visions. In this studio his painter-children had their first, if not their only, school.

The room was huge, two stories high, redolent of paints, linseed oil, turpentine, and books by the thousands along the walls. Weapons of various periods, and objects suitable for still-life groupings, and a great desk littered with correspondence, and double-decked racks for storage of paintings behind a half-drawn curtain; a few worn easy chairs, a sizable terrestrial globe, a battered model stand; and a high easel, always with a large canvas on it concealed by a worn cloth— all bespoke the climate of work that Henriette Wyeth knew from her earliest years.

Wyeth was a man of great amplitude of nature that his physical self seemed hardly able to contain. The energetic extension of this was of germinal power in the fostering of his children's talents from their earliest age of reason. He was tall, heavy, with a heroic head, thrusting shoulders, much emphasis of gesture, rushing eloquence of speech in a tumult of ideas. The lightness and certainty of his movement and the vivid quickness of his mind seemed to belie his physical weight and shape. In repose his face was somber, deeply marked by runnels of intense concentration and contemplativeness, his eyes dark and all-engrossed in perception beyond seeing. His features were rather heavy, but when he gave forth his mind his face was lighted from within and his eyes danced with spirit. He was not conventionally good-looking but his homely animation was winning. Puritanical by heritage, he honored this both in his severe discipline in work and his interest in every aspect of available knowledge—traits which in time came evident in his young. And so did his wildly funny, Chaucerian delight in the bawdy as a proper ingredient in the lustiness with which he met and shared life. Fundamentally, his view of life was tragic, and his gods of art and intellect were those of heroic measure—Breughel, Michelangelo, Beethoven, Shakespeare, Goethe, Tolstoy, Dostoevsky, Whitman, Hardy (*The Dynasts*), Stravinsky (*Le Sacre du Printemps*), Alban Berg (*Wozzeck*), and such. Living in the fullest daily communion with his large family and its unfolding talents, he dwelled, in his inward life, on the heights—from which in unsparing honesty and commitment he contended critically with his own work. When he listened to someone talking to him, his round eye-glasses doubled the gleam of his taking eye, and he attended so closely that his face, his lips, took on the changing expressions of the speaker. He received as he gave—that is, wholly.

Such was the man from whom his gifted offspring took their natures and the horizons of their thought and vision. It was the eldest, Henriette, who first inherited his complex, searching nature, as she was the first pupil to receive his definitions and examples of the act of seeing, feeling, and giving a second life to persons, places, things seen.

Carolyn, the mother, made her own daily gifts that lived on in the children. Her joy of home and family equaled her husband's gusto. She performed prodigies of housekeeping in the large, handsome house set on the hill below the studio. With or without servants in the kitchen, she produced meals whose bountiful excellence positively demanded high spirits of all as they gathered at the refectory table in the narrow, Tudor-paneled dining room. There were often guests at meals, but with visitors or without, the table-times were festivals of abundance in spirit, gaiety, food, story, comic outrage (of which the child Andrew, known as "Sprout," was a virtuoso inventor); and in the air a love so imaginative that alone it could serve to pose a vision of life, leaving to the future any of life's darker elements.

In the midst of the superior gifts alive in her children, Carolyn Wyeth at times expressed dismay at their headlong variety and energy, lamenting that she, herself, could not "do anything—look at them, they all can *do* something," and she was never comforted when reminded that it was she who had accomplished the most in bearing and fostering such a brood. Her dark, wondering eyes looked with impartial sympathy upon all her household, where all encouraged each other in their work. In the evening they listened to Beethoven played by Ann at the great Mason & Hamlin piano, or heard music from the phonograph while the father's concentrated listening was in itself instructive. All spent hours facing newly drawn or painted pictures, discussing them with hot cheeks and voices constricted by passionate interest pro or con, the while having access to the mother's "vast piles of doughnuts and sand tarts," as a son-in-law once remembered.

ii

So enfolded, Henriette Wyeth came through childhood and early youth acquiring a myriad of references and strengths that with time composed a nature as sensitive as it was expressive. As a child she was lovely to look upon, and after a growing girl's period of abnormal weight, entered into her presence as a slight, brightly active young girl of extraordinary beauty. (An international photographer chose her later as one of his published group of the "Ten Most Beautiful American Young Women With Brains," which put a glow about her in the spirited social life of her burgeoning days.)

But what mattered was the necessity to work that began early and has never ceased. In general knowledge, aside from art, she had no schoolroom but her father's studio—and it was enough. Simple association with him was an education. He was her drillmaster in drawing, her mentor in general awareness, the source of the swift, pointed thought and the precise and acute vocabulary that have served her always as expressive means hardly less gifted than her painting. Like her father, she has always seized upon the incidental, the peripheral, aspects of common experience to find meanings that greatly extend the significance of things seen and acts done.

Nothing was felt or observed by itself alone; everything had its metaphor, and thus perception was empowered. This habit of thought, of entering into the essence of the objective life, added an enlarging value to the painter's sight and work. Of all her legacies from her father, this style of meeting life and framing concepts was perhaps the most powerful in the shaping of her approach to her art.

From the time when she was six or seven years old, she and the others at home were, as she recalls, "constantly fed reproductions—prints and color. My father talked about painters and sculptors constantly, all the Old Masters of great quality."

In her drawing studies, she was set to work at the start with the universal basic forms—sphere, cube, cone, and pyramid. Reminder of academic pedagogy, the process under Wyeth became something more than mechanical renderings of these shapes. For hours he would dwell upon the optical marvels of light falling on any surface, and he would indicate, and insist on the capture of, infinite subtleties in how common light and shadow made uncommon marvels of the observed world and its objects, even if these were only severe geometrical shapes. If it was a humble exercise, it was also an establishment of a visual grammar never to lose its power of projection in the drawn or painted likeness of more intricate forms.

When Henriette was a "little girl with fat cheeks and a

beaver hat," as she said, her family moved from Chadds Ford to Needham, Massachusetts, in a return to the eighteenth-century house of the father's forebears, and lived there for two years before returning to Pennsylvania. At thirteen she was sent to study life drawing at the Normal Art School in Boston. For a year she worked in the class of Richard Andrew, a brilliant teacher who guided her in forming her mastery of the figure. Intuition touched by unsentimental compassion for the vulnerability of the visible being has ever since informed her painting of people.

It was a rich period of her youth. She had the great Boston collections to visit, and she found ecstatic heights in performances of the Boston Symphony Orchestra and Boston's opera seasons, to which she brought an already accustomed ear. She was often allowed to go alone to hear music. The ceremony of the great orchestral concerts under Pierre Monteux, and the transporting apparatus of the opera theatre, particularly in the works of Richard Wagner, with their almost smothering intensities, gave her a revelation of a theatre within herself. It was a dimension of imaginative power that, briefly, made her long to be a singer; and in all other ways it lingered as a factor in her vision, and in the way she arranged ever after the materials of her paintings, whether in portrait or still life.

This was a natural development, for even as a child she had had a theatre of the imagination in the way she would see the intimacies of earth, going alone into the little woods at home; and "loving the earth, the smell of the earth," she would lie down, "having my face hanging over a brook, and looking down into the little wet stones under the rippling waters—a simple, beautiful relationship with what I was living in." But more: such dreamlike intimacy with small natural objects was lifted in imagination into a greater scale, and she came to know that the transformation was in essence theatrical, larger than life, and she felt that she "had this great appetite for the artifice of blue light," and when she came to see live theatre in a heroic frame she thought of the transforming art of arrranged light and painted atmosphere of all theatre. "This is my world, really." It has never ceased to be so, though in the various periods of her work the dramatic statement has had its different uses.

After the Boston years, Henriette Wyeth, again in Chadds Ford, resumed daily work at her easel in her father's studio. She responded to contemporary painters, though without derivative affinity in her painting—though one gave her "an extraordinary, an electric shock." It was Georgia O'Keeffe, when Henriette saw for the first time "great paintings of hers: petunia, iris, something in New York. I never felt that I imitated her, but she gave me an imaginative shot in the arm, as it were, a hypodermic of advance sight in simple flowers and leaf forms. She affected me very much, very important, and I told her that when I met her for the first time. She released, released."

iii

Convers Wyeth sent Henriette to the Pennsylvania Academy of the Fine Arts in Philadelphia for further informal study.

She was coming into her late teens, her social style assured by her beauty, her quickness of thought and original word, her style in expensively simple high fashion. Her taste was quite thoughtlessly for the best. It was fostered by family habit. Wyeth was immensely in demand as an artist, and commanded fees sumptuous for their time. He denied his family nothing. For them there was an air not of extravagance but of great natural bounty.

First of all, what was most beautiful was most worth acquiring, whatever the cost. Then, the toys most stimulating to these imaginative children were imperatives, particularly to Andrew, whose collections were copious enough to bulge the walls of his basement playroom. So, too, the kitchen larder and pantry ached with profusion, and yielded accordingly to the family table, where the father, carving at the end with a musketeer's play of blade, kept the air blue with every sort of gusto, from the profoundly aesthetic to the wildly Rabelaisian. Henriette early learned how to honor the absence of thrift, to the satisfaction of her need for materials truly essential to her life and work, and, in time, to the formation of her husband's and her children's values of comfort and style.

The scheduled journeys to Philadelphia for her Academy hours were managed by little local trains that ran through the Brandywine Valley and junction points north. One day, returning from the Academy, she encountered a young man who was on his way to an interview with her father to propose the idea of becoming a Wyeth student. He was unsure of how to find the Wyeth place. She was able to tell him. In any case, her father was waiting at the station. They all drove home together.

The stranger was Peter Hurd, a born New Mexican, formerly a West Point cadet, now a student at Haverford College. He was tall, slim, charged with energetic charm, and with determination to become an artist. His artistic evidence at the time was meager, but Wyeth perceived the latent burn of talent in him, felt the strong will behind it, and accepted him first as an occasional visitor for criticism and within the year as a full-time student. Hurd left college, moved to Chadds Ford, and soon became a daily familiar in the master's lively household. They all took to him—he was high-spirited, outgoing, actually beautiful in a sinewy virile fashion. Someone called him "Shelley in cowboy boots."

His happiness was great. He had found his world. At first he must have seen Henriette as hopelessly out of reach, for he was a proudly impecunious student in the very early stages of an earnest apprenticeship, while she was already a professional painter of extraordinary gifts and a scintillant figure in the gayest society of Wilmington and the Brandywine as presided over by the elegantly conventional clan of the Du Ponts. In the 1920s she was a hybrid of a stylish society (whose standards of luxury became hers) and the inner, passionate life of mind and art, which was hers at home.

But she was wiser than needed to be known in all her gifts of understanding and expression so early developed under her father's ample nature; and in Peter Hurd she saw not only the hard-driving student from an unimagined distant background, but also a young man with yet hidden powers as a serious painter, and a being rampant with conviction and allure; and as passionately as he, she fell in love.

Their romance was observed, but it was not until 1927 that they were formally engaged. Peter was absorbed into the Wyeth family, to all of whom, especially the father, he would owe so much. Yet in time Peter began to long for independence—but independence that included Henriette, which meant having her with him wherever he might go; and by the time of their engagement he knew where he must go.

The misty beauties of the pastoral Brandywine still appealed to him, but awakening in him more strongly by the day was the memory of the Southwest plains and mountains where he came from. In Chadds Ford he would be among loving friends, but there he would always remain a lesser Wyeth. What he learned from them would always be his; but his vision must be his own, and he must return to find it in New Mexico, with Henriette beside him.

Yet the Wyeth family adhesion was powerful, and it seemed unimaginable to Henriette that she could ever want to be free of it, and to her father, impossible. Strong tensions resulted, and in the end, though the engagement held, Peter returned to his parents' place at Roswell, New Mexico, still determined that she must marry him and live with him in his own land. It was a trying dilemma that required years to resolve, as it finally was, in a hard-earned balance between commitments to differing styles, definitions of amenity, devotions to long-cherished but contrasting heritages. Resolutions came through what the young pair held in common—

their love of each other, and their work as artists no matter where they might be.

They were married in a Unitarian church at Wilmington on 28 June 1929, with a reception following in the Wyeth house. As guests left in the late afternoon, Andrew, aged twelve, was found to be drinking up any champagne left at the party, and next morning was reported to be not at his best. The bride and groom, beginning their honeymoon, sailed at once on a coastal steamer for Galveston. From the Gulf they traveled overland by car to New Mexico, where they spent the summer and autumn, most of the time in an isolated rustic cabin at the head of the Ruidoso canyon in the Capitan mountains.

It was an idyllic time. Both painted or drew every day. They hauled wood and cooked for themselves. They stayed into early autumn. Snow fell. Their first child was conceived. Henriette's happiness brought her a growing love of New Mexico. For the birth of Peter Wyeth Hurd, they must return to Chadds Ford and a reunion joyful for all. They both belonged once again to the Wyeth world. The young couple rented a small farmhouse a quarter of an hour from the Wyeth place. Henriette was content to be, with Peter, embraced by the patriarchal life once again. With energy and gaiety Henriette and Peter established themselves in the life of the countryside. For the most part it was a country-squire sort of existence: fine houses, widely separated, with gentleman-farming, horse shows, stables of thoroughbreds for fox hunting, a prevailing liveliness in exchanges between the establishments. It was not the scale that so much mattered as the style. Henriette and Peter gave much hospitality in their small, three-story farmhouse on a rise overlooking a fine, long meadow.

The little rooms were white. In them Henriette sparely placed fine antique furniture kept in high luster. Books gleamed behind the glass of an important breakfront. Whole shelves were given to the limited and regular editions of a most favored guest, the then celebrated novelist Joseph Hergesheimer, of West Chester, who gave all his books to Henriette. He romanced her in the way of a famous middle-aged lover of beautiful textures who was more amused by the game than by the candle. It suited him that Henriette's perfection of taste, her decisive eye, arranged the character of the house through simple elegance.

A figure more than portly but always fastidiously turned out, Hergesheimer often came to dinner, sometimes without his handsome wife, Dorothy. If there were other guests, he might present a problem, rather like having a trained bear to dinner, for it was never certain that the bear, or Joe, as he was inelegantly known, would be contained within amenity, or would suddenly lash out unprovoked and bare his claws at an unoffending guest who for obscure reasons he found unpleasing. Still, he was worth the risk, for when in form he was conversationally brilliant; at moments of small-eyed penetration, almost disconcertingly sympathetic; and always highly original in spoken style. Of a summer evening he would arrive dressed in a white suit with an emerald-green woven cravat ("necktie" would never do it) such as he wore for his superb portrait by Henriette. He was conveyed in an excessively smart town car, with a body by Brewster on a Ford chassis. The radiator cap supported a glass ornament by Lalique, which, Joe admitted with half-lidded gaze, cost more than the whole rest of the equipage. A uniformed man was on the box. In the dove-grey cabin Joe took his ease, with one well-fleshed hand expansively spread on the velours seat cushion. Entering the Hurds' immaculate small drawing room he set his huge round spectacles on his forehead the better to read, ran his eye along the back of his own books importantly published by Alfred A. Knopf, as though to greet his own preeminence. When his hostess appeared, he would put his heavy arm around her most slim of waists, examine her perfect frock, and ask banteringly, "What are you dressed as, babe?"—for all his Jamesian literacy, affecting slang to make play of his sybaritic nature.

Hergesheimer elaborately dramatized his taste and style in fictions concerned with the luxurious, the aesthetically exotic; and his romantic values, along with his lavishly handsome mode of living, had much effect on Henriette, then and later. She, too, had a natural taste for fine objects, original thought, and a standard of irreducible distinction in living. The home she created suited Peter also, for he came from a family out West who lived with high manner derived from his father's well-born Boston heritage and his mother's upbringing as the Gibson-girl daughter of turn-of-the-century society. For his part, Peter's inherited quickness of mind and habit of precise, fresh, witty speech sealed for life the temperamental pleasure of civilized companionship that, along with their shared perceptions in art, made of Henriette's marriage to him a true bond.

During their early married life in Chadds Ford they established daily work in their studios. Each had one half of an old schoolhouse to work in, provided by Wyeth the owner. The days were regular. After chores in earliest morning, when gold light dissolving in the Brandywine mists made long shafts in the dense air, Henriette and Peter drove to their schoolhouse for their daily work, leaving the baby with his nurse and the kitchen with a risible Negro cook. The little white schoolhouse was divided down the center, making parallel studios that were connected by double doors. From the very first, these painters were of supportive value to each other's work—an asset in their joint careers that served them all their lives.

At work, the air of concentration was intense, occasionally broken by visits between the studios for comments on work in progress. When summoned, Pa Wyeth, as he was intimately called, came to either studio to give criticism, which while unsparing in technical matters, always included hearty encouragement. His approval sometimes exploded with "That's a corker!"

When the day's work was done, Peter rode—he kept a pair of hunters and, a superb horseman, rode to hounds with the local hunt clubs—while Henriette would hurry up the hill a little way to the big house for an afternoon visit, drawn by the claiming family sense of all the Wyeths. Their meetings, even daily, held always fresh interest in each other's concerns. Whenever Henriette had to be away from that family she missed them all acutely, and whenever possible she worked to keep her marriage, her little son, her husband, within the enclosing Wyeth embrace. It was a state that did not wholly suit Peter's irrepressible need for independence—but given the happier aspects and advantages of the Wyeth family's love for him, life went on for some time with visible content and gaiety.

Affairs moved well professionally. Peter's studies with Pa Wyeth advanced him fast into technical aptness, and he benefited from commissions steered his way by Pa. Soon, also, he was painting decorative panels for neighborly patrons and in 1932 he was invited to show a canvas at the Corcoran Gallery in Washington—a recognition that did much to confirm his course, for him and for those about him. He worked incessantly, though, longing for New Mexico, he said, "I keep wishing for more daylight." The intensity of his commitment, the artist's urgency, moved him, he said, to a "sudden realization acute and terrible of the value of this moment in which we live bordered by the two eternities."

From the very beginning of her married life Henriette demonstrated her remarkable ability to hold to a daily schedule in the studio and at the same time to conduct a beautifully ordered household as a mother, wife, and hostess. For her the acts of life were never compartmented. Her day was all of a piece, an enclosing vessel in itself an aesthetic achievement. All things of her concern supported and enhanced each other in her vision of grace, bringing particular meaning to the world she made with her share of her father's prodigious energy and her mother's warm intuitions of the joys and needs of others.

iv

In the time before her marriage and during its early days, Henriette Wyeth, when not absorbed in portrait painting, brought to canvas a series of works that expressed her continued "great appetite for the artifice of blue light"—again, the transporting fantasy of theatre. These were large pictures, worked directly from the imagination, without models or arranged backgrounds. They were like arrested moments of ballet: fragile girls with great pools of questioning eyes, misty figures, little hands floating like petals supporting dreams of flowers, against atmospheres almost abstractly suggesting stage light and painted settings out of never-seen dramas. In them was an implied mourning for girlhood and its knowledge beyond innocence, overlaid by a lyric prophecy of the decay which however distant must overtake all things. In this measure, these works were mindful of the exquisitely decadent, and no less real for that, in art as in life. They were technically marvelous in their suggestion of theatre colors under sourceless light. As decorations they had a tapestry-like effectiveness. As expressions of her invention, they reflected a pent-up store of Henriette's childhood fantasies, which had been fostered for her by all the luxuries for the child spirit that her father could provide. These paintings were filled with both love and melancholy, and they contained the seeds of attitudes which, if the idiom would change with maturity, yet remained fruitful as sources of her lifework, whether in portraiture, still life, or the creation of her own domestic scene.

She said of such fantasy paintings, "I think they were a very honest part of my life." If they were flights of invention to free her from studio actualities, a means to find her own authority, she believed that no such purpose was at the time

"intellectually realized." She thought they might have represented "a retreat into a kind of world that was, perhaps,
not very wholesome. It was concerned with *shadows*." But
because they held such strong conviction, they had the reality and power of dreams that survived the daylight. Joseph
Hergesheimer was particularly fond of these works, and said
of the pallid girls who existed amidst the painted light and
shade of theatre, "Their bodies were like moths' bodies."

One of the last of the fantasies was painted in 1935. It is
called "Death and the Child," and it may represent a transition from memory of the final theatrical questions of adolescence to full knowledge of the tragic certainties which
have their determining moments in the cycle of life, including that of motherhood: an ineffably touching figure of a
naked child in late infancy is being taken with hands like
eternal light into the embrace of a golden angel descending
as an act of the air, all radiant with loving compassion
against the ultimate dark from which the angel has come
and to which it will return with its small beautiful burden.
The painting is a statement of profound emotion, with no
sentimentality whatever in its acceptance of the beginning,
and the end, of being.

v

With all its diversions, amenities, nourishments, the life at
Chadds Ford would not forever hold Peter Hurd from his
imperative need to live and paint in the light of the Southwest. A mural commission from his old school in New Mexico called him home. He went alone to make preliminary
plans. After another Chadds Ford interlude, he returned
West to stay and was followed in time by Henriette and
their two childen—a daughter, Carol, had been born—to
begin family life on a small ranch that he had acquired in
the foothills of the Capitan mountains west of Roswell.

For Henriette, the change was a strenuous uprooting.
Across the continent from her parental family with their

habits and standards, their informed support in all the arts, she was given into cultural isolation, amidst an alien Mexican-American village life, and a landscape whose immanent and arid forms at first seemed harsh. But even dearer commitments were with her, and in her strength of spirit, she came to love all that was most strange and challenging; for she was with Peter, who was endlessly intriguing, and her children, who were full of absorbing needs.

Initially the ranch house consisted of only three rooms—a bedroom and a long narrow kitchen at right angles to each other, joined by a small square room first used as a storage bin for the annual apple crop from the ranch orchard. Peter effected changes before his family's arrival. Plumbing was arranged for, the apple room was cleared, he built himself a two-story studio and, opposite the house, across the compound, a studio for Henriette. Over the years the establishment put out new rooms, patios, gardens, a greenhouse and orangery, with live water in an acequia, plantings of poplars, cottonwoods, and tamarkisk trees, guest quarters, corrals, and finally a great *sala* from a noble design by Robert Hunt of Santa Fe. Every room duly reflected Henriette's decorative imagination. She quickly joined Peter in his love for Mexico and its artifacts in their brilliant colors; much of the Mexican atmosphere enlivened the patio. Flowers were everywhere in the rooms. The ever-dramatic light of the vastly seen sky gave the hills of the ranch and the long perspective of the Ruidoso Valley a power inexhaustible in their fascination for a painter's eye. Here were subjects for infinite variation in Peter's pictures, and aspects of an earth that in time Henriette came to love more than any place she had ever known. At San Patricio she created a life which drew countless friends and guests. Portrait clients came to be painted by Henriette or Peter, and more often than not were enchanted by the daily life they were made to feel part of. If at first the ranch seemed far removed, it soon created a sense that what lay far away from it was isolated, not the other way round, so self-sufficient was it in the arts of civilized existence.

At the heart of the family life, with Michael, a third child arriving late on the scene, there was every rewarding joy in hard daily work in the studios, along with zestful meals whose table echoed the convivial Wyeth style, faithful even to the hilariously bawdy; high conversation laced with scandalous mimicry (at which both Henriette and Peter were brilliant); Mexican folk songs to Peter's recklessly effective guitar playing; long rides in the hills; and polo on the field Peter had built, having taught the game to native cowboys who went at it demonically; and over all a sense of fulfillment.

So for decades Sentinel Ranch—named for the highest of the hills which lay back like a lion against the horizon facing the rambling house and its compounds—thrived with its varied lives in their common purpose, which is the creation of art.

vi

Henriette Wyeth's articles of faith in her art are uncommonly certain as she speaks of them. Much—most, in fact—of an artist's source for expositions necessarily remains mysterious in the domain of the subconscious. But in the driving travail through which Henriette Wyeth achieves her paintings there is much disciplined thought, and she is able to articulate this with fluent force. It is her habit to express herself with captivating energy, whether in conversation devastating in its comedy, or in probing discussion of the serious affairs close to the reason of her being. Her dark eyes can be as tender as those of her mother, or as charged with the light of passionate conviction as her father's. Her mind is very much her own, but the traits of discipline, of often painful analysis, and of self-unsparing honesty sharply recall Convers Wyeth. (Much the same powers dwell in Andrew Wyeth, who in his maturity has become for a vast international public the visionary of the universal as seen in the humbly intimate evidence of one man's emotion confronting the common face of life.)

With reference to her own work, "I never talk about painting to painters," Henriette Wyeth has said. "I feel very cross, very down-the-nose, very *secret* about it . . . an invasion of privacy, and I don't like it." As for subject matter, she adds, "I don't know what is important and what is unimportant, so I call it all immensely important."

Yet her inner vision is so clear that she is able to speak with certainty about the thought behind her approaches to painting. It is of course evident from her work that she is entirely given to homage for the objective world, not in representation alone, but in countless supporting and interpretive aspects that reflect her play of spirit and mind. "It seems to me that reality is so exciting, always—it is *not* particularly understood, even by scientists. It is still an incredible mystery." Further, she is sustained by an ever-present feeling—"A kind of tribute to my delight in life, in all kinds of important aspects of my life, and also the very superficial, the delightful, the, the charming, the nonessential, except that I never know what's nonessential. Nothing is unimportant, or nothing should not be painted. It's all paintable. It's all part of an artist's life."

She wonders if there may be "a certain fuzziness" in such views, which she feels may lack conciseness. Yet when all things call to her in terms of their particular natures, and so must be responded to for what they are and given celebration, she knows that any evidence of life about her may "just take me in hand," and she admits with rueful humor that the process "sometimes leads to disaster." Nevertheless, the imperative is to contain and keep the truth, and do it honor. In this response there is deep emotion, and it harks back to her father's primary lessons with the cube, sphere, cone, and how he would "talk about the way the pyramid shadow would fall over the sphere, so that you felt you were traveling with a great philosophy, a curious sense of tremendous importance. And of course, it *is* important. The source of light from the sun in outer space"—here the most mundane simplicities have their organic share in the cosmic dimension—"falling on an object in front of you, and the shapes it makes over forms. That in itself makes your hair sit up."

Thus an object of smallest inherent consequence can be enough to summon association and abstract importance that set the visual imagination in motion toward a "realized representation." As for the abstract (so exclusively a measurement of worth in fairly recent aesthetic theory), "a realized representation is simply the sum of details which are in themselves little abstractions."

Of the genesis of a work, say, in still life, Henriette Wyeth has said, "There is always one object—it can be anything—that has stirred my imagination and feeling, of nostalgia, perhaps, or it may be a totally new perception of a precious stone or shell or feather. But it keeps gnawing at me, nibbling at me—how to release that with surrounding color other than its own, and perhaps to have a kind of drama between objects; and how shadow falls from one remarkable, immaculate, sharply cut shell, for instance, against another curve of fabric or perhaps grass, or even the bare floor. It needs almost nothing, because there isn't one square inch of anything I look at that doesn't constantly play back and forth to me. Sometimes it becomes just simply a shambles of dead nothing, I can't get anything to work. And perhaps the next morning, I can come into the studio and move something, or take away something, and the whole thing is fused. . . ."

She illustrates the process further with a fondly amused recollection of her long-deceased mother-in-law, Lucy Chew Knight Hurd, the decorative Gibson girl of years ago. She thinks of "a satin slipper of Lucy's; I had a pale, lemon-colored satin slipper of Lucy's about eight inches long, all toe. And I am going to do that slipper with her French fan and relate it to one of her underskirts of apple green, or possibly a little pale jacket of blue taffeta—and this is Lucy. She was made of feathers and stays and gold lace and all that sort of thing, and I feel in those, there's a kind of baroque little composition of color, an edge, a baroque quality of the way Mozart did those dry, brilliant, little—*not* sweet: a great many people seem to think it's sweet music. It *isn't*. It's the bare, lovely, delicate bones of feeling. Utterly Gothic. It builds in *bone lace*, you know."

In such words Henriette Wyeth states the very qualities—delicate, feminine, strongly designed, sharply thought out—which makes her paintings important in their combination of masterly technique with a nature at once deeply sophisticated and probingly emotional.

So: feeling, set to work with sureness of taste and vital empathy, plays its critical part in her work. She speaks of the experience of painting an ancient Mexican woman from the village of San Patricio near Sentinel Ranch—a tiny, fragile creature close to ninety years in age: Doña Nestorita, a woman of poverty, simple, illiterate, life-worn.

"I do feel I have become occasionally *really* emotional—for instance, in painting Doña Nestorita. She was charming, of great dignity, in a pitiful, tiny, blind person. Eyes that could see the print of my studio window, the light of my window, but that is all. Posing, she preferred to stand instead of sit; she hurt less, she said. And then, one morning, all of a sudden, she began singing in a high, curious, flute-like voice, an old lady's voice, those songs in Spanish that she learned as a little girl, concerning love, and butterflies, and flowers, and perhaps a religious allusion, and it was so extraordinary, so dramatic, such a touching protestation of life, of still believing in life. She'd had a very bad life, she was cruelly treated and misused by her husband. —To have that tiny old lady singing about something that was eighty, ninety years ago in her life overcame me. I had to mop my eyes and swallow and stop. —Said to myself, *Now for heaven's sake, paint while this goes on, don't be absurd, hang on to this.* And it was all right in half a minute. But that was one time that really . . ."

The eroded life, the dignity of time itself, are in the painting. It is one of Henriette Wyeth's most famous. It has been exhibited widely and is in the permanent collection of the Roswell Museum. Such a work reveals the crucial difference between the sentimental and the occasion of feeling.

"I suppose I sing the praises of the obvious," reflects Henriette Wyeth without apology. "But I believe in obvious things. I love obvious things, I love obvious rich colors, I love gold, I love diamonds, windowpanes"—in their common value as vehicles of light—"all of the exquisite variations of color, lilacs, roses, all of the transcendental rainbows, all of the lyric things that are supposed to be so obvious, so banal, no one paints them any more: well: let me have a translation of their quality and I don't care what anyone . . . They are all great verities. I love parched bones; I've seen dead things, and people, and birds, and they are exquisite; but I think that if I paint the obviously beautiful, or perhaps the sweet (that dreadful word)—if I do it painfully enough, then it may be as good as I want it to be. It's purged of the rubbish, purged of the sweetness, purged of the marshmallow content that I suppose. . . ."

Matter which, in other words, has come by popular response to be commonized beyond critical acceptance. But it is clear that still-life painting is as important to Henriette Wyeth for the philosophy of things as for their simple likeness. Thus another legacy from her father, who, standing before one of his own still lifes which showed a simple blue Chinese porcelain bowl in a vast ripple of chatoyant silk, once talked for the better part of an hour about the universe implicit in the hollow of the bowl, and the arrested spin of the universal light on its rim, and the analogy of space in the background where in any excerpted area the texture could stand in its own importance. Such impassioned relation to common matter was not instantly visible to the viewer; but that it was alive in the painter's conviction gave inexplicably present life beyond skilled realism to the result. It illustrated how a second vision, long in coming to focus, dwelled behind the first, which saw surface. With Henriette Wyeth, it is a conscious process, but not a facile one. Much furrowed thought goes into it, and the ripening of an understanding of even inert objects. "Germination," she says, "you know, that fungus thing." Life must assert. "It cannot be negative."

Ideas added to feeling, then, inform both her still lifes and portraits, and the most constant impulse is the desire to record that which must change and go.

"The reason I paint flowers is that I see them fading. This reminds me of the eternally renewed, the springtime, all of that, because I feel death and disaster lurk right behind them." Her work is testimony to the enduring power which abides strongly in certain forms of fragility. In a flower detail of a still life, in a child's wrist, she makes a little essay on mortality, but one reclaimed from morbidity by its celebration of present beauty.

"One of the reasons I love painting children: there is an inherited character bone, I can always feel that under those petal-soft faces, you know? Those brilliant eyes, and the exquisite gilt hair, the breadth of eyebrows, and the fold of lips like a flower petal's, and all the future is before them, and *I must get this while it is this way.* A downy—what are the little?—the pussy willow, the grey silk of the pussy willow: all this is a great truth, part of a development. So, too, I love a dry husk at the end of a flower. I've been painting dead flowers; it's no less important, and I'm bored to death at the people who are bothered by mere subject matter. Certain subjects have to remind me of how remarkable they once were, and are gone forever. . . ."

What is revealed in such reflections is this painter's many-veined approach to all visible forms. Abstractly, design is inherent in everything, but its revelation requires respect for the way forms grow in nature. It is this impelling love and respect for organic life that commits Henriette Wyeth to her aesthetic of the objective, against all the influence of the inward psychological chic of the nonobjective art which until recently commanded reputations through galleries, museums, reviewers. Without any degree of condescension to either painting or patron, she respects the all but incommunicable secrets of the common vision. "The painter should have a sense of responsibility toward people—the people who look at pictures, buy them, hang them. I feel that is not unimportant. Of course, most contemporary painters who stick a piece of burlap up in a rather dramatic arrangement across a square, or perhaps it's a map shape, I don't know, seem to me totally wrong." There is a sense that she regards such a procedure, illustrated by her broadly caricatured example, as a self-indulgent, ego-centered activity that, while it may express the naïve, even the troubled, state of the modern collective psyche, has small relevance to the universal imperative of nature toward ordained order. "You know," she declares, "a blade of grass doesn't grow untidily; it's very efficient. There's a thrust of clean, beautiful reason."

vii

Henriette Wyeth has created a population of portraits, most of them through commissions; but perhaps the most remarkable in her canon of likenesses in a series of paintings of members of her family, done at the various stages of their lives. All of her three children—Peter Wyeth Hurd the musician, and the painters Michael Hurd and Carol Hurd Rogers—have been recorded as they grew; her husband and her brother Andrew several times (one of her oil portraits of Andrew and an early charcoal drawing of Peter Hurd have recently been added to the permanent collection of the National Portrait Gallery), her grandchildren, and, in a grave, brooding presence, her father, who is seated on the edge of a model stand before one of his own paintings of the simple, epic life of Maine fishermen ("Island Funeral"). She has made a profuse record of a family, and as such it has historical value in relation to twentieth-century American art. Further, it is a connected chronicle of her enduring and inexhaustible love for those lives born into her responsibility.

She has always met the demands of daily life with the same fervid response she has given to her painting. There is no separation between the two duties. Or, to change the figure, her family, household, beloved friendships, the needs of dependents, the trusting wants of animal pets, and the unceasing claims of her art, all together, travel the same circumference about her life. As thought plays so great a part in the quality of her vision, her daily concerns enter into her sense of the person she paints, and even if inexplicit, find their way into her very concept of light, color, space, to inform her judgment of her subject.

Those who have sat to Henriette Wyeth always testify to the astonishing degree of her involvement with them. With driving energy and swift certainties of touch on the canvas she captures the confronting reality. But that reality is not an isolated goal. It must be supported by the mining of the thought and spirit of the one posing. In a sense it is the way this painter might hear music—notes in themselves, but with interior revelations of an order beyond literal components. There is a running conversation during the sitting. It is a useful device for distracting attention from the challenge of the artist's eye as it dartingly estimates the evidence of face, body, attitude. A mystery is present. It is one never wholly solved; but salient truths come clear, and along with always satisfying details of likeness, the subject's nature takes visible form.

The form, for purposes of painting, is not entirely left to ordinary posture. Henriette Wyeth in apprehending the double truth about her portrait subjects brings her own interpretation of how they should be arranged for painting.

As formally as with the materials of her still lifes, she decides on a statement for the body. It is not a capricious arrangement. It is an intuitive act of release for the marvelous uniqueness of every person. It rests, first of all, in a love of the human form for its own sake.

"I love the feeling of a round arm. I love the very feeling of a body under dress, in a woman, man, or child." It is a tactile response. As a very young person she wanted to do sculpture, and made a few tries. They arose from her exposure in her father's studio to the Old Masters through countless reproductions—Malraux's museum without walls. "The Michelangelo things, all of the photographs. Why do I have so many enthusiasms? Have I possibly room for them? I go absolutely mad, I get tearful, my voice shakes, I almost die—"

It is not uncommon for the conviction about the making of a work in any art to be signaled by a physical response, a thump at the solar plexus, a sign not only of readiness but of necessity to go to work. It is a possessing excitement that brings all faculties into harmony.

In entering upon a portrait, Henriette Wyeth is subject to this. The feeling can be an odd mixture of the painful and the joyous. In any case, it delivers a charge of energy, and the most modest detail of the task becomes as enthralling as the greatest overall conception.

"I'm afraid," she has said, "that in order to be excited, and this happens naturally, I never plan it, but I impose it on the person who interests me, either in commission or in just asking someone to sit, a kind of other . . . another concept—" She allows a hiatus of thought to occur which yet clearly conveys the idea that a qualifying idea comes to mind to be united with the image of the actual sitter. "For instance, in the head of a young girl that I was just working on, I had a feeling perhaps of Botticelli, I had a feeling of an unhappy young person that I know she is, this was all intermingled, and I can't *un*—" she gestures—"it's a fabric, I cannot separate." And she means separate the great past from the immediate problem. "Perhaps it is wrong to think of a head by Leonardo or a mask by Michelangelo or Rodin but such things *do* become involved." But since she draws, paints, like no one else, such great tributaries to the main flow of her perception take on a structural, nonimitative relation.

As important to such great matters are the many characterful details which together reveal the presence for a portrait. Something like the penetrating mimetic gift of a fine actress comes into play here, when Henriette Wyeth is able to inhabit something of the very quality of the sitter.

"To understand what the other person—how the dress *feels* on her, how it fits her: I am extremely critical about anything like that. I save very carefully anything that seems extremely personal in the sitter, even if it destroys perhaps the design of the Dior, or whatever [costume] I'm painting. I try to balance this, decide what is more important: how So-and-so's shoulder works into the sleeve, or should I have someone come and fix the sleeve so that it fits the way Dior wanted it to? Well, the *character* usually wins out."

Clues are often projected inadvertently by the sitter. How people walk, how they sit in a chair, of course how they speak, even their taste in food, the way they feel about music, or about almost anything at all—"all is extremely telling. It informs me of them, of their background, what kind of school they went to, what their nurse was like. Everything. It is terrifying how people reveal themselves."

To bring a coherent character out of so many impressions, the artist must conceive a synthesis, or, to use that piece of cant which she dislikes, "an artistic concept." Still, it is a necessary step, and is taken through a process of sifting the ingredients, "as if there is a fine gold sieve, and, perhaps, with a person who doesn't really basically interest me very much, putting it through a gold sieve makes it all come out very exciting for me, and I shamelessly paint it that way.

There is, then, of course, a very deep, deep struggle I have in projecting character." But she has her consolations. Great predecessors must have done the same thing. She cites Goya, no doubt thinking of the transcended ungainliness of the royal family of Charles IV, and she is consoled by Velasquez, who had to "elevate and translate the little bilious girls into exquisite creatures. And they were exquisite creatures, anyhow, because a small, blond, bilious child is often absolutely beautiful in this pallor. It is all so strangely mixed."

Henriette Wyeth cannot help but think that her portraits of others contain a strong element of the autobiographical, then. The dramatic gift, the theatre's "artifice of blue light" in her youth, the social acuity of her mimicry (not a frivolous gift, since it seizes character in accurate comedy, which is the other face of reality) all come into play as she translates a life into its icon. "My relationships with people, my awareness of them, my trying to become them, projecting myself into them, are entirely autobiographical. Completely involved; as far as I can go. And then I wonder after I have painted a portrait, How can I possibly have the audacity to think that I could *become* the sitter? But if I have any understanding whatsoever I do feel that it is projected from my side of the equation." She considers that in the artist there has to be a buried versatility, a protean persona, which can make its vicarious harmony with the opposite subject. "Oh, I feel that everything that happens to you, and everything you live with, contributes to that. The very fabric I put on my body, the way I comb my hair, what shoes I wear, *everything* relates because [of how] I understand the other person."

And not only the visual thing. Qualities of thought, opinion, belief find their way into a wholeness of view of the portrait subject—even to traits of speech. One Texan client was so expressively painted that her very voice was a factor. In one of her most scandalously accurate phrases, Henriette

Wyeth said it was a sound like "tearing a shingle off a roof," and something of the temperament capable of that sound made its way into the portrait.

Discipline is totally necessary. "You go every day [to the studio] whether you're disgusted with your painting, and feel uninspired, uncreative, not wanting to work at all. You go and sit and you look. You simply have to, because this is as necessary as being alive every morning, and getting up after sleeping, eating breakfast, keeping yourself walking: *alive.*" A life of painting cannot be "impulsive or sporadic. This is built up just as carefully as the crystals in a rock form. I believe utterly in it, and you have to know, try to know, what you are painting about, which means that you do need all of the possible visionary discipline as well as mental."

There can be misadventures. "In terms of hours dedicated, sometimes feeling dull, almost ill, I've had a picture begin to go bad. I keep trying to rescue it, like Doctor Handy"—a beloved family doctor long ago in Chadds Ford—"saving a dying baby. It is perfectly dreadful but you do hang on as long as you possibly can . . . and sometimes you can save it. Sometimes it begins to breathe. Actually, this happens constantly. You have to fight for it to the very end. You've got to *complete.* I don't like the word 'finish' because it sounds as if to *finish* something means dead."

But when idea and performance have both been completed, something has been given life proper to its medium. Stravinsky once said, "There is only one possible way to discuss music, and that is in technically musical terms." Apart from scholarly searches and conclusions, it is almost as impossible to describe the art of painting. And yet when beyond technical values we have been given, over the centuries, meaning in subject matter, we do have a valid avenue of entry into the degree and quality of the artist's achievement.

Of her recent portraits, none has more essential revelation

of Henriette Wyeth's power to arrest in paint the whole nature of a subject than her painting of her husband, Peter Hurd, done in his early seventies. The land of his lifework is beyond his figure. He stands to one side so that it is revealed. His wonderfully luminous vitality is expressed in the thrust of his head above his powerful, lean shoulders. His face is sober, marked with the gouges of his age, and his capacity for severity and purpose is drawn in the set of his mouth and the fixing power of his eyes. The years have not destroyed, they have only changed, the splendor of appearance which gave his abounding youth its appeal so long ago. He wears a Mexican jacket of leather richly frogged in silver thread. His folded arms suggest only a temporary agreement to be still. Strongly shadowed on the left side, his figure—it is a three-quarter-length portrait—stands like a metaphor of power against a vast clear sky. His shadowed left hand holds the wide-brimmed black hat which in itself is an expression of his cavalier temperament. As objective as it can be, it is an image of the painter's lifelong companion and father of her three children; and yet because of its embracing truth, rather than through any confession of sentiment, it is also a statement of love. It stands most poignantly in all these values because Peter Hurd died a few years after it was painted.

viii

The hills of the ranch, once badly overgrazed, were slowly restored to new herbage by Peter Hurd's sense of custodianship of his land. The house, the studios, the gardens, the flowing water of the acequia made the home where he and Henriette spent a life full of convivial grace. For those who knew the Wyeth family life in the time of the Hurds' young days there, an arc of style reached from that tradition to the manner of the Sentinel Ranch at San Patricio in its fullest days. In addition to her full-time work as a painter, Henriette always conducted a household in harmony with her standards as a Wyeth and an artist, to create a seamless fabric of taste, style, comfort, and civilized charm.

In the early days, when the ranch house was being slowly enlarged, the meals were taken at a refectory table of unstained pine at one end of the long narrow kitchen. Superlative food was prepared and served by warm-hearted Mexican maids who were loved by the family. Peter remarked, "We do not eat in the kitchen; we cook in the dining room." In later days the old apple bin became a beautiful dining room, gleaming with family silver and ancient polished wood, and alight with flowers in colored glass set against the old long windows. In the Wyeth idiom, enriched by the Hurds' own originality, rapid talk and robust merriment filled the air, whether the family was alone or expanded by guests.

In the porcelain clarity of summer evenings, the party—there was always a feeling of party—adjourned to the patio, where Peter often played the guitar and sang his songs of Mexico, and the fountain played, and the Mexican stone angels on the patio wall knelt before the starlight and the looming rise of Sentinel Mountain, from whose crest a century ago Mexican *rancheros* kept watch against raiding Indians. Winter evenings drew the company into the splendid *sala*, with its immense fireplace, its ceilings so high that the candles in the chandeliers had to be reached by ladder for lighting. The paintings on the plain walls included one by the founder, Pa Wyeth. His power continued to extend throughout the family. One of his great-grandchildren, at the age of ten, drawing and painting with more than a child's precocity, stated dynastically to his grandmother Henriette Hurd, "*Abuela*, I am the eleventh Wyeth painter." A transmitted richness of temperament and talent illuminated not only the work but the quality of life achieved by N. C. Wyeth's descendants; and none expressed this with more distinction of mind and spirit than his daughter Henriette.

First of all, people marvel at the copious flow of energy she pours into her work. How can a figure so small, so slim, contain it all? In her late seventies, she retains the elegant vigor of her young days. Her animation of mind is echoed by the lively play of expression in her face. Her mother's eyes—again those dark pools express encompassing sympathy for whatever lives. Her clothes, richly simple, sometimes brilliant in color, belong to her vivid temperament. In conversation she is dashingly literate; decisive in opinion; mistress of comedy, and deeply serious when proper. Her extraordinary range of general knowledge seems to come out of the air, for she has known formal study only for her art. She is a constant if highly selective reader of contemporary authors. The great world is much with her. It is as important as private thought. She enjoys it by virtue of her friends and the renown of such as her brother Andrew and her husband, Peter, as well as by her own work.

Most of all, the strong bond uniting her work with her personal life is her feeling for her family and all its branches. She goes often to Chadds Ford. Her love and veneration for her brother Andrew are boundless. She feels responsibly concerned for the affairs of all her brothers and sisters, their spouses, children, sons- and daughters-in-law. With both her parents gone, she is in a way, despite her distant residence in New Mexico, so far from the Brandywine, rather like the head of the family. She is the oldest child of them all; but more, she is the one to whom everyone turns for understanding, advice, inspiriting support. This is even more strongly true in relation to the memory of her husband and to their sons and daughter, and the direction taken by their lives. She is the fount of strength, the example for them all, the one who can make a significant career and at the same time keep open her mind and heart for personal duties as she sees them in relation to lives dear to her. As in all families, troubles have come and gone, and after they've gone, and are perhaps forgotten, it is Henriette, the wife, the mother, the sister, the grandparent, the mistress of the hacienda and its working dependents, who has given strength, and in turn has taken it, with a lifelong enrichment of her spirit.

ix

Henriette Wyeth's deeply personal art is a statement of her response to life, whether to living subjects or inert objects, all revealed in the light of her inmost nature. Granting the beauty and power of her technique, it is the radiant personal reflections in her paintings that lift her into the company of artists whose truth lives after them, and becomes ours.

MRS. L.

————————

𝒮

i

Washington is a city of transient persons, fugitive ideas, and enduring monuments. Of this third category, the most enlivening through many years was the Dowager Patroness of the United States, Alice Roosevelt Longworth. Administrations came and went, political philosophies clashed and changed, but Mrs. Longworth for seven decades provided that continuity which stood for more than itself, in an historical sense; for, coming to brilliant visibility as a girl, during and after the tenure of her father, Theodore Roosevelt, as president, she had three great phases of effect in the capital, each with its special character.

The first of these was her young womanhood, during her White House years, when she was known around the world as Princess Alice; gave the energy of her style to a shade of blue; established her high originality in public as a lifelong attribute; released her great share of the Roosevelt vitality into the national character; and without working for what other ladies—opera prima donnas, theatre stars, British suffragettes—had to seek professionally, she became the embodiment of the sort of glamour that demands imitation, though her particular graces of wit and intelligence, both often reckless as she expressed them, remained unique.

The second phase came when, as wife to Speaker of the House Nicholas Longworth, she spent her middle years in active politics, whether making campaign speeches from the brass-balustraded platforms of private railroad cars or, in evening drawing rooms, bringing legislators into line with deadly banter. She campaigned for her father against William Howard Taft; she campaigned for her husband in his biennial suits for his seat in the House; she gave loud and merry aid and comfort to the opponents of Woodrow Wilson; she twice, in famous verbal cartoons, did hilarious damage to a presidential nominee—it was Thomas E. Dewey—helping him to lose his two runs for the White House by describing him, in his first, as "the little man on the wedding cake," and, in his second, by declaring that he could not win even then, since "a soufflé never rises twice." With her closest friend and political ally of the old days, Ruth Hanna McCormick (Simms), she worked in every sort of job of participatory democracy except that of seeking office herself. Her names, Roosevelt and Longworth, were of value in these undertakings; but they would not have worked in and of themselves. It took her spirited character, her civilized gaiety, and her all-out convictions to make her a figure of political consequence—one of the first American women to achieve this position.

As the years drew on, she knew personal sorrows—the loss of her father, her husband, her daughter, her son-in-law, her best friend. The third style of her life seemed to emerge in her sensitive and sensible survival of such changes. Her life became symbolic, as it remained to her dying day—a matter of presiding socially, rather than of acting politically. Her unsparing realism—in which she spared herself least of all—continued to see life as an affair deserving of serious judgment delivered with the lightest, most precise of witticisms. In these, the great range of her mind was marvelously evident. Her originality of thought and statement was supported by a fine tangle of reference and style coming out of her acquaintance with the world's interesting persons and her appetite for reading. All the new books poured in upon her. It was said she read all night, consenting to take a nap from daybreak until noon. It was then that the morning's letters, telegrams, and phone messages had their turn, and the liveliest personal life in Washington its daily send-off.

For many of her friends, it reached its peak late in the afternoon, when Mrs. Longworth received in her upstairs drawing room. Her house was obscured by heavy, deliberately unpruned vines—a miniature jungle over the recessed approach to her door, masking it from the incessant traffic of Massachusetts Avenue.

ii

The door is opened for you by a uniformed maid. You say your name as if it were Strether or Selden, and give her your hat, gloves, and stick (these accessories are often more ideal than real, but they suggest the atmosphere of a house out of pages in Henry James or Edith Wharton). The light is dim as you mount stairs to the next floor. At the turn of the stair you pass by a great pelt of a grizzly bear, hanging in reference to the trophied life of T.R., the Rocky Mountain hunter. From the stairwell you enter a first drawing room facing the avenue. Here, between the windows, is Peter Hurd's coolly elegant portrait of Mrs. Longworth, painted when she was eighty-one years of age. Against an abstract background of pearl grey, she is shown wearing a heather tweed jacket, a short string of pearls, and a model of that famous black hat, with its round crown and wide, down-turned brim, which she has adopted as her hat for occasions. Her eyes are grey-blue. Her hair, swept lightly past her ears, is silvery. Her face is pale, with a remote coral glow. In repose, her expression is faintly melancholy, even in the hint of the smile lifting her cheeks. The portrait is a lovely first glimpse of her, and of the depth of feeling rarely otherwise seen in the high spirits that play across her face in conversation.

You turn to the left, perhaps hearing voices already there before you, including her own, the strongest, in words spoken at high speed to keep pace with her flow of ideas, accompanied by hoots of Rooseveltian laughter, and you enter the second drawing room, where, near a superb portrait of her granddaughter Joanna Sturm by Henriette Wyeth, Mrs. Longworth presides at the tea tray set before her at her small, low settee. She may, or may not, be wearing the black hat. She hails you, as she does every guest, in a burst of gaiety; you are introduced around, told what is being talked about as you arrive, given your tea and the thinnest known buttered slices of a particular white bread, of which there is a generous pyramid on a silver dish amidst all the other apparatus of the tea ceremony. The company—it is never large for tea—is ranged on low chairs or ottomans, facing the hostess.

The first element of the room is comfort, with no attempt to state a style except that most genuine of all styles: the expression, here the profusion, of diverse objects adhering to a biography. Small standing photographs, most of them presenting recognizable personages, on cloth-covered surfaces; a grand piano; some old shadowy paintings, probably "good," in dim gold frames; lamps with pleated silk shades; a Chinese painting, almost wall-high, of a glaring tiger; flowers on several tables; dark, rich rugs; a mild golden light; nothing "matching;" everything well used; the chairs and sofas so placed that even when empty they suggest continuing conversation, for this is a house of talk. The temperature cool. On a small table to Mrs. Longworth's left is a telephone. This may ring several times during tea and be dealt with briskly, in a manner that may even include for the invisible caller a description of who's here and what is being talked about. Mrs. Longworth's telephone "presence" is strong, her voice vibrant, her laugh caught up in her words. Telephone calls are not protracted; end abruptly, with no tapering off in any word of conclusion. Back to the tea circle, and the drawn curtains, which have established evening within, though late afternoon may still be rushing by in the avenue traffic outside. Out of separate occasions a composite hour, its scandals and credulities, its romping dialogue, come into memory's compass.

iii

To suggest her grasp on life itself, you have only to note that, in her late eighties, Mrs. Longworth is delightfully pretty. People always speak of "good bones" as the great lasting ingredient of beauty in age; and the item has its place here. But there is more. It is her whole bearing, which carries dashing comeliness. She sits erect on her sofa against the wall, looking very small, and, but for the energy of her every word and gesture, she might appear frail—which taken objectively she surely must be. Yet the animation in her pale eyes, full of the light of her darting intelligence, and the quick turn of her small, neat, finely shaped head, and the onrush of her speech, with its hilariously precise vocabulary, delivered in an accent comfortably placeless though unmistakably aristocratic, and in a strong, finely placed voice, get rid at once of the notion that age, apart from matters of long experience of people and style, has anything to do with how you regard her. She is a master of the art of dialogue, in the high tradition of drawing-room comedy, though you sometimes hope she will go in for the monologue, and, yes, at times she creates a sort of aria, or in the classical French dramatic sense, a *tirade*, in which by lightning-quick association of ideas, she spins out an anecdote, a characterization, a judgment, which unhappily lacks its Boswell. All this is far from artless. She knows her powers, plays them according to her audience, and carries off her effects through astute improvisation. "As good as a play," in the old Briticism; and all too often, her callers have come for a show, though the most frequent ones are those who love her beyond all the rhetoric and her status as an institution. It is a measure of her absolute self-awareness that she once said, after some reported exchange that made the tears roll down her listener's cheeks in laughter, "You know, *I sell myself. . . .*" So she shares in the sense of a performance that attends her amidst people.

At her gatherings, her granddaughter is often present. Joanna Sturm, in her twenties, is the closest "family" left to Mrs. Longworth, and has lived with her grandmother for a number of years. There is no sense of one "taking care" of the other, but on the part of the elder, there is now and then a mock challenge of the young woman's presence. Joanna often knows what is coming, sits a little removed, saying little, gazing steadily with her clear grey eyes, sometimes prompting her grandmother to say, with a small howl of drollery, "Joanna disapproves of me when I say" whatever it is. Joanna makes no move to contradict this. When she does speak, it is as rapidly as her grandmother, with as much crisp sense and charm. She reads as voraciously as Mrs. Longworth, is a frequent traveler to far places—the American West, the Arabian Near East—and at large parties in the house, when several groups necessarily form, one such always gathers around her for her calm beauty and quickness of mind. She bears a strong resemblance to an early photograph of Alice Roosevelt.

It is never long until the subject of the other Roosevelts comes up—the FDRs. Here there is always matter for damage. In her autobiography, *Crowded Hours*, published in 1933, Mrs. Longworth remarked that she had "a proclivity toward malice that occasionally comes over me"—a simple acceptance of a trait that, reported second hand, sometimes seems cruel, but that, received direct, with all the lively airs of zestful comedy, finds itself invested with skill and charm, and what remains is not always wounding, but only amusing, with nothing of the serious attack about it, or the attempt to missionize opinions. In her many references to the non–Oyster Bay branch of the family, there does remain, though, a strong flavor of old partisan loyalties to her father's first political home, the Republican party. In her response to the fact that her cousin Franklin won his way as a Democrat to what Mrs. Longworth always refers to as "The House" (and we know she means her childhood home of seven years at 1600 Pennsylvania Avenue), there is a chaffing mockery of what must always have struck her as a wild aberration of politics. She and Franklin and Eleanor were close in their youth. Perhaps she once admired him; perhaps she once felt sorry for her plain female cousin. These days, giving a scene on her sofa, Mrs. Longworth says, after the Lucy Mercer story became public:

"Oh! I was so glad for Franklin. Poor creature. It was time he had a little fun."

That this fun was what broke the heart and changed the life of the president's wife makes no change in a lifelong opinion. Eleanor was *always* earnest. She was *"oh, so good."* She was *"worthy"*—an inflection on this, which mocked the whole idea. There is a little hint of never-lost wonder that so handsome, amusing, light-hearted, if not too bright, a cousin should have married Eleanor.

"Have I ever done you my Eleanor face?"

"Oh, no. Would you?"

An immediate transformation, hard to credit. The exquisite small head, with its finely proportioned features, turns into a caricature of her cousin Eleanor—teeth prominent, eyes soberly searching, body slumping, head thrust forward from hunched shoulders as if in search of worthiness itself. It is a scandal, and when in a few seconds the pose is dropped, the general laughter includes none merrier than that of the actress.

"I do a number of others. Remind me one day."

Various presidencies play a large part in Mrs. Longworth's

life and talk. She accepts them all, not entirely impartially, but with a sense that since they come and go, and since she remains on stage and who she always has been, it is a sort of obligation for her to be nonpartisan and grant due attention to the incumbent. Her judgment, of course, goes farther in personal terms. The Lyndon Johnsons are mentioned.

"I like them both," she says. "I've known them, of course, forever. He's an enormously effective man. It is amazing how many people who think they have judgment miss the fact that he is highly intelligent. . . . *She* is an extraordinary woman. I do like her so much. She does ring true."

The Kennedys?

"Of course, they all delight me. Jack was a *charmeur.* Some people can impersonate intelligence and then wake up to find they possess it. I did love what Mrs. K. did to The House. And there was always what was so often lacking in other regimes."

"?"

"Good talk." A gust of amusement. "Did I ever tell you about Bobby and the mountain? . . . You of course remember that preposterous affair of the Canadian mountain which the brothers and some of the rest went out to climb after Jack's death, and how they took along a flag specially run up for the purpose, and unfurled it at the top—a Kennedy flag, something no one had ever heard of before, with a device—I suppose a fantasy of heraldry run up by loving hands at home. Soon after the conquest of the mountain, and the planting of the flag, when they bestowed the name Mount Kennedy on the helpless rock, I saw Bobby; he was here at a party. I attacked him." Her eyes dance with merriment. "I said to him: 'Very well for naming the mountain, I suppose, but really: the flag is too much of a muchness.'" She always loved provoking a response, and had one then. "Bobby was intantly in a rage with me; all black glares and an Irish flush. He was speechless for a moment, looking for some way to come back at me. Then he found it. I could see his thoughts on his face. He was talking to a very old woman, and this gave him the clue. He said in a fury, 'Alice, have you made plans and given instructions for your funeral?' For he thought the best way to wound me was to make me think of my own death. 'Don't be an idiot,' I said; 'of course I have, even down to the pallbearers.' He glared at me, and I said, 'It is all arranged for you to be one, and I've given you a partner, and you'll both sit side by side in the front pew, the two of you, you and Dick Nixon!'" She laughs briefly at the high ceiling. "Ah, how furious that made him! . . . I love Bobby; we are the best of friends." This is before the second tragedy of the brothers.

A snub of a more lethal kind is described with joy. During the Eisenhower administration she was invited to a state dinner at The House, and the White House arranged for Senator Joseph R. McCarthy to escort her that evening—a masterpiece of obtuse ineptitude. Bringing a senior-prom nosegay in cellophane, the luckless man, then at the height of his obscene antics in the Senate, came to call for her.

"He wore white tie, carried a tall silk hat, and bore up under an opera cape with white satin lining thrown back on his shoulder: an elderly chorus boy with a blue jaw. When I came down the long stairway, he greeted me by my first name. I paused on the lowest step. Could I believe my ears!" She smiles in delight at what is to come. "'Senator McCarthy,' I said, 'my secretary calls me by my first name. My hairdresser may do so if he likes. My father's chauffeur used to do so. To you, I am Mrs. Longworth. Come along.'"

As to presidents, her own father was not immune from her analytical strikes. She once said of T.R. that he always had to be the corpse at every funeral and the bride at every wedding. In her book of the thirties, she described how cronies from the Congress came to play poker with Nicholas Longworth, one of whom was Senator Warren G. Harding, who as president held for some time the championship for presiding over a corrupt administration. She didn't find him personally culpable. He was, in her judgment, not a bad man—"he was just a slob." His wife, who got herself up like a walking floor lamp in the period of tassels and fringe, was a relentless shrew. She pronounced her husband's name most remarkably. It went, says Mrs. Longworth, something like this—"Wurr-rran. Wurr-rran." And the impersonation actually evokes that unlucky woman, with her fussiness of dress, her pince-nez, which, gathering a pinch of flesh at the low center of her brow, gave her a look of permanent head-ache, and her black band, which held her neck together. Another presidential wife comes in for a performance, too— Mrs. Longworth's face disappears; in its place, the dropped eyelids, the mindless adoption of whatever might be occur-ring, the thick loose outthrust lower lip, together with a slow, mechanical turning of the head from right to left, back and forth, conjures up, absolutely, the look of a passive camel.

"How on earth can you do it?" people ask at such trans-formations when she resumes herself. She shrugs. She sup-poses it is some knack of not only looking like, but *feeling* like, her victims, for an instant or two. This kind of skilled farcing stands for more than japery; it is proof of a gift for knowing very sharply the essential life in anyone else. She could describe it in words, she could enact it in being.

iv

This sort of hilarious communication played a large part in an audience she gave to a British journalist, a young man named Aitken, a grandnephew of Lord Beaverbrook. He came to Washington with a CBS crew to tape a television interview with her. It was a virtuoso performance by both participants. She filmed very handsomely. Her spontaneous remarks, spoken at her usual lightning speed, sparkled and danced right off the screen. She had moments when she would speak seriously, looking earnestly at her visitor, lean-ing forward a trifle, her brows raised, her eyes luminous and sober; and in another moment, the old mischief was back, and the style once again was epigrammatic, irreverent, the very essence of civilized badinage. She talked politics, and about the life in Washington; she candidly weighed presidents, and their wives, and public characters, and policies. Aitken asked her if she thought her father was a Great Man, and she replied that she didn't know; nobody knew; it was too soon to know for another hundred years; perhaps he was, perhaps not; but she did know that he gave his best. It was a startling objectivity to come from a presidential daughter, and it gave a sudden insight into her character, capable as it was of a pragmatic realism, which, beyond comedy or malice, explained, if it might not always excuse, the mockeries, funny or harsh, in her inexhaustible repertoire of social commentary. (Sample: those who "talked" a cause that others enacted were "echo-activists.")

When the television episode was over, I telephoned her from Connecticut, saying among other things that she was the last great actress of drawing-room comedy. I was referring to how such comedy had to rely mostly on manner. Manner, above all, carried the text. Without manner even the most brilliant scene fell flat. With it even the poorest scene went along with sustained energy and wit. When manner and text were equal to each other, as they always were for Mrs. Longworth, high style was the result. I had in mind such artists as Mrs. Fiske, Ethel Barrymore, Gladys Cooper, Edith Evans, Katharine Hepburn. Mrs. Longworth never acknowledged a compliment directly, but there was a sense that all this pleased her, and she turned it aside by asking,

"Don't you think young Aitken altogether good at it?" (I.e., his job.) "Most of those inquisitors are so banal. Asking the right question has everything to do with it."

"Your answers were marvelous."

"But you've no idea," she said, "how much they cut out of the tape! All the best parts, by which I mean the wicked parts. I said whatever came into my head, and I did some of my faces, but they thought much of it too dangerous"—she laughed—"and the twenty minutes you saw was a much edited version. Too bad. Still, I suppose."

Within two weeks, I received a telegram inviting me to dinner at her house, black tie, eight o'clock, and when I telephoned to accept, she told me with glee that CBS had given her a tape of the full, uncut interview, and she would have it run off after dinner "and we will all howl."

There must have been twenty-four for dinner, including the Peter Hurds from New Mexico, the Andrew Wyeths from Chadds Ford, and the Douglass Caters (still in Washington, with Douglass brewing the materials for his excellent Washington novel *Dana*, which would include a brief but living sketch of Mrs. Longworth as Lady M.). She received everybody in the first upstairs drawing room. She was resplendent in the evening dress she had settled upon as her permanent model, always the same design, if in many varying color schemes. It was a high-necked, long-sleeved, floor-length dress of metallic brocade. It had pockets along the side, and she often stood with her hands thrust into them, her feet stanced apart, a figure of happy authority and strength. She took care that people met, if they didn't know each other already. Joanna was there, and some vital young Roosevelt men cousins. Mrs. Longworth moved about the two drawing rooms while the cocktails went around, and then when guests began to sit down in clusters, she took to her little sofa with Henriette and Peter Hurd, for all they had to talk about since they'd last met.

Dinner arrangements were on the grand side, rather like an intimate version of the banquet gear displayed in Apsley House—much bossed silver and gold, which spoke of family, and The House; the wines in heavy crystal; footmen working along in back of the chairs. Best of all, talk went on at normal voice levels but nonetheless animated for that. As for animation, the hostess, with Andrew Wyeth beside her, was enjoying the event more visibly and volubly than anyone else.

During dinner, matters were going forward in the front rooms—a movie projector was set up, chairs were turned to face an unrolled screen, and cushions thrown down for those who would have to sit on the floor to see the uncut CBS interview. When everyone was settled for the show, Mrs. Longworth called out to one of her young great-nephews, at his post of operator, to start the reel. She stood, she wandered in the little spaces among the chairs and cushions, and delighting in the film as much as anyone there, she cried out from time to time, "Oh! This was cut! You'll see why" or "Watch for this, now!" or "I could have said more at that point," and, in general, providing a running commentary to supplement the entertainment, and leading the laughter, which time and again erupted from the audience. It is almost useless to try to describe live *performance*, and a synopsis of the epigrams, impersonations, subject matter would take as much space as this whole piece. One sample on the film characteristic of the outspoken, self-unsparing play of her memory was this: when, vacationing in the Adirondacks, Vice-President Theodore Roosevelt and his family received word that President William McKinley had been shot and was on his deathbed, the young Alice (she was seventeen years old), exclaimed, "Oh! Hurrah! We're going to be president!"

Put simply, the screen gave us a recorded personality at its fullest play; and alive in our midst, enjoying it as much, if not more, than anyone else, was the original personality itself, embodied in a being of immense style who had no truck with either hollow vanity or false modesty. That was the point of the affair: she was beyond caring about the terms of her effect, so long as it amused her to animate it for the amusement of others.

Conversation followed the film. Everyone had seen and

heard much to set it going. She had done a sequence about the Hardings which reminded her that recently she had received a new biography of President Harding, which, by a court injunction in favor of the Harding heirs, had had to be published with many excisions. The publisher dramatized this censorship by leaving large blank spaces in the book to show where the forced cuts had been made. But never mind: she knew what was left out: come along—and she led Douglass Cater, Peter Hurd, and me up to her bedroom on the next floor. There, in a profusion of books on a wide table, was the Harding book, and, with it, she had a set of proofs sent her by the author.

"These are the uncut proofs," she said gleefully, "I've had a wildly good time collating the two texts. Look here!" And she found a blank half-page in the book, and the exiled paragraph in the proofs, and showed them together. On any level, to any degree, the passion to know exhilarated her; and so did any opportunity to subvert pompousness, flout repressiveness, or deflate pretension. I looked around. The room was crowded with books and memorabilia. It was otherwise unremarkable in its old, simple, not even "good," furniture. It had the air of being undisturbed for decades. Books stood in rows or lay in piles wherever possible. I remembered with amusement that it was my habit to send an occasional bundle of books to Mrs. Longworth and Joanna, to share copies of some I had particularly liked. One time, after something of an interval, came a note from Mrs. Longworth saying, "I grovel—for never telling you my enjoyment and gratitude for BOOKS." Someone in Washington once repeated to me how Mrs. Longworth had declared with light irony, "Paul Horgan is educating me." Ha.

v

Dining one night in Washington at the Caters', I was amazed to hear that Mrs. Longworth was coming, though she had only three weeks earlier endured surgery for breast cancer—

a double mastectomy. When the guest of honor arrived, she was established by Libby Cater on a sofa near the fireplace, and Libby took me to her, saying, "You won't be sitting with Mrs. L. at dinner, so I want you to have a chance to talk with her now." Mrs. L. looked splendid, not at all like a convalescent patient.

She said to me, "I must give you my outrageous remark for the evening immediately and have it done with. The subject is surgical."

"I'm all ears."

"Well, then," she said, bracing her diminutive figure in its long metallic folds, "I claim to be the only topless octogenarian in Washington."

If there was any vanity here, it lay only in the extremity of the wit. Her indifference to ailments, or perhaps her power of discipline, showed strikingly on the occasion of another evening. Vera—Madame Igor—Stravinsky was to have an exhibition of her paintings in Washington. I was going there with her and Robert Craft for the opening. I telephoned Mrs. Longworth to ask if I might bring them to tea.

"No! I'll give you a dinner party!"

A date was fixed; the event took place as planned. It was another evening for a couple of dozen particularly interesting people. Madame and the hostess hit it off splendidly from the first moment. Mrs. Longworth came downstairs a little late, after my party arrived. She was in tearing spirits throughout the evening. All the more, then, was I astonished to hear from my dinner partner how she had been told on the telephone earlier the same day by Mrs. Longworth that the dinner would have to go on without her, for she felt too ill to leave her bed—because of a chronic ailment, which was unpredictable but which sometimes forced her to cancel engagements. Joanna would take over.

"I never expected to see Alice this evening," said the lady.

"But look at her!" I said. "Listen to her!" For I sat at her side, and she was at that moment having a swift bout of verbal Ping-Pong with her other neighbor—I think it was William Walton—which had them both laughing. And so it went all evening. Her vitality flowed through the whole gathering, and the effect—not imposed or intended—was to lift spirits, let others sound at their best, create an airy fabric of dialogue and sense, which some few can do, and most cannot, of themselves. Toward midnight, when people began to drift away, as Madame and Craft and I went to her to say good night, Mrs. Longworth stood in the wide doorway between the two drawing rooms, and as if reluctant to see us go, gave a little supplementary show, saying:

"Have you ever seen my gorilla?"

When we said we had not, she, in her subdued robe of gold and silver threads, did a face, and made a lumbering parentheses of arms and a hulking of her tiny shoulders that, like all artful dramatic transformations, abolished for the observer the original scale or proportion of the performer, so that only an astonishing view of the representation remained. I suppose it was in something of this sense that Maurice Baring said of Sarah Bernhardt—who was plain and unremarkable offstage—that "she could act beauty. Great beauty." So we saw a most convincing gorilla for seconds, in our moment of leaving. Mrs. Longworth seemed not to want the party to be over. How to let go any moment of amusement or response? She glanced about. Her eye fell on the long Chinese painting of the tiger, with its fierce eye and swept mustache.

"Oh: see that," she cried. "That is my portrait of Dean Acheson"—and in truth the likeness, the caricature, was more than fanciful. But, alas, good night, good night.

vi

With cavalier grace, she managed any absurdities visited upon her from forces of the times, such as commercial restlessness in her neighborhood on Massachusetts Avenue.

Mrs. L.

Some old houses adjoining hers were torn down to make way for a new hotel. During occasional visits to Washington, I would see the hotel going up, and marvel how they could build it actually adjoining her north wall without inflicting every sort of inconvenience. But nobody imagined the one that actually occurred. The builders, about their enthusiastic work, knocked a great hole through her bedroom wall.

What on earth!

Yes, but they were most chagrined. Shambled becomingly. Made offers.

Offers? Repairs?

Yes, of course, to close up the hole, which seemed the minimum. But they went further, and proposed to paint not only the new plaster, but all the rooms on that floor, to match.

And they did?

No. Too much bother. Think of moving everything; it was not worth the trouble. It would, perhaps, even have led to repainting the entire house, which would be unendurable.

There it rested—though not forever. The hotel people, perhaps feeling that something promising had been struck up through the mishap, came around when the building was finished and declared that they intended to have a Grand Opening, and they thought it would be fine if their distinguished neighbor would agree to be present at the dedication, and cut the ribbon.

It struck her as highly amusing.

Did she do it?

Oh, yes, certainly. How pompous not to have! But a while later, they were back with another idea, and she wasn't sure about this one.

"What was that?"

"You see, they are going to have a new dining room in the hotel, and they want to name it 'Alice's Restaurant,' and have me cut the ribbon there, too. What do you think?"

"Good God, no." There was at the time a hit movie called *Alice's Restaurant*, which was a rock musical trading on all the dejected and sometimes ruinous hang-ups of the youth counterculture, including drugs. "You can get anything you want / At Alice's Restaurant," ran the nudging refrain of the musically illiterate title song of the piece. "Do you know about the movie?" I asked.

"No, I haven't seen it. Of course I have heard of it," she said.

Having seen it, I explained what it was, what it stood for.

"At best," I added, "the hotel is again exploiting your good nature, and at worst, in this case, making a vulgar joke. Since you've asked, I'd strongly advise against doing it."

I believe that was the end of the matter; though not of Mrs. Longworth's encounter with the youth culture. Some time afterward, in a long-distance conversation, she asked if I had ever seen the rock musical called *Hair*?

"No."

"But you must. I saw it last night," she cried. "There is a road company now playing in Washington. It is ravishing. They really *are* flower children! I quite fell in love with all of them. Why haven't you seen it?"

"I am sure it is too loud for me."

"Yes, true, it is deafening. I kept closing my eyes and falling asleep to get away from the noise. Though I did wake up in time for the nude scene. Yes, I found them all utterly beguiling, and after the play I went back to see all the young people, and I asked the whole company to tea with me, and they came yesterday. It was enchanting. . . . Why don't you come down and see it with me again, and I'll ask them all to tea for *you*?"

This happened not to be possible. There is no doubt that it was sad to miss an opportunity to see Mrs. Longworth casting her spell over a group four generations removed from herself. But I did not marvel, any longer, over her brisk and familiar watch upon the world as it ran along before her. In the late spring of 1973, I was in Washington again, and was asked to come round late in the afternoon. As I came in, she heard me, and before any other word, she declaimed in delight, with no hint of sentiment for or against, but only with zest for the spectacle itself,

"Aren't you absolutely loving it all?" She meant Watergate.

vii

On her eighty-ninth birthday, after everyone's fond marvelings, she disposed of these, and looked ahead, like a presiding lady in her own city, leading its public antics.

"On my ninetieth," she said in ringing tones, "we're going to put a tent over Dupont Circle and dance in the streets!"

The spirited plan did not come off. She died in her sleep on 20 February 1980, at ninety-six.

But well before that, wondering about her increasing frailty, I telephoned late one Sunday evening. It was reassuring when she herself answered.

"Oh," I said. "It is you!"

"Yes. I'm in the kitchen."

"The kitchen?"

"Yes. I sent them all off for the evening. I said to leave just a bite for me. I'm after it now—meat for the cat." Laughter.

ROUBEN MAMOULIAN

IN THE ROCHESTER

RENAISSANCE

i

Rouben Mamoulian, who died at the age of ninety in Hollywood on 4 December 1987, was of course widely known as the director, for the stage, of such productions as *Porgy*, *Porgy and Bess, Oklahoma!, Carousel,* and *Marco Millions*; and, for the screen, of *Applause, City Streets, Dr. Jekyll and Mr. Hyde, Love Me Tonight,* and *Queen Christina.* All these, and many others of his films, had international limelight played upon them. But for three years, long before these famous undertakings began, he was at work in America in one of the most interesting periods of our modern culture. I was so lucky as to be closely associated with him in those first years of his life in this country. In these notes I try to communicate how he began here, what he was like, and something of the nature of his extraordinary gifts.

ii

During the period 1923–1926, the city of Rochester, New York, was the scene of a promising cultural ferment. What was taking place was in a sense a one-man renaissance, and the man was George Eastman, the Kodak magnate. He had reigned for decades as the undisputed first citizen of the town, and his benefactions were many and intelligent. His labor policy at the Eastman plant was said to be a model that other American industrial titans would do well to imitate. His gifts to the University of Rochester were numbered in the tens of millions of dollars; but he gave more than money. He gave his character, that rational, dry, cool, shrewd, and modest view of life, which, combined with his industrial originality, and his immense fortune, made him a remarkably effective man—though occasionally, like all men, he had unaccountable opinions, which in his case were magnified by his powerful position from the merely personal to the official and compelling.

But on the whole he set by his mere presence in the city a standard of decorum, self-respect, and prestige that reached down through the levels of Rochester society. Everyone, from bank presidents to newsboys to hostesses, spoke his name with its democratic title: "Mist' Eastman." He lived in sober magnificence in a great house on the town's most important residential avenue. His austerity of character was carried over into his social life. The daily papers ran little news of his private activity, but everyone knew that he gave large parties enlivened by music played by his personal organist upon a concealed console; or sometimes there was a string quartet. In a life of industrial efficiency, without many comforts or pleasures aside from big-game hunting, and the freedom of movement that attended his life as a septuagenarian bachelor, Mist' Eastman had one taste that gave him much pleasure to gratify, and that brought grace and

[*196*

warmth into a life otherwise, according to any available evidence, unemotional. It was his fondness for music.

But even here he believed that people should first of all help themselves, as he had done throughout his entire career. Once they gave earnest signs of doing so, he was, if convinced of the probity of their purposes, usually ready to help with that of which he had more than they, which was money. (During his last years it was a Rochester belief that his income was one million dollars a month.) And so when it seemed a good idea to found a symphony orchestra, he subscribed heavily after he was shown that a large bloc of citizens had pledged substantial sums to support the Rochester Philharmonic Orchestra, not leaving him to support it alone, as he could well have afforded to do.

A self-educated man, he believed in education, as his gifts to the University of Rochester attested. Among them was the Eastman Theatre and School of Music, a beautiful establishment designed by McKim, Mead and White housing a grand auditorium, a chamber-music hall dedicated to the memory of his mother (oddly perpetuating not her married but her maiden name, Fanny Kilbourn), and studios and classrooms for every branch of musical culture. Over the colonnade of pilasters let into the main front of the building were engraved the words "For the enrichment of community life." Culture was once again the end product of commercial energy, as if history said, "Secure the markets, and then spend your gains for the benefit of the spirit."

The classical limestone shell of Rochester's cultural institution was rapidly filled with all the human elements, which in their temperamental complexity finally worked out to the performance of music. It was the era of the most sophisticated of the silent movies. The Eastman Theatre was for six days a week a temple of the cinema, with an impressive orchestra accompanying the films. That orchestra was the nucleus of the Philharmonic. On the seventh day, classical music took over the theatre, in concerts by local and visiting celebrities, the local Philharmonic, opera by the visiting Metropolitan company. Students in the music school had great opportunities under a distinguished faculty in sumptuous surroundings to learn their art—in every branch but one: the opera.

It was not long until that lack was filled. Not only was an opera department established in the school, but also a company was founded—the Rochester American Opera Company, which Mist' Eastman agreed to back for three years. He would then turn it loose, on the theory that during its growing pains it deserved patronage, but if in that period it had not proved itself popularly indispensable and self-supporting, then it had better be allowed to vanish. Here again was the democratic geometry that governed Mist' Eastman in so many of his activities. If the theorem cannot prove itself by demonstration to fulfill the desires of the people, it must fail.

The brilliant Russian tenor Vladimir Rosing had met and convinced Mist' Eastman on a transatlantic liner that the brilliant theatre and school of music in Rochester should be the seat of America's first modern opera company, whose artistic standards would be fresh, whose taste would refresh the dramatic conventions of the traditional opera, and whose members should be young, handsome, plausible figures of drama. The concept appealed to Mist' Eastman.

The following autumn found Rosing in Rochester. He had visited cities all over America to audition young singers for his company. He found two or three dozen promising principals, and counted on the vocal students of the Eastman School of Music to fill out the chorus. The ideals of the repertory company were egalitarian. Singers had modest but adequate scholarships. There were to be no stars. Carmen herself this week might next week find herself in the chorus of *Rigoletto*. The musical resources of orchestra, conductors, répétiteurs were all available. But opera was to be at least half drama in the Rochester scheme, and to bring dramatic values to the company, Rosing imported from London a young Russian-Armenian stage director whom he had met abroad, whose work had already commanded respect and interest in Moscow, Paris, and London, and whose name was Rouben Mamoulian. Together these two Russians would serve as co-directors of the new-style opera theatre.

iii

Mamoulian was then in his mid-twenties. He had a distinctly European look, underlined by the beautiful London suits he wore. He was tall, slender, black-haired. His face was pale, and his finely shaped head was always held high. What otherwise might have seemed a bearing of cold, remote superiority was saved and animated by the brilliance of his dark eyes, and by the sympathetic warmth of his smile, when he gave it; when, in effect, his smile was earned by the person he was with. He wore, at first, pince-nez, which seemed like a badge of culture, a symptom of intellectual maturity for a very young man in a very authoritative position. To citizens like us, who had not been particularly used to nose-pinching glasses on anyone but President Wilson, there was almost something exotic in the habit. What we judged by, at first, of course, were mere externals. He wore black fedora hats. His long black overcoat was lined with fur, which turned over to make a great collar. He carried fresh gloves always, and a gold-headed black stick. Proud of such directorial grandeur, the young gentlemen of the company felt more like opera singers under such a man. He wore spats. Baritones and tenors from Altoona, Oberlin, Sacramento, Dallas, began to wear spats, too, as if under sanction from the great artistic capitals of the Old World. In the lapel of his lounge coat he habitually wore two or three dried and faded violets, a highly personal and individual touch, that (for all we knew and in much we said) hinted at a love affair left behind in Europe, a ballerina, a leading actress, a marchioness. Youth and music and theatre together broadened the appreciation.

The exciting days of the convening of the company were bounteous with promises for the future. Rosing made an address to the school of music at large in Kilbourn Hall, describing the aims of the company and its policies. As a newly enrolled music student, I was in that audience, listening with the same excitement as the members of the company. In all his plans, Rosing mentioned nothing about scenery, an art director, the physical mounting of the operas about to be undertaken. I needed a job to see me through my study of music. I produced overnight a sheaf of drawings for various operas I knew, and took them to him the next day. My authority for this bumptious venture was based wholly on my having planned and painted the scenery for two plays, a year or two before in school. After several hilarious incidents having to do more with me than with Rosing or Mamoulian, but within forty-eight hours, I was engaged to do the designs and paint the scenery for the opera company.

I remember that when Mamoulian saw my drawings, he reserved his countenance, looking at me over his glasses, smoking his pipe, and smiling with an eloquent shade of opinion that seemed to say, "You are a pretty self-confident young man, to submit things like these, and I am not fooled by their assumption of experience and skill. Still, they have spirit, and show a love for the theatre, and perhaps something may come of it." I was then nineteen years old, an unpublished writer, an unexhibited painter, an unheard singer, an unseen actor, and, above all, an unrevealed scenic artist. But I was entirely at home in the conception of myself in any of these roles, with literature as my chief love. From the first, with humor and sympathy, Mamoulian took me on such various terms, so that our friendship grew the more I learned from him.

After the first administrative phases of the company, the

schooling of the members began. Here Mamoulian showed us the great and real aspect of himself. The gravity and restraint of his casual contacts with us, the sense of exquisite manner and formality, vanished; and in the drama classes, he became a column of energy. His English was at that time thoughtful and cultivated, but it was not yet fluent. You felt that he was always just ahead of his sentences, consciously selecting and arranging his words. Later, of course, he became fluent and wonderfully expressive, idiomatic, and at the same time original in his wit and exactness of statement. But that early search for the language made him even more expressive in other ways. His power of concentration was extraordinary. He was so possessed by the ideas and the atmosphere of the dramatic exercise he was working on that the whole company (including me, for I was a singing scenic artist and one day might, and did, have a role or two) felt separately and powerfully the impact of his intellect and his disciplined emotion.

He seated the class (the company) all about the walls of a large studio in the wing reserved for the opera company, and stood in the center, revolving slowly in his smart London shoes as he spoke. You felt that his dramatic method was his own, though based on his training in the Vakhtangoff Studio of the Moscow Art Theatre. You felt that he had a crystal-clear image of what a given character was like, what whole-life background created it for the author, what farthest ripples of dramatic meaning it would have in its spreading touch with other lives, and what common human experiences in all of us it could refer to, so arousing in us its primary meaning.

He was even then a profound student of psychology. He came to his artistic problems with the double resources of intellect and emotion, and that very consciously. He knew that other people—actors, singers—were the materials of his art as a director. He knew that in them he must bring alive his vision. To do that, he knew he must share with them the maximum of his own experience and understanding, and so he reached us with every possible means. Discussion of ideas. References to other arts—painting, sculpture, literature, philosophy—in order to shed light from all possible quarters upon the musical and theatrical problem at hand. Wonderfully clear, immediate sketches or pantomimes of character, in which he would become a personality—a technique the apprentice singing-actors must learn to inhabit for themselves. Above all, exercises, exercises, exercises, and with all, concentration, concentration, concentration.

There were dullards in the group who wondered what on earth concentration had to do with acting. In their experience, concentration had to do with scowling over a geometry book, or memorizing something. For such misplaced Babbitts of the arts he would resort to demonstration. He said one time, "I will show you a scene, a commonplace from everyday life. You will not believe what I show you—you won't know what it is—if for a single second I drop my concentration of mind and feeling upon what I am trying to represent. But if at every second and with every gesture I concentrate wholly upon my own dramatic problem, you will see everything and you will believe everything, though I will use no props, no speech, no co-actors, and no program notes. One false move, or false idea, or incomplete memory, and my whole act will fall to pieces. Now watch."

He then took the center of the room and became someone. In his fine, rather finical British suit, with his faded violets, his pince-nez, and his spats, he changed before our eyes; he became a barber, receiving, seating, sheeting, and shaving a customer. The whole thing was in pantomime, yet we could see the instruments in his empty hands. We could glance with him out the window at the passing world on the sidewalk. We could hear the soundless conversation of the obsequious barber and the grunts of the reclining victim. We could hear the steam in the sterilizer and the clock on the wall. We could smell the eau de Cologne and the bay rum. We had a sense of the shape, size, and color of the barbershop. When the razor was getting dull, we knew it, and winced at its pull, and were relieved when the barber, smiling tolerantly at life's little trials, wiped the blade and stropped it to a singing sharpness. Our spirits rose as the sharpened blade went flashing and expert again at its task on the sodden jowl of the man in the chair. We knew every bulge of the recumbent figure and every protuberance of the heavy chair from the way the barber stepped—danced—around them, avoiding clumsy touches and contacts unwelcome to the customer. We knew the self-satisfaction, the self-respect and the social character of the barber himself. He was sly, and he was happy; he was clever, and he was a sadly limited man; he was vain, and his vanity was satisfied by small successes; he was an expert craftsman, and next year would probably add another chair and have someone under him to bully except when clients were present.

The astonishing performance took about fifteen minutes. It never faltered. There was not a false note, or a half-considered movement, or an incomplete gesture. The real barber, had he been before us, would have made his little fumbles, his inaccuracies of movement; but we would not have remembered him, or known much of anything about him. The pantomimed barber was perfection; raw material, observed, considered, and re-created with more meaning than any of us would have detected in actual life. The difference, of course, was art—an art moving in a human character, through a little period of time, before our eyes. And—said Mamoulian, after the customer had gone, and the barber had examined his money, his public charm laid off and his native distrust visible when he was alone—granting talent, the determining factor among all the others that must be brought to bear upon a dramatic problem was concentration. "Do you see?"

We saw. Even the skeptics saw. Such mastery of impersonation was an instrument of authority. Who among us could resist direction from a man who knew so clearly what he wanted and, himself, could do it better than anyone he was teaching?

How hard the simplest things were. He told us that it took the very best actors to cross a room and sit down in a chair in such a way as to be entirely convincing in the purposefulness and achievement of that commonplace act. What was so difficult about it? In natural life, people did it all the time. But in stage life, how many actors did you see who knew at a glance, with the unconscious exactness of real life, how many steps it should take to walk to the chair and sit down, without having to take, at the end, a longer step, or a shorter step, or a sidling step, to reach the chair naturally? Smiles of skepticism again. Very well, try it. The smiles vanished. Nobody came out even. The distance, the chair, the *act of doing it consciously*, defeated our novices. He asked us—any of us—to take the chair and place it anywhere. He would then walk to it with neither a step too few nor a step too many, and sit down. Extraordinary as it sounds, we were astonished and moved when he did just that.

What was he doing for us? Showing us clearly how many problems—and meanings—lie latent in commonplaces, once they are really perceived and their use in art is controlled, until perfect appropriateness and proportion come to define and limit and release those human reminders which are the materials of the artist.

iv

"Art is cash; not credit" was one of his dictums. Nothing could be taken for granted; the artist could not succeed on hearsay.

The statement could as properly have been applied to Mamoulian's own reputation in Rochester, professional and social. His achievements abroad were those of a young man, just making his first successes. (St. James's Theatre in London, Théâtre des Champs Elysées in Paris.) They did not then have international réclame, and his local effect in Rochester had to be built from scratch. But it was not long before his prestige among the company was high. He was patient but exacting. When he became irritated at a bad rehearsal or a poor performance, you always felt that it was on behalf of a high ideal that he scolded; not against a poor youngster who was differently educated from himself, and less talented. You felt that he had worked so hard for years to bring himself to his sharp perception and personal expressiveness that he had every right to expect that you would do the same. So the tears of a soprano, the chewed curses of a baritone, rarely indicated any resentment toward him; especially when after his analysis of unfaithful artistic attempts he would encourage the unsatisfactory wretch to try it again, again, again, and this time move a little closer toward both release and control. He would smile with real tenderness at the bothered girls who failed him, and with heartening stoutness at the boys. Very often the satisfaction of knowing improvement did follow.

There were occasional insurrectionists, of course; for the ego of the singer is enclosed in coolly impermeable glass, through which it looks out upon rivals and composers and conductors and directors as potential enemies. "I'm sorry, Mr. Mamoulian. I can't seem to grasp what you want. I do not *feel* it that way"—implying that such a grubby excuse would pass for artistic integrity. It was an unwillingness, of course, to yield the ego to that concept of the ensemble which was the director's responsibility. Patience; patience; self-control; and a few rehearsals later, the bridling ego was not only *feeling* it that way, but beginning to translate that feeling for others.

Aside from his intimate personal qualities, what gave him real authority as a creative director was the richness of his own culture. He knew more about the various contributing elements of a stage production than any of the artists separately charged with creating each. His knowledge and taste in music were superior, though he was not a performer (barring his boyhood study of the violin; he had been called upon to play it before the Tsar in Tiflis upon the occasion of an imperial visit to the capital of the Caucasus). He was widely read in dramatic and operatic literature, as well as in other kinds; and on many a day could tell American students things about their own national literature that they were uneasily short on. He was an amusing draughtsman, and liked to draw (as I did) on restaurant tables, menus, paper napkins; but beyond this, his love of the art of painting was nourished by a penetrating knowledge of the great visual art of the European past; and the authority of such taste made him immediately articulate in plans and criticisms of stage décors. We felt that he was closer than anyone we had ever heard of to embodying Gordon Craig's ideal for the régisseur—that he should know more about the writing of plays than the playwright, more of music than the composer, more of painting than the painter, more of acting than the actor.

News of such attainments was not slow in filtering through the school of music, the theatre, the society of the town. Very early, he became a personage. His vitality charged the young people working under him. The city began to be proud of the latest of Mist' Eastman's ventures, the Rochester American Opera Company, and awaited its first production eagerly. There was a fine atmosphere of talented energy all around it. The Rochester Renaissance had an ozone good to breathe.

v

He quickly became a figure of distinction in the houses of Rochester society. The grand street of the town was East Avenue, which reached its climax in Mist' Eastman's large stone house, with its park, greenhouses, and pipe organ. Mamoulian lived in rooms on the second floor of a hand-

some house in East Avenue. I remember them as full of heavy mahogany, green carpets, heavily silk-shaded lamps. Here he would spend studious evenings at home, surrounded by souvenirs of his far-away life in Europe. He would sometimes decree a winter literary evening, and invite me to join him. While the clock ticked distantly on the landing of the elegant 1910 stairway of the mansion, we would, in silence, but exchanging occasional looks of encouragement, confirmation, and progress, proceed with our separate compositions. Mine were likely to be sonnets, none of which survives. His, lyrical prose sketches of characters, or aphorisms of the theatre art, or philosophical tales in the style of Villiers de L'Isle-Adam or E. T. A. Hoffman. At the end of an hour or two, while snow fell outside the windows of Rochester, we would return to one another's society and read our efforts aloud. After an exchange of opinions ("Wonderful, but—", and "Admirable; yet don't you feel that if—"), I would take my leave and wander back to my lodgings, musing upon the many facets to his mind, the spontaneous and spirited humor he played over his friendships, and the deep solid core of disciplined talent from which came his primary energy.

On other evenings, he would go forth from his rooms to the drawing rooms and dinner tables of Rochester society, splendidly dressed, with a higher collar, a whiter tie, longer and better-pleated tails than anyone else's in town, excepting only possibly those of Eugene Goossens, the elegant British conductor of the Philharmonic. He carried with him a sort of unspoken protocol, a grand-ducal dignity and reserve that made his arrival anywhere something of an event, and that—once friendship had penetrated it—set off the warm ingenuities and generosities of his companionship delightfully.

It was interesting to see him becoming an American. Like all foreigners, he enjoyed our slang, the undressed aspects of our thought, humor, and speech. He quickly picked up

something of our style, and would deliver himself through it of two things—the sense of becoming at home among us, and a fresh appreciation of how we said things. He responded immediately to our sort of vitality, the headlong energy with which Americans undertook things, and he revealed many things to us about ourselves which perhaps we had not noticed through taking much for granted. He came with fresh vision from another environment. But he came with more than that. He came with an artist's understanding of those universal and common qualities of humanity that took him past those aspects of our life that to him were picturesque, and led him to the heart of meaning and feeling in American ways. This gift of his explains his later triumphs with such regional folk traditions as those of the Southern Negro (*Porgy* and *Porgy and Bess*) and of the Western children of the pioneers (*Oklahoma!*). What has always been spoken of as his versatility I prefer to identify as his completeness of vision and understanding.

I don't think I ever heard him give an equivocal judgment, even for the sake of tact and good manners, when the critical values of art were involved. Rochester now and then bridled at such honesty. It was natural for so important—and so recent—a provincial capital of the arts to consider its orchestra, its concerts, its taste, as unimpeachable. He could have had an easier and an earlier popularity if he had permitted himself a trifle of flattery now and then. But he never did. Consequently he was viewed as formidable, here and there. One of the great catchwords of the time was "cooperation." Perhaps he did not wholly "cooperate" with the local *amour propre*. Perhaps Mist' Eastman himself might at moments have preferred a little more courtierlike enthusiasm. But as always when people come up against firm character, they could not help but admire it.

For there was never any nonsense about him of the kind popularly associated with foreign geniuses. No mannerisms of exotic and shocking interest. No tantrums. No eccen-

tricities about which hostesses need warn each other. Dignity was a constant factor in his distinction, and so were the habitual good manners of adopting those details of American social behavior that felt natural to him.

As I recall, it was not very long before the European pince-nez gave way to United States horn-rimmed spectacles, which he wore ever after.

vi

The first season of the opera company was modest. The productions were limited to one-act excerpts from opera, given as *divertimenti* on the motion-picture bills of the Eastman Theatre. The members of the company were still learning ensemble, acting, musical characterization, and the rest. Just as the Philharmonic supplied all the players of the Eastman Theatre Orchestra, and thus integrated the activities of the more serious musical aims of the institution with the popular culture of the movies, so the opera group would entertain the public with stage acts on the movie bills at the same time as the young singers got experience in operatic idiom and stage appearance without facing quite yet the challenge of a whole operatic production.

It was an intelligent compromise. The result was all that was hoped for in the way of entertainment and experience; and even more, the Eastman Theatre set a standard in those days that was never equaled for the taste, ingenuity, and charm of stage productions on movie bills.

The first operatic excerpt to be given was the last act of *Rigoletto*. Like all our offerings, it was in English. This was one of Mist' Eastman's first conditions of foundership. It seemed to him (and to all of us, indeed) the worst of affectations to insist that only in the United States should opera continue to be given in languages foreign to its listeners. Let the public in on the secret of the plot, action, and dialogue, in spite of cultural upstarts who thought that their own language was not singable. It is true that some of the texts were absurd and absurdly translated. In such cases, effort was made to improve them. *Rigoletto,* in English, could have stood more of it.

The last act of the opera calls for a double scene—the inside of the inn of Sparafucile, and the country outside, with the lights of Mantua twinkling in the distance. I measured the stage of the Eastman Theatre, which in its width was magnificently ample for opera, but which in its depth was barely able to take a vaudeville act. I made my drawings. They had the germs of atmosphere in them; but time and again Mamoulian told me to go back and try again. When I showed signs of weariness, or lack of confidence, he would remind me that the search for the real thing was never easy, and every step repeated was progress. At last satisfaction visited my efforts. I made scale drawings to which the built pieces of the scenery were made. I was given a large floor space in the basement of the theatre to paint them on. I had to paint a representation of something two or three hundred square feet in area, flat on the floor, with no way to back off and judge the effect. The ceiling was too low to let the scenery stand up. There was one electric light to paint by. With no one to help me, I labored away in my Piranesi dungeon between the times when I was upstairs at rehearsal, singing lessons, dramatic classes, Goossens's conducting class.

Our act from *Rigoletto* was to open on Monday afternoon just after three o'clock. On Sunday night we had our scenery and light rehearsal on the big stage, after the movies had ended for the night, and while the cleaning women were gossiping among the grey velvet stalls. The organ tuner was at work on the wind box upstage, and the man was in for the night to work on the immense chandelier, which had been let down from the golden sunburst in the middle of the ceiling.

What excitement as the stagehands moved my set pieces into place! The work light was on, overhead in the flies. The sky drop was in place behind. One by one my flat pieces were raised and anchored. Sparafucile's tavern. The bushes outside. The hills beyond. The towers of Mantua with their peepholes covered with tracing paper to make the distant lights of the city. Tall poplar trees at stage left. One by one each revealed hideous, amateurish painting, and drove my spirits farther down to despair. These were the fruits of my audacity, the wretched working facilities under which I had to realize my designs, the stubbornness of watercolor paint, lampblack, and glue sizing, about which I knew nothing. The stagehands exchanged professional looks of amused gratification at what was clearly a failure of the new long-haired cultural venture—opera in English in the movie house. I was ready to cut and run—and actually at one point went into hiding in the corridor outside the grand auditorium.

All this time, no opinion from Mamoulian or Rosing.

The hour grew late—very late.

We were opening tomorrow afternoon—no, *this* afternoon, at three. Where would they find a new scenic artist, and materials, and resilience enough to do the whole stage picture over, and save the day? For I never doubted that I had ruined America's most promising theatrical and musical enterprise beyond repair, and that on the very eve of its début. I gather that my horrified misery was so extreme as to be noticeable. I heard Mamoulian calling me, and went to him, hardly daring to face him. My pride was suffering; but more than that, I felt that I had betrayed him. When he saw my face in the wan light from the single thousand-candlepower lamp hanging high above the stage, I saw his. I thought he looked very grave. But with one look at me, he burst out laughing, and struck me on the shoulder.

"Paul, Paul, cheer up. What is so dreadful?"

"The flats. The painting. They're awful. And it's too late."

He seemed to believe that I really should be saved from suicide, but not at the expense of his honesty.

"Well, they are not too good, really, to tell you the truth. We had hoped for better. Your poplar trees are somewhat pe-cu-li-ar. The inn has a funny tex-ture. And Mantua is not such a me-tro-po-lis as all that."

It was all true.

"But do not lie down and die quite yet. We have not yet tried the lights on them."

That was so. My heart leaped. He was speaking altogether in professional terms, I knew. Perhaps something could be salvaged after all. It was between one and two o'clock. He stationed himself in the second row, standing; and feeling my wretchedness, he kept me by him as if I were a valued colleague. Then he began to call out his orders to the electricians for the lights he wanted.

The work light was cut off, and the stage rested in a darkness merciful to my handiwork.

And then he wrought the miracle that restored me. One by one, they placed the olivets, floods, spots that he called for. The inn of Sparafucile began to glow with a sinister atmosphere, and my daubs looked less inept and more like the scars and stains of a villain's life, revealed by dim candles and smoky lamps. The bushes outside became mysterious silhouettes against an indeterminate moonlit landscape. The far horizon was a lifting and falling line of hills against a night-blue sky under which anything—murder—might take place. The poplar trees rose like sentinels of doom, with faint moonlit edges. And when he called for the lights of Mantua to twinkle in the distance, a tiny magic resulted, for there in the towers and squares lost against the sky were gleams of innocence, ironical commentaries on the fearful deed to be done a few leagues nearer to us. Finally, slowly drifting clouds were projected on the dark vibrant blue sky. It was a realization that trembled with atmosphere. I think to this day that he placed his lights with a double purpose— first, and more important, to create the right mood in the

[212

setting; second, and very generous to me, to create a mood of restored confidence in me by keeping in darkness the worst passages of my work. It took two hours, for lighting a set thoughtfully and even with certainty is slow work. By three o'clock I was, though still shaken, a rather weakly happy young man.

But characteristically, he was not satisfied. Now that the set was lighted, and undeniably effective, he took me to the stage and pointed out places where touching up was needed. Reprieved and grateful, I raced to my Piranesi prison and got my brushes and pots, put down spatter cloths on the stage, and went to work, while everyone left me. By eight o'clock in the morning I was through, exhausted but virtuous. The propman returned to work as I was leaving for a little sleep, and enriched the set with last-minute props that Rosing and Mamoulian had ordered last night.

And at three o'clock in the afternoon, we were all assembled in the mezzanine balcony of the theatre to see our first production's first performance. It was actually a dress rehearsal, with a scattered audience, and a chance before the two evening shows to have a conference with the cast.

To that simple melody for strings which is one of Verdi's most eloquent strikes of theatre feeling, the curtains parted on the scene. So short is the memory of vanity, I thought of it as mine, and I could not believe the beauty, the suggestibility, of what was revealed before us. As a half-dozen or so handclaps greeted the stage scene from various parts of the house, I felt elated, though it is true that they might have come from loyal members of the company, all of whom came excitedly to the opening. We all saw Mist' Eastman himself sitting alone in his usual mezzanine first-row chair, with his little black skullcap over his white hair and his unknown opinions. We thought our singers did very nicely, in both song and action. We were launched; and so was Rouben Mamoulian, in America.

vii

That first year, excerpts were given from *Rigoletto, The Barber of Seville, Faust, Il Trovatore,* and *Tannhäuser*. I remember them all as having been richly handled, and the *Barber* in particular, for here there was a fine outlet for Mamoulian's sense of comedy, which was always quite special. There was a sunshiny brilliance playing through his jibes. He made scandals out of his characterizations of the wretches and rascals in the *Barber*. Rossini's witty music was charmingly echoed in the stage action. His rogues were got up in the spirit of Daumier. The sentimentality that Rossini both represented and satirized was projected by droll exaggerations in the action that yet remained human and believable.

Along with these operatic acts, the Eastman Theatre presented other sorts of stage *divertimenti* in those years, and Mamoulian was the director of these also. They ranged through many styles and subjects, from serious musical moments, to comic ballet, to little stage anthologies of folk song suitably dramatized.

In the second season, full-length operas were undertaken. I was by then relieved of my assignment as scenic artist, and a professionally experienced artist brought in. My duties became more various. In effect, I was Mamoulian's Figaro, his general assistant, responsible for any number of details of the productions. At the same time, I was supposed to think up and even write the stage acts for the movie house each week. In a few of them I appeared myself. The job was fascinating, if exhausting. I had an intensive apprenticeship in production, design, acting, singing, writing, musical selection—the blend of the arts that go to make up the vocabulary of the stage. I remember that I was charged with designing make-ups for the productions of the operas, and every time we gave one, it was I who, with Mamoulian himself, "did" all the major people in their characters, applying grease paint up to the very minute of the curtain.

The full productions of the second season included *Faust, Carmen,* and *Boris Godunov.* The casts were very promising, especially George Houston in the role of Boris. Characteristic of all of the productions Mamoulian directed (Rosing handled some of them, but discussion of their virtues, while tempting, does not enter into this piece) was a grand over-all conception. These operas had a *mise en scène,* a line, which you never saw in the traditional opera houses. The music was evoked not only by the singers' voices. It came alive with meaning in every gesture, in every movement of the stage crowd en masse, in the rhythm of the acting. Long before *Porgy and Bess, Oklahoma!,* and *Carousel* (of the theatre) and *Love Me Tonight, The Gay Caballero,* and his other musical films revealed again and again Mamoulian's marvelous grasp of the interaction of drama, music, and plastic movement, his theories were being put to work in Rochester. The young people of the company felt greatly stimulated working under him. They knew he was making a new theatrical synthesis. It was exciting to be a part of its development. On performance nights, on the great stage, with the sumptuous orchestral resources of the Philharmonic in the pit, and a first-class conductor like Goossens at the desk, the hope was very bright that, under such artistic direction as we had, there would really come to pass in this country a great satisfaction for the people as a whole in the art form of the musical drama.

Two of the best of the Gilbert and Sullivan operas were given, also, an act at a time, on the movie bills of the Eastman Theatre: *The Pirates* and *Pinafore.* Any traditional Savoyard must have died of chagrin and indignation if he saw Mamoulian's productions of these. They had little to do with the sacrosanct traditional stage business of the 1880s, which is so feebly and faithfully echoed by professional Gilbert and Sullivan companies. Mamoulian started entirely afresh. He brushed off that curious blend of solemnity and low comedy which is the familiar Gilbert and Sullivan idiom. He called for gaiety, brilliance, wit in the action to match the wit in the music—which is so often played, and taken, straight. How often has it been remembered that some of Sullivan's most incomparably expressive moments are also outrageous burlesques of Donizetti and the florid school of nineteenth-century Italian opera? Mamoulian, of course, relished the point, and made much of it, losing nothing of the musical quality of the score, and yet illuminating the sentimental parodies in the text with fresh comic action. The choruses were massed in delightful pictures. There was a balletlike precision and flow in the movements of the principals as they gave tongue. The settings were brilliant and droll at the same time. The costumes were delicately exaggerated, little decorative satires on the period and the styles they were to represent.

I remember these productions with particular pleasure because I was in both, as the First Lord in *Pinafore* and as the Major General in *The Pirates*. Detail by detail, Mamoulian evolved these characters as walking caricatures of the official mind and attitude. To see him sketching what he meant for me was in itself an hilarious experience. He became the last of the Bourbons, in developing Sir Joseph Porter, K.C.B.—tired, vain, complacent, yet dutiful with social response, and victim of a hollow elegance. He would show me how this must go, walking like a gouty pigeon, and I would laugh until I ached, and could not wait to try it myself. For General Stanley, he evoked the self-pity of the eternal sentimentalist, the darting glance of the uncertain man of authority, the self-confessing pretensions of the false and the feeble. He would sketch all that in action, and overtone it with the boredom of the London swell, the smart commander, and it all became a dramatic garment. I worked

[*216*

and worked to make it fit me perfectly. I kept thinking of
what a season of Gilbert and Sullivan this man would stage,
if he had the opportunity. I believe that a whole new excitement and charm, a perspective with new values and vitali-
ties, would bring these delightful operas alive all over again
from the ashes of their outworn original conventions.

Along with the operation of the opera company and the
stage acts of the theatre, Mamoulian had presently a large
new responsibility. He interested Mist' Eastman in establish-
ing a school of the theatre. It was, rather oddly, called The
Eastman School of the Dance and Dramatic Action. Mist'
Eastman did not much like the sound of the word "acting,"
or the word "theatre," or "theatre art." "Dramatic Action"
appeared to encompass more, and to sound somehow more
respectable. Anyhow, there was a full-fledged school, with
Martha Graham as the dance directress, and Mamoulian as
general director, and classes in the whole range of ballet and
stage presence. In the third year of the Rochester period,
Mamoulian undertook the most beautiful of all his local
productions, enlisted me in quite a new way as his coadju-
tor, and called upon all the resources of the music school,
the theatre school, and the dance department to activate his
project.

It was a production of Maurice Maeterlinck's play *Sister
Beatrice*, in which Mamoulian wanted to effect another of
his masterly blendings of the atmospheric, the plastic, and
the musical. The existing translation of the play was the
official one included in Maeterlinck's published works, and
though it respected the original, it reflected the taste of an
earlier period, and sounded rather like those bookish translations that appear in the English versions of the *Lieder* of
Schubert and Schumann. Mamoulian asked me to make a
new translation. He sketched for me how he felt about the
play, what he would do in the production, the flavor he
wanted in the text. I gathered that a marriage of the styles of

217]

Northern European Gothic and of Claude Debussy would approximate what he was after, and with dedicated enthusiasm went to work on my translation. I enjoyed and respected no task of that period more. The play is really a modest retelling of an old and touching legend. Everything would depend on atmosphere, in the text, the setting, the musical score, the flow of the bodies on the stage. But somewhere in the simple frame of the play there lies, smoldering and glowing, an ageless compassion. It was a proper task to try to find it and release it once again.

As I completed my acts, I would read each one to Mamoulian, he holding the French text, and weighing my English against it. I was happy when he liked what I was doing with it. His ear was by then acute and expert at the English language. We would debate and test possible choices for a word or a phrase, and together arrive at the purest translation compatible with the Van Eyckian tone of the whole production plan.

Otto Luening was asked to compose a score for organ to accompany the drama, and wrote a fine period suite that supported and defined the mood as arches lift and give shape to a stone vault.

The students of the dramatic school made up the cast, with a few from the opera company.

Sister Beatrice was given in Kilbourn Hall in January of 1926. It was Mamoulian's first full-length stage presentation in play form in this country, and it was an artistic success of the truest quality. I do not know whether members of the Theatre Guild came from New York to see it. But if they did, it may well have been one of the factors that obliged them later to engage this director for some of their most distinguished and successful productions.

I heard him say in after years that he still carried the hope that he might someday produce our Rochester *Sister Beatrice* before a wider public.

viii

In the season of 1925–26, though a number of full-dress productions had been done, and the interest of the local public was reasonably responsive, the Rochester American Opera Company was far from paying its way. I was not privy to the high fiscal councils of the theatre and music school, but evidently it was recognized that Mist' Eastman, true to his original premise, would not finance the company beyond its third year. Plans were accordingly set going by Vladimir Rosing to reorganize the company as a touring institution to take opera in English across the land, under the management of a New York impresario.

We heard that there were amicable disagreements on policy between Rosing and Mamoulian. Each made unexplained trips to New York and returned without releasing any news. I left Rochester in midwinter of that season and gathered the rest from a distance. It was suddenly known that Mamoulian was no longer connected with the Rochester establishment. He was to be the head of a new dramatic school established in New York by the Theatre Guild. His departure did not surprise anybody. It had seemed only a question of time until he took flight for broader fields. His superior gifts must sooner or later find a national public. Perhaps Mist' Eastman was past the age of being an innovator. The grand if brief era of the Rochester Renaissance was at an end.

Others departed. Goossens went to another orchestra. Rosing took his delightful opera company on the road, where it had a genuine success until the crash of 1929 caused mass cancellations of heavy booking for the next season. Martha Graham resumed her public career elsewhere. The opera activity in Rochester was reduced to a worthy but hardly exciting department in the school of music. Sound films replaced much of the orchestral activity in the Eastman Theatre movie bills. I returned to life in New Mexico and the writing of books, always my first interest. And Rouben Mamoulian within a year was the nation's most distinguished and original stage director. When the Theatre Guild assigned him to direct *Porgy*, the play by DuBose Heyward (from which the later Gershwin opera was fashioned, and also directed by Mamoulian), there was wonder that a Caucasian Russian, in this country only three years, should be expected to understand and interpret the folk life of the Southern American Negro. *Porgy*'s first night ended any doubts on the part of New York's knowing critical circles.

But those of us who had worked with him during his American apprenticeship were not astonished; we were proud of his enormous success.

We had intimately watched his work, and had ourselves been its raw materials for a little while; we knew the penetration, the ingenuity, and the superb taste he brought to every theatrical problem, dramatic or musical. We had had a glimpse into the nature of the director's task, and we had seen how, in perfecting his design with his human materials, Rouben Mamoulian brought to his work not only his inspiring imagination and his infinite technical skill, but also the prime resource that harmonized them beautifully and expressively—that was a human nature in him so warm, so various, and yet so well integrated that his life and his art flourished together.

THREE

A CERTAIN

CLIMATE

THE CLIMATE OF BOOKS

He was not alone of his kind, but none ever set down for his own recollection a greater delight in the books and libraries that he encountered throughout his life. When he was a young man he made two excursions to the Continent, the first in 1641, lasting four months, when he was twenty-one; the second in 1643, when he set forth on an extended tour that spanned five years. He brought with him from Balliol an excellent general education, so that as he came upon monuments of culture, fascinating oddments of behavior, and historical associations, in places new to him, he was able to tell his diary about them with lively understanding. He may not have seen everything on his tours, but unfailingly he examined libraries wherever he went, and often took note of their particular character and most striking possessions.

His first brief tour took him to the Low Countries, where he paid tribute to one who "left so Many Monuments of his Worth behind him," Joseph Scaliger, "more lasting than Marble," who bequeathed his library to the University of Leyden. Setting out again two years later, he traveled to Paris, where he found "a very Noble Library" at the College of Navarre, and donned mourning for the death of

Louis XIII. In the "incomparable" palace of Luxembourg, where he admired the great gallery of the immense panels painted by Rubens to commemorate the florid glory of Marie de Medici, he rejoiced in the library of the Duke of Orleans, which was "rarely furnish'd with excellent bookes, all bound in Mar[o]quin and guilded: the valans of the shelves being greene velvet, freing'd with gold. . . ."A week later, he was in Orléans, much interested to find that the "very antient" university was composed of four administrations according to distinct student populations from France, Holland, Normandy, and Picardy. The university housed two public libraries, "reasonable faire," but with a reckless policy: "whence one may borrow a booke to on[e]s chamber, giving but a note under hand, which is a custome extraordinary, & a confidence that has cost many Librarys deare."

Italy, always the English traveler's summons to the golden south, awaited; and the diarist proceeded south by way of Lyons, Marseilles, Genoa, Pisa, and finally came to Rome.

There, at the Palazzo Barberini, "superbe" in Bernini's design, the library was "full of worthy Collections, Medails, Marbles, and Manuscripts, but above all for its unknown material, and antiquity an Ægyptian Osiris." On 21 November 1644, he "was carried to a great Virtuoso one Cavalliero Pozzo, who shew'd us . . . a choice Library, over which are the Effigies of most of our late men of Polite Letters," and—enviable by any man given to reaching upper shelves—"a pretty folding ladder, to be put in a small compasse." Three days later he inspected two Jesuit libraries, and then came to the Vatican library, where he was guided by a certain Signore Vitellesco, "afterward Bibliothecary" of the great papal establishment, who led him to "one of the best collections of statues in Rome." The Bibliothecary is so in love with "these Antiquities &c" that to them "he frequently talkes & discourses, as if they were living, pronouncing now & then Orations, Sentences, & Verses, sometimes kissing and embracing them: Amongst many he has an head of Brutus scarr'd in the face by order of the Senat for his killing of Julius, this is esteem'd much. . . ."

Oh, "this Library is doubtlesse the most nobly built, furnish'd, and beautified in the World." He marveled at the painted walls and ceiling; the largest room, which was three hundred yards long; the manuscripts of illuminated texts, and books from China, Mexico, Abyssinia, in the collection left by Pope Urban VIII. "As to the [ar]ranging of the bookes, they are all shut up in Presses of Wainscot . . . nor are the most precious mix'd amongst the ordinary, which are shew'd to the curious only"—a rare book and manuscript collection including two Virgils and a Terence written on parchment, more than two thousand [*sic*] years old; the epigrams of Petrarch "written with his owne hand;" the book written by Henry VIII against Luther, "what we English do much enquire after;" and in another wing two hundred yards long a collection of books "taken from Heide[l]berg." The entire Vatican palace was a revelation, with its paintings and sculptures, but the library holdings above all, as cited, most rewarded the diarist, who nonetheless recorded with devouring interest the character of the libraries of his time as museums of curiosities and rare objects as well as enclosures for books.

After seven months in Rome, he set out again and by 21 May 1645 he was in Siena admiring the black-and-white-striped *duomo*, which looked best when wet by rain, and noting the frescoes of the cathedral library. In a few days he was in Florence for the second time; on his way into Italy he had paused briefly the year before, had examined the great manuscript collection in the Laurentian Library, mostly in Greek and Latin, and in particular "The Comedys of Terence interlined they say by his own hand." Now he returned to the Biblioteca Mediceo-Laurenziana, where he counted eighty-eight shelves, as he called the ranks of lecterns with their chained books, and a total collection of thirty-five hundred volumes. The design for the library he attributed to Raphael, whether through misinformation or his own confusion in a land prodigal of masterpieces, for it was Michelangelo who had designed for the Medici that palace of the intellect. The diarist commented that "the ascent to the library from [the vestibule was] incomparable," and it would have been much to his taste if he had known that the plan for it came to Michelangelo "as it were in a dream."*

In Bologna he hoped to see the "Library of St Saviours famous for the quantity of rare Manuscripts," but for unstated reasons was unable to do so, though he was rewarded in the "most stately" Piazza of Bologna by the sight of a "young handsom person of the most stately mine" he had ever seen: it was a young Persian most richly dressed "which did exceedingly please. . . ."

The wonders of Venice were not far away. They included a "Library of excellent MSS & books that belong to it, & the publique." He climbed the campanile, which had an "Angel which turns with the wind," and the "prospect down the Adriatic" was so encompassing that he was moved to a marvelous description in a phrase of "this Mira[c]ulous Cittie which lies in the bosome of the sea in the shape of a Lute." It was the week of the Feast of the Ascension, and all Venice was in festival. Monuments, masterpieces, and libraries gave way momentarily to a young man's proper attention to "the *Venetian* Dames," whose costumes and cosmetics were fascinating in their imperative way, for the ladies washed "their heads in pisse" to make their hair stand out in varicolored streaks, and they wore voluminous gowns that yet showed much flesh, "their petticoates comming from their very armpits, so high as that their very breasts flub over the tying place. . . ." Pages and pages and days and days were given to Venice, and also to a singular disappointment; for he heard of a ship being readied to sail for the Holy Land, and at once he took passage, bought provisions, including a stock

---

*Michelangelo, letter from Rome, 28 September 1555, to Giorgio Vasari.

of snow "to coole our drink," and looked forward to seeing "Jerusalem, & other parts of Syria, Egypt, & Turkey." But the voyage was canceled when the ship was pressed into Venetian service; and his travels continued in Italy.

Milan enchanted him, with its city wall ten miles round, its many-pinnacled cathedral, and inevitably the "Ambrosian Librarie . . . a goodly Librarie, furnish[ed] with rare *Manuscripts*," and amazing religious relics, including a letter addressed to Pope Alexander (Borgia) VI, which contained "a most honorable mention of Christ." He knew about books of drawings by Leonardo da Vinci at the library, and must see them; but this turned out to be impossible, "the keeper of them being out of Towne, who allways carried the keys with him." But he was told that "all but one booke are small, & that an huge folio contain'd 400 leaves, full of Scratches of Indiane [ink] &c." The Leonardo sketchbooks were a celebrated item, and King Charles I was supposed to have offered "1000 pounds for them."* The diarist's informant "having seen them since, did not think them so much worth." But there was better luck at the refectory of the Monastery of Our Lady of Grace, for there on perpetual view was the "Last Supper" of Leonardo, which took up "the intire wall at the end"—the same fresco of which Francis I of France, "the greate *Virtuoso*," was "so inamoured" that he once planned to "remove the whole Wall, by binding about with ribs of yron & timber, to convey it into France." But now—in May 1646—"this incomparable piece is exceedingly impaired."

Soon it was time to undertake the long homeward journey, north to Domodossola, up into mountains over the snowy pass [Simplon] from which he could see the great chasm of ice from which issued the Rhone to flow across all France; and he came again to Paris. There he made his will

---

*It is not known how the Leonardo drawings came into the Royal Collection at Windsor Castle.

and left for the Channel, where on 11 October 1648 he embarked, and arrived by one o'clock the next day "safe to *Dover*," for which he gave thanks heartily to God.

Taking up his life again at home, which would provide him with every notable fascination: social, political, scientific, (discreetly) amorous, and bibliographic: for sixty more years, until his death in 1706, the diarist recorded his lifelong surveys of the libraries of England. Through the years he toured all the college libraries of Cambridge and Oxford, notably the Bodleian ("no less than 1000 MSS: in 19 languages"); Gloucester Cathedral library, with its whispering gallery; Coventry ("faire free-Schoole & Librarie"); College of Physitians library, London; The Royal Society, London (where he moved to save "a noble library" otherwise doomed to "imbezilment" by an owner who had "little inclination to bookes"); the Earl of Bristol's library at Wimbledon (not worth purchasing as it was a "very broken Collection consisting much in books of Judicial Astrologie, Romances & trifles &c."); the private library of King Charles II at Whitehall ("which I did now at my full ease ... spent 3 or 4 intire daies locked up, & alone among these bookes &c.," including many "pompous Volumes").

When asked to serve as a planning consultant for a Royal Hospital to house old soldiers, he "would needes have a librairie," and specified acquisitions of a suitable nature, "since some souldiers might possibly be studious, when they were at this leasure to recolect." In 1684 he was shocked that London possessed no proper public library; and he joined the rector of St. Martin's parish in a plan to erect a public library there, whose first purpose was to provide alternate distractions for "30 or 40 Young men in *Orders*" given to "Taverns or Coffe-houses," who "would study & employ their time better, if they had books." The diarist was asked to advise Sir Christopher Wren on a suitable architectural solution to the challenge. Sometimes, if not simply absent, books were mistreated: during anti-Popish riots in 1688 the library of the Spanish ambassador was "pillaged and burnt." But there were always collectors, and the library of Lord Spencer was "incomparable," particularly after being enriched by the addition of "the very best collection especialy of Mathematical books which was I believe in all Europe: once designed for the Kings library at St James but the Queene dying (who was the great patronesse of that designe &c.) it was let fall, and so miserably dissipated." In a later time, Lord Spencer bought more books, among whose rarities were incunables—"several, that were printed at the first Invention of that wonderfull Art. . . ."

ii

By now it must be an open secret that the diarist was John Evelyn, himself a virtuoso, or, in the original meaning, a connoisseur in his own right, along with such bookmen as Francis I, Michel de Montaigne, Voltaire, Anthony à Wood, to name only an eminent few. Francis sceptered a law that required printers to deposit in the royal library a free copy of every book produced. Montaigne so strongly felt the living presence of books that they became the other half of a dialogue for him; he marked his copies, answering Guicciardini, Commines, Joachim du Bellay, saying, "I speak to them in my turn." He sought ready understanding of what he read, had little patience with struggles after meaning, and preferred reference books to other kinds: "In general I ask for books that make use of learning, not for those that build it up." But if this was severe, it was mitigated by his declared delight in Boccaccio, Rabelais, and Virgil, Martial, Catullus, and Horace, and "Plutarch is the man for me," he said. As for Cicero, he was wise but dull—a judgment endorsed by the centuries. Anthony à Wood, a contemporary of John Aubrey, spent his life in the Bodleian, so to speak, when he wasn't dancing in a rickety way through the observable scandals of Oxford, which he recorded with birdlike ferocity, noting among other things the perils of literature, in the example of how John Dryden was beaten up by three louts in a tavern for having "reflected on certaine persons in his 'Essay on the Satyr.' " Wood loved trivia and had a genius for the detail that captures a life—he found in a library book a pair of eyeglasses left there by a reader.

The type is here sufficiently identified. The history of libraries begins with those who in farthest antiquity and ever since have regarded the compilation of mankind's autobiography through incised or drawn or written record not so much as a duty but as a profound satisfaction of man's faculties for an orderly sense of the past; for pleasure in answers to often creative questions; for what Cardinal Newman called knowledge for its own sake; and for beauty in the arts, not least of which was always the art of giving increase and order to the collections of the virtuoso, for which, in our present interest, read the librarian.

iii

In the light of history, from the earliest Assyrian collections of Assurbanipal, and the hundreds of thousands of volumes or their equivalents at Alexandria, whose destruction in A.D. 640 crystallized the value of the word "library" for all time, to the monastic collections which held civilization in amber for later ages, to the sudden grand disseminations of books with the discovery of printing, the idea of a library needs no defining or defending, certainly not by any librarian or other bookman. Libraries were always spoils of conquest—a conqueror proved their virtue by carrying them away, or their danger by destroying them. They were thus judged in the same scale as works of art, as indices of civilization.

Not to mention sources of pleasure. Voltaire called the public library of the King of France "incontestably the most precious monument" in the nation. If it was true, as he said, that in its collection of two hundred thousand books there were about a hundred and ninety thousand that would never be read, still, the astounding multitude of books should not frighten; for "one may need to consult some of them in a lifetime." It was like choosing one's friends: Paris contained about seven hundred thousand men; one could not live with them all, accordingly one chose three or four. As for books, "Choose which suits you," he declared, "and try not to be bored." His image in this civil advice translates itself into his likeness by Houdon: leaning slightly forward in a marble armchair, his long fingers suggesting the skeletal figure under the flowing, classical folds of his robe, his immense brow presiding innocently above the smiling bones of his face and the benign gaze of his full eyes: an expression which in life signaled his dangerous amiability.

To proceed from the nature of this author of eighty-eight volumes of polemic, poetic drama, fictional parable, satire, and thousands and thousands of letters, we come to the nature of that reader who abides in humanity at large. The act of reading is surely one of the most private of man's influential activities. It is, then, the reader in whose image every library should be designed. The combination of man, book, and privacy is what a library must protect as far as possible. Thomas Carlyle, as quoted in an essay by E. M. Forster, on the London Library, which Carlyle helped to found, said, "A book is a kind of thing which requires a man to be self-collected. He must be alone with it. A good book is the purest essence of the soul." (We shall not pause to attend the cries of those who would claim for music this superlative.) A further dimension of this idea takes us to the writer in the act of producing a book, and by free association what comes to the mind's eye is a memory of a painting in the Scuola di San Georgi degli Schiavone at Venice. The subject of the painting, by Vittore Carpaccio, is Saint Augustine at the moment he is flooded by the light of a vision of another saint—Jerome. Augustine is at his writing table in his study. His manuscript lies before him, his pen is in his hand, but his hand is suspended in midair, for he is fixed in wonder at the light that pours in upon him from his window, beyond which the vision holds unseen. It throws long shadows in the ample room, which is furnished with Augustine's priestly credentials: his miter and crozier—for he is a bishop—and his prie-dieu, his altar, his Mass bell, his incense pot, his chalice and ciborium, his lavabo and his statue of Christ. But more: he is a scholar, a writer, and in addition to two manuscript folios of music, the painter has given him seventy-five books within immediate reach or only a few steps away. They stand on shelves or on tables, or rest on a lectern, or lie on the floor, or lean against the wall. By their number and place—some are left open like recent thoughts—they declare a reader: of all the circumstances of the exquisitely imagined picture, it is this that seems to come most eloquently out of that room suffused with two kinds of power—that of supernatural vision and that of organized thought. The whole is one more assertion, in glory through its own particular medium, of a consuming love for the faculty of man's mind, and an abiding respect for the reach of anyone toward any manifestation of it.

Given the materials, then, the librarian could well be the educator of his whole town or academy. A teacher of mine once said that if he were to design a school, he would build a library in the middle and put everything else around it, reaching like spokes to a hub.

If I were to design a city, I would do the same thing. (I have a notion that John Evelyn, if he were to do likewise in the context of his time, would place the king's palace in the center—but as in the case of the royal enclosures he explored, a great wing would be designed as a library.) This design has its greatest power perhaps in its symbolic aspect; for the corporate mind of any community can be no brighter than the idea it holds of the human heritage. The temple of man's thought must be the most appropriate center for any community of men of diverse persuasions. Who does not pause to create the present out of what is known and demonstrated of the past? Time itself waits for man to create his future also by learning the lessons of history.

As, recalling Carlyle again, the university is dependent on the library, instead of the other way round, so the civil government, the school system, all public agencies, in my new city, would be posed in their true relationship to the central source of historical energy about which they would gather.

As public educator-in-chief, the librarian would create an atmosphere of the sensibilities in which the patron would learn more than he was aware of learning. This would have to do not only with collections and their disposal, but also with the way they are architecturally contained. Informal education comes about as much by indirection as by programed pursuit of a goal. I am reminded of a note in an intimate book by Bernard Berenson called *One Year's Reading for Fun*. In this daily record of his pleasures as he went from book to book (for like all great readers he kept a dozen or two books going at the same time, using them according to his changing thought, or even to their random proximity to his momentary armchair or couch) Berenson made this entry about a letter he received from Ben Nicholson, the painter, who had been staying at I Tatti, with its marvelous conversation, its gardens, its paintings, and above all its superbly marshaled library: "When Ben Nicholson went away he wrote that although he had almost never heard me speak of art, he had, through the months he had passed with us, learned more about it than he had ever acquired elsewhere."

This is the kind of informal teaching I mean; and it suggests through its very climate of books alone, a library's power to represent civilization itself and to promise its extension. By the nature of custodianship, a library must tend toward governing use through one or another system of standardization. The librarian's role therefore must include a demonstration of the value of originality and even improvisation in his approach to the solution of his professional problems. E. M. Forster, in his tribute to the London Library, said, "It would be possible to have . . . admirable ideals, but to render them inacceptable through red tape. That is the great snag in institutionalism. There may be fine intention and noble provision, but they often get spoiled by the belief that the public cannot be trusted, that it is careless, dishonest, grubby, clumsy, that it must on no account be allowed access to the shelves, and is best served behind a wire netting. . . . There is a price to be paid; books do get stolen, or taken out without being entered or taken out in unauthorized quantities, or kept out too long, or dogs-eared [*sic*], or annotated in the margins by cultivated scribes who should know better; but it is worth it, it is worth treating the creatures as if they were grown up, the gain to the humanities outweighs the financial loss. Moreover, it is the tradition of the library to help the student rather than to snub, and this promotes a decent reaction at once."

It is a comment once again reaching toward the ideal for the public or institutional library—that in its arrangement and operation it resemble as closely as possible a personal collection whose continuing growth as a living organism reflects its constant use.

iv

A building design for the socially open library must answer to multiple problems, most of them concerning technical operations. These vary according to the character of the given library. But there is one aspect of the design that should be met to the advantage of all, though it is rarely achieved. This is an architectural statement that proclaims the enclosure of thought in its union with knowledge, and in both exterior and (where suitable) interior design it should be made with unapologetic nobility. All stylistic periods are capable of such a statement in contemporaneous terms. Michelangelo's palace of books rising above the cloisters of San Lorenzo speaks with the greatest genius about the suitability of magnificence in its Renaissance context, and his interior hall of the eighty-eight desks and the approach to it by the staircase with its curved steps and its double banisters, which our virtuoso Evelyn called "incomparable," speak as much for the purpose of the library as for the splendor of its design. The painted barrel vaulting of the Vatican library and the library of the Escorial (where book shelving against the walls was first used) have similarity of elevated style. The Austrian National Library in Vienna and the Abbey library of St. Gall in Switzerland enclose their collections in the curvilinear splendors of early and late baroque, to the honor of their times, and their contents, and the uses of both. The library of Trinity College, Dublin, and the John Rylands library at Manchester show in their long nave-like forms their derivation from the church, the one with its Roman barrel vaulting, the other with its Gothic groining. In the British Library (formerly called the British Museum Library), an architectural metaphor for universal light over the reading room is cast by the high circle of arched windows in the drum of the vast dome. For America, one thinks of the soaring volume of the Library of Congress reading room in the original building (Smithmeyer and Pelzi); the Beinecke Rare Book and Manuscript Library (Gordon Bunshaft) at Yale; and of the entrance hall and main reading room of the Olin Library (McKim, Mead and White) at Wesleyan University.* Countless examples could be cited to recall the respect that high art has paid to the library's place in the values of culture.

All those here noticed have one august characteristic in common—the volume of their central interiors is determined by soaring height. It is the analogy of the questing spirit made manifest by the lofty mystery of great space al-

---

*These descriptions are contrived in part after photographs in *Great Libraries*, by Anthony Hobson. New York, 1970.

lowed above the usable territory of man's encounter with knowledge. An implied idea of what human sensibility is like rests in the visions behind such designs.

Nowadays we are seeing prevailing architectural reflections of what this generation thinks man is like. From such evidence he seems chiefly to be a combination of a patient in a clinic, a worker in a sanitary factory, an itinerant motorist in search of highway lodging, and a high-rise hive dweller. The idiom, too, often results in libraries set down as rectilinear brick or concrete boxes obviously created in the name of a budget in panic. Local problems are embedded in the values of the society as a whole—a society that regards instruments of culture not as the last resources to be sacrificed during hard times, but the first.

Which is not to say that the only architectural need to be fulfilled for a library is a visible analogy of grandeur. The design problem is complex. The great spaces intended for use in common call for one kind of spatial imagination. Other spaces ought to be provided for those who would read and work in intimate privacy, beyond visual distraction or easy interruption. Recently built academic libraries that I have seen run to "areas" instead of to rooms. Perspectives of uninterrupted wall stretch away in empty space under eight-foot ceilings, and may have the effect of emptying the mind as the eye drifts with them. Furniture groupings take the place of partitions. It will not be simple, and it will not be inexpensive, to devise plans that will provide not only for communal use but also for separate, individual use of the library's interior. The ideal of man reading in privacy should be satisfied. The burning glass of meaning finally focuses on a single inclusive purpose. It is to establish and protect the unimprovable combination of man, book, and solitude—the condition that permitted our old scholar Anthony à Wood to exclaim in his notes (July 1656), on reading a certain book, that he found himself thereby "ravish'd and melted downe." The state could not be commonly achieved in an atmosphere given only to efficiency. Style—deliberate enhancement of functional mode—is an indispensable element of all lasting aesthetic achievements, including those of architecture. It is, as A. N. Whitehead implies in his *Aims of Education*, quite possibly contagious: "Style, in its finest sense, is the last acquirement of the educated mind; it is also the most useful. It pervades the whole being. . . . Style is the ultimate morality of mind."

v

But what, we can hear from technologists, does a concept of style and its atmospheric dimensions have to do with the library of the future? Knowledge is no longer retained only within printed pages. All talk of grand spaces becomes irrelevant if not mischievous when everything man has ever known can be kept on film in optically minimized form within a few shoe boxes. Only go to the appropriate machine with your slip of film and sit down and press various buttons, and there in enlarged characters on a panel of light you can find anything you want to know. It is surely a remarkable technique—it saves space, it offers fewer errors in a library's technical operations, and it feels like today. It makes the book collection in its great reaches of shelving seem wasteful and clumsy and constantly subject to the inconveniences of misplacement. What is more, the entire range of information on a given matter can now be provided by computers using synopsis, and this instantaneously, when the initiate punches the appropriate key. The genuine marvels of technology are as applicable to the storage and retrieval of information as they are to all other processes of the age of the machine. Certain areas of library usage are properly subject to such storage and retrieval.

But: those who justify such procedures carry their arguments too far, for they take it as a given that the book as such will be eliminated as a consequence of the perfection of information machines. The argument assumes that man, too, is a machine; that the retrieval of information is the only purpose of reading; that nobody will mind going to a machine in a fixed position when he wants to trace a thought or enlarge one; that a portable computer in a vest pocket provides aesthetic satisfaction as it answers questions or projects texts; that the energy of a cunning transistor is perdurable; and that the rate of comprehension, reflection, and original thought in all men is the same. For electronic transmission is relentlessly instantaneous, has no time for a pregnant pause, affects by its very means of expression the required speed and even mode of human comprehension; and in the process has no need for, and therefore no tolerance of, that aesthetic communion that exists between reader and book.

The very form of the book is supremely satisfying on many counts. It fits the hand. It is an object of individual design, and the design often reflects artistry and taste of the highest quality. Typography is a fine art among the graphics. Bookbinding is a beautiful craft. A single book can be a work of art to see. A rank of books is always an invitation to eye and curiosity. A wall of books is the most pleasingly decorative side for a room after a mural painting or a tapestry by master hands. A book can be read and annotated for rereading at the reader's pleasure in text, place, and frequency. Is is easily portable. If it is a great book, or even a good one, it is revered by literate persons for its own sake. To destroy or burn it for any reason is a sin in civilized society. Even a trivial or ephemeral book, by extension, calls forth a degree of common respect simply because it *is* a book. A library of any sort is a valued institution because everyone understands the importance of a book, five books, a great collection of books. If among them there should be a book of the greatest rarity and beauty, such as a unique copy of a medieval book of hours with illuminations in gold and miniature landscapes and scenes of natural or supernatural events, or if it might be an ancient missal bound in boards studded with jewels and clasped by wrought gold, its exhibition is an occasion of wide interest, drawing crowds to do reverence to history, art, and simply the idea of a book as such. In brief, the written record which can be individually handled, in all its historical forms from clay tablets to sheaves of papyrus, parchment scrolls, or gathered sheets of laid rag paper printed before 1501, to signatures fed out by high-speed presses—the written record is not a candidate for obsolescence, however useful and efficient later forms of information conveyed through fixed apparatus may be, despite the physical limitations they impose upon the user.

vi

It remains only to consider the ideal images of those drawn to govern and serve the library, which, fulfilled, would hold their places of honor for them in our culture. They are nothing less than universal persons, for whom no record of man's experience, in whatever form, is separated from any other record. They are people whose love of books is enriched by their sense of style in the accompanying fields of music, painting, and all the rest, including science. They are those who must teach others because they themselves have never ceased learning. In their desire to communicate their cultural faith to their fellows, they will, if a choice be necessary, choose passion over method. They can look at a library as a reader as well as an administrator. They are men and women who, in their vocation, remember how Burton, in *The Anatomy of Melancholy*, wrote: "Heinsius, the keeper of the library at Leyden in Holland, was mewed up in it all the year long; and that which to thy thinking should have been a loathing, caused him a greater liking. 'I have no sooner' (saith he) 'come into the library but I bolt the door to me, excluding lust, avarice, and all such vices, whose nurse is idleness, the mother of ignorance, and melancholy herself; and in the very lap of eternity, amongst so many divine souls, I take my seat, with so lofty a spirit and sweet content that I pity all our great ones and rich men that know not this happiness.' "

Librarians are those who, in the penetralia of their own taste and feeling for the acts of thought, would do all they could to release to all others the happiness of Heinsius of Leyden—the custodian of that library, which was the first seen by John Evelyn on the Continent in 1641.

A WRITER'S MARGINS

In Venice, on 3 October 1786, the traveler declared, in his journal: "On a quay overlooking the water, I have several times noticed a low fellow telling stories in a Venetian dialect, of which, unfortunately, I cannot understand a word. His audience consisted for the most part of people of the humblest class. No one laughed; there was rarely even a smile. There was nothing obtrusive or ridiculous about his manner, which was even rather sober; at the same time the variety and precision of his gestures showed both art and intelligence."

The traveler had come from Weimar by way of Munich, through the Brenner Pass across the Alps to Verona, and on through Vicenza and Padua to Venice. He was at the beginning of a great experience in his life—a journey into Italy. In the course of a long and illustrious life he would write novels, poetry, drama, and become a major source of the wisdom of his epoch. He was Johann Wolfgang von Goethe, and like the low fellow on the Venetian quay, he in his turn would be a storyteller, though it is doubtful whether his audience "consisted for the most part of people of the humblest class."

Low fellow or not, the modern storyteller—and it is he whose margins of experience and expression along which we'll be ambling here—has much in common with Goethe's Venetian. As we'll be concerned with prose fiction, we may, like Goethe, take as givens the writer's need and possession of both "art and intelligence." Given the second, the first can to an individual degree be approached. The matter is a large one to all who write, and we'll be hearing about it from several witnesses as we go along, but again, just now, we listen to Goethe, a master of the qualifying word, who wrote later: "It is the highest task of every art to employ appearances to create the illusion of a higher reality. But it is a false endeavor to carry the realization of appearance to such a point as to leave nothing in the end but ordinary reality." It is ordinary reality that the inventive writer works to escape. His vision must be his own, which means that it is *not* ordinary—not like everyone else's; yet it must contain that outline of the recognizable that will make readers exclaim, "Yes, that is what it is like; he says what I have always felt, or known, or wished for." Lord Byron is good on this. In a letter to his publisher, John Murray—also written, incidentally, at Venice—he says on 2 April 1817, "There should always be some foundation of fact for the most airy fabric, and pure invention is but the talent of a liar." And he adds, "I hate things *all fiction*."

What it comes down to, for a writer, is to discover for himself how he sees the world. This is a matter not so simple as it might seem. His margins are teeming with so much information, fact, fancy, desire, that to find a point of view, or even a pattern, takes some doing. There are dozens of answers for how to find the proper lens through which to view experience—for purposes of literature, that is. It is easy enough in writing a letter or making a statement in conversation to let character itself give voice, and the naturalness and spontaneity of this often make excellent reading or listening. That is why books of letters by interesting persons are so engaging. They give us living creatures, present and performing without rehearsal. Whatever organization exists in a published collection of letters is provided by its editor, who, although he or she may seem to work at second hand, as an arranger of the gathered correspondence, is actually creating a work of the highest literary quality. One thinks of the work of Leon Edel with Henry James's letters, of Rupert Hart-Davis with Oscar Wilde's, of Leslie Marchand with Byron's, and of Francis Steegmuller with the letters of Flaubert—monuments all to the art of editing. But it is art of a quite different order from that of the storyteller who has even a minimal amount of serious aspiration.

The question is, What is to be made out of Byron's "foundation of fact"?

Here enters the act of meditation. The writer need not spend time and agony in trying to answer the question "Who am I?" It will automatically be answered for him—and the world—in what he finally writes. But he does well to commune with such questions as these:

Do I believe in my own responses?

What has helped to create them?

How worthy or trustworthy are the influences behind them?

Do I know the conditions of my characters so well that the story they create almost of themselves, by coming together, cannot help being a true story in the larger sense—that is, of invention arising out of enough awareness of real experience?

Is there a satisfying inevitability in what comes to pass on my pages? Could every one of my characters write an autobiography if I needed to have this in mind as I use only that which is necessary to my fiction? A note by the way: Federico Fellini once said, "The pearl is the oyster's autobiography."

And—a question of some finality—are all the influences that converge in me worthy of a serious love of the world? For I believe that no artist can fulfill his own vision unless he loves the world. It is no argument to say, "Yes, but some great artists have been crushing satirists." The fact is that the bitterest satire is often evidence of such a love of life and respect for it that it is the very failures of ideal fulfillment that beget the mockery. We do not here countenance cynicism—that is too cheap a response to the marvels of life to yield an act of art.

Experience is another word for raw material. It is Byron's "foundation of fact" or the oyster's grain of sand. For those who write it is a double source, consisting on the one hand of external events in their own lives, and on the other of their own response to them, enriched by every possible awareness of the conditions by which to "see" and evaluate experience. Everyone has experience. The humblest person has a right to say as impressively as possible, "In *my* experience . . ." but only the artist makes of it something new which is yet recognizable if what he makes keeps alive his own original truth.

If the inventive writer knows experience in two general ways, the first is through what we might call the moral imagination—that faculty which creates a world out of the inquiry "What if?" and then evaluates the logic, the truth, and the beauty inherent in the projected answer to the speculative question. The second way is of course that of personal action and vision in the observed world.

These two kinds of experience—the external and the internal—come together for the writer when he immerses himself in history's best evidence of the human spirit. I refer to the fine arts in general as collective experience. The writer is surely the beneficiary of what the arts other than his own can show to him by analogy. The painter's vision, the composer's rhythm, the sculptor's sense of dimension, the architect's formal symmetries, the theatre's required entry into impersonation of character—all yield qualities that can enhance, not through imitating, but through understanding, the writer's sensibility. Above all, literature—the books produced by various cultures—requires of the writer that he read incessantly, over as broad a range as possible, in as many forms as may interest him, in at least one other language than his own. He will read not to copy but because words on a page, whether written by himself or by others, are the central obsession of his life. Reading is the writer's second great preoccupation, the first being writing itself. And it is probable that through reading (in what form, who can define for everyone?) the writer may be so lucky as to encounter an intense spiritual experience, a sort of conversion to a vision of his craft and that aspect of it which is uniquely his, and thus come to discover the nature of his own best expression. When this happens to him, he is done with his apprenticeship and can look to a lifelong process of refining his work—a conscious process bespeaking the highest maturity.

The seed of such growth is of course present in most children. In a certain way children are like, if in fact they are not actually, beings of genius. What experience is so intense as that of the child? How often it is expressed with dazzling freedom and directness, whether in drawing or rhyming or impersonation, as a kind of release of open dreams, done without assessment or restraint or critical arrangement! Drawings and paintings by children have a freshness in their view of the world that has the immediacy of original discovery. The child's concept of words and the dimensions they represent is often startling in its authority and wonder. A very small boy once said to his parents in my hearing, "There was an elephant in the patio." "Oh?" said his father, with encouraging amusement enclosed in an expected convention. "And was it huge?" "Oh, no," said the boy, "it was tiny." The effect was that of a stunning literary formulation, and it was gravely received by his parents—both artists of the first order.

The pristine talent of children in a vast number of cases vanishes when puberty arrives with its changes for the body and spirit. Those destined to become conscious artists safely endure the passage through the second of life's three great traumas—birth, adolescence, and mortality; and according to the degree of their talents, they still see with childlike intensity; and then with adult awareness of experience, both inner and outer, they assess what they see and give it form.

What is seen is often captured out of the corner of the eye, as it were. A flash of perception of person, place, event, observed obliquely, can often be an experience as generative as a totally absorbing preoccupation that lasts hours or days or even years. The instant is complete in itself. There is no time for immediate analysis, rearrangement, projection—all of which may follow if the impact of the instant is great enough. The fleeting impression has its own over-all accuracy, and that can be enough. We think of what Eugène Delacroix said in his *Journal*: "What I require is accuracy for the sake of the imagination"—that grain of truth from which a whole flowering form can arise. Later he quotes Boileau's "Nothing is beautiful but the truth," and we are again in touch with the artist's own truth as it grows from his perception of actuality.

So if everything is experience, then everything is material for the writer. But as Pablo Casals said, in conversation, "Sometimes, looking at a score, I say to myself, 'What marvelous music. But I must *make* it so.' " It is all marvelous for the writer, too, but only if he makes it so. One more word from Goethe: "The more closely and precisely one observes particulars, the sooner one arrives at a perception of the whole." This meticulousness reminds us of Henry James, and the extraordinary depth and fineness of that agency through which he acquired—as he might have said late in life—the significance of the circumambient totality. In 1884 James wrote:

The power to guess the unseen, to trace the implication of things, to judge the whole piece by the pattern, the condition of feeling life in general so completely that you are well on your way to knowing any particular corner of it—this cluster of gifts may almost be said to constitute experience, and they occur in country and in town and in the most differing stages of education. If experience consists of impressions, it may be said that impressions *are* experience, just as . . . they may be the very air we breathe. Therefore, if I should certainly say to a novice, "Write from experience and experience only," I should feel that this was rather a tantalizing monition if I were not careful immediately to add, "Try to be one of the people on whom nothing is lost!"

It is an instructive privilege to look behind the finished page of an interesting writer and live along the margins of his thought. In his notebooks and journals such a writer makes for himself a stockpile of experience, intention, point of view, and opinion. Much of what he sets down may never be used; bits of it may be used; all of it gives an intimate view of his intellect and his temperament, and leads to the conclusion that every writer would profit by the habit of keeping notebooks; for he can never predict what may one day be of generative power for him in the sometimes stubborn job of writing a finished work.

Some of the most exemplary and engaging notebook pages available to us were kept by Nathaniel Hawthorne. These copious notebooks were edited by his widow and published in several volumes, divided up as *American Notebooks, English Notebooks,* and *French and Italian Notebooks.*

I want to look at some of the entries in the *American Notebooks,* the volume published in 1868 by Ticknor and Fields of Boston. Here are events of the mind and of the observed world—the double experience again. We enter the capacious margins where he has his stock of impressions, memories, and notions for character, story, and design. Hawthorne interspersed such notes with dated diary entries. The margins from which he could draw included morbid fancies, supernatural events and embodiments, violent paradoxes, contradictions within character, moralistic visions and symbols, simple magic, and imagined inducements to madness. Most of such were recorded to serve symbolic ideas, with an accent on that tendency hazardous to art—conscious symbolism. He dwells, too, on what might happen to an individual in a group of people as a result of a revelation about him. Again and again he defines a parable or an allegory in terms of an abstract plot which later could be embodied by characters and scenes; and we wonder whether this might not be the wrong order of events in the making of literature. But who is qualified to prescribe a procedure for him? It is for us to note the thoughts that command his literary imagination.

It is for us to note also the enriching value of notebooks to any writer's idea for a new work. An abundance of notebook entries not only keeps alive the writer's faculties of observation, invention, and expression; it also gives him a sense of imagining and knowing more than enough than is needed for his new work. He will speak out of riches, mostly unseen, instead of out of visible poverty. The greatly gifted American novelist Willa Cather gave us something to consider about the whole and the sum of its parts when she said, "Any first-rate novel or story must have in it the strength of a dozen fairly good stories that have been sacrificed to it." The rich undersoil of the notebooks provides nourishment for what surfaces in strength.

Here are a few examples of Hawthorne's schemes for tales: "A person writing a tale, and to find it shapes itself against his intentions; that the characters act otherwise than he thought; that unforeseen events occur, and a catastrophe comes which he strives in vain to avert. It might shadow forth his own fate—he having made himself one of the personages." This concept from 1835, as do many others of Hawthorne's, suggests the tone in much of Poe's fiction.

Another, of the same year: "The scene of a story or sketch to be laid within the light of a street-lantern; the time, when

the lamp is near going out; and the catastrophe to be simultaneous with the last flickering gleam." Again, the climac-
tic idea of a catastrophe, as a regular piece of this writer's
furniture.

A fanciful note, from 1842: "A stove possessed by a Devil."

An illustration, from 1837, of his basic sequence—a symbolic idea before the fleshing out with individual humanity:
"Meditations about the main gas-pipe of a great city,—if the
supply were to be stopped, what would happen? How many
different scenes it sheds light on? It might be emblematical
of something." "Emblematical" is the operative word for
many of Hawthorne's ideas.

In 1838 he saw something that suggested a detailed process
for a story:

On the road to Northampton, we passed a tame crow, which was
sitting on the peak of a barn. The crow flew down from its
perch, and followed us a great distance, hopping along the road,
and flying, with its large, black, flapping wings, from post to
post of the fence, or from tree to tree. At last he gave up the
pursuit with a croak of disappointment. The driver said, perhaps correctly, that the crow had scented some salmon which
was in a basket under the seat, and that this was the secret of his
pursuing us. This would be a terrific incident if it were a dead
body that the crow scented, instead of a basket of salmon. Suppose, for instance, in a coach traveling along, that one of the
passengers suddenly should die, and that one of the indications
of his death would be this deportment of the crow.

In a farthest ironic incongruity of history, Hawthorne
noted an idea in 1839: "Some moderns to build a fire on
Ararat with the remains of the Ark."

In 1843 he notes a familiar exasperation of the writer's
job: "This forenoon I began to write, and caught an idea by
the skirts, which I intend to hold fast, though it struggles to
get free. As it was not ready to be put upon paper, however,

I took up the Dial [a periodical] and finished reading the article on Mrs. Alcott."

Eleven years before a famous story of his was published, he made this note: "[The] semblance of a human face to be formed on the side of a mountain, or in the fracture of a small stone, by a *lusus naturae* [freak of nature]. The face is an object of curiosity for years or centuries, and by and by a boy is born, whose features gradually assume the aspect of that portrait. At some critical juncture, the resemblance is found to be perfect. A prophecy may be connected." It was, of course, the germ of "The Great Stone Face," published in 1851. Hawthorne was beautifully sensitive to landscape, much as a painter might be, and in addition to his methodical geographic observations, he captured mood and spirit with descriptions of the natural scene.

Certain notions recur often—on one page he has two different entries in which a character's body is subject to petrifaction, and one is reminded of the popular interest in a folk marvel that early in our century traveled the nation in sideshows and was a feature of museums of curiosities: the huge recumbent stone image of "the Cardiff giant," which the gullible were assured and convinced was the petrified body of an exhumed monstrosity—a satisfying hoax. Repeatedly Hawthorne dwelt on the idea that "there is evil in every human heart, which may remain latent, perhaps, through the whole of life; but circumstances may rouse it to activity." We recognize one of his most pervasive themes: that of secret guilt that torments, alters, and in the end may destroy its host.

He has an emblem or symbol of evil. It appears in notebook entries in 1836 as a "snake, taken into a man's stomach and nourished there from fifteen years to thirty-five, and tormenting him most horribly. A type of envy or some other evil possession." Again, in 1842: "A man to swallow a small snake,—and it to be a symbol of a cherished sin."

Perhaps to remind himself of the writer's need to weigh

his values, he notes, "Bees are sometimes drowned (or suffocated) in the honey which they collect. So some writers are lost in their collected learning."

Throughout his informal pages, Hawthorne records his American fellows, and the cumulative effect is a likeness of a population, in a delightful vision suggestive of the way George Caleb Bingham painted his rivermen and farmers and politicians. We think, too, of John James Audubon's diary, in which he describes American eccentrics on the frontier—the ones who imagine themselves externally, and are dramatizers of solo democracy; the work-molded and also those sanctioned in the outlandish who flourish as rudely inquisitive citizens.

Serious as Hawthorne is most of the time, he is, when seized by comedy, light and funny. "Mrs. Prescott has an ox whose visage bears a strong resemblance to Daniel Webster—a majestic brute." He is taken by an odd name—"Miss Asphyxia Davis," and he invents another, "Miss Polly Syllable, a schoolmistress." In the barnyard, he finds a sketch of the "queer gestures and sounds of a hen looking about for a place to deposit her egg; her self-important gait; the sideway turn of her head and cock of her eye, as she pries into one and another nook, croaking all the while—evidently with the idea that the egg in question is the most important idea that has been brought to pass since the world began. Speckled black and white tufted hen of ours does it to the most ludicrous perfection; and there is something laughably womanish about it." (As to the last bit, we can only hope that Sophia Hawthorne laughed forgivingly as she edited it.) About other creatures, Hawthorne was very good when he portrayed dog nature. About his fellow human beings, he was, as everyone knows, profoundly wise, and when he catches a superb specimen, he gives him to us with loving economy: on a day in 1843, "Mr. Emerson came, with a sunbeam in his face."

His felicity of expression has a great range, from the immediacy of his private pages to the sometimes daunting and heavy texture of his finished tales and novels. The contrast between these works is striking, and in *The Scarlet Letter*, for example, there are passages of rhetoric so elegantly dense that it is difficult to recognize in them the author of the swift, clean, surely delineated persons, places, and ideas that make the notebooks and diaries so swiftly rewarding. But Hawthorne was a particularly complex man, as a note for 19 May 1840 tells us:

Lights and shadows are continually flitting across my inward sky, and I know neither whence they come nor whither they go; nor do I inquire too closely into them. It is dangerous to look too minutely into such phenomena. It is apt to create a substance where at first there was a mere shadow. . . . If at any time there should seem to be an expression unintelligible from one soul to another, it is best not to strive to interpret it in earthly language, but wait for the soul to make itself understood; and were we to wait a thousand years, we need deem it no more time than we can spare. . . . It is not that I have any love of mystery, but because I abhor it, and because I have often felt that words may be a thick and darksome veil of mystery between the soul and the truth which it seeks. Wretched were we, indeed, if we had no better way of communicating ourselves, no fairer garb in which to array our essential being, than these poor rags and tatters of Babel. Yet words are not without their use even for purposes of explanation,—but merely for explaining outward acts and all sorts of external things, leaving the soul's life and action to explain itself in its own way.

What a misty disquisition I have scribbled! I would not read it over for sixpence.

Surely it is a statement born of exasperation at the falling short of the artist's vision, which is never fulfilled entirely.

It is instructive here—and it may be consoling in its way—to review in capsule form the natural history of one of the world's masterpieces of fiction. The author first called it *All's Well That Ends Well* as he was working on it in 1866; but the next year he changed the title to *War and Peace*, and a year later he wrote, "I am still held enthralled by my yet unfinished work (which has recently progressed near to its conclusion)." Even as he progressed, there were revisions—so many and so radical that his copyist (his wife, Countess Tolstoy)—had to copy the whole work half a dozen times. Finally published in serial form and then in volumes issued separately, the huge panoramic work was completely before the public with the appearance of the sixth volume in 1869. The author was drained. He turned to studies in German and Greek. "I am not writing anything, only learning," he wrote in 1871. "How glad I am that God inflicted this madness upon me! Firstly, I enjoy it, and secondly, I'm convinced that until now I knew nothing of all that the human language has produced that is truly and simply beautiful, and thirdly, because I've stopped writing, and will never again write verbose nonsense like 'War and Peace.' I'm guilty, but I swear I'll never do it again." But two years later, he was "on the point of writing something again," and at the same time preparing revisions for a new edition of *War and Peace*, about which he said, "I find 'War and Peace' utterly repugnant now. . . . I can't tell you the feeling of repentance and shame I experienced as I scrutinised many passages! It's a feeling not unlike what a man experiences when he sees the remains of an orgy in which he has taken part. One thing consoles me—that I was carried away by this orgy heart and soul, and thought that nothing else mattered besides it." However, the orgy receded in memory, and after three years, he was able to write in a letter, "You are right that 'War and Peace' grows in *my* eyes. I have a strange feeling of joy when people remind me of something from it . . . but it's strange, I remember very few passages from it, and the rest I forget."

But it was now 1876, and he was deep in writing *Anna*

Karenina—"Oh, let me hurry and finish this book so I can start another"—and for the next twenty-three years he poured forth philosophical, religious, and aesthetic works; returned to the short story and the short novel; wrote plays; and finally wrote his last novel, *Resurrection*, which was revealed in 1899. It is no wonder that Maxim Gorki, meeting the aged Tolstoy, remarked, "He has energy enough for three lifetimes—so much that he seems to sweat sparks like red-hot iron." Looking at him, Gorki thought, "The man is godlike."

These samplings have been necessarily limited in range and number; but the point of them is that, marginally, any writer can find something of himself in their suggestions of the literary nature. It is always edifying for mortals to look at a god, as Gorki did, and if it so happens that a writer now and then measures himself by living, however briefly, with his betters, he is consoled for his shortcomings by awareness of the grand variety of the visions expressed through the art of writing, and by the saving fact that if, in the end, he manages to express truth, it will be his, and his alone.

AN ALLEGORY

The value of books to the civilized life can hardly be exaggerated. I once saw this value declared in a living allegory by an expression of great joy. When we see allegory in living form—some principle of our nature symbolically illustrated in an event before our eyes—we are moved and confirmed in the way poetry moves and confirms us.

So, I remember with emotion how such an experience came to me, and seemed to bring with it an affirmation of what the life of the mind means.

In August of 1945 I was proceeding across France toward defeated Germany as an army officer on a mission of inspection for the director of my War Department staff division at Washington. With a lieutenant and a corporal-driver I had come from Paris in a command and reconnaissance car. At the Rhine we crossed the temporary bridge of Strasbourg and proceeded northeast toward Frankfurt and SHAEF Headquarters.

Along our road the devastation was everywhere appalling but I saw none in the dimension beyond imagining until the corporal began to bring us into the streets of the city of Mannheim during the late afternoon. We moved through a hanging atmosphere of dust the color of the rosy brick of the city—a haze of particles that seemed to have been suspended there ever since the end of battle in May.

Along street after street we saw no whole structure. We drove along the beds of canyons formed by hills of rubble that sloped away on both sides toward the choked sky. The sun was lost and found behind low clouds now thin, now thick. We found it hard to believe the degree of ruin all about us as we crawled ahead on broken paving.

Inhabitants were slowly moving along the precarious walks. Where did they go at night? Who could sleep on the shards of a whole city? What was left to them? What could indicate, much less create, a future for them? How could they ever think? What would ever help them to do so?

Presently we turned a corner and entered another long avenue between dwellings collapsed from on high. By the height of their wreckage they must have been towering apartment houses. We looked up at the skylines of ruin. How could anything abide there?

But then I saw a child—a very small boy in a pullover shirt, shorts, and sandals—who was grubbing in the detritus of a near slope. He was scratching for anything he could find in the silence left by the bombs. And then I met my allegory.

For the child, climbing higher, came upon the edge of something that protruded from the rubble. He leaned down to learn what it might be. He clawed it free. He saw what it was. With a gesture more exultant than any I ever saw, he lifted it above his head to the very sky and gazed at it as if it were treasure saved from oblivion, which it was.

It was a book.

Incredibly, at the same instant a shaft of sunlight, made visible as a ray by the dusty air, broke through and in a pool of glory illumined the child, his precious find, and the crest of a hill made by ruins.

I will add only that among the notions illustrated by this

[256

picture we may find suggestions of why in honor of the book all civilized communities need, want, maintain, and respect libraries; for these contain the past, illuminate the present, and promise the future, of mankind.

ACKNOWLEDGMENTS

"Preface to an Unwritten Book" and "A Writer's Margins" were originally published in the *Yale Review*. "Journey to the Past—and Return" first appeared in the *Texas Quarterly*. "Rouben Mamoulian in the Rochester Renaissance" appeared in slightly different form in *Films in Review*. "Yankee Doodle: Early Models of American Style" is drawn in part from *Great River: The Rio Grande in North American History*, originally published by Rinehart and Co.; the current fourth edition by the Texas Monthly Press.

Certain essays—"Maurice Baring Reconsidered," "The Climate of Books," and "An Allegory"—were prepared for occasions at Wesleyan University.

ABOUT THE AUTHOR

Paul Horgan is the author of more than twoscore books, including seventeen novels, four volumes of short stories, and twenty books of history and other nonfiction. Two of his books are juveniles. His first novel, *The Fault of Angels*, published in 1933, was a Harper Prize novel. The Pulitzer Prize for History has been awarded to him twice, in 1955 for *Great River: The Rio Grande in North American History*, which also received the Bancroft Prize, and in 1975 for *Lamy of Santa Fe*. His most recent books are a novel, *Mexico Bay*, published in 1982, in his seventy-ninth year; *Of America East and West; The Clerihews of Paul Horgan* (Wesleyan, 1985); and *Under the Sangre de Cristo*.

Born in Buffalo, New York, in 1903, Paul Horgan moved west with his family at twelve to Albuquerque, New Mexico; the history of the Southwest thereafter became a central subject of his writing. He attended the Eastman School of Music and worked in the Eastman Theater in Rochester, New York, and in 1926 became librarian of New Mexico Military Institute, which he had attended as a boy. He served in the U.S. Army, from 1942 to 1946, as Chief of the Information Branch of the Information and Education Division, for which he received the Legion of Merit. He had the rank of Lieutenant Colonel at war's end. From 1962 to 1967 he was Director of the Center for Advanced Studies at Wesleyan University, where he has been Adjunct Professor of English; he is now Professor Emeritus and Author-in-Residence. He lives in Middletown, Connecticut.

ABOUT THE BOOK

A Certain Climate was set in Linotype Baskerville and printed by letterpress on 60-pound Glatfelter Offset Vellum by Heritage Printers of Charlotte, North Carolina. The design is by Cynthia Krupat of New York.

WESLEYAN UNIVERSITY PRESS, 1988